D1601631

About Guilt
and Innocence

About Guilt and Innocence

The Origins, Development, and Future of Constitutional Criminal Procedure

Donald A. Dripps

KF
9619
.D75
2003
WEST

PRAEGER

Westport, Connecticut
London

Library of Congress Cataloging-in-Publication Data

Dripps, Donald A., 1957–
    About guilt and innocence: the origins, development, and future of constitutional criminal
    procedure / Donald A. Dripps.
        p. cm.
    Includes bibliographical references and index.
    ISBN 0–275–97730–7 (alk. paper)
    1. Criminal procedure—United States.   2. Constitutional law—United States.   I. Title.
    KF9619.D75   2003
    345.73′05—dc21   2002068625

British Library Cataloguing in Publication Data is available.

Library of Congress Catalog Card Number: 2002068625
ISBN: 0–275–97730–7

First published in 2003

Praeger Publishers, 88 Post Road West, Westport, CT 06881
An imprint of Greenwood Publishing Group, Inc.
www.praeger.com

Printed in the United States of America

The paper used in this book complies with the
Permanent Paper Standard issued by the National
Information Standards Organization (Z39.48–1984).

10 9 8 7 6 5 4 3 2 1

Copyright Acknowledgments

The author and publisher gratefully acknowledge permission for use of the following material:

Excerpts from Donald A. Dripps, *Beyond the Warren Court and Its Conservative Critics: Toward a Unified Theory of Constitutional Criminal Procedure*, 23 University of Michigan Journal of Law Reform 591 (1990). Reprinted with permission.

Excerpts from Donald A. Dripps, *Akhil Amar on Criminal Procedure and Constitutional Law: "Here I Go Down That Wrong Road Again,"* 74 North Carolina Law Review 1559 (1996). Reprinted with permission.

Excerpts from Donald A. Dripps, *Miscarriages of Justice and the Constitution*, 2 Buffalo Criminal Law Review 635 (1999). Reprinted with permission.

Excerpts from Donald A. Dripps, *Constitutional Theory for Criminal Procedure*: Miranda, Dickerson, *and the Continuing Quest for Broad-but-Shallow*, 43 William and Mary Law Review 1 (2001). Copyright 2001 W&M L. Rev., used with permission.

This is for LAURA, who, like every other child, deserves to inherit a society that is both safer and freer.

Contents

Acknowledgments

I have received help and encouragement in preparing this book from so many people that the specific thanks recorded here will be sure to leave out some individuals who deserve to be recognized individually. I apologize, in advance, for those omissions.

This book would not have been written if Yale Kamisar and Jerry Israel hadn't excited my interest in constitutional criminal procedure at the University of Michigan Law School some twenty years ago. They were superb teachers from whom I continue to learn to this day.

I am grateful, too, to have had the benefit of an all-star roster of faculty colleagues interested in the constitutional regulation of criminal justice. Wayne LaFave, Gerry Bradley, Kit Kinports, John Nowak, and Andy Leipold, long-time colleagues at the University of Illinois, shaped my thinking in countless conversations. Barry Feld, Richard Frase, Mike Tonry, Jack Cound, and Mike Paulsen have engaged me in the same way for the last several years at the University of Minnesota. The book also has improved due to the comments I received during faculty workshops at the University of Minnesota and Washington University law schools.

Some of the initial research for this project was done during a sabbatical leave from Illinois. I am grateful to Dean Howard Hunter and the Emory University School of Law for providing an office and research privileges during that period. Tom Mengler and Tom Sullivan, deans respectively at Illinois and Minnesota, supplied generous research support at every point.

Both at Illinois and Minnesota, I have been blessed by access to superb libraries and by the assistance of superb librarians. Only the diligence of a team of excellent research assistants—Ryan Brauer, Derek Fitch, Jeff Harrington, and Nicole Saharsky—made the preparation of the final manuscript possible.

No one contributes to a body of scholarship without benefitting greatly from the existing literature. Whatever the weaknesses in the prevailing law and the literature concerning it, the fault does not lie in any lack of energy or intellectual power on the part of scholars in the field. I expect that I have learned most from those with whom I have disagreed. When debate remains intense, we do well to remember that passion in controversy stems from a common concern with the issues disputed. In the words of William Blake, "opposition is true friendship."

Introduction: Values and Doctrine in Criminal Procedure

Scholars and judges who agree on little else agree that the constitutional law of criminal procedure is in disarray. Although nominally grounded on the Constitution, the Supreme Court's criminal-procedure cases typically do not reflect much concern for text, history, or structure. And precedent, in criminal-procedure circles, is a bit of a bad joke. The Warren Court overruled precedent on a regular basis, while the Burger and Rehnquist Courts have distinguished the Warren Court landmarks in accord with theories that leave the old cases with no justification of their own.

If the resulting body of law were highly functional, few would care about the weakness of the constitutional justifications or the arbitrary distinctions in the cases. But the current body of law is highly *dysfunctional*. Consider three statistics.

Roughly speaking, half of all arrests don't lead to convictions.[1] That can only mean that the police detect many guilty offenders the courts fail to convict, that the police arrest a great many innocent people, or that arrest is routinely used as a kind of informal punishment. The most likely interpretation is that some combination of these phenomena explains the nonconviction rate.

Nationwide, 25% of the conclusive DNA tests performed at the request of the police exonerate the suspect.[2] There is no reason to suppose that the processes of police investigation are any better in cases that do not involve tissue samples that can be tested by the DNA technique. The same factors that implicate the innocent in rape and murder cases where DNA testing is often possible—misidentification, poor defense work, prosecutorial misconduct, informant perjury, and false confessions—are at work in other cases too. Our trial process is being asked to negate far more false accusations than criminal justice professionals previously believed.

Consider a final statistic. Although social science data suggest that black and white usage rates of marijuana and cocaine are roughly comparable, blacks are five times more likely than whites to be convicted of these offenses.[3] Police decisions to stop, search and arrest, and prosecutorial decisions to charge, clearly have a massively disproportionate impact on black Americans.

A variety of other evidence could be brought to bear on the point, but these three statistics alone suggest that our criminal process is not punishing enough of the guilty, exonerating enough of the innocent, or doing equal justice under law. How could this be, thirty years after the Warren Court's criminal-procedure revolution? This book argues that legal doctrine is in large measure responsible for the failure of the criminal-procedure revolution. Put another way, current doctrine does not reflect prevailing (and justified) values about the criminal process very well. The corollary is that changes in legal doctrine could both rationalize the law and improve the performance of the justice system.

For a long time the Supreme Court relied on substantive due process—the so-called "fundamental fairness" test—to regulate criminal procedure in the states under the authority of the Fourteenth Amendment. The test was in terms open-ended, but as applied it placed minimal restrictions on state procedure. At the same time in federal cases the Supreme Court interpreted the Bill of Rights in a libertarian spirit.

The failings of the fundamental fairness test led the Warren Court to incorporate the Bill of Rights criminal-procedure provisions as a matter of substantive due process under the Fourteenth Amendment. As a result, the Warren Court itself began to discard the old libertarian federal cases. The Burger and Rehnquist Courts have not questioned the unification of state and federal criminal-procedure law, but have relentlessly narrowed the scope of the Warren Court landmarks to the point where there are now very limited restraints on legislatures and law enforcement officials whether state or federal. It is quite rare nowadays for the government to seek certiorari from the Supreme Court on a criminal-procedure question, because the government rarely loses a case on procedural grounds in the absence of egregious facts.

The incorporation doctrine, although historically less implausible than some have assumed, is certainly not compelled by the text and history of the Fourteenth Amendment. The Warren Court's decision to rely in state cases on the Bill of Rights, rather than on due process and equal protection, lies at the root of modern law's incoherence and dysfunction. The current Court's continued reliance on the basic incorporation framework needs to change before the law can be made either more legitimate or more functional.

Now that I've impugned the Bill of Rights, I suppose you expect me take a couple of shots at motherhood and apple pie. What's so awful about the Bill of Rights? The Bill of Rights has two problems as a constitutional code of criminal procedure. The first problem is what the Bill of Rights does *not* contain, and the second is what it does.

The Bill of Rights doesn't include any requirement that police investigations be reliable. How could it, when the invention of the municipal police force was still decades away? The single biggest cause of false convictions—eyewitness misidentification—is completely unregulated by the Bill of Rights. The Sixth Amendment guarantees the assistance of counsel, but not an effective defense founded on a thorough investigation. There is nothing in the text of the Bill of Rights about racial equality.

What the Bill of Rights includes is sometimes as bad as what it omits. The Fifth Amendment privilege against self-incrimination is a prime example. If taken seriously the privilege would greatly damage the pursuit of truth, especially in homicide cases. Under the ragged compromise of *Miranda*,[4] the naive, slow-witted, or submissive (together constituting the great majority of suspects) waive their rights and are then subject to unrecorded backroom questioning by the police. The small minority of professional criminals, however, can completely insulate themselves from questioning, however polite, by uttering the magic words "I want a lawyer." Likewise the double-jeopardy clause prevents retrying a case no matter how manifest or even grotesque the jury's error, without securing real finality for the defendant, who can almost always be tried for several offenses arising out of the same transaction.

The criminal provisions in the Bill of Rights were adopted as part of a comprehensive set of limitations on the powers of the new federal government. The immediate backdrop for the criminal-procedure provisions was English political history, in particular the treason trials under the Tudors and Stuarts. The Bill of Rights criminal-procedure provisions are only partially concerned with preventing mere factual errors. Far more prominent in the minds of the framers was preventing the new government from becoming tyrannical.

This checking-value function of criminal procedure often hamstrings the search for truth. The self-incrimination privilege and the double-jeopardy bar clearly have this potential; and the framers revered jury trial less because juries accurately found the facts and more because juries could block politically oppressive prosecutions.

I have no quarrel with these historical purposes *in federal cases*. At a time when the Justice Department is investigating the Independent Counsel, it seems fair to say that we have yet to outgrow the practice of politically motivated prosecutions. The Bill of Rights criminal provisions deserve our full respect, and generous judicial interpretation, in the federal cases they were designed to regulate.

The manuscript for this book was prepared before September 11, 2001. Obviously the criminal justice system, along with many other features of our society, will change to reflect the fact that small numbers of fanatics, organized in subnational groups, have both the capacity and the will to commit mass murder for political or religious purposes. Whatever the precise changes required by the terrorism challenge, the investigation and prosecution of ordinary crime will remain profoundly important in its own right. The claims made in this book may have implications for handling terrorism cases, but at this point I would venture only some very general and tentative comments in that direction.

The normative position taken by this book in favor of an instrumental view of procedure may well draw additional strength from this new world of asymmetrical threats. On the other hand, a principled respect for the Bill of Rights in federal prosecutions may now seem a legalistic luxury we no longer can afford. Thoughtful people, however, might very well hesitate before investing the federal government with investigatory and adjudicatory tools powerful enough to combat international terrorism *if* those same sweeping powers can be used in ordinary law enforcement.

The case for distinguishing between federal cases, properly subject to the restraining influence of the Bill of Rights, and state cases, properly subject to an instrumental interpretation of due process, remains strong. In the first place, the Bill of Rights procedures, at least given their current rather anemic interpretations, make prosecutions more difficult, but not impossible. The McVeigh case and the convictions following the 1993 World Trade Center bomb plot show that the federal government can prosecute terrorism cases successfully under current law.

In the second place, prevailing Supreme Court doctrine recognizes that the national government has constitutional power to prosecute and adjudicate charges of war crimes, piracy, and so on without complying with the Bill of Rights procedures. The terrorism threat therefore seems unlikely to call forth constitutional amendments or other radical changes in the criminal process at large. If it turns out that the federal courts are incapable of handling foreign terrorism cases under prevailing procedures, the government has the option of turning to military tribunals of the sort proposed by the administration.

Dispensing with some of the Bill of Rights procedures in such cases is more than an unprincipled concession to expedience. Foreign nationals have only very limited entitlements to engage in domestic political activity. The checking value, ordinarily a prominent concern in federal cases, therefore has far less significance with respect to foreigners suspected of terrorism. Expanded investigative authority and military adjudication tribunals for foreign nationals do not threaten domestic political opponents of the government, who alone can oust the incumbents at the polls.

By contrast, domestic terrorism cases can be prosecuted in state courts. I argue that the state courts ought to work under instrumental due process constraints rather than the Bill of Rights. Under a due process regime dedicated to separating the innocent from the guilty, there would be far less concern that miscarriages of justice might permit getting away with mass murder. In domestic terrorism cases, moreover, suspicion of federal authority is only prudent, because distinguishing domestic terrorism from lawful political opposition may often be difficult, even when the authorities are acting in good faith (which may not always be the case).

Rather than permit the risk of domestic terrorism to provoke still further federalization of the criminal law, we should require the federal authorities to respect the Bill of Rights procedures in domestic cases. If federal prosecutors can make their case under more demanding procedural rules, well and good. If they cannot, a state process more fully devoted to instrumental purposes would provide an alternative safeguard for the public interest. If neither process is adequate to the challenge, then the appropriate course would be to adopt carefully-considered constitutional amendments to authorize broader law-enforcement powers in a limited class of cases.

In state cases political prosecutions are the exception and garden-variety felonies the norm. The states must hold regular elections under the guarantee clause, cannot discriminate against out of state residents under Article IV, face the practical check of emigration by both persons and their capital, and in general pose less of a threat of a thorough-going tyranny than the federal government. In the first place, state responsibility for prosecuting the familiar felonies suggest a more instrumental and less libertarian approach in state cases. In the second place, a state advantage in criminal procedure vis a vis the federal government might create a practical incentive to slow or even reverse the creeping federalization of the substantive criminal law.

It turns out that the right place to look for criminal procedure doctrine is right there in the text of the Fourteenth Amendment. Due process means no punishment without a fair trial, and equal protection means no racial discrimination in criminal justice. The current reliance on the Bill of Rights has meant that due process and equal protection have been marginalized, even if they have not yet fallen into complete desuetude.

Under current law police practices consistent with the Bill of Rights do not violate due process unless they "shock the conscience" of the court. Consciences formed since the Holocaust are pretty hard to shock. The Supreme Court has never held police practices unconstitutional under the test. Yet the Court has defined many troubling police practices as neither searches nor seizures, leaving them practically unregulated by the Constitution. Examples include informants, examination of bank and telephone records, and so-called "consensual" encounters between citizens and police who "ask" for "consent" to search.

In adjudicatory proceedings due process is now primarily informed by history, not reliability. Consistency with founding-era practice (whether 1791 or 1866 is left a little vague) will ordinarily insulate a state procedure from due process challenge. By contrast, a purely instrumental assessment of procedural reliability and the consequences of error governs such lesser administrative liabilities as discharge from public employment or suspension from public schools. It is a revealing comment on the state of our criminal process that conservative judges were worried that a test explicitly concerned with instrumental reliability would require judicial activism.

Current equal protection law is little changed since the 1880s. Invidious discrimination in policing, charging, or jury selection is unconstitutional, but the defendant has to prove invidious discrimination and can rarely do so simply by proving disparate impact.

I suggest a doctrinal strategy that reduces the primacy of the Bill of Rights in favor of greater reliance in state cases on due process and equal protection. Police practices should be regulated under a substantive due process test far more focused than the fundamental fairness test. When the government justifies an invasion of liberty on grounds of criminal law enforcement there must be a reasonable expectation, proportionate to the intrusion, that the police tactic will lead to the prevention or prosecution of an offense. This would entail current Fourth Amendment law, but it would also impose some limits on such practices as the use of informants, which are currently wholly unregulated by the Constitution.

Both police investigations, prominently including identification procedures, and state trial procedure should be subject to the instrumental procedural due process test of *Mathews v. Eldridge*[5] that the Court applies in administrative law. Just as in the entitlement cases, after consulting the risks and consequences of error, and the costs of additional procedural safeguards, the courts should describe the required safeguards in general, rule-like terms. *Mathews* directs the appropriate analysis, while *Miranda* suggests the proper model of doctrinal form.

Equal protection doctrine in criminal cases should move generally in the direction of adopting Title VII type burdens of proof. The long history of discrimination in the criminal law, and the profoundly disturbing disparate impact of the criminal justice system, suggest regulating police investigations as well as charging decisions under some sort of burden-shifting regime. There will be limits on how much progress equal protection analysis can achieve, but it can surely achieve more than it has done so far.

Of course legal doctrine does not exist in a vacuum. There are sociopolitical and institutional, as well as doctrinal, limits on what the Supreme Court can do. I do not claim that doctrinal changes by themselves will make the criminal process completely reliable or fully egalitarian. I do claim that whatever the political orientation of the justices, and whatever the sociopolitical or institutional limits on their choices, *within those constraints* a turn away from the Bill of Rights to the Fourteenth Amendment would promote legitimacy, reliability, and equality. In my view it is no coincidence that the modern Supreme Court's two most enlightened decisions are *Batson v. Kentucky*[6] and *Ake v. Oklahoma*,[7] which rest respectively on the Fourteenth Amendment's equal protection and due process clauses.

The first three chapters trace the history of constitutional criminal procedure from its origins in fundamental fairness, through the Warren Court's turn to selective incorporation, to today's regime of conservative balancing, in which the felt necessities of law enforcement have utterly extinguished the old libertarian interpretations of the Bill of Rights in federal cases. Chapter 4 examines the transition from fundamental fairness to selective incorporation, then from selective incorporation to conservative balancing, in more detail, by concentrating on the illustrative example of police interrogation.

Chapter 5 develops a normative framework for evaluating criminal-procedure decisions and applies that framework to criticize all three of the models the Court has thus far developed. Chapter 5 defends a conventionalist theory of constitutional interpretation and an instrumental normative theory of procedure. Judged by these standards, none of the models had strong support in the legitimate sources of constitutional law, none gave sufficient protection to the innocent from unjust conviction or police overreaching, none gave broad enough scope for state practices that enhance reliability without oppression, and none did much to prevent racial discrimination. To this list of deficiencies, the current model adds a plethora of arbitrary distinctions between cases. Given the intellectual powers of those responsible, one must assume that what is arbitrary is also disingenuous.

Chapter 6 develops a criminal-procedure model based directly on the Fourteenth Amendment. That model looks to substantive due process to limit police overreaching, procedural due process to ensure reliable investigations and fair trials, and to Title VII type procedures to implement the constitutional command of equal protection. To the extent possible, judgments about the application of these principles should be expressed as rule-like generalizations, and enforced by a new constitutional remedy—the contingent exclusionary rule. Chapter 7 illustrates the application of the model in the contexts of informants, identification procedures, the right to counsel, confessions, and confrontation.

In a nutshell, the old fundamental fairness standard describes the governing values too generally, while selective incorporation describes the governing norms too particularly. For those who value reliability and equality in criminal justice, the second sentence of the Fourteenth Amendment enshrines those very values. Mediated by the substantive due process, procedural due process, and equal protection standards I suggest, those values would be described at a level of generality that would canalize judicial discretion without freezing the law in the image of common-law procedure.

Before the Warren Court we gave the wrong answers, and since the Warren Court we have asked the wrong questions. The great clauses in the Fourteenth Amendment don't guarantee anything. But they enable us to ask the right questions, without which the right answers will never come.

Constitutional Criminal Procedure from the Adoption of the Fourteenth Amendment to 1947: The Strange Career of Fundamental Fairness

THE DOCTRINAL FOUNDATIONS OF FUNDAMENTAL FAIRNESS

On the twentieth of February, 1882, the state of California, in an *ex parte* information rather than a grand jury indictment, charged Joseph Hurtado with murdering Jose Antonio Stuardo.[1] At trial, Hurtado was convicted and sentenced to death. He attacked the validity of the judgment on the ground that the Fourteenth Amendment's due process clause required grand jury review of criminal charges.[2] The United States Supreme Court had not previously given plenary consideration to a Fourteenth Amendment challenge to a state conviction.[3]

The briefs and the opinion in *Hurtado* raise the basic arguments that continue to perplex scholars and judges. At the outset, the litigants agreed upon the origins of the phrase "due process of law."[4] As the Court's opinion expounds with considerable erudition,[5] Lord Coke, in his Second Institute, commenting on Chapter 39 of Magna Charta, equated the King's pledge not to injure any freeman except according to "a judgment of his peers or to the law of the land" with the commitment to "due process of law." It follows that the basic meaning of due process corresponds with that of Magna Charta's Chapter 39, i.e., restraining the unlawful exercise of official power.

The leap from Magna Charta to the Fourteenth Amendment, however, spans a course of history in which representative democracy had its modern origins. As Justice Matthews wrote in *Hurtado*, "[i]t did not enter the minds of the barons to provide security against their own body or in favor of the Commons by limiting the power of Parliament; so that bills of attainder, *ex post facto* laws, laws declaring forfeitures of estates, and other arbitrary acts of legislation which occur so frequently in English history, were never regarded as inconsistent with the law of the land[.]"[6]

The fundamental challenge in interpreting the due process clause is to reconcile the idea that the government is subject to the law with the idea that the elected legislature makes the law. Antebellum American legal thought supplied the *Hurtado* Court with three possible responses to this challenge. The first of these was a historical understanding of procedural due process. The legislature, on this account, has plenary authority to determine the substantive content of laws regulating the primary conduct of individuals, but is constrained by the due process clause from departing from the common-law forms of procedure the United States inherited from England. Joseph Story, in his *Commentaries on the Constitution of the United States*, had taken this view.[7] The Supreme Court, in its most important due process decision antedating the adoption of the Fourteenth Amendment, had approved this interpretation with respect to the Fifth Amendment due process clause.[8]

A second alternative recognized in antebellum legal sources was an instrumental, rather than historical, conception of procedural due process. Like the historical approach, the instrumental approach conceded the legislature broad power over the substantive rights and liabilities of citizens. When it came to procedure, however, what was crucial was not the historical pedigree, but the practical fairness, of the procedure provided by the legislature to test the application of its substantive rules. Webster's argument in the *Dartmouth College* took this view of due process: "By the law of the land is most clearly intended the general law; a law which hears before it condemns; which proceeds upon inquiry, and renders judgment only after trial."[9] The bare fact that the legislature provided the procedure would not suffice; bills of attainder, *ex post facto* laws, acts reversing judgments, and so on, were not due process.[10] But on the Webster account the forms of procedure need not be frozen in the image of the common law. Judge Cooley adopted this view in his *Constitutional Limitations*, first published while the Fourteenth Amendment was pending in the states.[11] Webster's reference to "a general law" and Cooley's views on vested rights suggest that they may also have entertained substantive understandings of due process. Antebellum legal theory, however, clearly included some understanding of due process as a requirement of fair procedure as distinct from historically sanctioned common-law procedure.

Yet a third antebellum understanding of due process viewed "the law of the land" as natural law, so that legislation contrary to fundamental principles of justice was made invalid by the due process clause. Although most of the state courts to consider the matter under "law of the land" provisions in state constitutions appear to have rejected this approach,[12] opposing factions in the slavery controversy had relied on substantive understandings of the Fifth Amendment due process clause. Most prominently, Chief Justice Taney had relied on due process to invalidate the Missouri Compromise in the *Dred Scott* decision.[13] Antislavery lawyers had also found a substantive component to Fifth Amendment due process. For example, the Republican Party platform declared that due process *forbade* slavery in the territories.[14]

The *Hurtado* Court took this latter, substantive due process approach to resolve the case before it. The thesis of this book is that the turn to substantive due
process was a mistake, and that the instrumental theory of procedural due
process offers the most appropriate doctrinal premise for constitutional criminal
procedure. To understand why the *Hurtado* Court chose as it did, to appreciate
the difficulties of the doctrinal choice, and to expose the deep roots of what went
wrong in the century that followed, we must consider five recurring topics of due
process argumentation. I shall refer to these topics as the positivist trap, the parade of horribles, the indeterminacy objection, the constitutional straightjacket,
and the Bill of Rights problem. All five make prominent appearances in the
Hurtado decision.

The Positivist Trap and the Parade of Horribles

The simplest response to the paradox of limiting legislatures to following the
law is to admit that due process is whatever process the legislature provides.
Thus the label "positivist trap"; the law of the land is positive, not natural, law,
and therefore legislation that does not violate some other constitutional provision
can never violate the due process clause. Government agents may violate positive law, but in the Fourteenth Amendment context, the state courts provide the
highest authority on the meaning of the state's laws.

This approach has enjoyed significant support in the context of administrative
entitlement decisions,[15] in which the power of the legislature to decline to provide some benefit arguably includes the power to offer the benefit subject to
some specified procedure.[16] The Court at one time flirted with the positivist approach in criminal cases as well,[17] but the affair was short-lived and necessarily
so. This is because the positivist approach encounters two convincing objections,
the first holding that the positivist account renders the due process clause nugatory and the second holding that accepting the positivist approach would invite
unacceptable consequences.

As Hurtado's lawyer put it in his brief:

The same reasoning which would give to a state, notwithstanding this provision of the
Constitution, the right to set aside and disregard this institution, would also necessarily
concede to the state the same power to abolish the right of trial by jury, and as well also
the right to be informed of the charge against him before he would be put upon his trial.
If, notwithstanding the amendment, these rights may be taken from the citizen, it is evident that the words "due process of law," as used in that amendment and applied to the
protection of life and liberty, are useless and meaningless.[18]

Both objections attack the idea that the legislature is not bound by the due
process clause. The first variation asks if there is *any* injustice the state legislature is constitutionally precluded from enacting. The second asks why intelligent
people would condition the application of a constitutional provision designed to
limit state power on the acquiescence of the state legislature.

The Indeterminacy Objection
and the Constitutional Straightjacket

The twin objections to the positivist trap are persuasive, but they invite a response I call the indeterminacy objection. If due process is not whatever process the legislature provides, what is due process? Commissioning the judges to identify the law of the land independently of legislation effectively transfers from the legislative to the judicial branch ultimate law-making power. In short, while the positivist account fails because it reduces the due process clause to meaning *nothing*, any alternative account must avoid the tendency to make the due process clause mean *anything*.

One natural response for nineteenth-century lawyers was to take the historical approach and identify the law of the land with the common law. Hurtado pressed this argument because common law procedure required grand jury review in felony cases. Quoting Pomeroy, Hurtado's brief interpreted the due process clause as constitutionalizing common-law procedure in criminal cases: due process does "not mean any law which the legislature may see fit to pass, but that common law course of proceedings known in England for centuries and described by our organic law[.]"[19]

Substituting the information procedure for grand jury review was an excellent example of a reasonable procedural reform that departed from the common law. In *Hurtado*, counsel for the state defended the information procedure as an improvement on the grand jury, and predicted—accurately—that the states would move toward its general adoption unless precluded by a constitutional ruling.[20] The Court found this argument persuasive. Justice Matthews wrote that to hold that common-law pedigree "is essential to due process of law, would be to deny every quality of the law but its age, and to render it incapable of progress or improvement. It would be to stamp upon our jurisprudence the unchangeableness attributed to the laws of the Medes and Persians."[21]

The Court could have reached this conclusion on instrumental grounds. If anything was a mere variation in the form, but not the fairness, of proceedings, the substitution of information for indictment was just such a change. The Court, however, did not read due process as a limit on legislative choice of procedures within the range set by instrumental considerations of accurate adjudication. Instead, the *Hurtado* Court met the indeterminacy objection by turning to substantive due process and crafting the standard of fundamental fairness.

Justice Matthews did not use these very words, but fundamental fairness is the gist of the middle ground taken between the positivist trap and assuming a vast, standardless judicial power. The law of the land

refers to that law of the land in each State, which derives its authority from the inherent and reserved powers of the State, *exerted within the limits of those fundamental principles of liberty and justice which lie at the base of all our civil and political institutions*, and the greatest security for which resides in the right of the people to make their own laws, and alter them at their pleasure.[22]

Thus "[i]t is not every act, legislative in form, that is law."[23] Rather,

Law is something more than mere will exerted as an act of power. It must be not a special rule for a particular person or a particular case, but, in the language of Mr Webster, in his familiar definition, "the general law, a law which hears before it condemns, which proceeds upon inquiry, and renders judgment only after trial," so "that every citizen shall holds his life, liberty, property and immunities under the protection of the general rules which govern society," and thus excluding, as not due process of law, acts of attainder, bills of pains and penalties, acts of confiscation, acts reversing judgments, and acts directly transferring one man's estate to another, legislative judgments and decrees, and other similar special, partial and arbitrary exertions of power under the forms of legislation.[24]

Due process therefore does not forbid *either* procedures that are "sanctioned by age and custom, or newly devised in the discretion of the legislative power, in furtherance of the general public good, which regards and preserves these principles of liberty and justice[.]"[25]

According to this interpretation, the states, as well as the federal government, are governments of limited powers. The states, however, are not, like the federal government, governments of enumerated powers. Rather, unenumerated limits on state power always have formed part of the law of the land. The Fourteenth Amendment due process clause posits those limits with the force of federal constitutional law; legislation is constitutional only so long as it respects "those fundamental principles of liberty and justice which lie at the base of all our civil and political institutions." The federal courts have the responsibility for identifying and enforcing "those fundamental principles," for "[t]he enforcement of these limitations by judicial process is the device of self-governing communities to protect the rights of individuals and minorities, as well against the power of numbers, as against the violence of public agents transcending the limits of lawful authority, even when acting in the name and wielding the force of the government."[26]

The doctrine announced in *Hurtado* is that of substantive due process. Having held that due process excludes state legislation for inconsistency with an unwritten law, and that the federal courts are responsible for the exposition of this unwritten law, the Court confided to the federal judiciary a plenary power to review state legislation. The information procedure was upheld, not on the narrow ground that the information process enabled a fair, reliable trial, but on the broader, perhaps limitless ground that the information procedure was consistent with "fundamental principles of liberty and justice."

I believe the justices recognized the problem. The majority noted that elected representatives best secure compliance with the unwritten law incorporated by the due process clause, emphasized that the limiting principles were "fundamental" rather than controversial, and in the event upheld the California procedure against Hurtado's claim.[27] The *Hurtado* opinion also gives some specific

examples of state practices that would constitute clear violations of these fundamental reservations of popular sovereignty. Nonetheless, invoking a federal judicial power to enforce implied limitations on the popular grants of sovereignty to
the states necessarily sowed the seeds of a motley garden of decisions invalidating state legislation for no more authoritative reason than that the justices disagreed with its policy.

Due Process and the Bill of Rights

The Bill of Rights provides one opportunity for constructing the content of the
unwritten law invoked by the *Hurtado* majority. Hurtado did not press such an
argument; the incorporation claim makes more sense with respect to the privileges and immunities clause, which the Court only recently had laid to rest in the
Slaughter-House Cases.[28] Indeed, the *Hurtado* Court took an approach completely incompatible with the theory that due process includes limitations on
state power coincident with those on federal power expressed by the first eight
amendments.

The *Hurtado* Court reasoned that if due process included grand jury review,
the founders would not have included an express grand jury requirement in the
Fifth Amendment.[29] As Justice Harlan responded in his dissent, accepting this
argument logically committed the Court to permitting the states to dispense with
any of the Fifth Amendment guarantees.[30] Indeed, it is equally logical to conclude that the framers would not have included *any* constitutional provision redundant with the due process clause, and so the redundancy argument counsels
permitting the states to abridge the freedom of speech, press, and religion, to execute unreasonable searches and seizures, and to inflict cruel and unusual punishments. The parade of horribles returns, more unappealing than before.

The redundancy argument based on the Fifth Amendment due process clause
collides with the fact that the Fifth Amendment due process clause is itself redundant with other provisions of the Bill of Rights. Due process was thought, before *Hurtado*, to require grand jury presentment and jury trial in serious criminal
cases, but the Fifth Amendment provides for indictment by grand jury and both
the Sixth Amendment and Article III require jury trials. The Sixth Amendment
also requires that the accused "be informed of the nature and cause of the accusation," something indispensable to due process.

If the Court had continued to reject the possibility of redundant constitutional
provisions, incorporation, selective or otherwise, would never have become an
issue. The due process clause might even have gone the way of the privileges-
or-immunities clause. But once the Court adopted a natural-law interpretation
of due process, the redundancy argument proved too insubstantial a chock to
prevent the descent down the slippery slope. For doctrinal purposes, the next important step in the development of constitutional criminal procedure was establishing the legitimacy of overlapping interpretations of related constitutional
provisions. This development deserves a brief digression.

THE DOCTRINAL FOUNDATION
OF SELECTIVE INCORPORATION

Selective incorporation, like fundamental fairness, is a substantive due process doctrine; indeed, selective incorporation is one expression of fundamental fairness doctrine. The theory underlying selective incorporation holds that state action inconsistent with some of the rights guaranteed in the first eight amendments exceeds the implied limits on the powers delegated to the states by the people, and thus violates the law of the land that is given positive expression in the Fourteenth Amendment's due process clause. To the degree that this approach excludes fundamental fairness analysis, it has the virtue of determinacy; the content of the first eight amendments is accessible.

But selective incorporation has the same rabbit-from-the-hat problem that plagues fundamental fairness, because there is no inevitable connection between the first eight amendments and natural law. The determinacy advantage, moreover, has never been realized, because the Court has viewed selective incorporation as a supplement to fundamental fairness, rather than as an alternative.

This assessment of selective incorporation should disturb even the most modest civil libertarian. The criminal procedure cases are not the only expression of selective incorporation. The effectiveness of rights against the states to freedom of speech, press, and religion has depended on the same doctrinal predicate. The unvarnished truth is nonetheless that the selective incorporation decisions rest on the same theory of the Fourteenth Amendment as *Lochner v. New York*.[31] Illuminatingly, the first provision of the Bill of Rights that the Court applied to the states under the Fourteenth Amendment was not the First Amendment's guarantee of freedom of expression or of conscience, but the Fifth Amendment's protection of private property against condemnation except for a public purpose and with adequate compensation.[32]

In November of 1890, the city of Chicago ordered the improvement of Rockwell Street. The improvements required establishing railroad crossings over tracks owned in fee simple by the Chicago, Burlington & Quincy Railroad Company. The city condemned the railroad's rights of way; under Illinois law the compensation afforded the owners of property taken for public use was established by jury trial. The jury awarded the railroad one dollar in damages, and the state courts upheld the award. The railroad then sued out a writ of error in the Supreme Court, alleging that the award was inadequate and therefore a denial of due process.

The Court was unanimous in holding that due process incorporates the takings clause of the Fifth Amendment. Justice Harlan, the dissenter in *Hurtado*, authored the court's opinion, in which the redundancy argument is not mentioned. But the Court's approach is perfectly consistent with the general approach taken in *Hurtado*. Due process was not satisfied by notice and an opportunity for the railroad to be heard, because a state's "judicial authorities may keep within the letter of the statute prescribing forms of procedure in the courts and give the parties interested the fullest opportunity to be heard, and yet it might be that its final action would be inconsistent with [the Fourteenth] amendment. In determining what is due process of law regard must be had to substance, not to form."[33] The Court bolstered this render-the-provision nugatory argument with the parade of horribles.[34] There followed the holding that the right to just compensation for property taken for public use was an essential component of the law of the land—"a principle of natural equity, recognized by all temperate and civilized governments, from a deep and universal sense of its justice," "a settled principle of universal law, reaching back of all constitutional provisions."[35]

The Court nonetheless affirmed the judgment on the ground that the validity of the award depended on the facts, i.e., whether a real possibility existed that the railroad would ever use its land for anything but a right-of-way, with which the street crossing would not interfere. Deferring to the jury's verdict on this issue, the Court nonetheless left open the possibility that the federal courts might review factual findings so arbitrary as to undermine federal constitutional rights.

What does this have to do with criminal procedure? Everything; for when, in *Twining v. New Jersey*,[36] the Court considered the question of whether the Fourteenth Amendment imposed the Fifth Amendment's privilege against self-incrimination on the states, the Court cited the *Chicago, Burlington & Quincy* case for the proposition that "it is possible that some of the personal rights safeguarded by the first eight Amendments against National action may also be safeguarded against state action, because a denial of them would be a denial of due process of law."[37] The Court nonetheless refused to incorporate the privilege, ranking it as something less than "fundamental," in part (illogically, given the *Chicago, Burlington & Quincy* cite) because the framers had thought it necessary to constitutionalize the privilege independently of due process.[38]

The *Twining* Court did not treat redundancy as dispositive; its analysis of fundamental fairness considered the role of the privilege in the history of English law, the extent to which state constitutions included the privilege prior to the adoption of the Fourteenth Amendment, and the cases thus far adjudicated applying the due process clause to criminal cases.[39] Nearly twenty years would pass before the Court would apply another of the provisions of the Bill of Rights to the states as a matter of due process;[40] and more than forty would go by before the Court did so with respect to one of the criminal procedure provisions in the first eight amendments.[41] Even though selective incorporation would lie dormant for generations, its doctrinal predicates were established by the end of the first decade of the twentieth century. The *Twining* resolution of the Bill of Rights problem is significant because it kept open the possibility of federal judicial intrusions into state criminal procedure, which the scope of the criminal procedure provisions in the Bill of Rights otherwise would have precluded as beyond the independent meaning of due process.

Fundamental fairness and selective incorporation thus are cut from the same substantive-due-process cloth. What modern students think of as competing paradigms in constitutional criminal procedure share a common interpretation of the due process clause; they differ only in their assessments of what counts as fundamental.

PRIVILEGES OR IMMUNITIES: THE ROAD NOT TAKEN

The growth of selective incorporation out of substantive due process might have surprised the framers of the Fourteenth Amendment. They did, after all, include a broadly worded substantive limitation on state power—the privileges-or-immunities clause. It would have been more natural to develop the substantive limits on state power, whether or not derived from the Bill of Rights, under the authority of the privileges-or-immunities clause, rather than under the authority of the due process clause. Why did Hurtado's lawyer rely on due process? Why did the *Hurtado* opinion interpret due process as imposing substantive, as well as procedural, limits on the states?

An obvious, but I believe only partial, answer lies in the *Slaughter-House Cases*,[42] decided by the Supreme Court in 1873. In that decision, a bare majority of the justices had upheld a New Orleans ordinance that created a butcher's monopoly within the city. In so holding, the majority construed the privileges-or-immunities clause as protecting only rights that arise out of national citizenship—such as the right to travel between states and the right to petition the federal government.[43] As the dissenters bitingly pointed out, this interpretation pretty much nullified the clause.[44] This was, apparently, the majority's very object, for Justice Miller's majority opinion openly admitted the fear of standardless judicial power to overturn state legislation.[45]

Given *Slaughter-House*, it seems natural enough for Hurtado to have turned to due process, especially in light of the historical connection between due process and grand jury presentment. And it could well be that the *Hurtado* opinion opened the door to substantive due process as a way of circumventing the *Slaughter-House* opinion's artificial limitations on substantive review of state legislation under the privileges-or-immunities clause.

Nonetheless, the more likely explanation for the focus on due process in the early criminal procedure decisions is simply that to the extent that good lawyers thought the Fourteenth Amendment limited criminal procedure in the states, they thought it did so through the due process clause rather than through the privileges-or-immunities clause. *Slaughter-House* was a five-to-four decision subject to widespread criticism.[46] That decision did not involve criminal procedure, or any claim based on the Bill of Rights. The Court could have maintained the *Slaughter-House* holding under much broader theories of the meaning of "privileges or immunities of citizens of the United States."

That *Slaughter-House* did not foreclose the incorporation question is made clear by *Walker v. Sauvinet*,[47] decided but two years after *Slaughter-House*. Walker kept a coffee house in New Orleans and refused to serve Sauvinet because Sauvinet was black. Sauvinet sued under a state statute requiring public accommodations to serve persons of color. Given the difficulty of persuading a southern jury to award damages for such a claim, the statute provided for judgment by the court in case of a hung jury. The jury in the *Sauvinet* case did not agree, and the judge entered a verdict for plaintiff in the amount of a thousand dollars. The publican sought a writ of error on the ground that section one of the Fourteenth Amendment incorporated the Seventh Amendment right to jury trial.

The Supreme Court rejected the claim, but it did not rely on, or even cite, *Slaughter-House*. Indeed, not even the plaintiff argued that *Slaughter-House* was dispositive.[48] The Court, however, concluded that under the Seventh Amendment, the states "are left to regulate trials in their own courts in their own way. A trial by jury in suits at common law pending in the State courts is not, therefore, a privilege or immunity of national citizenship, which the States are forbidden by the Fourteenth Amendment to abridge."[49]

Thus *Slaughter-House* did not preclude incorporation claims. On the contrary, litigants turned to the privileges-or-immunities clause *after* the *Hurtado* decision had taken a narrow view of due process limits on state criminal procedure, *Slaughter-House* notwithstanding. The claim that the privileges-or-immunities clause applied the Bill of Rights criminal procedure safeguards to the states was made before the Supreme Court for the first time in *Spies v. Illinois*,[50] decided in 1887, three years after *Hurtado*. The defendants were anarchists who had been convicted of murder. They challenged the convictions under the Fourth, Fifth, and Sixth Amendments, as applied to Illinois through the Fourteenth. The specific claims were that the state courts had denied defendants an impartial jury by permitting jurors to sit who were prejudiced by pretrial publicity, in violation of the Sixth Amendment; that cross-examination of one defendant went beyond the scope of direct and thus violated the Fifth Amendment privilege against compelled self-incrimination; and that this cross-examination was based on a letter seized without a warrant, and so violated both the Fourth and Fifth Amendments as construed in the *Boyd* decision.

John Randolph Tucker, who taught constitutional law at Washington and Lee, and would later serve as President of the American Bar Association, made a famous argument on behalf of the petitioners.[51] Tucker advanced two distinct but related claims for incorporation. On the one hand, he argued that the provisions in the Bill of Rights declared rights of the person against all governmental authority, but made those rights enforceable only against encroachment by the United States and not by the states.[52] The Fourteenth Amendment then made these declared rights enforceable against the states. On the other hand, Tucker asserted that the privileges-or-immunities clause protected fundamental rights against state violation, and that the items in the Bill of Rights were, *ipso facto*, fundamental.[53]

Neither of these claims is implausible; they are the same points emphasized by modern defenders of total incorporation.[54] Representative John Bingham, the progenitor of the privileges-or-immunities clause, subscribed to the declaratory theory.[55] Senator Jacob Howard, who introduced the Fourteenth Amendment on the floor of the Senate, subscribed to total incorporation under the fundamental-rights theory.[56] Some contemporary commentators endorsed incorporation under the privileges-or-immunities clause,[57] as did Justice Bradley's dissenting opinion in *Slaughter-House*.[58] Tucker did not invoke legislative history; but he did raise what are now thought to be the strongest arguments for total incorporation.

Slaughter-House did not stand in the way. Indeed, Tucker even relied on *Slaughter-House*. Rights secured by the Bill of Rights, he argued, qualify as distinctively federal privileges or immunities,[59] and both the majority and the dissent in *Slaughter-House* agreed that the clause protects fundamental rights.[60]

The Court, per Chief Justice Waite, began by recognizing that under *Barron* and its progeny, the Bill of Rights did not limit the states.[61] Indeed, one of the cases Waite cited was *Twitchell v. Commonwealth*,[62] in which a unanimous Court had rejected the petition of a Pennsylvania man convicted of murder who claimed that the failure of his indictment to specify the method of causing death violated the notice requirement of the Sixth Amendment. *Twitchell* was unexceptional in rejecting a Sixth Amendment challenge against a state conviction; but it has special significance because the case came to the Court in April of 1869, less than a year after the Fourteenth Amendment became effective. Evidently, Twitchell's lawyer didn't think the Fourteenth Amendment had anything to do with criminal procedure. More significantly, a unanimous Supreme Court thought that *Barron v. Baltimore* remained good law after the passage of the Fourteenth Amendment.

The *Spies* Court, however, frankly admitted that Tucker was making an argument that *Barron* did not foreclose—that the Fourteenth Amendment had altered the underlying premise of underlays *Barron* and *Twitchell*.[63] The Court did not reach this argument regarding the impartial jury or the search-and-seizure claim. The record did not establish that any of the jurors were actually biased;[64] and the search-and-seizure claim had not been raised in the state courts.[65]

The *Spies* Court did, however, reach the self-incrimination claim based on the cross-examination of Spies. It held that "whether a cross-examination must be confined to matters pertinent to the testimony-in-chief, or may be extended to the matters in issue, is certainly a question of state law as administered in the courts of the State, and not of Federal law."[66] This holding cannot be squared with Tucker's argument. There can be no question that whether cross of the accused beyond the scope of direct violates the privilege is a federal constitutional question if the Fifth Amendment privilege is in play. To hold that the issue is a state law question clearly implies that the Fifth Amendment privilege does not apply to the states.

Tucker did not prevail in *Spies*, but five years later Justice Field invoked his argument as the true interpretation of the privileges-or-immunities clause. Field, however, was dissenting from the Court's holding in *O'Neil v. Vermont* that "as a Federal question, it has always been ruled that the 8th Amendment to the Constitution of the United States does not apply to the States."[67] The Vermont courts had sentenced O'Neil to fifty-four years hard labor for shipping liquor from New York, where liquor was legal, to Vermont, where it was not. Despite the sympathetic facts, only Field, Harlan, and Brewer voted to vacate the sentence.

Charles "Gunplay" Maxwell was convicted of robbing a Utah bank. He was charged by information, and tried by a jury of eight, rather than twelve, jurors. If the total incorporation theory were accepted, he would have won on both Fifth Amendment presentment and Sixth Amendment jury trial grounds. Maxwell's lawyer supported his case in the Supreme Court by quoting Senator Howard's remarks equating privileges or immunities with the Bill of Rights.[68] More than thirty years after Congress debated the Fourteenth Amendment, the Court was finally confronted with the principal piece of evidence supporting the total incorporation theory.

The Court was unimpressed. Howard was only one of many in Congress, and in any event a constitutional amendment ultimately is ratified not by Congress but by the people acting through state conventions.[69] Harlan, the lone dissenter, made no reference to legislative history.

What seems clear from the early case law on the Fourteenth Amendment is that while an argument for incorporating the Bill of Rights criminal procedure guarantees via the privileges-or-immunities clause can be made, that argument was not obvious or inevitable. Even before *Slaughter-House*, the Court had reaffirmed *Barron* in the *Twitchell* case. After *Slaughter-House*, in *Hurtado* both counsel and the justices looked to the due process clause for constitutional limits on state criminal procedure. *Slaughter-House* did not bar the total incorporation claim in criminal procedure cases, for in *Spies*, *O'Neil*, and *Maxwell* counsel made the claim, and in *Spies* and *O'Neil* the Court did not treat it as barred by precedent. Only one justice, Harlan the first, consistently maintained the incorporation position. If incorporation were widely thought to follow from the Fourteenth Amendment, the judicial record is inexplicable.

The incorporation claim was a lawyer's argument, and by the turn of the century it was a dead letter. In 1899, John Randolph Tucker's treatise on constitutional law was published posthumously. In his book, Tucker repudiated as a jurist what he had avowed as an advocate. Regarding the privileges-or-immunities clause, Tucker wrote that "any denial of a right in a State court, which by any one of the ten amendments is forbidden, is not unconstitutional, for those amendments are limits upon federal power only, and the State court may do, contrary to the terms of those amendments, what the Federal court is forbidden to do."[70] The supporting footnote cites *Spies v. Illinois* and *Walker v. Sauvinet* for this proposition, without the faintest intimation of critique.

RACE, FEDERALISM, AND THE ILLUSION OF EQUAL PROTECTION

In the immediate wake of the Fourteenth Amendment racial discrimination in criminal justice took a variety of forms.[71] Criminal acts by whites against blacks went unpunished, while blacks were punished with disproportionate severity. Sometimes these two disparities came together, when whites went unpunished for lynching blacks (sometimes innocent), often with grotesque cruelty. Blacks were routinely excluded from jury service.

Relief from private violence lies in the first instance with the executive authorities. After the withdrawal of troops from the states of the old confederacy in 1877, the southern authorities turned a blind eye to lynching.[72] Without investigation or prosecution by the law enforcement agencies of the state, the courts, whether state or federal, were incapable of taking steps to punish private violence on their own.

The Supreme Court, however, did condemn racial discrimination in prosecution and jury selection. *Yick Wo v. Hopkins*[73] famously reversed a criminal conviction under a law that was almost exclusively enforced against Chinese. *Strauder v. West Virginia*,[74] in rhetoric noble enough to be quoted repeatedly in *Batson v. Kentucky* more than a century later,[75] declared that the exclusion of blacks from jury service violates the Equal Protection Clause. *Neal v. Delaware*[76] rejected the "violent presumption" that the total absence of blacks from juries could be attributed to the racially neutral application of general qualifications such as intelligence and good character.

Yet discrimination in criminal justice persisted.[77] As late as 1965, a case reached the Supreme Court in which the record showed that no black had served on a petit jury in Tallageda County, Alabama, for more than a decade.[78] How could discrimination persist in the face of the Supreme Court's clear announcement of a contrary constitutional norm?

The very same justices who recognized the right withheld practical remedies. Justice Harlan, the great dissenter in *Plessy v. Ferguson*, wrote the *Neal* decision inferring discrimination from complete absence of black jurors in an entire state for a period of years. But the portion of the opinion that mattered most was the holding that the erroneous denial of a motion to quash the venire did not justify removing the state prosecution to the federal trial court under a Reconstruction statute.[79] Justice Harlan explained this holding by saying that *de facto*, as opposed to *de jure*, discrimination was not state action for purposes of the removal statute—even though he held a few paragraphs later that it was state action for purposes of the Constitution. How were the federal courts supposed to know that the state appellate courts would not correct the error on their own?

This did not leave victims of discrimination without a theoretical remedy. They could raise their claims in state court, and, if they lost there, seek review in the Supreme Court of the United States. In subsequent cases, however, the Court refused to second-guess state court factual findings, however improbable, provided the state courts observed the formality of receiving the defendant's proof in support of motions to quash a venire or an indictment on equal protection grounds.[80] Federal habeas corpus relief was unavailable because defects in jury selection were not deemed jurisdictional.[81]

This gap between rights and remedies can be described as hypocrisy,[82] but there are at least two principled explanations for the *Neal* Court's course. First, in the historical circumstances it is not quite clear just what else the Court could have done. A broad construction of the removal provision might have prompted its repeal, but of far more pressing importance black jury service would certainly have resulted in retaliatory violence against blacks bold enough to serve, as well as the lynching of defendants likely to have black jurors hear their cases. Without federal troops to oppose force with force, Justice Harlan simply lacked the power to enforce the equal protection clause.

Rather than hold that the state was justified to presume that all blacks lacked the judgment or honesty to serve as jurors, the *Neal* majority chose to issue an opinion more aspirational than juridical. That can be called hypocrisy. It can also be called prudence. Justice Harlan's opinion in *Neal* has a tragic quality, not wholly unlike Justice Jackson's famous dissent in *Korematsu v. United States*.

Second, it may be mistaken, but it is not necessarily hypocritical, to say that the Constitution honors both the antidiscrimination principle and federalism, but that when these conflict, it is federalism that deserves priority over the antidiscrimination principle. Since *Carolene Products* we have taken a different view, but we should not attribute hypocrisy to justices operating under a very different set of constitutional premises. Justice Harlan surely knew that the southern courts would not enforce the equal protection clause. He might, however, have decided, without hypocrisy if not without error, that the federal judiciary's assumption of the power to try state criminal cases on a routine basis was a greater evil than racial discrimination in jury selection.[83]

One striking feature of the early jury cases is the automatic assumption that race matters—matters a lot. *Strauder* and *Neal* take the view that the black defendant has an equal protection right to freedom from invidious exclusion of blacks from the jury that hears his case, and that the appropriate remedy is reversal for a new trial untainted by racial unfairness. The idea of the criminal defendant as an enforcer of the rights of potential black jurors is a long way off.

The deference to state court fact-finding finally ended in *Norris v. Alabama*,[84] in which counsel for the defense proffered the forged jury lists to the Supreme Court during oral argument. The justices personally inspected the documents, and Justice Van Devanter was heard to whisper "Why it's as plain as punch" that the state officials had falsified the jury rolls.[85] Per Chief Justice Hughes, the Court unanimously reversed.

Norris coincided with the constitutional sea-change wrought by the New Deal. It coincided, also, with the increasing rigor of the fundamental fairness due process test. Norris was one of the "Scottsboro boys," retried after the *Powell* decision reversed his first conviction. As the Court turned from review of social and economic legislation to the field of human rights, it was obvious that southern justice was due for a searching examination. Ultimately—and, as I shall argue, unfortunately—that review took the form of incorporating the Bill of Rights into the due process clause, rather than the form of direct application of due process and equal protection to the criminal process.

FROM *HURTADO* TO THE MODERN INCORPORATION DEBATE: CONTRASTING APPROACHES TO STATE AND FEDERAL CASES

The natural law interpretation of due process approved in *Hurtado* did not immediately yield any revolutionary change in state criminal procedure. Quite the contrary, until 1923, the Court did not reverse a state criminal conviction because of a due process violation. A host of petitioners sought such relief, but the Court consistently refused to find that state prosecutions violated the Fourteenth Amendment.[86] Yet the same Court engaged in the frequent and capricious nullification of state economic regulations on substantive due process grounds.[87] This same Court also took a noticeably pro-defense approach to federal criminal cases. In these federal cases, the Court reached holdings under the Fourth, Fifth, and Sixth Amendments that presaged results not reached under the Fourteenth until the highwater mark of the Warren Court's intervention in state administration of criminal justice. Indeed, some of the early federal decisions turned out to be so favorable to the defense that modern Supreme Court majorities, even of the Warren Court, felt compelled to overrule them.

To begin with search and seizure, just two years after *Hurtado*, the Court in *Boyd v. United States*[88] held that a subpoena for documentary evidence amounts to an unreasonable seizure under the Fourth Amendment, and that the Fifth Amendment privilege against self-incrimination forbids the admission in evidence of such a subpoena's fruits. The government claimed title by forfeiture to thirty-five cases of plate glass, allegedly imported without payment of the applicable duty. Edward and George Boyd claimed title to the glass and a trial followed on the issue of whether the appropriate duty had been paid. At the trial, an issue arose as to the quantity and value of a previous shipment of glass imported by the Boyds.

Pursuant to a statutory authorization, the government moved for a court order directing the Boyds to produce the invoice for the earlier shipment. Under the statute, failure to comply with the discovery order would be treated as confessing the truth of the facts set out in the government's motion. The Boyds complied with the order, but objected both to the order, and to the introduction of the invoice in evidence at the trial, on constitutional grounds.

The Supreme Court unanimously agreed with the Boyds. Justice Bradley's opinion, for seven of the justices, analogized the compelled production of a business record to the house-breaking search for a political tract that Lord Camden had condemned in *Entick v. Carrington*:[89]

It is not the breaking of his doors, and the rummaging of his drawers, that constitutes the essence of the offense; but it is the invasion of his indefeasible right of personal security, personal liberty and private property, where that right has never been forfeited by his conviction of some public offense; it is the invasion of this sacred right which underlies and constitutes the essence of Lord Camden's judgment. Breaking into a house and opening boxes and drawers are circumstances of aggravation; but any forcible and compulsory extortion of a man's own testimony or of his private papers to be used as evidence to convict him of crime or to forfeit his goods, is within the condemnation of that judgment. In this regard the Fourth and Fifth Amendments run almost into each other.[90]

Private papers were wholly different from stolen or smuggled goods, for the government had title to the latter but not to the former.[91]

The Court saw little distinction between the Fourth and Fifth Amendments:

We have already noticed the intimate relation between the two amendments. They throw great light on each other. For the "unreasonable searches and seizures" condemned in the Fourth Amendment are almost always made for the purpose of compelling a man to give evidence against himself, which in criminal cases is condemned in the Fifth Amendment; and compelling a man "in a criminal case to be a witness against himself," which is condemned in the Fifth Amendment, throws light on the question as to what is an "unreasonable search and seizure" within the meaning of the Fourth Amendment. And we have been unable to perceive that the seizure of a man's private books and papers to be used in evidence against him is substantially different from compelling him to be a witness against himself.[92]

The individual's sphere of autonomy encompassed both physical security, personal liberty, and private property. To use his property as evidence against his will was indistinguishable from forcing incriminating words from his own lips—at least when the property took the form of documents.

Boyd laid the foundation for a distinctive, and extraordinarily liberal, federal model of criminal procedure. Initially, the Court did not interpret *Boyd* to require suppression of illegally seized evidence. In *Adams v. New York*[93] police, pursuant to a warrant, searched the defendant's office and seized illegal "policy slips," or lottery tickets. They also seized letters, which were used at the trial both as handwriting exemplars and as admissions of ownership of the policy slips. The Court, per Justice Day and without dissent, held that *Boyd* did not require exclusion of illegally seized evidence, and so it was not necessary to determine whether the Fourteenth Amendment incorporated the Fourth.

In the ground breaking *Weeks*[94] decision, however, the Court viewed *Boyd* as authorizing the modern exclusionary rule. The defendant's home was searched twice, once by local police and once by police accompanied by the U.S. Marshall. Justice Day once again wrote for a unanimous Court, but this time held that the defendant's pretrial motion for the return of his property—the papers showing his guilt of the crime charged—should have been granted, with the practical effect (given the *Boyd* limit on the subpoena power) of suppression. *Adams* was distinguished, unconvincingly, on procedural grounds; an objection at trial was untimely, while a pretrial motion for return of property was timely.[95] The *Weeks* Court also noted that in *Adams* the police had acted under warrant;[96] but if the evidence in *Adams* was untainted the Court could have passed *both* the exclusionary rule and the incorporation issue.[97]

There is another, and better, explanation for the flip-flop than those given by the *Weeks* Court. *Adams* was a state case, in which the defendant claimed that the

Fourteenth Amendment applied the Fourth to the states. Reversing the conviction would have required the *Mapp* holding fifty-eight years early. In *Weeks*, the Court carefully distinguished the evidence seized by the local police in the initial search from the evidence seized later by the U.S. Marshall. Only the latter must be returned, as the "Fourth Amendment is not directed to individual misconduct of such [state] officials. Its limitations reach the Federal Government and its agencies."[98] Thus the *Weeks* Court gave a negative answer to the incorporation question reserved in *Adams*; the Fourth Amendment holding of *Adams* was effectively overruled.

In subsequent cases, the *Weeks* exclusionary rule grew beyond the Fifth Amendment theory announced in *Boyd*. In *Silverthorne Lumber Co. v. United States*,[99] the Court held that a corporation, which did not enjoy the Fifth Amendment privilege,[100] could nonetheless invoke the rule of *Weeks*. In *Agnello v. United States*,[101] the Court suppressed cocaine seized during a warrantless search of a home. *Boyd*'s predicate was the defendant's rightful ownership of the evidence; only a Fourth Amendment deterrent theory could justify suppressing contraband. Yet in a move more consistent with treating use of the owner's evidence against him as a Fifth Amendment violation than with a theory of deterring future Fourth Amendment violations, the *Agnello* Court held the tainted evidence admissible against the defendants other than the home-owner.[102]

Likewise consistent with *Boyd*'s focus on property rights was the 1921 decision in *Gouled v. United States*.[103] An undercover agent obtained entry on the pretext of a social call, and seized incriminating papers during the owner's brief absence from the room. The Court had no difficulty applying *Boyd*'s self-incrimination theory. But the *Gouled* Court went further, and declared that "mere evidence," as distinct from contraband, could not be seized even under the authority of a warrant based on probable cause.[104]

All of the early exclusionary rule cases assume a warrant requirement. For example, in *Weeks*, the Court declared that the "United States Marshall could only have invaded the house of the accused when armed with a warrant issued as required by the Constitution, upon sworn information and describing with reasonable particularity the thing for which the search was to be made."[105] In *Silverthorne* and *Agnello* the searches apparently were illegal for want of a warrant, rather than for want of probable cause.

In *Carroll v. United States*[106] the Court held that a search of an automobile on the highway was legal if supported by probable cause, even though the government agents had no warrant. Chief Justice Taft relied on federal statutes dating to the founding, which authorized warrantless searches of ships to enforce customs duties. From these he inferred that

the guaranty of freedom from unreasonable searches and seizures by the Fourth Amendment has been construed, practically since the beginning of the government, as recognizing a necessary difference between a search of a store, dwelling house, or other structure in respect of which a proper official warrant readily may be obtained, and a search of ship, motor boat, wagon or automobile, for contraband goods, where it is not practicable to secure a warrant because the vehicle can be quickly moved out of the locality or jurisdiction in which the warrant must be sought.[107]

Given the cases that had come to the Court, however, the warrantless search was thought to be the exception rather than the rule.

The federal model thus presumptively required a warrant, and so, logically enough, probable cause, even in cases like *Carroll* in which no warrant was required. How could government agents do without judicial authorization what no court could command? Any evidence—even contraband—seized in violation of the warrant-probable cause standard was to be suppressed, at least against the victim of the illegal search.

The feedback from this rigorous model was that the Court adopted a narrow definition of "searches and seizures." In *Olmstead v. United States*,[108] the issue was whether government agents could testify about conversations overheard by tapping a bootlegger's telephone line. Given the special place of private papers in *Boyd* and *Gouled*, any proof of private conversations against the parties at trial would have been of very doubtful constitutionality. But if the Fourth Amendment did not forbid *acquiring* the evidence in the first place, the Fifth Amendment would not forbid *using* the evidence later at trial.[109]

So the property-based conception of the Fourth Amendment prevailed. Chief Justice Taft equated "searches and seizures" with common-law trespass; unless the agents had illegally entered private premises, or seized "material things,"[110] there was no search and thus no violation of the Fourth Amendment. Holmes and Brandeis both dissented, in opinions now more famous than the majority's. For Holmes the key point was that the government agents had violated a state statute;[111] for Brandeis the key point was that the Fourth Amendment was about privacy rather than about property.[112]

Olmstead marked the crest of the liberal tide that had begun with *Boyd*. During the years between *Boyd* and *Olmstead* the Court also took a liberal view of the Fifth Amendment privilege against self-incrimination. *Boyd* itself had held that the privilege protects documents uttered without compulsion from compulsory disclosure. In *Counselman v. Hitchcock*,[113] the Court held that a witness before a grand jury could invoke the privilege, even though the text of the Fifth Amendment could be read to apply only to compelled testimony at one's criminal trial.[114] *Counselman* also held that only transactional immunity (immunity against conviction for the crimes disclosed by compelled testimony) as distinct from use immunity (exclusion of the compelled testimony at any subsequent trial of the witness) could satisfy the constitutional privilege.

Initially, the Supreme Court tested confessions in federal cases according to the common-law standard, which excluded coerced confessions because of the risk of unreliability.[115] In *Bram v. United States*,[116] the Court, presaging *Miranda v. Arizona*[117] by nearly ninety years, reversed a murder conviction because the admission of a confession violated the Fifth Amendment privilege against self-incrimination.

Compared to the facts in some of the *state* cases in which the Court later approved admission of confessions under the due process "voluntariness" standard, *Bram* presented an exceedingly pale case of official misconduct.[118] Wigmore sharply criticized *any* scrutiny of confessions on Fifth Amendment, as opposed to common-law, grounds.[119] Thus federal law was no less liberal in Fifth Amendment cases than in the Fourth Amendment context.

Sixth Amendment doctrine during the period separating *Hurtado* and *Adamson* also took a path favorable to the defense. The Court did not treat the confrontation clause as absolute, but rather as consistent with traditional common-law hearsay exceptions such as those for former testimony and dying declarations.[120] Nonetheless the clause was held to keep out highly probative evidence of guilt. In *Kirby v. United States*,[121] decided in 1899, the government charged Kirby with receiving stolen postage stamps. Under the federal statute, the conviction of the thieves was entered into evidence, and established *prima facie* proof that the stamps were stolen. The Court reversed Kirby's conviction on the ground that the statute denied his right to confront the witnesses against him, inasmuch as Kirby had not been a party at the trial of the thieves.

With respect to the Sixth Amendment right to counsel, standard practice in felony cases—in both federal cases and quite commonly in the states—appears to have involved appointing counsel for indigent defendants who went to trial rather than plead guilty, although there was a split in authority on the question of whether appointed counsel had an action for fees against the appointing authority.[122] In the Supreme Court's first Sixth Amendment right-to-counsel case, *Johnson v. Zerbst* (not decided until 1938)[123] the issue was whether the defendant's waiver of the right to counsel was effective when the trial court did not clearly explain the right and make sure that the defendant was waiving "competently and intelligently."

Because the case came up from the denial of a petition for habeas corpus, the Court could quash the conviction only if the failure to admonish the defendant ousted the trial court of jurisdiction. At the time it greatly strengthened the case for finding jurisdictional error if the claimed error was constitutional, rather than a violation of statute or court rule. The Court, per Justice Black, therefore treated the case as a constitutional one, and had no difficulty finding that the Sixth Amendment required appointing counsel for the indigent unless, after an explicit admonition from the court about the right to court-appointed counsel, the defendant made a competent and intelligent waiver. As a historical matter this may have confused prevailing practice with a constitutional requirement. The casualness with which the issue was resolved reflects the libertarian spirit of the pre-incorporation federal criminal procedure cases.

This undeniable doctrinal difference between state and federal cases suggests considerable difficulty for explaining doctrine as the product of class bias, whether unconscious or well-disguised. In the late nineteenth and early twentieth centuries, the law-abiding population tended to view criminals as representatives of an alien species, like Grendel preying on the good people across the border.[124]

Racism and social Darwinism contributed to this view. But however prevalent this conception of the criminal-as-outcast may have been, the justices scarcely could have distinguished between the evil beings prosecuted in state court and their federal counterparts.

Nor is it fair to suggest that the *Boyd* regime was simply the logical application of *Lochner* to the criminal law.[125] In the first place, substantive due process applied to state as well as to federal action. For example, *Lochner* itself struck down a state labor standards law. By contrast, during the *Boyd* era the Supreme Court scrupulously (if unfortunately) avoided interference with the administration of criminal justice by the states. Seven months after handing down *Lochner*, the Court held in *Jack v. Kansas*[126] that a state could compel immunized testimony despite the state's inability to immunize the witness against federal prosecution. *Weeks* and *Twining* made the federal model possible, precisely because those decisions exempted the states from federal interpretations of the Fourth and Fifth Amendments.

If *Boyd* and *Lochner* were cut from the same cloth, one would have expected the Court to cast the protection of *Boyd* around corporations. Less than a year after handing down *Lochner*, however, the Court, in *Hale v. Henkel*,[127] held that only natural persons could claim the privilege, despite the applicability of the due process and the takings clauses to corporations.[128] *Hale* suggests that the justices were sensitive to the practical problems *Boyd* posed to federal regulation of businesses at a time when popular concern with trust-busting was intense.[129] Rufus Peckham, the author of *Lochner*, joined the majority in *Hale* and wrote the Court's opinion in *Jack*.

Moreover, the federal model's generosity to the criminal defendant was not confined to white-collar crimes. As many of the defendants before the Court were charged with street crimes as with business crimes. Agnello was charged with trafficking in cocaine; Bram with murder; Kirby with theft. In *Davis v. United States*,[130] an 1895 common-law evidence decision rather than a constitutional law ruling, the Court reversed a murder conviction because the government had not disproved, beyond reasonable doubt, the defendant's claim of insanity. In an 1893 case involving federal substantive criminal law, rather than constitutional procedure, the Court reversed a conviction for aiding and abetting murder because the trial judge instructed the jury in a way that permitted a guilty verdict even if the jury concluded that the defendant did not intend to aid the killing.[131]

These federal cases strongly suggest that the Court's refusal to intervene in state criminal proceedings was neither unprincipled nor disingenuous. The guiding principle under the Fourteenth Amendment due process clause was constitutional withdrawal of state power to impair *fundamental* liberties. The judicial refusal to intervene in state criminal procedure reflected a sincere belief that in criminal cases, procedural protections, except of the most basic sort, are not fundamental, as are the rights to hold private property and enter into contracts.[132] The facts of the cases did not at first compel any contrary conclusion. In general the cases that came before the Court prior to 1915 resembled *Hurtado*; they were cases in which the state had departed from common-law procedure in a manner that did not increase the chance of an unjust conviction.

Frank v. Mangum[133] broke this pattern, but not the Court's indifference to the claims of the criminal defendant. Leo Frank, a Jew, was convicted of murdering a young woman by a Georgia court after a trial dominated by a hostile mob, and sentenced to death. The evidence strongly suggested what subsequent history confirmed, that Frank was innocent of the charge. Nonetheless the Supreme Court of Georgia affirmed the conviction, and the Supreme Court of the United States denied Frank's petitions for a writ of error.

Frank then applied for a writ of habeas corpus in the federal district court. The district court rejected the petition. On appeal, the Supreme Court of the United States affirmed the district court, over the dissent of Holmes and Hughes.

Characterizing *Frank* as expressive of bigotry or authoritarianism would not be difficult, but the decision is susceptible to a reading grounding the result on the neutral principle of federalism. The procedural posture of the case—collateral review of a state court judgment—implicated the same respect for federalism inspiring the Court's narrow construction of the due process clause. At issue was the relationship between Frank's constitutional *right* to due process, and his entitlement to the statutory *remedy* of habeas corpus.

Habeas corpus originated as a device by which the common-law courts of England could compel the trial or release of individuals detained by agents of the King.[134] The remedy of habeas corpus corresponded precisely with the classic understanding of due process; due process meant no punishment without trial according to law, and habeas corpus was available to compel trial according to law or the release of the prisoner.[135] But when the Reconstruction Congress authorized the federal courts to issue writs of habeas corpus on behalf of state prisoners detained in violation of the laws or Constitution of the United States, the Great Writ was assigned a novel and paradoxical purpose.[136] Instead of forcing the government to invoke the legal process or release the prisoner, now the defense might test the end product of the legal process—a judgment of conviction.

The writ of error, in common-law practice, hitherto had served this function.[137] Indeed a facially valid conviction of itself defeated an application for habeas relief, for the whole point of habeas was to compel trial.[138] The modern federal habeas petition of a state prisoner duly convicted after trial in the state courts is, from a historical perspective, a very strange creature indeed.

The federal courts confronted a dilemma. Either habeas corpus would take over the functions of appeal, or the congressional intention to provide a federal forum for the constitutional claims of state convicts would be defeated. The nineteenth-century legal mind solved this conundrum by invoking the slippery concept of jurisdiction. Habeas would only lie in the absence of a trial, but the defendant might have been convicted after a trial infected by constitutional error so fundamental that no trial could fairly be said to have occurred.[139] If constitutional error ousted the trial court of jurisdiction, the resulting judgment was not merely unconstitutional but void as well, and thus no bar to a habeas petition. Thus was the square peg of habeas corpus fitted to the round hole of federal review of convictions rendered by state courts.

Ultimately this jurisdictional account could not accommodate the expansion of due process rights to include security against police practices that occur long before the trial process ever begins. But so long as due process meant little more than notice and an opportunity to be heard, the states scarcely could violate due process without forfeiting jurisdiction in the ordinary sense of the word. A committee of vigilantes may call its own proceedings a trial, but that does not invest the gang's deliberations with jurisdiction.

Frank claimed that he had been convicted by just such a kangaroo court, after a formal trial that was in reality only the ritual indulgence of a mob. Georgia had violated his right to due process by preparing his execution without a genuine opportunity to be heard; and the remedy of habeas corpus was appropriate because the formal judgment of conviction was a sham, a nullity. In effect Georgia proposed to execute Frank without trying him first.

The *Frank* Court accepted all of this. What divided the majority from the dissenters was the subtle question of how the federal court is supposed to know when the state court proceedings were in fact dominated by a mob. The majority reasoned that the state supreme court, in which, all agreed, the proceedings were not dominated by the mob, had rejected Frank's claim that the trial was mob-dominated. Given no question as to the jurisdiction of the state appellate courts, habeas was unavailable to attack the judgments those courts affirmed.[140] The *Frank* Court could find no middle ground between converting the habeas remedy into a plenary appeal and accepting a remedial version of the positivist trap.

The justices in the majority opted for the latter alternative, effectively accepting the formal judgment of the state appellate courts as conclusive that the trial court had afforded the substance of a meaningful hearing. Presumably the result would have been otherwise had the case reached the Court on a petition for a writ of error rather than appeal from the lower federal court's rejection of a petition for habeas; the *Frank* holding meant that the only federal forum in which state convictions could be reviewed for constitutional error was the Supreme Court itself.

Had the Court maintained this position, the development of constitutional criminal procedure might have changed little, for most of the major cases decided before the 1950s reached the Supreme Court on direct review of state court judgments. But there would have been no ability in the lower federal courts to enforce new constitutional rules announced by the Supreme Court. As a practical matter, due process without habeas corpus is paralyzed force, gesture without motion.

After the Court's decision, the governor of Georgia conducted an investigation that raised grave doubt about Frank's guilt.[141] The governor commuted the death sentence. Unimpressed, a Georgia mob abducted Frank from state custody and lynched him.

This odious affair, truly a parody of due process, left a permanent mark on constitutional criminal procedure. Eight years later, in *Moore v. Dempsey*,[142] a virtual rerun of the *Frank* case, Holmes authored the majority opinion rather than the dissent. Of *Frank* Holmes wrote that

We assume in accordance with that case that the corrective process supplied by the State may be so adequate that interference by *habeas corpus* ought not to be allowed. . . . But if the case is that the whole proceeding is a mask—that counsel, jury and judge were swept to the fatal end by an irresistible wave of public passion, and that the State Courts failed to correct the wrong, neither perfection in the machinery for correction nor the possibility that the trial court and counsel saw no other way of avoiding an immediate outbreak of the mob can prevent this Court from securing to the petitioners their constitutional rights.[143]

The Court therefore remanded the case to the district court to determine whether the defendants' allegations of mob domination were true.

"[T]he corrective process afforded to the petitioners" was not "sufficient to allow a Judge of the United States to escape the duty of examining the facts for himself when if true as alleged they make the trial absolutely void."[144] *Moore* repudiated the positivist trap that *Frank* had accepted; even when passing on collateral attacks on state court judgments, the federal courts were not required to accept a state's formal judgment of conviction as conclusive of constitutional questions.

Between 1923 and 1947, the Court gradually expanded the constitutional protections of the accused.[145] During this period, the cases in which the Court reversed state convictions on due process grounds involved either grave doubts about the reliability of the trial verdict, or the oppressive abuse of official power in obtaining evidence against the accused. But just as concrete cases of abuse induced the Court to reverse particularly offensive convictions, the Court's decisions were limited to reversing the particular conviction in the instant case. The Court made no effort to reach beyond the case to be decided, no attempt to reform state criminal justice in any general way.

In 1932, the Court decided *Powell v. Alabama*,[146] the famous case of the "Scottsboro boys."[147] The defendants were illiterate young blacks from other states, accused of raping two white women on a train. The character of the trial is suggested by the fact that the local authorities thought it prudent to call out the militia, so that "every step taken from the arrest and arraignment to the sentence was accompanied by the military."[148] State law required the appointment of counsel in capital cases, but that requirement was defeated by the trial judge's appointment of "all the members" of the local bar to assist the defendants. In effect, none of the defendants had counsel prior to the day of his trial. The Court held that due process required the appointment of counsel prior to trial, at least on the facts presented.

In so holding, the Court confirmed that the *Chicago, Burlington & Quincy* decision marked the rejection of the redundancy argument approved of in *Hurtado*.

The Court, however, stopped short of incorporating the Sixth Amendment into the Fourteenth, even though the language of its opinion suggested generally that counsel was essential to a meaningful hearing and therefore qualified as a "fundamental" right. "All that it is necessary now to decide," Justice Sutherland wrote for the Court, "is that in a capital case, where the defendant is unable to employ counsel, and is incapable adequately of making his own defense because of ignorance, feeble mindedness, illiteracy, or the like, it is the duty of the court, whether requested or not, to assign counsel for him as a necessary requisite of due process of law."[149] The Court's response to a particular case of abuse thus was to reverse the conviction in that particular case.

The Court reacted to the problem of coerced confessions in the same way. *Brown v. Mississippi*,[150] decided in 1936, brought to the Court the ugliest conviction ever reviewed there. Brown was convicted on the basis of a confession obtained by torture. The deputy in charge of the questioning testified on the record that Brown had been whipped, but added that the whipping had not been "too much for a Negro; not as much as I would have done, if it were left to me."[151]

The Court refused to countenance this grotesque compound of racism and brutality. Chief Justice Hughes wrote, for a unanimous Court, that "[i]t would be difficult to conceive of methods more revolting to the sense of justice than those taken to procure the confessions of these petitioners, and the use of the confessions thus obtained as the basis for conviction and sentence was a clear denial of due process."[152] The conjunction in that sentence, however, bridges an important doctrinal gap; for unlike *Moore* or *Powell*, there was nothing irregular about Brown's *trial*. Simply put, the *Brown* Court equated due process with "the sense of justice."

Holding that the admission in evidence of a coerced confession violates due process committed the Court to a major involvement with state criminal justice. *Brown* was the easy case, a pristine atrocity. But, substantively, how far did the new rule reach? Did it cover any physical abuse of the suspect? Any psychological abuse? If not, how much abuse was consistent with due process? Procedurally, how could the Court enforce its new rule, given that police willing to torture a suspect are probably willing to lie on the stand, and that the lower courts tended to look the other way when police brought in a guilty criminal's confession?

The Court's next confession case, *Chambers v. Florida*,[153] answered the second question by holding that the Court would independently examine the record to determine whether a state conviction depended on a coerced confession. Independent review of the evidence bearing on coercion can reach some police coercion that might otherwise go undetected. But it also means that the Court must in each case come to factual conclusions about the particular case. General rules did not emerge from this approach. The Court did no more than look to the facts of each case, consult its collective "sense of justice," and classify the police methods as coercive or noncoercive.[154]

So it is appropriate that the phrase "fundamental fairness" appears first in a confessions case, *Lisenba v. California*.[155] It is also appropriate that in *Lisenba* the Court upheld the death sentence of a particularly vicious defendant[156] who had confessed only after two marathon interrogation sessions, during which he at one point was struck by the police and at another fainted from exhaustion. I call *Lisenba* an appropriate inaugural case for the "fundamental fairness" label because *Lisenba* illustrates the vacuity of the Court's criminal procedure doctrine under the Fourteenth Amendment. While the cases decided during the thirties and forties broke new ground in response to particularly outrageous cases, during this period the Court also upheld state practices that many would label—and some dissenting justices did label—fundamentally unfair.

The confessions cases afford one illustration. *Betts v. Brady*,[157] counterpointing the case of the "Scottsboro boys," offers another. Betts was charged with robbery; at his arraignment he informed the court that he lacked funds to pay for a lawyer and requested court-appointed counsel. The local practice provided free legal assistance only in rape and murder cases. Betts relied on *Powell v. Alabama*, but the Court rejected his claim. For a six-justice majority, Justice Roberts wrote that "due process of law"

formulates a concept less rigid and more fluid than those envisaged in other specific and particular provisions of the Bill of Rights. Its application is less a matter of rule. Asserted denial is to be tested by an appraisal of the totality of facts in a given case. That which may, in one setting, constitute a denial of fundamental fairness, shocking to the universal sense of justice, may, in other circumstances, and in the light of other considerations, fall short of such denial.[158]

Now you see it, now you don't.

Applying this doctrine, born of apparent necessity in *Hurtado*, the Court through the forties functioned in criminal cases as a court of errors. To be sure, only gross error could justify reversal, but the Court articulated no criteria for distinguishing gross errors from mere errors. Indeed the Court celebrated the unpredictability of its doctrine.

Fundamental fairness, on a case-by-case basis, permitted the Court to reverse any conviction it found particularly offensive. But it did not allow the Court to regulate the police and the state courts in any general way. The most striking difference between the traditional fundamental fairness analysis and the incorporation approach is that incorporation provides rules applicable to every criminal prosecution.[159] The interpretive foundations of selective incorporation coincide with those of fundamental fairness, but treating the absence of specified procedures as denials of fundamental fairness independent of any other facts in a case gave the Court the opportunity to reform state criminal procedure on a wholesale, rather than a retail, basis. The reemergence of the incorporation debate therefore signals a new chapter in the development of constitutional criminal procedure.

Constitutional Criminal Law from 1947 to the Early 1960s

THE THEORY THAT THE FOURTEENTH AMENDMENT INCORPORATES THE BILL OF RIGHTS

Dissenting in *Betts v. Brady*,[1] Justice Black casually suggested that the Fourteenth Amendment had imposed on the states the restrictions imposed on the federal government by the first eight amendments to the Constitution. He did not present a thorough defense of this theory, however, until the 1947 decision in *Adamson v. California*.[2] Adamson claimed that the prosecutor's comments on Adamson's failure to testify in his own defense violated the due process clause.

A bare majority of the Court, adhering to long-standing doctrine, disagreed. First, the majority refused to reconsider the decisions in the *Slaughter-House Cases*[3] and *United States v. Cruikshank*.[4] In those early cases, the Court had read the privileges and immunities clause of the Fourteenth Amendment to forbid only state interference with the privileges or immunities of federal citizenship—privileges and immunities that owe their "existence and protection" to the federal government, such as the right to petition that government for redress of grievances. Second, the majority, citing *Twining v. New Jersey*[5] (which had held clearly that the privilege against self-incrimination was not incorporated) and *Palko v. Connecticut*[6] (which had clearly held that only "fundamental" rights were incorporated), ruled that compelled self-incrimination does not violate due process.

In Justice Black's view, the incorporation of the Fifth Amendment's privilege against self-incrimination by the Fourteenth Amendment required overruling *Twining* and reversing Adamson's conviction.[7] Justices Douglas, Murphy, and Rutledge endorsed Black's argument on the incorporation question.

Black advanced three basic arguments for incorporating the Fifth Amendment privilege. First, he argued that fundamental fairness cases such as *Powell v. Alabama* and *Chambers v. Florida* had undercut the authority of *Twining v. New Jersey* by recognizing in state cases rights to counsel and against self-incrimination that the Fifth and Sixth Amendments protect in federal cases.[8] Second, Black claimed that the framers of the Fourteenth Amendment had intended to incorporate the Bill of Rights.[9] Finally, he argued that the fundamental fairness regime gave too much power to unelected judges.[10] Judicially enforced limits on state legislation should therefore be limited to protecting rights declared in the first eight amendments.

The fundamental fairness cases, however, really were fundamental fairness cases rather than incorporation decisions in disguise. *Betts v. Brady*, for instance, clearly established that the Fourteenth Amendment right to counsel was much narrower than the Sixth Amendment right to counsel. The Court had indeed incorporated the First Amendment and the Fifth Amendment's takings clause, but it just as clearly had not deviated from the holdings in *Hurtado, Maxwell, Twining*, and *Betts*.

Black's other two arguments are plausible, but they contradict one another. The historical case for incorporation relies primarily on what the congressional sponsors of the Fourteenth Amendment said during the floor debates. Congressman Bingham thought that *Barron v. Baltimore* had denied Congress power to enforce the Bill of Rights against the states, even though the states were obligated to respect the rights it declared.[11] Bingham had opposed the civil rights bill on the ground that Congress lacked constitutional power to legislate on civil rights; he thought the Fourteenth Amendment would cure the deficiency.[12] Five years later, in a debate about congressional power under the Fourteenth Amendment to adopt a civil rights measure, Bingham asserted that his purpose in 1866 had been to apply the Bill of Rights to the states.[13]

Senator Howard introduced the Fourteenth Amendment in the Senate.[14] He equated privileges or immunities with fundamental rights, following Justice Washington's circuit court opinion in *Corfield v. Coryell*. Howard refused to give an exhaustive catalogue of fundamental rights, but said that they did include the rights declared in the first eight amendments, many of which he specifically mentioned.

None of the speakers in the congressional debates ever suggested that section one's protections were *limited* to the Bill of Rights. Senator Howard specifically denied this.[15] There was general sentiment that section one, coupled with section five, gave Congress unquestionable authority for the Civil Rights Act,[16] which protected such private-law rights as the right to enforce contracts and hold property—rights not mentioned in the Bill.

Justice Black was hostile to substantive due process but sympathetic to individual liberty. He sought to accommodate these commitments in his total incorporation thesis, which he knew was wildly out of sync with the case law.[17] To overcome precedent, he invoked original intent; but original intent supports incorporation only with the baggage of federal judicial power to identify and enforce unenumerated rights. Justice Douglas, another New Dealer, joined Black's opinion, while the more thoroughly libertarian Murphy, joined by Rutledge, endorsed incorporation but held out the possibility that the Fourteenth Amendment also protects unenumerated rights.

Justice Reed's majority opinion relied on precedent and on federalism; Justice Frankfurter concurred on the same basic grounds but with more pointed reference to Black's dissent. Black's historical claim, however, was not to go without rebuttal. Two years later, Charles Fairman published one of the most influential law review articles ever written, concluding that a "mountain of evidence" weighed "overwhelmingly against" Black's thesis.[18]

Fairman had waded through the documentary record of the congressional elections of 1866 and of the ratification of the Fourteenth Amendment in state conventions.[19] He found no direct references to the possibility that the amendment would incorporate the Bill of Rights. He also found that several states had departed from the Fifth Amendment's grand jury requirement either before, or immediately after, ratifying the amendment.[20] Bingham was "confused,"[21] and Howard was idiosyncratic.

The sheer mass of Fairman's research, and his magisterial tone, lent his conclusion something like oracular authority. A few years later, William Crosskey published a long and cogent rejoinder[22] to Fairman that did nothing to forestall the general opinion that Fairman had "refuted" Black, as though the question of the Fourteenth Amendment's meaning were like a chess problem, susceptible of demonstration.[23] Not until the 1980s would acceptance of Fairman's work, by then supplemented by his Holmes Devise volumes on the history of the Supreme Court during Reconstruction,[24] be shaken by contrary scholarship.[25]

In truth, Bingham and Howard did endorse incorporation, but the ratification process did not in the least concern itself with the incorporation question.[26] The technical consequences of the amendment were of far less contemporary moment than its political significance as the Reconstruction policy of the Republican party. Even good lawyers, however, would have compelling reasons not to give extensive thought to the incorporation question.

In the first place, everyone understood that section one forbade state racial discrimination in civil rights—then understood as the rights of citizens exclusive of political rights such as suffrage. Every state had a bill of rights very similar to the federal one. Clearly the states could not grant jury trial or the privilege against self-incrimination to whites but not to blacks. In practical terms, equality meant that the state versions of the Bill of Rights would bind the states with respect to every citizen.[27] The technical differences between the state bills of rights and the federal Bill could not have interested anyone but Abundance of Caution.

Second, the framers of the Fourteenth Amendment did not devote much thought to what the federal courts might do with the amendment. They concentrated on what the Republican congress might do (and had done, in the Civil Rights Act), under the authority of section five, even though Congress had revised section one to be self-executing. Thus the question raised in *Adamson*—whether the Supreme Court should invalidate a state practice that departs from the federal Bill of Rights but does so across-the-board, without invidious discrimination—is not a question to which we should really expect to find an answer in the historical record.

If we look at how good lawyers reacted to the Fourteenth Amendment immediately after its adoption, we can see how far the modern incorporation thesis was from their minds. In federal prosecutions in the South under civil rights statutes, two federal circuit courts disagreed about whether the Fourteenth Amendment gave Congress power to punish interference with the exercise of rights protected by the first eight amendments.[28] These cases did not question state court convictions on federal review. Instead, prosecutions under congressional enactments to further Reconstruction were the very sort of case the framers of the Fourteenth Amendment had in mind. If incorporation were expected in any context, it would be in the context of protecting freed slaves and southern unionists in the exercise of their rights. That incorporation was debatable even in this context suggests the absence of any general expectation that the Bill of Rights, *in toto*, would become enforceable against the states.

When state court defendants did invoke the Bill of Rights, courts, state and federal, consistently rejected their pleas. Only months after the amendment became effective, the Supreme Court itself, in *Twitchell v. Commonwealth*,[29] upheld a state criminal conviction on the authority of *Barron v. Baltimore*. Twitchell challenged the constitutionality of his murder conviction on the ground that the indictment had not specified the manner in which death was caused. This failing, Twitchell claimed, violated both the Fifth Amendment right to indictment by grand jury and the Sixth Amendment right "to be informed of the nature and cause of the accusation."[30] The Court, in a terse opinion, rejected the claim, relying on, and quoting extensively from, *Barron*.[31]

Maybe all that was going on in *Twitchell* was gross incompetence by defense counsel, who failed to invoke the new amendment. But the Court did not rely on a waiver analysis, which would have been a harsh approach indeed to a capital case. Instead, a unanimous Court—including justices Swayne and Field, who both would later dissent in *Slaughter-House*—relied on *Barron* for the proposition that the Fifth and Sixth Amendments did not apply to the states.[32] In his 1873 edition of Kent's *Commentaries*, Holmes cites *Twitchell* as confirming *Barron*—without any discussion of the Fourteenth Amendment.[33]

Judge Cooley, in the 1868 edition of his *Constitutional Limitations*, with the amendment not yet in force, had noted the rule of *Barron v. Baltimore*.[34] In the second, 1871, edition, he reaffirms the *Barron* rule, citing *Twitchell*.[35] In this edition Cooley treated the Fourteenth Amendment as protecting fundamental rights against discrimination under *Corfield*,[36] i.e., as an equality provision, prohibiting the states from denying the freedmen the protections of the state constitutions.[37] At the end of the footnote supporting the *Barron* rule, he added that "[f]or instance, though the right of trial by jury is preserved by the Constitution of the United States, the States may, nevertheless, if they choose, provide for the trial of all offences against the States, as well as the trial of civil cases in the State courts, without the intervention of a jury."[38]

In his 1873 edition of Story's *Commentaries on the Constitution*, Cooley interpreted the privileges-or-immunities clause as establishing the constitutionality of the Civil Rights Act, as mandating equality in civil rights, and as requiring states to observe fundamental rights as set out in *Corfield*.[39] While he recognized the possibility of substantive due process,[40] Cooley expressly rejected the view that the due process clause requires state conformity with the federal Bill of Rights criminal procedure provisions.[41]

In an 1874 decision, Cooley rejected Fourth and Fifth Amendment challenges to a state statute authorizing warrants for the seizure of goods to satisfy tax liabilities.[42] For a unanimous Michigan Supreme Court, Cooley wrote that "[t]here is nothing to this objection. It is settled beyond controversy, and without dissent, that these amendments are limitations upon federal, and not upon state power[.]"[43] Citations to *Barron* and *Twitchell* follow.

State courts throughout the country took the same path Judge Cooley took. Sometimes state defendants invoked the Bill of Rights provisions directly, without relying on the Fourteenth Amendment. Between late 1868 and 1877, courts in South Carolina,[44] Ohio,[45] Louisiana,[46] and Iowa[47] rejected such arguments. If you count the nine justices in the *Twitchell* case, twenty-seven judges heard claims of state criminal defendants grounded directly on the Bill of Rights. Not one of the twenty-seven agreed with the defense. These decisions do not rest on the defendants' failure to rely on the Fourteenth Amendment. Rather, they expressly reaffirm the rule of *Barron v. Baltimore*.

When state criminal defendants did plead the Fourteenth Amendment, the result didn't change. In California[48] and Wisconsin,[49] the state supreme courts unanimously held that the Fourteenth Amendment due process clause does not apply the Fifth Amendment grand jury clause to the states. The Supreme Court, in the *Hurtado* case, rejected this claim over a solitary dissent. So of the nineteen judges who were asked the precise question of whether the Fourteenth Amendment makes the Bill of Rights binding on the states while the question was open for decision, eighteen rejected the claim and only one affirmed it.

The great nineteenth-century writers on criminal law cast further doubt on the incorporation thesis. Joel Prentiss Bishop and Francis Wharton were the two leading criminal law scholars of their time. Both wrote widely on other legal topics, and both had international reputations.[50] If the Fourteenth Amendment incorporated the Bill of Rights, the transformation of criminal procedure in the states would have called forth some comment from leading scholars.

In the first edition of his treatise on criminal procedure, published in 1866, Bishop wrote simply that the Fifth Amendment grand jury "provision does not bind the states."[51] In the second, 1872, edition, after ratification but before *Slaughter-House*, Bishop again says that "this provision relates only to the proceeding before tribunals of the United States,"[52] but that many states have grand jury provisions of their own. Now, however, Bishop cites *Twitchell* for the proposition that the Fifth Amendment does not apply to the states.[53]

In the third, 1880, edition, Bishop again says that the grand jury clause "does not bind the States."[54] But he also for the first time discusses the possibility that due process might require grand jury presentment. "And there is room for doubt, whether under this provision in the United States Constitution, or a like provision in a State Constitution, the legislature can authorize a trial for felony, without indictment, contrary to the established course of the common law."[55] After noting that the Wisconsin Supreme Court had decided the question favorably to the state, Bishop adds that "it is not probable the question will escape further agitation."[56] A fourth edition does not appear until 1895. By then the matter is settled and Bishop tersely writes, citing *Hurtado*, that due process "does not in any case preclude the proceeding by information, when authorized by a statute or a State constitution."[57]

In 1868 Wharton published the sixth edition of his *Treatise on the Criminal Law of the United States*. On the relationship between the Fifth Amendment grand jury clause and the states he wrote only that the Supreme Court of Vermont had declared as a general rule that the Fifth Amendment does not apply to the states.[58] In 1874 the locution changes. Now, it is not the Vermont court that declared the general rule; instead it can be "stated as a general rule, that the provision in the federal Constitution [the Fifth Amendment] applies only to cases in the United States courts."[59] The supporting footnote cites *Rowan* and other state cases. In 1880[60] and 1889[61] editions, the treatment is identical. Different cases appear in the footnotes (oddly, the 1889 edition does not pick up *Hurtado*), but there is no change in the statement of the "general rule."

Total incorporation under the privileges-or-immunities clause never occurred to either Bishop or Wharton. In 1872 Bishop cites *Twitchell* as permitting state use of the information procedure. Only in 1880 does he see a possible constitutional issue, on the theory that the due process clause mandates common-law criminal procedure, including indictment. He withheld an opinion on this issue, and did not criticize its ultimate resolution. Wharton never thought the issue colorable.

Only one of the dissenters in the *Slaughter-House Cases* adopted language consistent with the incorporation theory.[62] Justice Harlan, dissenting later in *Hurtado*, did not invoke the incorporation doctrine, let alone on the basis of the privileges-or-immunities clause.[63] Harlan wrote for the Court in the 1897 case incorporating the Fifth Amendment's takings clause,[64] but he relied on the natural law approach to due process that had prevailed in *Hurtado*, rather than on the privileges-or-immunities clause. Not until *Maxwell v. Dow*,[65] decided in 1900, did Harlan link the privileges-or-immunities clause with total incorporation. A recent biographer describes Harlan as "his era's lone consistent advocate of incorporation,"[66] but he was consistent only as to result, not as to interpretation.

The views of contemporary lawyers offer powerful evidence about the amendment's intended meaning. Modern scholars can read the congressional and ratification debates only through twentieth-century eyes. Perhaps dedicated historians can empathize with the period deeply enough to recover what its inhabitants really thought, but that kind of empathy is difficult to achieve in those whose

interest in the past derives from interest in current legal doctrine. The judges in
Twitchell, Rowan, and *Weimer* had lived through the ratification of the Fourteenth
Amendment. We can hardly escape presentism; they cannot be suspected of it.

Nonetheless, the issue is by no means as one-sided as Fairman made it out. Total
incorporation is consistent with the language of the privileges-or-immunities
clause, and it was supported by Bingham and Howard in the congressional debates. The ratification process, however, apparently never considered the incorporation question.[67] Fairman made a lot of this silence, but it is perhaps less
important than it seems in retrospect. All of the states had their own bills of
rights, so that even understood solely as an antidiscrimination provision the
amendment would have had the effect of extending bill of rights protections to the
former slaves.[68] The difference among the federal and state bills of rights may have
loomed less important to a generation that conceived the law as general principles
given superficially various expressions in different jurisdictions. Cooley's *Limitations*, for instance, treats the state bills of rights as indistinguishable.

Aside from the congressional debates, there is some affirmative support for
the incorporation theory. Some contemporary commentators thought that privileges or immunities included the rights protected by the first eight amendments.[69]
One federal circuit court endorsed the incorporation theory.[70]

The opposing evidence includes the dozens of appellate judges who rejected
both direct Bill of Rights and Fourteenth Amendment incorporation claims in the
early cases. It includes also the views of the generation's most distinguished
legal commentators—Holmes, Cooley, Bishop, and Wharton. The great majority
of good lawyers on record who had lived through the ratification process did not
believe that the Fourteenth Amendment incorporated the specific criminal procedure provisions in the Bill of Rights.

Looking at the evidence for both sides, a striking fact emerges: The support
for incorporation is almost always general, rather than particular. While most jurists simply concluded that the amendment did not overturn *Barron*, at least a
few did insist that this was indeed the intended effect. Yet even the incorporation
proponents stopped short of saying that specific forms of criminal procedure
were to be made binding on the states. John Norton Pomeroy's 1868 treatise on
constitutional law[71] beautifully illustrates this tension. Pomeroy wrote that the
rule of *Barron v. Baltimore* was "an unfortunate one," but that the then-pending
Fourteenth Amendment offered a "remedy" for this "dismaying" result.[72] Pomeroy
does not quite say that the Fourteenth Amendment would overturn *Barron* with
respect to every element in the Bill of Rights, but that is certainly a cogent way
to read his remarks on *Barron*.

Only a few pages later, however, when Pomeroy turns to discussing the first
eight amendments, he has this to say about the Fifth:

It may well be questioned, however, if the grand jury is not now so cumbersome and inef-
ficient, that any theoretical advantages which may flow from it, are not far outweighed by
the practical defects and hindrances which are inseparable from its use in administering

the criminal law. Indeed, it has been already abolished in some states. I am strongly of the opinion, also, that some others of these time-honored principles of English and American criminal procedure have outlived their usefulness, and are obstacles to the proper investigation and punishment of crime. The provision that no person shall be compelled to be a witness against himself can only be supported by that intense reverence for the past which is so difficult to be overcome. This ancient rule of the English law has been entirely repudiated in civil cases, and there is no reason for preserving it in criminal trials. A judicial trial is in theory, and should be in fact, a means of ascertaining the truth; but this maxim of the law closes at once the most direct and certain road which leads to the truth. There can be no doubt that the states will gradually abandon this provision, and reject it from their constitutions.[73]

One could, I suppose, read Pomeroy as saying that the Fourteenth Amendment would require grand juries and the self-incrimination privilege even though they are outworn impediments to rational procedure; but why would states abolish the privilege or the grand jury if the new amendment were to perpetuate these institutions as a matter of federal constitutional law?

If contemporary lawyers consistently rejected incorporation claims in concrete criminal-procedure contexts, they were honoring another generalization about the Fourteenth Amendment that did command a consensus. Republican proponents of the amendment consistently denied the intention to curtail state power by granting broad new powers to the federal government. This respect for federalism was as integral to Republican thought as was respect for individual rights.[74]

The second half of the nineteenth century saw major reforms, and a spirit of experiment, in criminal procedure. Pomeroy did not stand alone in embracing Bentham's call for rationalization of the criminal process. Many states turned to the information procedure, and the states abolished testimonial incapacity rules, permitting the defendant for the first time to give sworn evidence. The *Hurtado* opinion reflects this spirit, celebrating a "quick and active age" in which legal reform must keep up with the times. It seems hard to believe that, just as the reform movement was gaining momentum, the framers could have intended to freeze criminal procedure in the eighteenth-century mold of the federal Bill of Rights.

Thus it was not entirely fair for Justice Black to point to general expressions favorable to the incorporation theory. When it got down to cases, lawyers and judges recoiled from equating the Bill of Rights criminal-procedure provisions with "privileges or immunities" or with "due process." It might be fair to say the total incorporation theory has not been disproved or refuted. It is fair to say that the thesis that a majority of those involved in framing and ratifying the Fourteenth Amendment intended to apply the Bill of Rights to the states has not been proved and seems on the whole very doubtful.

The case against incorporation, however, is basically negative. The great difficulty with *Slaughter-House* is that it trivializes the privileges-or-immunities clause. The hundreds of thousands of men who died for the Union cause did not lay down their lives to secure the right to travel to Washington, D.C. Such federal rights were in any event already protected by the antebellum constitution's supremacy clause.

There are, however, plausible interpretations of the clause that give it more meaning than *Slaughter-House* recognized, without resorting to incorporation. It would be reasonable to read the privileges-or-immunities clause as a fundamental rights provision. If section one provided solely for racial equality, it would not have prevented the states from leaving blacks to the mercies of private ordering in the Reconstruction South. All equality could have achieved would have been to require the states to permit blacks the same access to the benefits of government as was enjoyed by whites.

Equality would not prevent a state from acquiescing in anarchy, i.e., from denying all citizens, black and white, protection from crime, security of property, and access to the courts for the enforcement of contracts. The privileges-or-immunities clause can be read as mandating that the states provide to citizens the essentials of liberal government. With Blackstone, we might categorize these as the right of personal security, the right of personal liberty, and the right to hold and convey property, including the right to contract.[75]

These were the substantive rights the 1866 Civil Rights Act required the states to extend to blacks on the same terms as they were extended to whites; a frequently attributed purpose of the Fourteenth Amendment was to authorize the Civil Rights Act.[76] These were also the rights Justice Washington identified as fundamental for purposes of Article IV's privileges-and-immunities clause in the widely cited case of *Corfield v. Coryell*.[77]

Another substantive interpretation reads the clause, coupled with section five, as authorizing congressional enumeration of the rights of federal citizenship. This interpretation is not wholly coincident with the Supremacy Clause, because while the Supremacy Clause elevates federal over state law in cases of conflict, there must first exist a constitutional source for the exercise of congressional power. The federal government is a government of enumerated powers, and *Dred Scott* held that Congress had no expressed constitutional authority to regulate slavery in the states. The 1937 revolution in commerce clause jurisprudence renders the Fourteenth Amendment largely superfluous as a source of federal power to protect civil liberties in the states. But in 1866 this was not the case.

The clause, then, might require states to respect fundamental private-law rights, such as those recognized in the Civil Rights Act and in *Corfield*; or it might assign Congress power to legislate over civil rights; or it might do both of these things. These substantive interpretations identify a nonredundant significance to the clause, but they fall far short of justifying total incorporation.

Although private-law rights, as set out in the Civil Rights bill, seem to have exemplified fundamental rights to the framers, history does not suggest any clear limits on the fundamental-rights formula. Reading the clause as a fundamental-rights provision therefore invites the unconstrained judicial supervision of state legislation that Black regarded as illegitimate. It was precisely this fear of judicial legislation that moved the *Slaughter-House* majority to nullify the clause.[78]

The emergence of substantive due process, however, soon renewed the temptation posed by judicial authority to recognize unenumerated constitutional rights. If the turn to substantive due process lacks the support of original intent, it has made up for that deficit by its applicability, via the Fifth Amendment's due process clause, to the federal government as well as to the states. Justice Black went along with *Bolling v. Sharpe.*[79]

Against even a limited resurrection of the privileges-or-immunities clause there weighed by 1947 seventy years of precedent, much of it written by men who were closer to the amendment's purposes than we can ever come.[80] *Hurtado*'s unwritten law interpretation might justify *selective* incorporation under the due process clause, but not total incorporation. Indeed, the present selective incorporation regime depends on the fundamental fairness theory. But the language of the due process clause is no more a technical synonym for the Bill of Rights than is, say, the Lord's Prayer or *America the Beautiful.*[81] Justice Black himself seems to have acknowledged this,[82] and the modern defense of total incorporation rests primarily on the privileges-or-immunities clause.

The historical importance of the total incorporation theory is the gravitational force it lent to claims that due process incorporates *some* of the provisions in the Bill of Rights. Throughout the fifties, fundamental fairness continued to define the scope of due process. Experience with the fundamental fairness test gradually made Justice Black's dubious doctrinal thesis increasingly attractive to other justices. That experience is highly instructive.

FROM *ADAMSON* TO *MAPP:* FUNDAMENTAL FAIRNESS IN OPERATION

Only two years after *Adamson*, a Colorado doctor named Julius Wolf put the fundamental fairness doctrine to a severe test. Wolf conspired with his partner, Montgomery, to provide illegal abortions for a substantial fee. At his trial, the government introduced into evidence business records members of the district attorney's staff had snatched up while visiting Wolf's office to investigate the abortion charge. The records identified Wolf's patients, thus linking him to women who had sought abortions.

Wolf objected to the use of the books in evidence, but the Colorado courts rejected his claim.[83] Wolf sought review in the Supreme Court, arguing that under the test announced in *Palko* and followed in *Adamson*, the evidence was received in violation of due process. To support the claim that the Fourth Amendment's protections are "fundamental," "implicit in the concept of ordered liberty," Wolf quoted the argument of James Otis in the Writs of Assistance case. Otis condemned the writs as the "worst instrument of arbitrary power, the most destructive of English liberty, and the fundamental principles of law, that ever was found in an English law book."[84] If the founders thought that security from arbitrary search was "fundamental," how could the Court disagree? The Court indeed agreed that the Fourth Amendment was fundamental. "The knock at the door, whether by day or by night, as a prelude to a search, without authority of law but solely on the authority of the police, did not need the commentary of recent history to be condemned as inconsistent with the conception of human rights enshrined in the history and the basic constitutional documents of English-speaking peoples."[85] The exclusionary rule, however, was a different matter.

"[W]e have no hesitation in saying that were a State affirmatively to sanction such police incursion into privacy it would run counter to the guaranty of the Fourteenth Amendment. But the ways of enforcing such a basic right raise questions of a different order."[86] The federal courts adhered to the exclusionary rule, but the states were sharply divided, and other free societies completely rejected it. Therefore, "in a prosecution in a State court for a State crime the Fourteenth Amendment does not forbid the admission of evidence obtained by an unreasonable search and seizure."[87]

Justice Black concurred. His *Adamson* dissent explained why he agreed that the Fourth Amendment binds the states. As for the exclusionary rule, he agreed "with what appears to be a plain implication of the Court's opinion that the federal exclusionary rule is not a command of the Fourth Amendment but is a judicially created rule of evidence which Congress might negate."[88]

Justice Black's view that the exclusionary rule is not a constitutionally required remedy has been disputed ever since. What went undisputed in *Wolf* was the characterization of the exclusionary rule as a remedy for Fourth Amendment violations, rather than as the prevention of an independent Fifth Amendment violation stemming from the introduction of the accused's wrongly seized property against him at trial. Earlier cases such as *Silverthorne* and *Agnello* had heralded the separation of the exclusionary rule from the Fifth Amendment. *Wolf* made the divorce official, for none of the justices thought that the exclusionary rule issue was foreclosed by the *Adamson* decision, which but two years before had held that the Fifth Amendment privilege did not apply to the states.

What divided the dissenters from the majority was the pragmatic question of whether alternative remedies really could enforce the Fourth Amendment effectively. Douglas, Murphy, and Rutledge dissented. Justice Rutledge captured the gist of their view: "the Amendment without the sanction is a dead letter."[89] Events would quickly bring before the Court strong evidence that Rutledge had it right.

Rochin v. California[90] presented the following facts. Three Los Angeles deputies, acting without either probable cause or a warrant, entered Rochin's home through an unlocked door. They found Rochin in the bedroom with his common-law wife. On the nightstand were two capsules. When the deputies asked to whom the capsules belonged, Rochin swallowed them. The deputies sought to physically snatch the capsules from Rochin's mouth. Failing this, they took Rochin in handcuffs to a hospital where his stomach was pumped and the capsules, still containing traces of morphine, were recovered.[91]

The California courts upheld the admissibility of the capsules. The Supreme Court, *Wolf* notwithstanding, reversed. Justice Frankfurter, the author of *Wolf*, now wrote that the police behavior did

more than offend some fastidious squeamishness or private sentimentalism about combating crime too energetically. This is conduct that shocks the conscience. Illegally breaking into the privacy of the petitioner, the struggle to open his mouth and remove what was there, the forcible extraction of his stomach's contents—this course of proceedings by agents of government to obtain evidence is bound to offend even hardened sensibilities. They are methods too close to the rack and the screw to permit of constitutional differentiation.[92]

Rochin did not question *Wolf*; rather, the Court held that when state police violate the Fourth Amendment in a way that shocks the conscience, due process requires exclusion.[93]

In states that did not apply the exclusionary rule, the exceptional suppression remedy announced in *Rochin* left the Fourth Amendment as much a dead letter as ever. An illustrative case reached the Court but two years after *Rochin* was decided. California police suspected Patrick Irvine of illegal bookmaking. While Irvine and his wife were away from home, the police employed a locksmith to make a key to the home.

Lacking a warrant, but possessed of a key, the police installed a hidden microphone in the hall. They bored a hole in the roof and ran a wire to the neighbor's garage, which thereafter functioned as a listening post. The police twice repeated the illegal entry for the purpose of relocating the bug, on one occasion concealing it in the marital bedroom, on the other in the bedroom closet.[94]

On behalf of a four-justice plurality, Justice Jackson wrote that the police behavior "would be almost incredible if it were not admitted. Few police measures have come to our attention that more flagrantly, deliberately, and persistently violated the fundamental principle declared by the Fourth Amendment."[95] Yet Irvine's case was ruled by *Wolf*, not *Rochin*. *Rochin* involved a "physical assault"; "[h]owever obnoxious" the *Irvine* facts were, "they do not involve coercion, violence, or brutality to the person."[96] Suppressing the evidence "would leave the rule so indefinite that no state court could know what it should rule in order to keep its processes on solid constitutional ground."[97]

Justice Douglas dissented on the ground that *Wolf* should be overruled.[98] Justice Frankfurter, joined by Justice Burton, found the police conduct "outrageous" and dissented on the ground that *Rochin* was not confined to cases of physical violence.[99] Black dissented on an unrelated self-incrimination ground.

The deciding vote thus fell to Justice Clark. Although Clark agreed with Douglas that *Wolf* was wrongly decided, he refused to vote for reversal without mustering a majority to apply the exclusionary rule generally to the states. Reversing under *Rochin* might "vindicate the abstract principle of due process, but [would] not shape the conduct of local police one whit."[100] Clark followed *Wolf* while expressing the hope that "strict adherence to the tenor of that decision may produce needed converts for its extinction."[101]

Justice Jackson may have found the police misconduct in the *Irvine* case "incredible," but the unhappy truth is that the police actions were not aberrant. The police in fact had been advised by the district attorney's office.[102] In 1942, Roger Traynor authored the opinion for the Supreme Court of California rejecting the exclusionary rule.[103] The year after *Irvine* he wrote the opinion in *People v. Cahan*[104] adopting the exclusionary rule.

Traynor later explained this reversal:

My misgivings about . . . admissibility grew as I observed that time after time it was being offered and admitted as a routine procedure. It became impossible to ignore the corollary that illegal searches and seizures were also a routine procedure subject to no effective deterrent; else how could illegally obtained evidence come into court with such regularity? It was one thing to condone an occasional constable's blunder, to accept his illegally obtained evidence so that the guilty would not go free. It was quite another to condone a steady course of illegal police procedures that deliberately and flagrantly violated the Constitution of the United States as well as the state constitution.[105]

By 1961, Earl Warren and Hugo Black would have experienced the same "education" described by Traynor.

Until that time, the Court's focus on fundamental fairness would preclude any broad reform of criminal justice in the states. In the confessions context, just as with search and seizure, fact-sensitive adjudication under the general mantle of fundamental fairness provided no generalizations to limit the police or to guide the lower courts. The Court rejected confessions made when the "totality of the circumstances" indicated that the confession was "involuntary."[106] But other cases approved the admission of a confession obtained after a long period of incommunicado detention and marathon interrogation sessions,[107] and a confession given by a suspect who was kicked and threatened with a blackjack an hour before he was questioned.[108]

The Court consistently rejected pleas to approach the confessions problem through selective incorporation. Justice Douglas, dissenting, urged the exclusion of statements obtained during periods of unlawful detention on Fourth Amendment grounds.[109] In the federal practice, the failure to bring the suspect into court as soon as practicable after arrest would lead to the exclusion of any statement made during the period of unnecessary delay.[110] But this result rested on an interpretation of the Federal Rules of Criminal Procedure, and was not applicable to the states.[111]

Douglas also advocated extending the right to counsel to persons during questioning by the police. In 1958, the Court took two cases in which the suspect confessed only after the police denied an explicit request to consult with counsel.[112] In the first of these, *Crooker v. California*, the defendant was a college graduate who had attended law school and knew his rights, a fact that undoubtedly weakened his constitutional claim. Douglas mustered only four votes—those of Warren, Black, Brennan, and himself—for the proposition that the "demands of our civilization expressed in the Due Process Clause require that the accused who wants a counsel should have one at any time after the moment of arrest."[113]

The majority rejected any analogy between the right to counsel secured by the *Powell-Betts* line of cases and a right to counsel during interrogation: "[T]hose decisions involve another problem, trial and conviction of the accused without counsel after state refusal to appoint an attorney for him. What due process requires in one situation may not be required in another, and this, of course, because the least change of circumstances may provide or eliminate fundamental fairness."[114] Any right to counsel during interrogation "would have a . . . devastating effect on enforcement of criminal law, for it would effectively preclude police questioning—*fair as well as unfair*—until the accused was afforded opportunity to call his attorney."[115]

In the second case, *Cicenia v. LeGay*, the police secured the defendant's confession during a period in which the suspect was asking to see his lawyer and the lawyer was asking to see the suspect.[116] Expressing "strong distaste"[117] for the police behavior, Justice Harlan wrote for a five-justice majority that "[t]he broad rule sought here and in *Crooker* would require us to apply the Fourteenth Amendment in a manner which would be foreign both to the spirit in which it was conceived and the way in which is has been implemented by this Court."[118]

Adamson itself had of course rejected any reliance on the privilege against self-incrimination by state defendants seeking federal relief. So by the end of the fifties, the cases had rejected incorporation of the Fourth, Fifth, and Sixth Amendments as approaches to the interrogation problem. Federal review of police practices, whether interrogation or search and seizure, was conducted under the standard of fundamental fairness. Under that standard, "the least change of circumstances" could spell the difference between one outcome and another. As the *Irvine* case suggested, a doctrine so fluid, contingent on application in so remote a tribunal, was at best a modest guarantee of civil liberty.

BROWN V. ALLEN AND THE EXPANSION
OF FEDERAL HABEAS CORPUS

Whether carried out under the rubric of fundamental fairness or selective incorporation, federal constitutional rules of criminal procedure express skepticism about state respect for federal constitutional rights. Ironically, the fundamental fairness regime, precisely because of its insistence on individualized adjudication, demanded a federal forum for review of state court criminal convictions to at least as great an extent as a selective incorporation regime. When the "least change of circumstances may provide or eliminate fundamental fairness," federal review of the record in each case seemed the only way to enforce the dictates of the Constitution.

The federal habeas statute provided the salient, indeed unique, possibility for grounding any such general review power. But, as *Frank* and *Dempsey* had shown by the early twenties, the historical functions of the writ coexisted only uneasily with its modern role as a safeguard against state action inconsistent with federal rights.

The nineteenth-century theory that some, but not all, constitutional errors might nullify the jurisdiction of the trial court proved unequal to the task of harmonizing habeas corpus with federal review of state convictions. It failed in part because of the doctrinally embarrassing parallel between the habeas petition of a state prisoner and that of a federal prisoner. Logically, the erroneous rejection of a coerced confession claim, a right-to-counsel claim, or a search-and-seizure claim would nullify the jurisdiction of a federal trial court as much as of a state trial court. Yet the federal courts were loath to convert the habeas remedy into a second tier of appellate review for prisoners whose constitutional claims had been adversely adjudicated by a *federal* court.[119]

The jurisdictional theory also labored under the growing weight of the substantive constitutional law of criminal procedure. When due process could be satisfied by an inquisitorial proceeding on a cold record, so long as the tribunal was impartial, constitutional error could scarcely occur without a complete breakdown in the judicial process. But as the requirements of due process became more generous to the accused, constitutional error became less and less a question of procedural regularity and more and more a question of factual guilt, and even of civilized police practices.

I doubt very much that the unanimous Court that decided *Brown v. Mississippi*[120] would have reversed a decision by the federal district court granting Brown a writ of habeas corpus. But there was nothing violent or disorderly about Brown's *trial*. So if the expansion of due process protections in criminal cases required some expansion of the claims cognizable on federal habeas, the precise scope of the broadened remedy was very much a matter of conjecture and debate.

Largely for want of a principled alternative, the Court drifted into the position that *any* constitutional violation was cognizable on a petition for habeas corpus. In 1939, the Court could still opine that "[t]he scope of review on *habeas corpus* is limited to the examination of the jurisdiction of the court whose judgment of conviction is challenged." There immediately follows this qualification: "But if it be found that the court had no jurisdiction to try the petitioner, or that in its proceedings his constitutional rights have been denied, the remedy of *habeas corpus* is available."[121]

Three years later, in a unanimous *per curiam* opinion, the court was more explicit. Holding that a petition alleging that the prisoner's guilty plea was coerced raised an issue cognizable on habeas corpus, the Court explained that when the petitioner averred facts that "are dehors the record and their effect on the judgment was not open to consideration and review on appeal," habeas corpus was appropriate. "In such circumstances the use of the writ . . . is not restricted to those cases where the judgment of conviction is void for want of jurisdiction. . . . It extends also to those exceptional cases where the conviction has been in disregard of the constitutional rights of the accused, and where the writ is the only effective means of preserving his rights."[122]

A conviction rendered after a state trial, followed by appeal, presented a different case. Nonetheless, the slippage from jurisdictional to constitutional error continued, at such a pace that by the early fifties judges and law enforcement officials voiced concern that the federal habeas jurisdiction was intruding obnoxiously on the administration of justice in the states.

In response to these concerns, the Supreme Court reviewed a trio of cases from the Fourth Circuit; the title case was *Brown v. Allen*.[123] On a variety of then-murky procedural issues the Court succeeded in clarifying the law. For example, in the *Daniels* case the Court held that failure to perfect an appeal in state court barred resort to federal habeas; the state courts must be given the chance to correct their own errors.[124] On the critical question of which constitutional claims might be considered in habeas corpus proceedings the Court also succeeded in dispelling the confusion in the lower courts, but not by restricting the scope of federal review.

On the contrary, the *Brown* court almost casually endorsed federal habeas review of *any* constitutional claim raised by a state prisoner.[125] In *Brown* the rhetoric of jurisdiction completely disappears. This was logically required by the Court's understanding of the state criminal process as neither void nor conclusive, but entitled to such deference as the federal courts deemed appropriate in each case.[126]

Some surprise may be occasioned by the fact that Felix Frankfurter, ordinarily a fastidious federalist, should have joined in this incursion into the state judicial process. But just as in *Frank v. Mangum, Brown* is explicable as rendering the habeas corpus procedure in the mirror image of the substantive law of due process.[127] For Frankfurter, the jurisdiction to issue the writ was consonant with federalism so long as due process meant truly *fundamental* fairness. Instead of gauging the state procedure for fairness in adjudicating federal constitutional claims, the federal courts under *Brown v. Allen* decided the claim as a substantive matter. State process was only a reason to be skeptical of the petition, and not the entirety to which the petitioner had a constitutional right.

Perhaps this had been the law since *Moore v. Dempsey* or even since *Frank* itself. I know of no case decided by the Supreme Court during this period in which the Court rejected a state prisoner's habeas petition in a case in which it would have reversed the conviction on direct review. Likewise in the lower federal courts, the petitions of state prisoners were usually rejected for reasons that would have supported affirmance on direct review in the Supreme Court.

Brown v. Allen made this equation official. Henceforth the constitutional rules generated by the selective incorporation approach would be enforceable on a general basis in the federal district courts. The procedural avenue would remain open long after fundamental fairness had given way to selective incorporation, enabling the wholesale reform of the criminal justice system.

CRIMINAL PROCEDURE AND EQUAL PROTECTION

The Warren Court, strictly speaking, began in 1953. New Chief Justice Warren's first signal accomplishment was the unanimous decision in the school segregation decision. Sympathy for egalitarian arguments became the distinctive feature of Earl Warren's Court, and one would expect that the equal protection clause provided the fountainhead of its doctrinal innovations.

The Warren Court did indeed rely on the equal protection clause to justify the desegregation decisions, but surprisingly, almost shockingly, the rest of its work—even its egalitarian work—rested on other provisions of the Constitution. With the significant but peculiar exception of the reapportionment cases,[128] outside the segregation field, and especially in the criminal cases, the Warren Court precedents speak the language of liberty, not equality.

There are, no doubt, a great variety of reasons for this doctrinal deflection. But one alone is sufficient to explain the sterility of equal protection analysis in criminal cases. Committed at once to the extinction of Jim Crow and to the preservation of progressive social and economic legislation, the Court of the fifties developed a rigid distinction between classes of state action subject to review under the "rational basis" and "strict scrutiny" standards. The very rigor of strict scrutiny—"strict in theory but fatal in fact"—limited the variety of government classifications that might be subjected to the standard.[129]

The development of a constitutional law of sexual equality has given us "tiers" of equal protection analysis.[130] These were inconceivable in the fifties, except perhaps to apologists for segregation. Actually holding state action unconstitutional for want of a rational basis was likewise unthinkable. The equal protection clause was, for the nonce, a citadel for blacks in the struggle to end segregation.

Of course racial injustice tainted the enforcement of the criminal law. It is anything but an accident that the defendants in *Moore v. Dempsey, Powell v. Alabama*, and *Brown v. Mississippi* were Southern blacks. But discrimination in the criminal justice system, in contrast to education and public facilities, was *de facto*, not *de jure*. There was no statute commanding police abuse or unjust conviction of blacks that could be struck down by a stroke of the judicial pen.

Moreover, much of the invidious discrimination in criminal justice disadvantaged the poor in relation to the rich. Such disadvantages impaired the defense of blacks in proportion to their poverty, but they could not be treated as racially discriminatory without very radical changes in the economic organization of the American society. It is hard to understand why the poor have a constitutional right to a lawyer as good as the rich can afford, but not to a comparable doctor, house, or education for their children.

Notwithstanding the troublesome difficulty of drawing such distinctions, discrimination against the poor prompted the Court's foray into equal protection analysis of criminal procedure claims. These equal protection cases arose from state-imposed financial barriers to the appeals of indigent defendants. In *Griffin v. Illinois*,[131] by a vote of five to four, the Supreme Court reversed the convictions of two defendants who claimed that they could not afford the transcription of the trial proceedings. For a four-justice plurality Justice Black wrote that "[i]n criminal trials a State can no more discriminate on account of poverty than on account of religion, race, or color."[132] Justice Frankfurter agreed but in narrower language; if the state "has a general policy of allowing criminal appeals, it cannot make lack of means an effective bar to the exercise of this opportunity."[133]

Frankfurter's rhetoric proved more prophetic. What may have seemed like a landmark decision about wealth and poverty turned out to be a ruling about appellate procedure in criminal cases. It was, and remains, well settled that the federal Constitution does not require appellate review of criminal convictions.[134] Indeed for nearly a century after the adoption of the Constitution federal criminal convictions were not reviewable by writ of error.[135] Those claiming that the right to appeal was unconstitutionally infringed had little choice but to rely on the "last refuge of the constitutional litigant."

Thus in earlier cases the Court had found a violation of equal protection, but not of due process, made out when state prisoners alleged that prison officials had prevented them from filing claims of error within the state's statutory limitations period.[136] If the state may not maliciously or arbitrarily deny the statutory right to appeal, may it deny the same right on the basis of poverty?

It would be cogent to answer "yes," precisely because there is a "rational basis" for making people pay for government services. Perhaps the resources of criminal defense—counsel, private investigators, and so on—differ from other services, because of the extraordinary hardship resulting from conviction. But the distinction is untenable. Relatively few criminal prosecutions lead to incarceration. Wealth-based classifications involving health care and education have far more dramatic adverse consequences for the poor.

The Court might have identified persons charged, or suspected, of crime, as opposed to the impoverished, as a suspect classification. This approach, however, would not address discrimination *among* those accused of crime. Moreover, the procedural safeguards against criminal conviction, however limited they may have been in a given jurisdiction, always were more elaborate than those afforded in any civil proceeding.

So, like *Shelley v. Kraemer*,[137] *Griffin* has survived on the basis of a doctrinal predicate that with only modest hyperbole may be described as commanding socialism on constitutional grounds.[138] Modern equal protection law might recharacterize *Griffin* and its progeny as declaring poverty to be a classification subject to intermediate scrutiny, a recharacterization that would of course have implications far beyond criminal procedure. In the alternative, the Court might, on due process grounds, require some form of appellate review of criminal convictions,[139] with transcripts and filing fees tested by their effect on the right to appellate review.

The Court has pursued neither strategy. Instead, confronted with the doctrinal equivalent of a land war in Asia, the Court simply announced victory and withdrew. In *Gideon v. Wainwright*,[140] the equal protection approach mysteriously disappears. The poor are entitled to lawyers not because the rich can afford them, but because without a lawyer no person is secure against unlawful punishment. But on the very day the Court decided *Gideon*, it perpetuated the *Griffin* principle in *Douglas v. California*,[141] holding that equal protection requires the appointment of appellate counsel for the indigent, even though due process does not require any appeal procedure at all.

The modern law can be restated by the proposition that wealth is a suspect classification *on which to predicate denying appellate review of a criminal conviction*, but not a suspect classification on which to predicate inferior representation during plea negotiations or trial.[142] The only reason for distinguishing the appellate process is the Court's refusal to require appellate review on due process grounds, and the major reason for the refusal is the universal practice of affording appellate review. Given this experience with the equal protection clause, it is not hard to understand why the Warren Court turned to the due process clause as authority for a revolution in criminal procedure.

3

Revolution and Reaction

In 1960 two distinct models described the constitutional law of criminal procedure. One model, based on *Boyd* and applicable in federal prosecutions, expansively defined the Fourth, Fifth, and Sixth Amendment criminal-procedure provisions. The other model, based on *Hurtado* and applicable in state cases, assessed the "fundamental fairness" of the state process on a case-by-case, totality-of-the-circumstances approach.

The Warren Court's criminal procedure revolution unified the constitutional law of criminal procedure in federal and state cases. In 1961 the Court held that the Fourteenth Amendment due process clause incorporates the Fourth Amendment exclusionary rule. In 1963 the *Gideon* decision incorporated the Sixth Amendment right to counsel, and in 1964 the *Malloy* decision incorporated the Fifth Amendment privilege against self-incrimination. By the end of the decade the only significant Bill of Rights criminal procedure safeguard not absorbed into the Fourteenth Amendment was the Fifth Amendment grand jury provision. *Hurtado* survives, but only as a museum piece, a relic from a bygone era.

Ironically enough, while *Hurtado* has been eclipsed, *Boyd* has been openly overruled. The liberal old interpretations of the Bill of Rights found in the pre-incorporation federal cases have gone the way of the buffalo. Harlan was right and Black was wrong; the "specific guarantees" in the Bill of Rights have not survived the pressures of policy considerations in state cases.

This chapter summarizes the Warren Court's revolution and the reaction that followed. The treatment is necessarily general but should suffice to establish the basic pattern of doctrinal development. The next chapter examines the historical process of legal development in greater detail by focusing on the example of interrogation and confessions.

OVERVIEW OF THE PROCESS

In the old federal model the Fourth Amendment was understood primarily as protecting property rights by the requirement of a judicial warrant founded on probable cause. The Fifth Amendment sheltered the citizen not only from compelled testimony in formal proceedings, but also against overreaching police interrogation and the coerced surrender of incriminating private property. In the federal practice, in all cases deemed not "petty," indigent defendants who went to trial could proceed *pro se* only after making an explicit on-the-record waiver, although apparently before trial the indigent defendant was required to request representation affirmatively.

The Fourth Amendment is now based on privacy rather than property, but privacy is quite narrowly understood. Procedurally, warrants are now the exception, not the rule. "Mere evidence," including private papers, can be seized under warrant. Substantively, "probable cause" doesn't mean "probable," and many searches and seizures can be justified by an even less demanding standard of "reasonable suspicion." Generous to the government as the Fourth Amendment has become, the fruits of its violation are admissible in a wide variety of procedural contexts. When the now nearly toothless jaws of the exclusionary rule do threaten a conviction in serious cases, a tolerant attitude toward police perjury can still save the day for the government.

While privacy has become the gravamen of the Fourth Amendment, it has been banished from Fifth Amendment jurisprudence. The Fifth Amendment privilege does not apply to preexisting documents at all—so much for *Boyd*'s high regard for private papers. Suspects in custody may waive the privilege, without consulting with counsel, even though the Court itself describes this environment as inherently coercive.

The Sixth Amendment right to counsel does not attach until the filing of formal charges, so that during the critical phase of police investigation the suspect is routinely denied counsel completely. During the adjudicatory phase, the indigent defense lawyers who represent a high percentage of all defendants are overworked, underpaid, and recruited from a talent pool willing to accept such conditions. Counsel's performance will not violate the Sixth Amendment unless it causes a "breakdown in the adversary process" that might have caused a miscarriage of justice.[1] Reviewing courts apply this test based on a record that was made by the very lawyer whose errors are challenged on appeal.

Meanwhile, due process and equal protection have fallen into virtual desuetude. Despite some promising experiments with procedural due process and equal protection, the Bill of Rights now totally dominates the criminal procedure landscape. Police practices will not violate substantive due process unless they shock the conscience, procedural due process claims are now subject to a test more concerned with history and judicial restraint than with avoiding miscarriages of justice, and defendants challenging their convictions on equal protection grounds are denied the discovery that alone could enable them to prove the invidious intent required to show a constitutional violation.

Despite the determined—sometimes desperate—effort to construe the Constitution to minimize the limits on police, prosecutors, and state courts, the criminal process has not become notably more efficient at convicting the guilty. The Fifth Amendment privilege still bars judicially regulated questioning of suspects, the Sixth Amendment right to counsel can taint evidence gathered by police who did not know that the suspect was charged at the time, and the confrontation clause and the hearsay rule make it difficult to overcome the witness cooperation problems that are the single largest cause of lost arrests.

Nor has the law become more consistent since the days of fundamental fairness. The Burger and Rehnquist Courts have proved as concerned with judicial as with ideological conservatism; they have refused to overrule the incorporation decisions. Yet they have frequently interpreted the Warren Court landmarks in ways contrary to any plausible justification of the original precedent. Arbitrary distinctions abound. For example, whether the suspect has the right to a lawyer at a lineup depends on whether formal charges have been filed or not, even though neither the police nor the suspect may know about the filing of an indictment or information.

To some extent the unfortunate state of the law is due to judicial ideology. I shall argue, however, that a major reason for criminal procedure's dysfunction has been the turn to the incorporation doctrine. The Bill of Rights is undesirable in some of its particulars, and inadequate in its entirety, as a constitutional guide to criminal procedure.

The recurring pattern of doctrinal development that has brought us to the present quagmire runs through three basic steps. First, the Warren Court incorporated a provision in the Bill of Rights that had been expansively construed when applied solely to federal cases. Second, typically during the tenure of Earl Warren himself, the collision between the incorporated provision and widely shared judgments about public policy moved the Court to reduce the specific language of the Bill of Rights to a generalized test of reliability or fairness. Third, typically during the Burger and Rehnquist years, reliability and fairness were given extremely narrow interpretations in favor of combating crime. The current model in criminal procedure is conservative balancing, in which the Bill of Rights procedural safeguards are applicable to both state and federal cases but are qualified at every turn by the felt necessities of law enforcement.

Academic criticism has often focused on this third stage standing alone. Certainly there is much to criticize in the Burger and Rehnquist Courts' treatments of criminal procedure. An exclusive focus on judicial personnel, however, would be misleading. For one thing, the Warren Court itself initiated the reaction against the federal model. Moreover, to a significant degree, the Warren Court's perceived activism was *responsible* for the political reaction that included Nixon's election and the appointment of Burger, Blackmun, Powell, and Rehnquist.

Even the Warren Court justices were willing to modify long-standing interpretations of the Bill of Rights to accommodate law enforcement interests. Indeed, no jurist or scholar, so far as I know, is inclined to bring back the *Boyd* model in all its aspects. The Warren Court's criminal-procedure decisions nonetheless did not backpedal fast enough to avoid conflict with powerful forces in electoral politics. Up to a point such collisions are precisely what judicial review is for; but in a democracy there are limits on the Court's power to take on unpopular causes. If the criminal-procedure revolution had secured decent and reliable police investigations, fair trials, and equal justice, it would be hard to imagine any political price that would have been too much to pay. The revolution, however, fell far short of such achievements, not least because the Bill of Rights provisions do not require reliability or equality.

THE FOURTH AMENDMENT

The text of the Fourth Amendment calls for four basic interpretive judgments. First, what government actions qualify as "searches and seizures"? Second, what substantive justifications for a search or a seizure make it reasonable or unreasonable? Third, how, procedurally, should the presence or absence of substantive justification be tested? In other words, what is the relationship between the warrant clause and the reasonableness clause? Fourth and finally, when the government violates the amendment, what is the appropriate remedy or sanction?

The pre-incorporation federal decisions had worked out answers to these questions in the libertarian spirit of *Boyd*—that the Fourth and Fifth Amendments run into each other, that books and private papers were constitutionally inviolable, that prior judicial authorization by warrant was required whenever feasible, and that the fruits of violations could be suppressed by means of a timely motion for return of the seized property. Although originally connected to the *Boyd* decision's vision of the self-incrimination privilege, the Fourth Amendment exclusionary rule came to enjoy a life of its own, and could be invoked both by corporations that did not enjoy the privilege and to suppress contraband in which the movant could not claim any lawful property rights.

The early federal cases made one major concession to law enforcement interests. The Supreme Court gave a narrow interpretation to the term "searches," requiring a trespassory invasion of the individual's property rights to trigger the protections of the amendment. Wiretapping was thus excluded from Fourth Amendment scrutiny. Given the rigorous demands of the Fourth Amendment at the time, this narrow definition made some sense. Under the mere evidence rule, for example, wiretapping could not have survived Fourth Amendment scrutiny even when authorized by warrant founded on probable cause.

Following the incorporation of the Fourth Amendment exclusionary rule in *Mapp v. Ohio*,[2] Fourth Amendment law went through an illustrative metamorphosis. In *Lopez v. United States*,[3] *Hoffa v. United States*,[4] and *Lewis v. United States*,[5] the Court adhered to the view that transactions and conversations between suspects and undercover agents are not searches. The combination of *Mapp* and the federal Fourth Amendment cases made this course virtually mandatory. Otherwise every informant and undercover officer could have operated only when authorized by warrants founded on probable cause. *Terry v. Ohio* was still years away.

Thus the Warren Court adhered to the old law in the one instance in which the old law favored the government. Soon enough stage two set in. In 1965 the Court refused to give *Mapp* retroactive effect, characterizing the exclusionary rule purely as a deterrent.[6] In 1969 the Court reaffirmed the standing doctrine, reasoning that suppression by the search victim was sufficient to deter.[7] By then Justice Black himself was characterizing the exclusionary rule as an optional deterrent remedy that should not be applied on habeas corpus, even for federal prisoners.[8]

Even narrowly defined, and even enforced by a circumscribed exclusionary rule, the warrant-clause-based interpretation of the Fourth Amendment posed an obstacle to law enforcement that the Warren Court was unwilling to accept. Building inspections could not be defined as anything but "searches," unless Newspeak was to find its way into the United States reports. No child of the New Deal could oppose building inspections as unreasonable. Yet to demand that the inspections be supported by warrants based on probable cause would defeat their purpose.

The Warren Court insisted that building inspections be authorized by warrants, but the warrants need not be based on any individualized suspicion of code violations.[9] Instead rational area standards for inspecting the entire housing stock satisfied the requirements of "probable cause." What had to be probable was cause, not the existence of a violation.[10]

This shift in emphasis from the insistence that warrants based on probable cause were the benchmark of Fourth Amendment reasonableness to an open-ended inquiry into reasonableness quickly migrated (or metastasized, depending on your view) to police practices. Prior to the 1960s, the police had the authority to enforce vagrancy and loitering laws that made it a crime to behave suspiciously.[11] Probable cause to believe that the suspect was a vagrant authorized arrest, and arrest carried the power to search, all without warrants under long-standing doctrine. During the 1960s, however, defendants mounted successful challenges to the vagrancy laws on void-for-vagueness grounds.

Coercive police encounters with suspicious characters short of formal arrest thus soon emerged as an important Fourth Amendment issue. Following the old model, the Court might have given a restrictive interpretation of "searches and seizures" and held that detention for investigation and protective frisk did not trigger the Fourth Amendment at all. Alternatively, the Court could have treated stop-and-frisk as a seizure requiring probable cause (exigency would typically have excused the absence of a warrant).

The first option would have tolerated arbitrary police authority to stop and search citizens on the streets, and the second option would have raised an unacceptable barrier to law enforcement. Faced with the challenges that confront the Cleveland police, rather than the FBI, the Warren Court basically disincorporated the Fourth Amendment in *Terry v. Ohio*.[12] *Terry* reasoned that searches and seizures, as a matter of the constitutional text, need only be reasonable. So construed, the

Fourth Amendment adds nothing to substantive due process except a narrower threshold category ("searches and seizures" as opposed to "life, liberty, or property"). *Terry* did not, however, go so far as to fall back on fundamental fairness in light of the totality of the circumstances. Instead, the Court crafted a distinct standard of substantive justification (the "reasonable suspicion" standard) applicable to a distinct category of police behavior (stop-and-frisk). Such a standard could just as easily have been derived from due process *simpliciter*. The important point is that Earl Warren himself excised both probable cause and preliminary judicial authorization from the Fourth Amendment.

Once the Warren Court had adopted reasonableness, rather than warrants and probable cause, as the Fourth Amendment's pole star, it became possible to expand the definition of searches and seizures. *Terry* illustrates this very practice, taking a broad view of seizures and a generous view of reasonableness. With the demise of the mere evidence rule (also thrown out by the Warren Court),[13] the reasonableness model allowed the Court to adopt a privacy-based, rather than property-based, understanding of searches.

The *Katz* decision[14] and the ultimate formulation of "reasonable expectations of privacy" derived from Harlan's concurrence are well known. What is less widely recognized is that the old secret-agent cases survived the transformation to a privacy-based regime. *United States v. White*[15] came down in 1971, before the retirement of Douglas or Harlan. Over Harlan's dissent, the Court reasoned that since criminals assume the risk that those to whom they admit their crimes may turn them in, they can have no Fourth Amendment right against an accurate recording of their admissions.

Justice Harlan strove to distinguish undercover agents from undercover agents supplemented by hidden recorders or corroborating witnesses. The claim of a constitutional right to plausible deniability seems unconvincing. The disturbing tension with *Katz* stems from the *White* plurality's major premise about the privacy of conversations with apparent friends, not the minor premise that accurate recording does not offend the Constitution.

Katz holds that when one talks to another over the telephone one has a reasonable expectation of privacy in the communications. *Lopez, Lewis, Hoffa,* and *White* all hold that this expectation is not reasonable when one's interlocutor is a government spy. But if the theory is that speakers assume the risk that their words will be repeated, why does the fact that the interlocutor is a spy make any difference? If the *risk* that one's audience includes a spy suffices to make conversations unprivate, the government should have the right to tap telephones at will, for there is always the chance that one party may betray the other.

The *White* plurality, unlike the justices who decided *Lopez, Hoffa,* and *Lewis,* had the benefit of the *Terry* standard. The Court might have admitted that society recognizes as reasonable confidences reposed in trusted friends, so that the betrayal of that trust at the behest of the government requires some justification in the way of antecedent suspicion. Instead the Court, long before the emergence of a "Nixon majority," went with Poor Richard and held that three can keep a secret, if two of them are dead.

Once a solid conservative majority *did* emerge, the Warren Court's doctrinal framework was given an emphatically pro-government interpretation. Anything entrusted to another person—be it transactions recorded by your bank[16] or garbage left for collection on your curb[17]—can be parsed by the government without triggering the Fourth Amendment at all. Searches can be "reasonable" with disturbingly little justification. For example, high school students can be subjected to urinalysis solely because they play on the school's sports teams.[18] There is now a home-and-office exception to the usual rule that no warrant is required.[19] The exclusionary rule has so many exceptions that tainted evidence still confers major benefits on the government.[20]

A few illustrative cases suggest just how far from the old model the Court has traveled. Under *Griffin v. Wisconsin*, the police may enter a private home without probable cause and without either a warrant or exigency, provided that the home contains a probationer.[21] Such a search, the Court held, is "reasonable" under the theory of *Camara* and *Terry*. There is a surface appeal to the idea that release from prison comes with reasonable conditions. But what about the obvious fact that most such homes contain people who are *not* on probation, or the less obvious but no less important fact that in some states *a majority* of the young black men are under the control of the criminal justice system?

United States v. Leon recognized a "good-faith exception" to the exclusionary rule for searches authorized by facially valid warrants. The majority reasoned that the police should not be required to second-guess judicial determinations of probable causes. Yet the text of the Fourth Amendment declares that "no warrants shall issue, but upon probable cause[.]" *Leon* holds that the exclusionary rule will not apply when this flat prohibition is violated, and other cases curtail the available tort remedies.[22] In effect *Leon* holds that the Constitution can be violated without any sanction or remedy whatsoever.

Together with the relaxed standard of probable cause in informant cases adopted in the *Gates* decision,[23] *Leon* makes it virtually impossible to win a suppression motion in warrant cases. So long as obtaining warrants was a difficult and time-consuming process, this may not have been a grievous result.[24] Increasingly, however, warrant applications are based on "confidential informants" and little else.[25] Under *Gates* police seeking search warrants need not establish either the informant's basis of knowledge or prior reliability. Under *Leon*, even if the warrant application fails the lenient *Gates* test, the exclusionary rule will not apply. The door to speculative searches of private premises is wide open. The old model was based on probable cause, warrants, and exclusion. *Gates* and *Leon* reveal just how thoroughly the modern Court has repudiated the old model.

The one residuum of the old model is a grudging definition of "searches and seizures." A young black man hectored on a bus by a pair of hulking sheriff's deputies, the Court maintains, is free to disregard the police.[26] Police who parse a suspect's discarded garbage, the Court insists, have invaded no reasonable expectation of privacy.[27] *Katz* might have supported what the *Camara/Terry* interpretation fully justifies—a broad definition of searches and seizures, and a flexible approach to defining the justification required for particular types of searches and seizures. Instead, Justice Black's faith in the specific guarantees of the Bill of Rights has not saved us from the worst of all Fourth Amendment worlds, in which the Amendment is hard to trigger, harder to violate when it applies, virtually impossible to enforce when it is violated, and yet is thought of as the Constitution's primary, almost exclusive, regulation of the police.

THE FIFTH AMENDMENT

In 1964 the Warren Court handed down *Malloy v. Hogan*,[28] which applied the Fifth Amendment privilege to the states. This required overruling two long-standing precedents, *Twining* and *Adamson*. It also raised the specter of applying *Boyd*'s libertarian model of criminal procedure to the states.

The development of confessions law following the incorporation of the Fifth Amendment privilege is taken up in detail in Chapter 4. *Boyd*, however, dealt with compulsion to surrender evidence by formal process, not through the informal processes of police questioning. In the context of Fifth Amendment claims raised during formal proceedings, the development of post-incorporation doctrine once again followed the three-stage pattern.

In the immediate aftermath of *Malloy*, the Warren Court adhered to traditional federal interpretations of the Fifth Amendment privilege. The key case was *Griffin v. California*,[29] decided in 1965. California practice permitted both the prosecutor and the court to point out that an inference of guilt could be drawn from the failure of the defendant to take the stand at trial. A *Boyd*-vintage Supreme Court decision[30] had forbidden this inference in federal cases.

The *Griffin* court held that the federal rule applied to the states as a matter of constitutional law. In effect, the inference of guilt imposed a penalty on standing silent, thus punishing the defendant for exercising the privilege. Of course, all incriminating evidence tends to force the accused onto the stand. A videotape showing the defendant committing the crime "compels" the accused to come forward with some evidence of justification or excuse, for instance. But the inference of guilt from a videotape is completely rational. For two different reasons, the *Griffin* majority concluded that the inference of guilt from silence is not rational.

First, an innocent defendant might expose himself to impeachment with prior convictions by taking the stand. Such evidence is generally banned from the prosecution's case because of the fear that juries will overvalue the probative value of prior crimes and because juries may decide to convict in a doubtful case because the defendant deserves additional punishment for past, as distinct from charged, offenses. The empirical evidence strongly supports the tendency of prior convictions to increase the likelihood of conviction.[31]

Second, an innocent defendant may be so slow-minded or inarticulate that testifying might do more harm than good to a justified cause. A fatal misstep on cross-examination is a sufficiently plausible scenario to persuade some innocent defendants not to testify. It follows that no inference of guilt should be drawn from the failure to testify.

Malloy and *Griffin* have effectively prevented state experimentation with formal system of in-court questioning as alternatives to police interrogation. The key to questioning the suspect after the appointment of counsel is to give the suspect an incentive to talk on the record. The most obvious way to do this is to authorize an adverse inference at trial from the refusal to answer pretrial questions. *Griffin* means that the accused cannot be put to this election, with the result that the only way to question the suspect is *before* the appointment of defense counsel, in the backroom of the police station.

Of course it would have been possible, as *Escobedo* suggested, to live with the loss of confessions that would have accompanied extending the right to counsel to the process of police interrogation. Given the necessity of interrogation to solve many serious crimes, especially homicides where there is by definition no surviving victim to serve as a witness, this is a price few would be willing to pay. As it turned out, this was a price the Warren Court was not willing to pay. *Miranda*, as the next chapter shows, should be understood as a second-stage decision retreating from *Escobedo*.

Shortly after *Miranda* the Warren Court began the process of burying *Boyd* itself. In *Schmerber v. California*[32] the Court held that drawing blood without the consent of the suspect did not violate the privilege against self-incrimination because the privilege protects only testimonial evidence. The blood of an intoxicated motorist could not be described as contraband, or the fruits or instrumentality of crime. A year later the Court made the connection to the Fourth Amendment's explicit by repudiating the "mere evidence" rule, holding that the discarded clothes of a fleeing felon were not immune to seizure.[33]

The essence of *Boyd* was the idea that violating a state-law property right to evidence was equivalent to compulsion to testify. Within three years of applying the Fifth Amendment to the states, this connection was a dead letter.

The application of the *Schmerber* doctrine to private papers represents the third stage of development. In a series of cases the Burger Court applied *Schmerber*'s logic to documents that exist at the time their production is compelled.[34] In such cases the evidence is testimonial, but the suspect was not compelled by the government to prepare the documents. If seized under a search warrant, the documents can be used freely as evidence. If demanded by subpoena, the custodian of the documents may claim that turning them over in response might help to authenticate them at trial. Ordinarily the government can authenticate the documents in other ways and so can afford to immunize the act of production, although this course might generate extensive litigation about derivative evidentiary use of the immunized act. In any event, there is a "foregone conclusion" exception to the privilege against the act of production.[35] In effect, the government can obtain preexisting documents by showing an independent ability to prove their authenticity, a kind of informal immunity for the act of production. As a result, in practice it is very difficult to keep preexisting documents out of government hands, at least when the government knows that the documents exist before issuing the subpoena.

Early on the Burger Court upheld a new federal immunity statute, which re-placed transactional immunity with use-plus-fruits immunity.[36] *Counselman v. Hitchcock*,[37] a *Boyd*-era decision that approved even transactional immunity with some qualms, was overruled. Justice Brandeis once wrote that *Boyd* "will be re-membered as long as civil liberty lives in the United States."[38] After the *Fisher* decision in 1976—only a dozen years after the Court incorporated the privilege— *Boyd* was dead, and with it, the libertarian federal model of criminal procedure.

THE RIGHT TO COUNSEL

The unanimous decision in *Gideon v. Wainwright*[39] reflected several underly-ing developments in the administration of criminal justice. Only a few Southern states still refused to appoint counsel for indigent defendants in felony cases. The *Daniels* trilogy made convictions without defense counsel routinely reviewable in federal courts, under the impenetrably vague standard of *Betts v. Brady*. As Abe Fortas argued in the brief for *Gideon,* a flat requirement of counsel in felony cases would overturn the practice of a few parochial jurisdictions, but avoid the friction between state and federal courts that inevitably attended federal review under the fundamental fairness standard.[40] Even Justice Harlan agreed that *Betts* should be overruled.[41]

Of the various questions raised by *Gideon*, two stood out as especially impor-tant. First, at what point in the criminal process did the right to counsel attach? Obviously the accused had the right to counsel at trial, but what about during po-lice investigations? In particular, what about an arrested, but as yet uncharged, suspect who is questioned by the police or paraded before eyewitnesses?

Second, given that the accused now had the right to a lawyer, how good did the lawyer have to be? At some extreme, incompetence or overwork would nullify the substance of the procedural safeguard. How was that extreme to be defined?

Betts had swept these questions under the rug. Indigent defendants who had no federal constitutional right to a lawyer *at trial* were certainly not going to enjoy appointed counsel during interrogation. Likewise, if the state had the power to force the indigent defendant to proceed *pro se*, it seems unimaginable that a lawyer's malpractice could make out a constitutional issue.

In the immediate aftermath of *Gideon* the Warren Court looked to the Sixth Amendment right to counsel as a check on police overreaching. The 1964 deci-sions in *Massiah v. United States*[42] and *Escobedo v. Illinois*[43] threw out convic-tions because the suspect was questioned before trial in the absence of counsel. In the *Massiah* case the defendant had been indicted, retained counsel, and been released on bail. While waiting trial he was engaged in conversation by an un-dercover agent. The Court suppressed these conversations on the ground that the right to counsel had attached at the time of the indictment at latest, and that com-munications between the government and the accused absent counsel therefore violated the Sixth Amendment.

Escobedo went further, inasmuch as Escobedo had not been formally indicted. Escobedo had once employed a lawyer named Wolfson in a personal injury case.[44] After his arrest for murder, Escobedo's sister telephoned Wolfson, who sought to speak to Escobedo at the stationhouse. At the same time Escobedo was demanding to talk to Wolfson. At one point the two actually caught a tantalizing glimpse of one another, before Escobedo was hustled behind closed doors, where, when confronted with an accomplice, he made incriminating admissions.

The Supreme Court held that the refusal to permit consultation with counsel violated the Sixth Amendment. It was not clear from Justice Goldberg's rambling opinion what fact was dispositive—the lawyer's request to see the suspect, the suspect's request to see the lawyer, or the fact that Escobedo had become the prime suspect. *Escobedo*, however, clearly held that the absence of formal accusation was *not* dispositive.

As the next chapter develops more fully, *Miranda* embodied the second stage of doctrinal development. If the uncharged but arrested suspect enjoys the Sixth Amendment right to counsel, logic would seem to require the demanding standard for waiving counsel at trial during interrogation. The suspect would need to consult with counsel or be admonished by a judge before waiving the right to a lawyer. Imagine the reaction to the suggestion that the police could obtain valid guilty pleas in the backroom of the stationhouse, or that a valid *Miranda* waiver irrevocably bound the suspect to proceed without counsel through the trial process.

Miranda holds that the uncharged suspect can waive the privilege against self-incrimination, and the right to counsel during interrogation derived from the privilege, without actually seeing a lawyer or a judge. Unlike the Sixth Amendment right to counsel at trial, which traditionally could be waived only after exacting inquiry,[45] the traditional test of Fifth Amendment is use-it-or-lose-it. If a witness before, say, a congressional committee answers a question, the privilege is waived, even though no admonition is given.

Thus, as a matter of the Fifth Amendment privilege, *Miranda* broke some new ground by requiring the warning before answers to questions amounted to waiver *ipso facto*. But as a matter of Sixth Amendment law, *Miranda* marked a major victory for the government. Police interrogation was saved from the jaws of *Escobedo*.

During this second stage, the Warren Court avoided ruling on the standard for effective assistance of counsel. The lower courts, following Judge Thurman Arnold's reasoning in a pre-*Gideon* federal case,[46] took the view that only if counsel's performance made the proceedings "a farce and mockery of justice" would a conviction be set aside for ineffective assistance.[47]

In the 1970s the Supreme Court sent deliberately vague signals about the standard for ineffective assistance,[48] and also developed a rule of automatic reversal for cases in which the government interfered with defense counsel's representation in one way or another.[49] Given room to maneuver by the Supreme Court, and as indigent defense programs became better established in the 1970s, the lower courts began to move in the direction of more exacting standards. Various approaches were adopted,[50] but all of them examined counsel's performance in individual cases on the basis of the record made by counsel.

In the third stage of development, the Burger Court formalized what was implicit in *Miranda* by holding that the Sixth Amendment right to counsel does not attach until formal charges are filed.[51] Even after charges are filed, the accused has the right to counsel's assistance only during so-called critical stages of the prosecution. This includes interrogation[52] and corporeal identification proceedings,[53] but not, significantly, photographic identification proceedings.[54]

The Burger Court also adopted a demanding test for ineffective assistance claims. The 1984 decision in *Strickland v. Washington*[55] requires a defendant challenging a conviction on ineffective assistance grounds to prove that counsel made errors so grievous as to cause a "breakdown in the adversary process that renders the result unreliable."[56] Thus negligence alone is not sufficient; the defendant must also show prejudice, i.e., that but for counsel's negligence the result of the proceeding might well have been different. The *Strickland* test generates an enormous amount of appellate and collateral litigation, is very rarely met, and has done nothing to address the systematic underfunding of the indigent defense system.[57]

How is an indigent convict supposed to show on appeal that his overworked public defender could have won the case by a more thorough investigation? If such a convict had the resources to mount a thorough post-conviction investigation and support the appeal with affidavits, he wouldn't have been represented by the public defender in the first place. And if the investigation *were* inadequate, there would be no way to prove exculpatory theories based on the very record alleged to be incomplete or misleading. *Strickland* simply presumes that the defendant convicted without a thorough investigation by the defense is guilty. Shades of *Betts v. Brady*!

The standard pattern also played itself out with respect to the Sixth Amendment's confrontation clause and jury trial guarantee. The Warren Court incorporated the confrontation clause,[58] but in 1970—with Black, Harlan, and Douglas still sitting after Warren's retirement—*California v. Green*[59] held that the mere opportunity to cross-examine a hearsay declarant, either at the trial or at the time of the prior statement, satisfies the clause. The Burger Court went further and drew a global and irrebuttable inference of reliability from the satisfaction of a traditional exception to the hearsay rule.[60]

In 1968 the Warren Court incorporated the jury trial guarantee, but only two years later the Court upheld state practices authorizing convictions by less-than-unanimous verdicts and by juries of fewer than twelve. During the days of the old federal model the Court had declared that the Constitution's reference to juries meant twelve as surely as if that number had been specifically named. But a majority of the Court could see no magic in the number twelve, while permitting conviction over the objections of one or two holdouts seemed a fair concession to rational adjudication.

As we have seen, incorporation repeatedly forced the Court to choose between traditional interpretations of the Bill of Rights or the apparently perfectly reasonable demands of law enforcement. The reasonable demands of law enforcement almost always won, and they started winning long before the Nixon majority took control of the Court. The other nonobvious feature of the turn to incorporation was the effect incorporation had on freestanding Fourteenth Amendment doctrine. While the Bill of Rights was being hammered on the last of policy considerations presented by law enforcement in the states, due process and equal protection fell into practical desuetude in criminal cases.

THE FOURTEENTH AMENDMENT

The consequences of incorporation were not limited to modifying the old interpretations of the Fourth, Fifth, and Sixth Amendments. The Warren Court's focus on the Bill of Rights, and the Burger/Rehnquist Courts' solicitude for the government, resulted in quite narrow interpretations of due process and equal protection in criminal cases.

The Warren Court's decision in *Schmerber* initiated this process by adopting *Rochin*'s "shock the conscience" language as the test of substantive due process rights against police practices. *Rochin* required no such interpretation. The issue in *Rochin* was not whether the warrantless midnight entry and the stomach-pumping violated Rochin's due process rights. There was no question that they did, because the *Wolf* case had incorporated the substance of the Fourth Amendment a few years earlier. What was at issue in *Rochin* was whether the exclusionary remedy would apply to the fruits of the illegality, and Justice Frankfurter adopted the conscience-shocking terminology to distinguish extreme Fourth Amendment violations from ordinary ones.

The pre-*Mapp* decision in *Breithaupt v. Abram*[61] had held that drawing blood to test for alcohol content did *not* shock the conscience so as to require excluding the evidence. *Schmerber* casually—and erroneously—read *Breithaupt* as controlling Schmerber's due process claim. After *Mapp*, however, there was no longer any constitutional question for the *Rochin* test to answer. Instead of permitting *Rochin* to pass to a deserved repose, the *Schmerber* opinion adopted a designedly narrow escape hatch from the purely remedial rule in *Wolf* as the test of substantive due process rights.

In his famous concurrence in *Poe v. Ullman* Justice Harlan described the "liberty" protected by substantive due process as "a rational continuum which, broadly speaking, includes a freedom from all substantial arbitrary impositions and purposeless restraints" as distinct from "a series of isolated points pricked out in terms of the taking of property; the freedom of speech . . . and so on."[62] On Harlan's view, it is the government that must justify deprivations of liberty, not the individual who must show that government action is shocking or outrageous.

Schmerber admits that some government action might violate substantive due process without violating the incorporated amendments, but practically speaking the conscience-shocking formula has effectively reduced substantive due process to the Bill of Rights. Since *Schmerber* the Supreme Court has never held that police conduct violates substantive due process because it was shocking or outrageous. In effect, freestanding substantive due process analysis in criminal cases has ceased.

For example, excessive force claims invite substantive due process analysis, because in these cases the constitutional concern is that the police have skipped the trial by imposing their own brand of informal punishment. Yet in 1985 the Supreme Court preferred to say that one shot to death by the police with insufficient justification had been "unreasonably seized" rather than "deprived of life,"[63] and soon after rejected the Second Circuit's well-thought-out test of substantive due process in excessive force cases in favor of Fourth Amendment "reasonableness" analysis.[64] Anything that can be shoe-horned into the Bill of Rights will be, and claims that admittedly fall outside the specific provisions in the Bill are judged under the shock-the-conscience test. Harlan endorsed *Schmerber*'s treatment of the due process issue, but the modern Bill of Rights regime is about as far from Harlan's *Ullman* account as it is possible to get.[65]

Procedural due process claims have had a more uneven record, but it is still fair to say that incorporation has marginalized claims grounded directly on the due process clause. The 1970 decision in *In re Winship*[66] involved a juvenile delinquency proceeding under a preponderance of the evidence standard. The Court held that the proceeding was in fact a criminal prosecution and that the government must prove guilt beyond a reasonable doubt as a matter of due process. Both Justice Brennan's majority opinion and Harlan's somewhat clearer concurrence took the position that, given the extreme consequences of unjust conviction, procedural fairness required the higher standard.

The Court, however, qualified *Winship* by holding, in *Patterson v. New York*,[67] that due process permits the state to shift the burden of proving affirmative defenses by a preponderance of the evidence to the accused. This result was supported by common-law practice and pre-*Winship* precedent. The Court has adhered to this theory even when the affirmative defense is self-defense,[68] a defense that the state, unlike such defenses as entrapment, insanity, or provocation, presumably has no constitutional power to abolish.

The tension between *Winship* and *Patterson* reflects the old tension between Webster's instrumental theory of procedural due process and the historical approach taken in *Murray's Lessee*. An instrumental approach would allow the courts to throw out antiquated procedures that run a high risk of error, and to require procedural safeguards beyond those known at common law. The historical approach, by contrast, makes common-law practice a constitutional safe harbor for the state.

Patterson's turn to the historical approach was called into question by the 1976 decision in *Mathews v. Eldridge*.[69] There, generally following the analysis of Judge Henry Friendly,[70] the Supreme Court announced a general three-factor test of what process is due before the termination of constitutionally protected interests in administrative proceedings. The test requires the reviewing court to consider the weight of the individual's interest, the risk of error, and the cost to the government of additional procedural safeguards. Although adopted in the administrative law context, the *Eldridge* test represented a general turn toward the instrumental theory.

The Court applied the *Eldridge* test to require court-appointed expert witnesses for indigent defendants raising defenses based on mental illness. Unlike counsel, which the accused has a right to under the Sixth Amendment, there is nothing in the Bill of Rights that provides a right to expert witnesses. *Ake v. Oklahoma*[71] held that, at least when the state relies on expert testimony about the mental condition of an indigent defendant, the defense has the right to retain an opposing expert at state expense. The *Ake* opinion openly consulted the *Mathews* factors.

It is a revealing comment on the Bill of Rights that the prospect of applying the *Mathews* test in criminal cases faced the Rehnquist Court with the uncomfortable specter of judicial activism. Bluntly put, a criminal prosecution can fully comply with the Bill of Rights and still be blatantly unreliable. To name only a few examples, there is nothing in the Bill about the collection of evidence, eyewitness identification procedures, discovery, expert witnesses, or pretrial publicity. The Supreme Court has approached each of these topics as a matter of freestanding procedural due process law, in each case adopting far less rigorous procedural safeguards than the *Mathews* test might well support.[72]

If the Court had followed through on *Ake* and subjected the criminal process to a thoroughgoing reexamination in light of the *Mathews* factors, we might have seen a second revolution in criminal procedure. Despite all the conservative rhetoric about criminal procedure being about guilt and innocence, judicial restraint has proved more valuable to the current Court than reliability in criminal cases. In *Medina v. California* the Court repudiated *Ake*'s reliance on *Mathews*, although the result in *Ake* was not overruled.

The issue in *Medina* was whether a state rule casting upon the defendant the burden of proving incompetence to stand trial by a preponderance of the evidence violated due process. The defendant attacked this allocation of the burden of proof under the *Eldridge* test.

Writing for the Court, Justice Kennedy rejected both the specific claim and the reliance on *Eldridge*:

In the field of criminal law, we have defined the category of infractions that violate fundamental fairness very narrowly based on the recognition that, [b]eyond the specific guarantees enumerated in the Bill of Rights, the Due Process Clause has limited operation. The Bill of Rights speaks in explicit terms to many aspects of criminal procedure, and the expansion of those constitutional guarantees under the open-ended rubric of the Due Process Clause invites undue interference with both considered legislative judgments and the careful balance that the Constitution strikes between liberty and order. . . .

The proper analytical approach, and the one that we adopt here, is that set forth in *Patterson v. New York*, which was decided one year after *Mathews*. . . .

It goes without saying that preventing and dealing with crime is much more the business of the States than it is of the Federal Government, and that we should not lightly construe the Constitution so as to intrude upon the administration of justice by the individual States. Among other things, it is normally within the power of the State to regulate procedures under which its laws are carried out, including the burden of producing evidence and the burden of persuasion, and its decision in this regard is not subject to proscription under the Due Process Clause unless it offends some principle of justice so rooted in the traditions and conscience of our people as to be ranked as fundamental. As *Patterson* suggests, because the States have considerable expertise in matters of criminal procedure and the criminal process is grounded in centuries of common-law tradition, it is appropriate to exercise substantial deference to legislative judgments in this area. The analytical approach endorsed in *Patterson* is thus far less intrusive than that approved in *Mathews*.[73]

Note how the Court repeatedly slips back into the language of "fundamental fairness," a substantive due process concept, to articulate the proper inquiry into procedural fairness. Note also how Justice Kennedy deploys the case for judicial restraint in substantive due process cases as a reason for taking a lamentably narrow approach to procedural due process questions.

In *Medina* the Court consulted common-law practice, found "no settled tradition on the proper allocation of the burden of proof in a proceeding to determine competence,"[74] and therefore rejected petitioner's historical argument. But the Court then rather pointedly went on to conduct a purely instrumental analysis. In the language of the opinion, "[d]iscerning no historical basis for concluding that the allocation of the burden of proving incompetence to the defendant violates due process, we turn to consider whether the rule transgresses any recognized principle of 'fundamental fairness' in operation."[75]

In this portion of the opinion, the Court frankly consulted instrumental considerations in light of the special character of the criminal process. The majority rejected the state's contention that precedents upholding shifting the burden of proving the insanity defense to the defendant compelled rejection of Medina's claim, because competence goes to the present ability to conduct one's defense, not the past ability to understand or control one's behavior. Nor was the case analogous to burden allocation cases involving suppression motions, where the object is deterring police misconduct. The Court considered, but rejected, the argument that competence is so vague a concept that borderline cases must be resolved in favor of the defendant. In the end what due process requires is "a reasonable opportunity to demonstrate that he is not competent to stand trial."[76] Given that the preponderance of the evidence standard makes the burden of proof only a tie-breaker, the state's procedure satisfied this standard.

The Court thus now takes a position somewhere between the Webster and *Murray's Lessee* interpretations. Procedural due process analysis looks first to history, and only secondarily to instrumental reliability. The desirability of this retreat from *Ake* and *Mathews* is debatable, but there can be little doubt that the current Court favors judicial restraint over instrumental reliability as the dominant value in procedural due process cases. Ironically, in administrative cases involving far lesser liabilities—such as a suspension from public school or discharge from public employment—*Mathews* controls and the focus is on instrumental reliability.[77]

What about equal protection? By 1960 there were two lines of equal protection precedents. The first, initiated by *Strauder v. West Virginia*,[78] forbade racial discrimination in selecting individuals for grand or petit jury service. The second,

initiated in *Griffin v. Illinois*,[79] forbade discriminating against the indigent in offering post-conviction review.

One might have thought that an egalitarian Supreme Court might have relied
on the equal protection clause for its criminal procedure revolution, but the truth
is the exact opposite. The practical difficulty with claims of racial discrimination
in criminal justice is the inherently difficult problem of distinguishing disparate
impact from invidious discrimination. *De jure* racial classification had long since
vanished; discrimination in jury selection worked through the forms of educational qualifications, voter registration lists, and peremptory challenges.

Back in the nineteenth century, in *Neal v. Delaware*,[80] the Supreme Court had
shown the willingness to infer invidious intent from catastrophically disparate
impact. In the 1930s, in *Norris v. Alabama*,[81] Chief Justice Hughes had made that
same inference for a unanimous Court. In *Neal* and *Norris* the record showed that
no blacks had served on juries (in the whole state of Delaware and in Morgan
County, Alabama, respectively) within living memory. In *Neal* and *Norris* the
prosecution had responded that there simply were no blacks, and never had been
any, within the jurisdiction who satisfied legitimate, race-neutral qualifications.
In both cases the Supreme Court treated this defense as a preposterous cover for
invidious intent.

Swain v. Alabama[82] came to the Court in 1965. Swain, a black defendant
charged with raping a white woman, was convicted and sentenced to death by an
all-white jury. During jury selection, six blacks appeared on the venire, and all
were peremptorily challenged by the prosecutor. Alabama employed a so-called
struck-jury system, in which, in capital cases, a hundred individuals were sum-
moned to the venire. After challenges for cause, the remaining members of the
venire were peremptorily challenged, with the defense striking two and the prosecution one, by turns.

The system certainly seems fair—could not the twelve out of a hundred Swain
felt least suspicious of give him a fair hearing? But the system was also nicely
calculated to keep members of a racial minority off of juries. The six strikes the
prosecution needed to purge the venire came nowhere near to exhausting the
state's peremptories. No blacks had served on a petit jury in Tallageda County
"since about 1950," even though the county's population was 26% black.

The record in *Swain*, however, was less clear-cut than the records in *Neal* and
Norris. The record showed that grand juries typically contained a few black citizens, and that in some instances the defense was responsible for striking blacks
from the venire. There was testimony in the record from defense lawyers to the
effect that some black defendants preferred white to black jurors in their own
cases. The process of calling the venire is wholly within the control of state
actors; peremptory challenges are exercised by both prosecution and defense.

Moreover, the peremptory challenge is especially difficult to subject to
equal protection scrutiny, because the nature of the challenge is that no
reason need be offered for its use. To demand an explanation would make the
challenge something less than peremptory. Relying on these considerations,

Justice White's majority opinion held that Swain had not made out a *prima facie* case of discrimination. The opinion cautioned, however, that if in some future case the defense could prove that "the prosecutor in a county, in case after case, whatever the circumstances, whatever the crime and whoever the defendant or the victim may be, is responsible for the removal of Negroes who have been selected as qualified jurors by the jury commissioners and who have survived challenges for cause, with the result that no Negroes ever serve on petit juries, the Fourteenth Amendment claim takes on added significance."[83]

As the dissent foresaw,[84] this burden of proof proved practically impossible to satisfy. Across the country prosecutorial peremptories resulted in the trial of black defendants by all-white juries.[85] The courts consistently found that these defendants had not met the burden of proof demanded by *Swain*.[86]

While the empirical evidence demonstrating the role of the peremptory challenge in excluding blacks from jury service accumulated, the Burger Court turned to the Sixth Amendment to strike down rules that made it easier for women than for men to avoid jury service. In this line of cases, the Court equated the "impartial jury" language of the Sixth Amendment to require that those called for jury duty be drawn from a "fair cross-section" of the community.[87] The test developed under the Sixth Amendment looked much more like the Title VII burden-shifting process than the traditional rule in the equal protection cases that invidious intent, in the absence of direct evidence of animus, will be inferred only from extremely disparate impact.[88]

Fed up with *Swain*, some of the lower courts began to apply the Sixth Amendment fair cross-section requirement to peremptory challenge cases.[89] The Supreme Court's cross-section cases all dealt with the venire, not the process of selecting the actual panel from the venire. The Supreme Courts of California[90] and Massachusetts,[91] and the Second Circuit federal court of appeals,[92] adopted a procedure modeled on the fair cross-section test. If, from all the circumstances in the instant case, the defense can make out a *prima facie* case that the prosecutor's peremptory challenges are based on race, the burden shifts to the prosecutor to show some nonracial reason for the challenges. The burden then shifts back to the defense to show that the purported explanation is pretextual, at which point an inference of discrimination is appropriate.

The fair cross-section cases looked like an end-run around *Swain*. The justices faced three choices. They could decide to live with the racial consequences of *Swain*, and hold that the cross-section requirement applied only to the venire, not to the panel. They could have extended the cross-section requirement to the panel, left *Swain* undisturbed, and imported equal protection logic into the Sixth Amendment. Finally, they could overrule *Swain* and adopt the burden-shifting approach on equal protection grounds.

Batson v. Kentucky[93] made this last choice, overruling *Swain* and adopting a burden-shifting approach. Justice White, the author of *Swain*, agreed with the decision, although Chief Justice Burger and Justice Rehnquist dissented. Soon thereafter the Court held that the Sixth Amendment fair cross-section requirement does not apply to the venire.[94] Thus in jury-selection cases, the Title VII burden-shifting approach had entered equal protection jurisprudence, imported from lower-court decisions that are no longer sound law as a Sixth Amendment matter. Legal history moves in mysterious ways.

How could the Burger Court, sympathetic to the state in criminal cases and yet unwilling to overrule even such pro-defense precedents as *Mapp* or *Massiah*, bring itself to overrule a conservative Warren Court precedent? With collective decisions there are always complex explanations, but two factors stand out as particularly important.

First, overwhelming evidence had confirmed that the *Swain* rule had the effect of imposing all-white juries on a great many black defendants. The justices surely appreciated how much damage this practice did to the appearance of justice.

Second, unlike police practices cases or confrontation clause cases where the effect of ruling for the defense is the exclusion of evidence, the *Batson* rule will ordinarily not result in the escape of the guilty.[95] If the rule deters the prosecutor, then the trial will go forward as usual. If the trial judge rules for the defense on a *Batson* motion, a new venire will be called and the trial will go forward with only a slight delay. If an appellate court reverses the trial court's denial of a *Batson* motion, the case will be retried, with considerable delay and expense but with every prospect of doing justice on remand.

When these factors have not been present, the Court has reverted to *Swain*-type equal protection doctrine. In *United States v. Armstrong*,[96] black defendants challenged the denial of their motion to discover evidence of prosecutorial charging decisions against similarly situated white suspects. The Supreme Court held that discovery on a discriminatory prosecution motion could be allowed only when the defense has first come forward with evidence of discrimination. How the defense is supposed to discover evidence of discrimination without discovery is, of course, a bit of a mystery.[97]

In *Armstrong*, however, there was nothing comparable to the twenty-year record of disparate impact presented in *Batson*. The defendants, moreover, were seeking to quash their indictments because guilty whites had not been similarly charged. Freeing the guilty without powerful evidence of discrimination was not a project for which the justices could summon much enthusiasm.

Batson's basic project—demanding reasons for some peremptory challenges—of course leaves room for prosecutors to get away with some racially motivated strikes. The Court has held that "I didn't like the way he looked" is a race-neutral explanation,[98] so it is hardly a surprise to learn that in four out of five cases in which a *prima facie* case is established the government's explanation is accepted by the courts.[99] What we do not know is how often *Batson* causes prosecutors to refrain from striking black jurors in the first place. Although this number is not known, it is not trivial.[100] Prosecutors, like any other public official, are averse to being accused of illegal discrimination. None of *Batson*'s critics, at any rate, propose a return to the days of *Swain*.

As for equal access to justice for the rich and poor, the Burger Court simply recognized the doctrinal incoherence of such cases as *Griffin* and *Douglas v. California*.[101] In a sequence of decisions dealing with the denial of appointed counsel to indigent defendants seeking discretionary review or collateral relief,[102] the Court made clear that poverty is not a suspect classification except when used as the criterion for denying an effective right to one round of appellate review. The underlying supposition is that, some Supreme Court dicta to the contrary notwithstanding,[103] due process requires one appeal, with counsel, but no more.[104]

HABEAS CORPUS, CAPITAL PUNISHMENT, AND THE CRIMINAL PROCEDURE REVOLUTION IN PERSPECTIVE

Originally, due process meant trial before punishment, and the common-law writ of habeas corpus had compelled the trial, or the release, of persons under arrest. The Reconstruction habeas corpus bill adopted the habeas procedure as a check on the practices of the recently subdued Southern states. As we have seen, the Supreme Court accommodated the common-law history of the writ and its new function under the rubric of jurisdictional error.[105] While habeas was not a writ of error, still if constitutional error ousted the state trial court of jurisdiction, federal courts were within their authority to issue a writ of habeas corpus, because the state conviction was a nullity and so imprisonment violated due process.

Brown v. Allen[106] effectively equated any constitutional error with jurisdictional error. Coupled with the explosive expansion of federal constitutional law governing criminal procedure during the heyday of the Warren Court, this equation greatly expanded the potential scope of federal habeas.[107] Under Warren Court habeas precedents, federal courts reviewed questions of constitutional law *de novo*,[108] had discretion to retry factual issues bearing on constitutional claims,[109] and could hear claims not presented to the state courts in the absence of a "deliberate bypass" of state proceedings.[110]

Federal habeas for state prisoners always has been controversial. While the Warren Court habeas decisions provoked judicial dissent and academic critique, they might have weathered the storm but for the Burger Court's intervention into the substantive law of capital punishment. Collateral review of convictions by persons serving prison sentences may waste judicial time and taxpayer dollars, but it does not defeat the ends of justice, because the petitioner remains incarcerated while the habeas proceeding goes forward. By contrast, the state's object in a capital case is to kill, not to confine, the petitioner. So long as the execution is stayed while the habeas corpus proceeding is heard, the petitioner wins and the state loses even if the petition is ultimately dismissed.

When the Supreme Court held, in 1976, that capital punishment for aggravated murder is constitutional so long as the states abide by some vaguely defined procedural safeguards,[111] the justices set the stage for major revisions in the law of federal habeas corpus. A state prisoner who challenges a state conviction on federal constitutional grounds raises a claim that either was, or was not, presented to the state courts. If the claim was presented to the state courts, the prisoner, by hypothesis, lost the claim on the merits. In this scenario, deference to the state court's ruling can lead to narrow review in federal court. If, by contrast, the claim was *not* presented to the state courts, a waiver analysis can lead the habeas court to refuse to consider the claim on the merits.

As the law stood in the early 1970s, this dilemma did not greatly obstruct state prisoners' access to a federal forum. Under *Brown v. Allen*, state court conclusions of law were entitled only to the deference that "federal practice gives to the conclusion of a court of last resort of another jurisdiction on federal constitutional issues."[112] Under *Fay v. Noia*,[113] failure to raise a federal constitutional claim in state court did not bar federal review on the merits unless the failure to raise the claim in state court was a tactical gambit—a "deliberate bypass."

The Warren Court's approach to federal habeas has been called nationalist, because that approach insisted that federal claims must be heard by federal courts. The nationalist approach has had two basic rivals—federalism and instrumentalism. Federalist theory emphasizes the value of finality and the dignity of the state courts. Instrumentalism holds that habeas review be structured so as to protect the falsely convicted but not to benefit the guilty. Each of these approaches has distinguished defenders.[114]

How the habeas structure changed under the pressure of the death penalty could be a book unto itself. Only a summary treatment is necessary here. While the Burger and Rehnquist Courts decided a welter of habeas corpus cases, the two that stand out as especially important are *Wainwright v. Sykes*[115] and *Teague v. Lane*.[116] *Sykes* rejected the deliberate bypass standard; instead, the habeas petitioner must show a good excuse for not raising the claim, and must also show that the failure to have the claim vindicated might have altered the outcome. The *Sykes* standard is usually referred to as the "cause and prejudice" standard.

Teague, following *Sykes* by almost a dozen years, held that on a habeas petition the state court's interpretation of federal law will not be overturned unless contrary to clearly established federal precedent. "New rules" of constitutional criminal procedure, announced after the state court's decision, do not justify issuing the writ unless the Supreme Court itself holds that the new rule should be given fully retroactive effect.[117]

Sykes and *Teague* together greatly narrowed access to the federal forum. If a state prisoner presents his claim to the state courts and loses, then there will be no review on the merits, only deferential review under *Teague*. It is not enough for the state court to be wrong, it must be manifestly wrong. If, on the other hand, the prisoner's claim was *not* presented to the state courts, it will typically be deemed waived under *Sykes*.

The pressure of the death penalty, however, works in two directions. On the one hand, the court felt the need to prevent habeas litigation from continuing until death row inmates died of old age. On the other hand, the specter of executing an innocent person—a specter that inherently attends a speedy death penalty—was something a majority of the justices could not accept. The Court *in dicta* maintains that a prisoner under sentence of death who can affirmatively prove his innocence of the crime charged would be relieved from the limits of both *Sykes*[118] and *Teague*.[119]

Responding to these conflicting impulses, and in general following the recommendations of a special commission chaired by former Justice Powell,[120] Congress in 1996 adopted major revisions of the Reconstruction-era habeas statute. In legislation marked by great complexity, Congress substantially ratified the Court's approach to procedural defaults and to deference to state court interpretations of federal law.[121] The Supreme Court rejected a facial challenge to the constitutionality of the statute.[122]

From the standpoint of legal history, federal habeas is now completely upside-down. The writ is technically still available for its classic role of challenging detention *outside* the criminal process, but it is rarely used for that purpose. At common law, it was axiomatic that habeas was not to serve the function of a writ of error. Now, federal habeas has become part of the error-correction process in state death-penalty cases. In this role, factual innocence has become more and more important to a successful petition. Federalism and instrumentalism have triumphed over nationalism.

Abolition of federal habeas jurisdiction with respect to persons detained on authority of state convictions makes a certain amount of sense, so long as one trusts the state courts to comply with federal constitutional criminal procedure standards under the remote threat of certiorari rather than the more immediate supervision of the local federal district judge. The great irony is that assigning the federal courts an error-correction mission in state cases implicitly admits that the state process is not reliable enough to trust on its own. If the Supreme Court had successfully moved to minimize false convictions—by, for instance, vigorous enforcement of the right to effective assistance of trial counsel, procedural safeguards against erroneous identification, and affirmative police duties to collect and preserve exculpatory evidence—then the state process might have been made reliable enough to deserve finality. The 1996 Act, by contrast, did nothing to improve the *trial process*, even in death cases.

Instead, the lingering role for federal habeas, coupled with the increasing importance of factual innocence in habeas litigation, admits what should now be obvious. Rhetoric notwithstanding, the Supreme Court's criminal procedure decisions have done precious little to prevent miscarriages of justice, whether on the street or in the courtroom. Instead, one hundred and fifteen years after *Hurtado v. California*, constitutional criminal procedure is dominated by the historically implausible, and practically unwise, incorporation doctrine, modified by a seemingly infinite set of qualifications, distinctions, and exceptions.

CONCLUSION

As we approach the fortieth anniversary of *Mapp v. Ohio*, the Bill of Rights dominates constitutional criminal procedure. Substantive due process review is a virtual dead letter under the "shock the conscience" test; procedural due process review is more concerned with history than with reliability; and, although in jury selection cases a more probing inquiry into official motive is allowed, the equal protection clause imposes practically no restraint on police and prosecutors.

Meanwhile, the Bill of Rights itself has undergone a metamorphosis. The libertarian model of criminal procedure from the old federal cases is long gone. The incorporation decisions have stood unquestioned, while interest-balancing has reduced the Bill of Rights provisions to flexible notions of reasonable police practices or fair adjudicatory procedures. The criminal-procedure revolution fell far short of securing measured police practices, reliable investigations, and fair trials. The reaction against it has given us an inconsistent body of law that still does too much to protect the guilty.

This chapter has developed this theme in summary fashion, ranging widely but necessarily not comprehensively over the entire field. The next chapter takes a more detailed look at how the pattern of doctrinal development played out in the representative instance of police interrogation.

The Historical Process Considered in Detail: Interrogation and Confessions

Chapter 3 outlined in summary fashion the transition from fundamental fairness to selective incorporation to conservative balancing. This chapter examines that process in more detail, focusing on the example of police interrogation. Here as in other areas dissatisfaction with fundamental fairness moved the justices to incorporate the Bill of Rights criminal-procedure provisions into the Fourteenth Amendment's due process clause. Here as elsewhere the Warren Court began the process of curtailing the scope of the incorporated provisions. Here as elsewhere the Burger and Rehnquist Courts have taken the process of reaction much further, without overturning any of the major Warren Court landmarks. Here as elsewhere the result is an inconsistent body of law that tolerates unnecessary risks of police excesses and miscarriages of justice, yet also raises needless barriers to convicting the guilty.

STAGE 1: FROM FUNDAMENTAL FAIRNESS TO SELECTIVE INCORPORATION

By the early 1960s, the Supreme Court had decided more than thirty cases in which defendants challenged the admission of confessions at state trials.[1] The test applied in these cases demanded exclusion of "confessions which are involuntary, i.e., the product of coercion, either physical or psychological."[2]

Lower courts, police officers, and commentators were never sure which foci of the test was more important—the subjective capacity of the suspect to resist police pressure, or the objective tendency of the police methods to cause a typical suspect to confess. Nor did the Court ever succeed in clarifying how much pressure amounted to "coercion." While the Court did come to focus on certain "hallmarks" of coercion, even physical violence to the suspect was never declared *per se* unconstitutional.[3]

The vagueness of the voluntariness standard had at least two unfortunate consequences. First, because the Supreme Court could review only a very few confessions cases—typically capital cases—enforcement of the voluntariness test was left largely to the state courts. This was not, to put it gently, a very strong guarantee against police coercion. Second, the police themselves had neither the ability nor any incentive to comply with the voluntariness test.[4]

The voluntariness standard's defects are well illustrated by the 1961 decision in *Culombe v. Connecticut.*[5] Culombe was "a thirty-three-year-old mental defective of the moron class with an intelligence quotient of sixty-four and a mental age of nine to nine and a half years. He was wholly illiterate."[6] On a Saturday afternoon, Connecticut police asked Culombe if he would come to the station for questioning about a double murder; Culombe agreed. He soon asked for a lawyer, and was told that he could have a lawyer if he would name one; but the police knew that Culombe was illiterate and thus unable to use the telephone directory.[7]

On Saturday night the police formally arrested Culombe on suspicion of committing a felony. On Sunday the police added a breach of the peace charge. On both days police questioned the suspect, but the interrogation was not continuous, involved no physical violence or deprivation, and was confined to reasonable times of the day. Culombe confessed to stealing some canned goods, but not to murder.

Not until Tuesday did the police present Culombe to a court. He was charged only with breach of the peace; at the behest of the prosecution, the judge continued the case for a week and committed the suspect to custody until that time. Culombe was not heard by the court and counsel was not appointed. Not until Wednesday did Culombe confess.

Justice Frankfurter wrote a sixty-seven-page opinion, loaded with the ballast of ninety-seven footnotes. He surveyed the policy considerations that make confessions a difficult subject; he reviewed the history of confessions in Anglo-American jurisprudence; he canvassed the decided cases of the Court; and then restated the process of applying the voluntariness standard. After a minute examination of the record, he found it "clear" that Culombe's "will was broken Wednesday afternoon."[8]

Only Justice Stewart joined Frankfurter's opinion. The other votes for reversal came from Warren, Douglas, Black, and Brennan, all of whom disagreed with much of what Frankfurter had said. Chief Justice Warren, in an opinion made rather droll by his later performance in *Miranda*, denounced Frankfurter's "treatise" as an "advisory opinion"; in Warren's view, "the reasons which have compelled the Court to develop the law on a case-by-case approach, to declare legal principles only in the context of specific factual situations, and to avoid expounding more than is necessary for the decision of a given case are persuasive."[9]

In stark contrast, Justice Douglas, joined by Black, thought the case "a simple one" not because of the voluntariness rule, but because the Sixth Amendment right to counsel protected Culombe against questioning after he requested a lawyer. Far from a fact-specific, case-by-case approach, the Douglas suggestion was that the

Court should replace the due process analysis with a selective incorporation analysis that would require in every case the availability of counsel during questioning. The Douglas position had been rejected by the Court in *Crooker v. California*,[10] and for a compelling reason. The "doctrine suggested by petitioner . . . would effectively preclude police questioning—*fair as well as unfair*—until the accused was afforded opportunity to call his attorney."[11]

Justice Brennan agreed only with that portion of the Frankfurter opinion dealing with the specific facts of Culombe's case, implicitly agreeing with Warren. Justice Harlan, joined by Clark and Whittaker, dissented; although he agreed with the generalizations in the Frankfurter opinion, Harlan thought those considerations led to the conclusion that Culombe's confession was voluntary.[12] As Warren tartly observed, this augured poorly for the project of clarifying the law of confessions.[13]

Given the dismal failure of this determined effort to clarify the voluntariness standard, the justices began to look for some alternative to the due process analysis. Selective incorporation suggested three; a Fourth Amendment limit on detention for purposes of investigation, a Fifth Amendment right to refuse to cooperate with the police, or a Sixth Amendment right to counsel that would attach at the moment of arrest.

At the time the Court decided *Culombe*, each of these avenues was blocked by precedent. Respecting the Sixth Amendment, *Gideon* had not yet announced an unqualified right to appointed counsel at trial, let alone before trial; and *Crooker* unequivocally rejected any right to counsel during police questioning. The Court's unwillingness to apply the federal rule excluding confessions obtained after unnecessary delay in presenting the arrested individual to a court obstructed any Fourth Amendment approach to the confessions problem.[14] And two Supreme Court decisions, *Twining v. New Jersey*[15] and *Adamson v. California*,[16] held that the Fifth Amendment privilege against self-incrimination was not incorporated by the Fourteenth Amendment.

In 1962, Byron White and Arthur Goldberg succeeded Charles Whittaker and Felix Frankfurter as justices of the Supreme Court. Although White would prove to be sympathetic to the concerns of police and prosecutors, the addition of Goldberg made for a decisive change in judicial arithmetic. Now there were five justices—Warren, Black, Brennan, Douglas, and Goldberg—who were disturbed by prevailing police methods and willing to pursue selective incorporation as their remedy.

Much of the Warren Court's criminal procedure revolution might have gone forward even if some centrist jurist had replaced Frankfurter. *Mapp* had come notwithstanding Frankfurter's dissent, and the next major step—*Gideon*—was taken unanimously.[17] In the confessions context, however, the division of opinions reflected in the *Culombe* case magnified the importance of a change in votes. As of 1963, a majority of the Court perceived the voluntariness test as wholly inadequate to the confessions problem.

The Fourth, Fifth, and Sixth Amendment approaches suddenly opened up. *Mapp* made the Fourth Amendment route plausible. Under *Wolf*, the physical fruits of an illegal arrest were admitted at trial; excluding statements that resulted from unlawful detention would, as a Fourth Amendment matter, have been arbitrary. But once physical evidence seized incident to an illegal arrest was subject to suppression, constitutionalizing the *McNabb-Mallory* rule became a plausible development under the Fourth Amendment.[18]

On the right-to-counsel front, *Massiah v. United States*[19] came down in March of 1964; June brought *Escobedo*. *Massiah* held that statements obtained by an undercover agent from a defendant who had been indicted and who had not waived counsel must be suppressed on Sixth Amendment right-to-counsel grounds.[20] Out-of-court dealings with the accused were seen as an end-run around the trial process.[21] The *Massiah* majority saw no distinction between police interrogation and the deliberate elicitation of incriminating statements by an undercover agent.[22]

Massiah posed a serious threat to the practice of police interrogation. Defense counsel inevitably would advise a client to stand on the Fifth Amendment privilege; and counsel's presence would inevitably vitiate the psychological pressure on the suspect that interrogation is designed to create.

True, at the time he made his admissions, *Massiah* had been formally charged with the offense for which each was tried. Whether the right to counsel protected a suspect during police questioning prior to indictment was an open question. All the *Massiah* opinion says on this score is that the questioning of an indicted defendant occurs "at a time when he was clearly entitled to a lawyer's help."[23] The Court did not say that an unindicted suspect is not "entitled to a lawyer's help."

Only five weeks later, in *Escobedo v. Illinois*,[24] the Court seemed to extend the right to counsel to the moment of arrest, rather than the moment a formal accusation is filed in court. On January 19, 1960, police arrested Danny Escobedo and Bobby Chan for the murder of Escobedo's brother-in-law, Manuel Valtierra. The arrest took place at 2:30 in the morning, and was not authorized by a warrant. Escobedo refused to make a statement to the police; his retained lawyer, Warren Wolfson, obtained his release at 5:00 in the afternoon by suing out a writ of habeas corpus.[25]

The police also suspected Benedict DiGerlando of involvement in the murder of Valtierra. DiGerlando told the police that Escobedo had done the shooting. Police again arrested Escobedo between 8:00 and 9:00 on the evening of January 30, 1960. Escobedo was interrogated and handcuffed for several hours; during this period he repeatedly asked to see his lawyer. Meanwhile, Wolfson was in the same building, attempting to talk to his client. Various police officers refused to permit consultation until the conclusion of questioning.

At one point the two actually saw each other at the Homicide Bureau, but police closed the door to the office in which Escobedo was being held. Eventually, the police brought Escobedo face-to-face, not with his lawyer, but with DiGerlando. Escobedo accused DiGerlando of doing the shooting, thus admitting his own involvement in the crime. Thereafter, Escobedo made additional incriminating remarks, including a formal statement taken by a prosecutor.

The Illinois Supreme Court eventually affirmed the conviction.[26] On the right-to-counsel question, the Illinois court cited *Crooker* and *Cicenia*, and stressed the fear that "the presence of an accused's attorney would preclude effective police interrogation even though the questioning be fair."[27] The state court's holding captured the gist of its reasoning: "Having given due weight to the various considerations involved, we are of the opinion that the right of a person in custody to see and consult with [his] attorney does not deprive the police of their right to a reasonable opportunity to interrogate outside the presence of counsel."[28] The court was unanimous, a notable point because one of its members, Walter Schaefer, was a keen student of constitutional criminal procedure as well as one of the most respected state court judges in the country.

The Supreme Court, over four dissenting votes, reversed. Justice Goldberg wrote for the majority, and relied on the right to counsel rather than the voluntariness doctrine to hold Escobedo's statements inadmissible. If Escobedo had been indicted at the time he confessed, then *Massiah* would control his case. But he had not been formally charged; and so the issue in *Escobedo* was whether a suspect, in custody but not yet charged, has the right to the presence of counsel during interrogation by the police.

The *Escobedo* majority answered this question squarely: "The interrogation here was conducted before petitioner was formally indicted. But in the context of this case, that fact should make no difference."[29] The majority summarized its holding by saying that "when the process shifts from investigatory to accusatory—when its focus is on the accused and its purpose is to elicit a confession—our adversary system begins to operate, and, under the circumstances here, the accused must be permitted to consult with his lawyer."[30]

"The circumstances here" were quite unusual. The suspect had retained private counsel, and asked to consult with counsel during the interrogation. At the same time, the lawyer was at the police station seeking access to his client. Nonetheless, combined with *Gideon*, *Escobedo* implied the end of police interrogation.

Gideon had held that even the accused who could not afford a lawyer had a Sixth Amendment right to appointed counsel. Nor, the Court had held in *Carnley v. Cochran*,[31] where it applies, may the right to counsel be waived by the failure to request a lawyer. Thus, the state reasoned in its brief for the Supreme Court, accepting Escobedo's right-to-counsel claim would mean "the end of confessions as a tool of law enforcement."[32]

The *Escobedo* opinion is quite vague as to what counsel is supposed to *do* during interrogation; after all, Escobedo's lawyer previously had advised him to claim his Fifth Amendment privilege during questioning. But nobody, on the bench or off, was under any illusions about the practical effect of permitting counsel for the accused inside the interrogation room.

The incompatibility of defense counsel and police interrogation does not derive from Justice Jackson's observation that "[u]nder [our] conception of criminal procedure, any lawyer worth his salt will tell the suspect in no uncertain terms to make no statement to police under any circumstances."[33] Escobedo's lawyer had given that very advice. What would be lost by permitting consultation at will with defense counsel during questioning is the psychological pressure, and the secrecy, without which interrogation cannot succeed.

Justice White, dissenting, echoed the argument of Illinois, and charged the majority with taking "another major step in the direction of the goal which the Court seemingly has in mind—to bar from evidence all admissions obtained from an individual suspected of crime, whether involuntarily made or not."[34] The majority did not deny the charge, but rather argued that interrogation was a practice that should be put behind us.

Interrogation, on this view, is an end-run around the requirement of an adversary trial: "The rule sought by the state here . . . would make the trial no more than an appeal from the interrogation. . . ."[35] "The fact that many confessions are obtained during this period," Justice Goldberg wrote, "points up its critical nature as a 'stage when legal aid and advice' are surely needed. The right to counsel would indeed be hollow if it began at a period when few confessions were obtained."[36]

The death of interrogation was not to be lamented, for "[w]e have learned the lesson of history, ancient and modern, that a system of criminal law enforcement which comes to depend on the 'confession' will, in the long run, be less reliable and more subject to abuses than a system which depends on extrinsic evidence independently secured through skillful investigation."[37] Commentators who took opposing views of the desirability of confessions agreed that *Escobedo* seriously endangered the practice of custodial interrogation.[38] Only the extraordinary decision in *Miranda*, accepting an uncounseled waiver of counsel in a situation where the suspect needs counsel, saved police interrogation from the jaws of *Escobedo*.[39]

June of 1964 also brought *Malloy v. Hogan*, in which the Court incorporated the Fifth Amendment privilege against self-incrimination. *Twining* and *Adamson* stood in the way, but Malloy argued that recent selective incorporation decisions, *Mapp* in particular, indicated that the old precedents rejecting the incorporation theory had lost their vitality.[40] The tenor of those constitutional times is echoed in the state's argument. Armed not with one, but with two Supreme Court precedents squarely holding that Malloy had no claim, Connecticut agreed that the privilege applies to the states through the Fourteenth Amendment.

In the state's view, the coerced confession cases in effect had applied the privilege to the states for years.[41] Connecticut claimed only that the federal privilege did not bind the states "in all its particularities and peripheral characteristics."[42] The National District Attorney's Association filed an amicus brief limited to a plea that the Court's resolution of Malloy's case avoid impairing the operation of state immunity statutes.[43]

Given this rollover by the law enforcement interests on the incorporation issue, the result in *Malloy* was foreordained. To support incorporation of the Fifth Amendment privilege, Justice Brennan's opinion for the Court relied on the coerced confession cases, which explicitly excluded the privilege from their rationale;[44] the exclusionary rule cases, which are now regarded as having no connection with the Fifth Amendment privilege;[45] and Dean Griswold's rather idiosyncratic statement that the privilege is "a symbol of the America which stirs our hearts."[46]

Only Justice Clark joined Justice Harlan's dissenting opinion, defending *Twining* and *Adamson*. Justices White and Stewart dissented on the ground that even applying the federal standard, Malloy had not suggested a sufficient risk of incrimination to support his claim of privilege.

Mapp, *Escobedo*, and *Malloy* exposed the practice of police interrogation to attack on three different fronts. Judges and scholars sympathetic to law enforcement feared that the Supreme Court might be prepared to accept *Escobedo*'s denunciation of confessions as a perverse influence on the administration of criminal justice. *Escobedo* became the object of a powerful legal counteroffensive.

On the judicial front, many lower courts fought a dogged rear-guard action to confine *Escobedo* to its facts. Emphasizing some of the limiting language in Justice Goldberg's opinion, these courts ruled that a statement by the suspect was not to be excluded on Sixth Amendment grounds unless the suspect, as Escobedo had done, requested counsel.[47] Some courts, state[48] and federal,[49] held that no request was required.

Meanwhile, law enforcement officials and academics sympathetic to their position mounted an effort to persuade the Supreme Court to go no further.[50] The most prominent element in this effort was the American Law Institute's proposed *Model Code of Pre-Arraignment Procedure*.[51] The reporters for the model code, James Vorenberg and Paul Bator, have been described as figures in "an interlocking directorate of criminal law institutions with a decided Harvard flavor and a plan to preserve the police's authority to interrogate."[52] Even the ALI draft code, however, included serious restrictions on police questioning.

The code required warning the suspect of the right to remain silent,[53] and limited to four hours the window between arrest and presentment in court.[54] It also accommodated *Escobedo* by forbidding questioning after a suspect "made it clear that he is unwilling to make a statement or wishes to consult counsel before making a statement."[55] Where the Model Code parted company with the evident drift of the Court was in denying the applicability of *Gideon* to the *Escobedo* situation.

The ALI draft provided that counsel for an arrested person would have access to the suspect, and that if the arrested person was not represented by counsel, similar access should be accorded a friend or relative.[56] At an initial level the drafters defended this provision on the ground of necessity: "Private and public resources for legal aid presently face serious problems in assuring competent representation in the courtroom; providing counsel at the stationhouse is not an end that can be readily attained."[57] But the drafters frankly admitted that even if the resources were available, the combination of the privilege against self-incrimination with counsel for suspects in custody was a dangerous idea.[58]

Escobedo marked the end of the first stage of the historical dynamic played out during the criminal procedure revolution. In *Escobedo* the justices gave the newly incorporated Sixth Amendment right full play. The ALI and the lower courts apprehended the end of interrogation. That prospect, however, was hardly congenial to the Warren Court. The second stage was about to set in.

STAGE 2: *MIRANDA* IN CONTEXT

By the time the ALI's Model Code was presented to the full Institute membership for approval, events had been brought to a head by the various interpretations the lower courts had given *Escobedo*. In the autumn of 1965, the justices and their law clerks waded through one hundred and fifty petitions for certiorari raising issues under *Escobedo*.[59] Four of the petitions were granted on November 22; a fifth petition was granted two weeks later.

In two of the cases—*Miranda v. Arizona* and *Vignera v. New York*—the criminal defendant challenged state court rulings that put the burden of requesting counsel on the suspect. The justices also chose to hear a federal case, *Westover v. United States*, in which the defendant challenged confessions given to agents of the FBI. The FBI enjoyed the prestige of the nation's most elite law enforcement agency; the warnings given by its agents were considered state-of-the-art. A fourth case, *Johnson v. New Jersey*, raised the question of whether *Escobedo* applied retroactively. In the final case, *California v. Stewart*, the state asked the Supreme Court to reinstate a conviction overturned by the California Supreme Court. In *Stewart*, neither party had introduced evidence to show that the suspect either had, or had not, been warned of the rights to silence and counsel. The California court reversed the conviction, in effect placing upon the government the burden of proving that a confession was preceded by a warning of rights.

This deliberate selection of representative cases as vehicles for the making of general policy was not quite unprecedented. The Court had done much the same thing in the trilogy of habeas corpus cases decided under the name of *Brown v. Allen*. It would take this approach again in the 1975 death penalty cases. Nonetheless, it was quite clear that in the 1966 confessions cases, the Court was engaged in an extraordinary project; not just to resolve some difficult cases, but to establish general rules to guide police and lower courts in handling confessions. Although adjudicatory in form, and styled as constitutional adjudication at that, the proceedings before the Court were in spirit not unlike those observed in an administrative rule-making proceeding.

Certainly no administrative agency could have generated a more thorough or more thoughtful survey of the confessions problem. The brief for Miranda, whom the police had not warned of a right to counsel, relied on the Sixth Amendment and argued that *Escobedo* applied to suspects who had neither retained, nor requested, counsel.[60] Counsel for Westover, whom the FBI *had* warned, necessarily went further, and argued that the Sixth Amendment could only be satisfied by actual consultation with counsel.[61] Vignera's lawyer advanced not only the Sixth

Amendment argument predicated on *Escobedo*, but also attacked the confession as the fruit of unlawful detention, and urged the Court to enforce the *McNabb-Mallory* rule against the states under the authority of *Mapp*.[62]

The American Civil Liberties Union filed what is now one of the most famous briefs in the history of the Court. In it, Anthony Amsterdam and Paul Mishkin characterized the right to counsel at the interrogation stage as a means of enforcing the *Fifth Amendment* right to silence.[63] They quoted extensively from police interrogation manuals to support their claim that custodial interrogation is "inherently compelling."[64] Only the presence of counsel, they argued, could dispel the compulsion inherent in custodial questioning and so vindicate the Fifth Amendment privilege against self-incrimination.[65]

In the brief for the United States in the *Westover* case, the Department of Justice took the position that the Sixth Amendment did not apply until the commencement of formal proceedings.[66] The government explained *Escobedo* as a case of deliberate delay by the prosecution in filing formal charges—that is, as an attempt to circumvent the ruling in *Massiah*.[67] *Escobedo* accordingly deserved very limited application.

Like the ACLU, the United States argued that the relevant amendment was the Fifth; but in the view of the government, compulsion, just like coercion under the due process test, must be evident from the totality of the circumstances. In some cases, the United States maintained, the suspect need not even be warned of the right to remain silent.[68] As for a warning about the right to counsel, since the government denied any Sixth Amendment right to consult with counsel before the filing of a formal charge, unindicted suspects need not be warned about a right they did not possess.[69]

Both the United States[70] and twenty-seven states that endorsed an amicus brief, authored by Telford Taylor,[71] urged the Court to await possible legislative action, especially in light of the pending ALI project. Along similar lines, the National District Attorneys Association urged the Court to adopt an "advisory rule"—whatever rule the Court deemed wise, so long as it would not be enforced with the exclusionary sanction.[72] Arizona defended Miranda's conviction on the ground accepted by many lower courts—that *Escobedo* only forbade police frustration of the suspect's request for counsel, and did not affirmatively mandate advising the suspect of the right to consult an attorney.[73] All of the government parties stressed the importance of confessions to law enforcement, and the incompatibility of defense counsel's presence with successful interrogation.

Early on in the oral arguments, it became clear that the heart of the controversy was the Fifth Amendment, not the Sixth.[74] Justice Goldberg, the author of *Escobedo*, had resigned to represent the United States at the UN. His replacement, Abe Fortas, was a deep believer in the privilege against self-incrimination. Perhaps the reason for the sea-change was this shift in judicial personalities; perhaps it was the force of the ACLU brief. No doubt these factors played their role, but it is certainly true that the right-to-counsel approach did not offer a satisfactory approach to the confessions problem.

The ultimate defect in the right-to-counsel approach in the confessions context is the same as it is in the lineup context; how is counsel supposed to "assist" the suspect during interrogation? Whatever answer is given presupposes some legal rights that counsel can assert on the suspect's behalf. The right to counsel, whether at trial or before, is derivative of other procedural safeguards. Counsel can never obtain more than the law allows; it follows that counsel is always no more than a means to secure some other legal right.

Thus the suspect's right to silence is logically prior to the right to counsel. Before *Malloy*, the state had the constitutional authority to check the privilege against self-incrimination at the door of the stationhouse. But after *Malloy*, federal constitutional law forbade any state compulsion of incriminating statements. Was police interrogation compulsion? If it was, could statements obtained by the police from suspects in custody ever be admitted into evidence? Remarkably, the Supreme Court answered both questions in the affirmative.

The *Miranda* majority consisted of just five justices—Douglas, Brennan, Black, Fortas, and Warren. Chief Justice Warren assigned the opinion to himself, and delivered a true essay in constitutional policymaking. Police interrogation *in general*, Warren wrote, constitutes compulsion. Therefore, the Fifth Amendment requires that safeguards mitigate the compulsion typical of police questioning; the famous warning is the minimum safeguard consistent with the Fifth Amendment.

To this day the *Miranda* opinion's treatment of the compulsion issue remains, well, compelling. Warren described the typical circumstances of custodial interrogation—the secret surroundings and the atmosphere of domination. He followed this account with a devastatingly effective survey of the interrogation manuals—manuals that are still in use today.

Confession is obviously contrary to the immediate self-interest of the suspect. Why then do so many suspects confess? The manuals advise the police to create and maintain an environment of total "privacy" and to convey the impression that the questioning will continue for as long as it takes for the suspect to confess. The officer should sympathize with the suspect and minimize the seriousness of the crime. "Good cop/bad cop" is played to heighten the suspect's anxiety while offering a sympathetic ear. The suspect can be confronted with made-up "evidence" to convince him that the game is over and confession is his last chance for sympathetic treatment.

Do these tactics amount to "compulsion" within the meaning of the privilege? Warren wrote that

all the principles embodied in the privilege apply to informal compulsion exerted by law-enforcement officers during in-custody questioning. An individual swept from familiar surroundings into police custody, surrounded by antagonistic forces, and subjected to the techniques of persuasion described [in the manuals] cannot be otherwise than under compulsion to speak. As a practical matter, the compulsion to speak in the isolated setting of the police station may well be greater than in courts or other official investigations, where there are often impartial observers to guard against intimidation or trickery.[75]

By way of comparison, a will drafted under circumstances similar to those of custodial questioning would certainly be held void for undue influence.[76]

What did police interrogation *in general* have to do with the cases for decision? Warren admitted that the records in the individual cases did not show "overt physical coercion or patent psychological ploys," but the "fact remains that in none of these cases did the officers undertake to afford appropriate safeguards at the outset of the interrogation to insure that the statements were truly the product of free choice."[77] In effect, compulsion is presumed from the facts of custody and questioning.

The *Miranda* Court described the famous warning as one way of dispelling the compulsion implicit in custodial questioning. "[W]e will not pause to inquire in individual cases whether the defendant was aware of his rights without a warning being given."[78] Warning of the right to silence "at the time of the interrogation is indispensable to overcome its pressures and to insure that the individual knows he is free to exercise the privilege at that point in time."[79]

A police-administered warning of the right to silence, although necessary, was not sufficient. The suspect must have the right to consult with counsel; but even this was thought insufficient protection for the privilege. The suspect under *Miranda* has the right not just to counsel's advice, but to the presence of counsel during questioning.[80] As had been anticipated, given *Gideon*, the right to counsel did not depend on either an affirmative request[81] or the ability to pay.[82]

Thus far the *Miranda* opinion tracks the ACLU brief. But the Court would not take the final step. Amsterdam and Mishkin had argued that "*the presence* of counsel is required to protect the subject's privilege against self-incrimination."[83] In other words, the suspect must see a lawyer before making an admissible statement. But the Court ruled otherwise: "An express statement that the individual is willing to make a statement and does not want an attorney followed closely by a statement could constitute a waiver."[84]

Waiver must be executed "knowingly and intelligently."[85] Waiver was not to be "presumed simply from the silence of the accused after warnings are given or simply from the fact that a confession was in fact eventually obtained."[86] The government must carry the "heavy burden"[87] of proving waiver. But waiver there might be without the intervention of counsel for the suspect; the fangs of *Escobedo* had been pulled.

The *Miranda* Court's waiver doctrine is plainly at odds with the rest of the opinion. As Justice White demanded in dissent, "if the defendant may not answer without a warning a question such as 'Where were you last night?' without having his answer be a compelled one, how can the Court ever accept his negative answer to the question of whether he wants to consult his retained counsel or counsel whom the court will appoint?" The majority made no answer.

The only explanation for the inconsistency in the *Miranda* rules is concern for effective law enforcement. The Court purported to deny that "society's need for interrogation outweighs the privilege."[88] Yet Warren took pains to argue that the new rules "should not constitute an undue interference with a proper system of law enforcement."[89]

The *Miranda* rules closely resemble the contemporary practice of the FBI.[90] The effectiveness of the FBI was unquestioned, enabling Warren to argue that the FBI practice "can readily be emulated by state and local enforcement agencies."[91]

The dissenting opinions made three basic points. First, they objected to the legislative-quality of the majority opinion. There was no proof in the record, Justice Clark protested, that the police manuals cited by the Court were even taught, let alone applied, by the police departments involved in the cases *sub judice*.[92] Justice Harlan scoffed at "the Court's new code,"[93] and was nettlesome enough to cite Warren's now thoroughly embarrassing concurrence in *Culombe*.[94]

The majority had invited the charge of legislating by admitting that "the Constitution does not require any specific code of procedures for protecting the privilege against self-incrimination during custodial interrogation."[95] The *Miranda* rules were only one alternative; Congress or state legislatures could provide for any other system, "so long as they are fully as effective"[96] in protecting the Fifth Amendment privilege.

Second, the dissenters defended the due process, voluntariness test as an adequate safeguard for the rights of the suspect.[97] Finally, the dissenting opinions stressed the importance of confessions to effective law enforcement.[98] In short, the *Miranda* dissenters denounced the new rules as both illegitimate and unwise.

Political opposition to the Court's criminal procedure rulings had grown increasingly intense. Even the *Mallory* decision, although it did no more than abide by the precedent set in *McNabb*, had drawn protests from the law enforcement community. *Escobedo* had been the target of a vigorous reaction; *Miranda* brought to a climax the political opposition to the criminal justice revolution.

Barry Goldwater had made crime an issue in the 1964 election. In 1965, President Johnson appointed a commission to study the crime problem and recommend legislation to combat it. The Commission published its report in February of 1967.[99] The majority saw the causes of crime in social conditions, and the principal need in the law enforcement area to be increasing the resources and improving the training available to police. A minority saw the Supreme Court's recent decisions, *Miranda* foremost among them, as an aid to crime and a major obstacle to law enforcement.[100]

That same month the administration proposed a crime bill, generally incorporating the recommendations of the Commission.[101] Money was to be allocated to improve state and local law enforcement. The administration bill included no provision authorizing wiretapping or other electronic surveillance; nor did it include any provisions designed to modify, let alone overturn, *Miranda*.

Early in 1967, members returning from the winter recess were keenly aware of an anticrime sentiment in the country. Hearings were held before both the House and the Senate Judiciary Committees. Street crime, riots, and antiwar protests were lumped together as a crisis in law and order. In August, the House passed a version of the administration proposal.

In the Senate, however, conservatives led by John McClellan and Sam Ervin (later to be lionized by liberals for his role in exposing the Watergate conspiracy) pushed a modified bill that directly attacked the Supreme Court's criminal procedure revolution. The bill reported out of the Senate Judiciary Committee provided that any confession voluntarily made would be admissible in federal courts; a warning of rights or a demand for counsel were only factors to be considered under the voluntariness standard.[102] This provision flew in the face of *Miranda*. The bill at that point also included a provision eliminating the jurisdiction of the federal courts to reverse state court criminal convictions because of the erroneous admission of a confession, as well as a section gutting federal habeas review of state convictions.[103]

The Senate debated the crime bill in May of 1968, in the wake of Martin Luther King Jr.'s assassination and the riots that followed. Early in that month, Richard Nixon's campaign issued a major policy paper, "Toward Freedom from Fear," exploiting the crime issue and blaming the Court for setting "free patently guilty individuals on the basis of legal technicalities."[104] On the floor, a scant majority composed of fifty-two senators voted to delete the jurisdiction-stripping provision.[105] Only fifty-four voted to delete the habeas provision.[106] The bill was also amended to provide that the *Mallory* rule would not apply until the suspect had been in custody for six hours, and that even then, a confession might be received if the delay in presentment was "reasonable."[107]

The Senate bill went to the House, which had thus far deliberately rejected both wiretapping and direct attacks on the Court. Robert Kennedy was assassinated on June 5. On June 6, the House voted 369–17 to adopt the Senate bill, without a conference.[108] Lyndon Johnson, anxious to see his own crime program written into law and aware of how the opposition party would use a veto in the coming campaign, signed the bill into law on June 19.

Whether its provisions were constitutional seems not to have mattered much to the proponents. Rather, they seemed to hope that the justices themselves would either reverse *Miranda* or retire and be replaced by justices who would.[109] On June 26, President Johnson announced the resignation of Earl Warren as Chief Justice. *Miranda*, at that moment, stood as a four-to-four decision of the Supreme Court, condemned in Congress, and the subject of bitter criticism in a presidential campaign in which Richard Nixon was widely favored.

Twenty-five years later, *Miranda* not only survives, but boasts a promising life expectancy. *Miranda*'s survival is largely attributable to two intellectual developments that took place in the years immediately following the decision, one empirical and one doctrinal.

The doctrinal development was the publication of Yale Kamisar's essay, *A Dissent from the* Miranda *Dissents: Some Comments on the "New" Fifth Amendment and the Old "Voluntariness" Test.*[110] Kamisar attacked the voluntariness standard as hopelessly vague, affording little guidance to the police, and in practice countenancing police abuse. He supported these arguments with pointed quotations from the dissenting opinions themselves, quotations from the authorities relied on by the dissenters, the unsavory facts of many of the cases decided for the government under the voluntariness standard, and statistics showing that the Supreme Court typically found confessions involuntary that the lower courts found voluntary—but that the Supreme Court could take only a handful of confessions cases a year.

The article "effectively demolished the dissenters' arguments,"[111] exposing their "central premise . . . as altogether unconvincing if not mildly ridiculous."[112] Thirteen years would pass before a respected academic published a defense of even a much-modified voluntariness standard.[113] By that time, *Miranda* had become a fixture in American police procedure, and Byron White had become a convert to the "bright-line rules" his *Miranda* dissent had disparaged.

The empirical development was the consistent finding that the *Miranda* rules did little or nothing to discourage confessions, at least in cases when a confession was needed to convict. In the immediate aftermath of *Miranda*, studies in New Haven[114] and Washington[115] reported that the warnings did little to discourage suspects from making statements. Another study in Pittsburgh[116] found a significant drop in the frequency of statements, but not in the conviction rate. Subsequent research has confirmed that *Miranda* has not seriously reduced the utility of confessions to the police.[117]

How can this be so? As it turns out, both the Amsterdam/Mishkin brief and Justice White's dissent were prophetic about the effect of the *Miranda* rules. The coercive environment, the stress and ignorance operating on most suspects, and clever police tactics can induce a *Miranda* waiver in most of the cases in which they previously secured a "voluntary" confession. Just as Justice Goldberg foresaw in *Escobedo*, what is critical for the police is also critical for the suspect. *Miranda* does little to hamper law enforcement because it does little to protect the privilege against self-incrimination.[118]

Miranda to be sure would pass through troubled times. But as time passed, *Miranda* became more and more a revered landmark, and did less and less to hamper the police. The absence of any credible alternative legal regime for confessions, and the demonstrated ability of the police to cope with the *Miranda* rules, sustained that decision despite the political currents running so strongly against it in the summer of 1968.

Nonetheless, the compromise struck in *Miranda* would soon be interpreted far more favorably to the government. The new conservative majority—which *Miranda*'s unpopularity helped to bring about—proved unwilling either to overrule a famous landmark, or to interpret and apply it in any principled fashion. The third stage of the historical dynamic had arrived.

STAGE 3: *HARRIS V. NEW YORK* AND THE PROBLEM OF THE ILLEGITIMATE PRECEDENT

Viven Harris was charged with selling heroin to a New Rochelle police officer on two occasions, once on January 4 and once on January 7, 1966.[119] On January 7, he was arrested and interrogated, without being first apprised of any right to consult with appointed counsel. From the police standpoint, there was no reason for such a warning, because *Miranda* had not yet been decided. In response to police questions, Harris said he had purchased heroin from a third party at the officer's direction and with money supplied by the officer.

At trial, the government did not offer the statement into evidence, so no hearing was held on its admissibility. Instead, the officer testified that Harris had sold him heroin on January 4 and 6. The petitioner took the stand and testified that he had sold nothing to the officer on January 4, and only baking powder on January 6. On cross-examination, the prosecutor, over defense objections, read the transcript of what Harris had said during the police questioning, and asked Harris if he remembered making the statements.

The trial judge overruled the defense objection on the authority of *People v. Kulis*,[120] a New York Court of Appeals decision permitting impeachment of the defendant's testimony with a statement barred from the government's case-in-chief by *Escobedo*. *Kulis* in turn relied on *Walder v. United States*,[121] in which the Supreme Court had permitted impeachment of the defendant's testimony with evidence seized in violation of the Fourth Amendment.

Walder deserves a brief digression. In 1950, the defendant was indicted for possessing heroin, but the indictment was dismissed after Walder succeeded in moving to suppress the heroin as the fruit of an illegal search. Two years later, Walder was indicted on new drug charges. He took the stand, and testified that "I have never sold any narcotics to anyone in my life."[122] Walder repeated this lie on cross-examination. The government then offered the testimony of the officer who had seized the heroin in 1950 and of the chemist who had tested it. Over defense objection, the trial court permitted this proof.

The Supreme Court affirmed. Two facts were crucial to the result. One is that the defense, and not the prosecution, had put Walder's history of narcotics dealing in issue.[123] The second is that the impeachment went to a collateral matter rather than directly to the charged offense. The jury could not convict on the basis of the illegally seized evidence, because proof that Walder had dealt drugs in 1950 could not establish that he had dealt drugs in 1952 as charged in the indictment.[124]

Given these peculiar facts, Justice Frankfurter wrote for the Court that

It is one thing to say that the Government cannot make an affirmative use of evidence unlawfully obtained. It is quite another to say that the defendant can turn the illegal method by which evidence in the Government's possession was obtained to his own advantage, and provide himself with a shield against contradiction of his untruths. Such an extension of the *Weeks* doctrine would be a perversion of the Fourth Amendment.[125]

Walder, then, was apparently intended as a narrow ruling allowing the government to expose perjury, but not to prove guilt, with illegally obtained evidence.

Harris was a different case. The government had not, as it had in *Walder*, already lost one case as a result of the unlawful police tactics. Nor could Harris, as Walder could, have denied the charge against him without contradicting the government's illegally obtained evidence.

Moreover, unlike a Fourth Amendment violation, a Fifth Amendment violation occurs not when evidence is illegally "seized" but when the accused is compelled to be a witness against himself. Thus, each use at trial of a compelled statement, unlike the use of illegally seized physical evidence, is itself a violation of the constitutional provision.

The Court's opinion in *Miranda* speaks directly to this consideration; there was to be no impeachment exception.[126]

Although Harris had lost in the New York courts, his case before the Supreme Court appeared to be a strong one. *Walder* was distinguishable, and *Miranda* had spoken against permitting impeachment with statements obtained without the required warnings.

A majority of the Court, however, now believed that *Miranda* was wrongly decided. Stewart, White, and Harlan had dissented in *Miranda*. Burger and Blackmun had replaced Warren and Fortas. These five justices composed the majority in *Harris*. They faced, for the first time, the problem confronted by conservative justices constrained by a Warren Court precedent of which they disapproved. Their resolution of that challenge set the pattern for decades to follow.

None of the five suggested overruling *Miranda*. Indeed, one index of the conflict between conservative criminal procedure and conservative judicial method is that until the year 2000 *no justice* had *ever* issued an opinion that urges overturning that decision. But the new majority did not exactly follow *Miranda*, either.

Instead, Chief Justice Burger reasoned that the passage from *Miranda* condemning use of unwarned statements for impeachment constituted mere dictum. In none of the cases decided by the *Miranda* Court had the suspect's statement been admitted solely to impeach. Thus discussion of the impeachment issue "was not at all necessary to the Court's holding and cannot be regarded as controlling."[127]

Miranda, however, is nothing if not dicta.[128] The bare decision to exclude the confessions in the cases then adjudicated would have occasioned no interest whatsoever. What made *Miranda* a landmark was the prospective announcement that confessions thenceforth would be excluded unless the *Miranda* rules were followed. Those rules included an exclusionary rule that the *Miranda* opinion applied to impeachment just as clearly as the opinion required the famous warnings.

Having distinguished *Miranda*, so that the use of the statements to impeach Harris was an open question, the majority then deployed two arguments that would become stock features of criminal procedure opinions. First, the Court discounted the benefit of excluding the challenged evidence. After citing *Walder*, the majority spoke to the key issue in the case—whether the *Walder* exception applied when the illegal evidence went to the merits of the case being tried:

The impeachment process here undoubtedly provided valuable aid to the jury in assessing petitioner's credibility, and the benefits of this process should not be lost, in our view, because of the speculative possibility that impermissible police conduct will be encouraged thereby. Assuming that the exclusionary rule has a deterrent effect on proscribed police conduct, sufficient deterrence flows when the evidence in question is made unavailable to the prosecution in its case in chief.[129]

The opinion does not elaborate on how much "deterrence" is "sufficient," or on how the justices know that permitting impeachment with illegal evidence would not diminish deterrence to an insufficient level.

Second, the *Harris* opinion exalts, as opposed to the "speculative" benefits of exclusion, the value of truth in adjudication. "The shield provided by *Miranda* cannot be perverted into a license to use perjury by way of a defense, free from the risk of confrontation with prior inconsistent utterances."[130]

Thus the *Harris* majority exploited a factual distinction with *Miranda*, and then balanced the "speculative" benefits of exclusion against the need to find the facts in the case at hand. The majority did not rescind the right to freedom from questioning without counsel, but severed that right from the remedy of suppression. This approach to the problem of the illegitimate precedent accommodated the competing conservative values of fidelity to precedent and truth-in-adjudication, but only by papering over the real, even profound, differences that divided the conservative justices from the Warren Court majority.

The essence of *Miranda* is the proposition that statements obtained by custodial interrogation are presumed to be compelled in violation of the Fifth Amendment. The *Harris* majority did not overtly question this proposition. But as subsequent cases would confirm, these same justices would not permit *any* use, for impeachment or otherwise, of a statement they regarded as genuinely compelled, whether by overbearing interrogation methods or by the threat of a contempt sanction.

In *Mincey v. Arizona*[131] the Court held that statements obtained in violation of *Miranda* could not be used to impeach the defendant's testimony when those statements also ran afoul of the due process voluntariness test. All four justices in the *Harris* majority still serving joined the majority opinion. And in *New Jersey v. Portash*[132] Justice Stewart wrote a majority opinion, joined by Justice White, holding that testimony compelled under a grant of immunity might not be used even to impeach the testimony of the immunized witness at his subsequent criminal trial.[133]

How is impeachment with a statement tainted under *Miranda* different from impeachment with an involuntary statement or a statement compelled by formal process under a grant of immunity? The upshot of *Harris* is that statements obtained in violation of *Miranda* are only *sort of* unconstitutional. For the new majority, "sufficient" deterrence of *Miranda* violations was not "sufficient" deterrence of hard-core constitutional violations.

The obvious hole in the majority's deterrence analysis is that the police will often have enough evidence to get to a jury, but not enough to be fully confident of a conviction. Frequently they will face this situation while the suspect is in custody, perhaps after invoking his rights under *Miranda*. What do the police have to lose by questioning the suspect? If they obtain useful statements that are inadmissible in the case in chief, at least the defendant will be kept off the stand if a trial takes place. The prosecutor's hand in plea bargaining will be strengthened by this prospect.[134]

In a bitter denunciation of the *Harris* opinion, John Hart Ely and Alan Dershowitz accused the majority of "at best, gross negligence concerning the state of the record and the controlling precedents."[135] The charge is harsh, but substantially justified. Harris did indeed claim, both at trial and before the Supreme Court, that his statements were not merely unwarned but coerced.[136] Both under New York statutory law, and under *Jackson v. Denno*,[137] the trial court must determine the voluntariness issue outside the presence of the jury. When the state decided not to offer the statement in its case in chief, no hearing was held before trial. After Harris testified, the trial judge permitted the impeachment without conducting a voluntariness hearing. Thus, the case could have been remanded for a voluntariness hearing, without reaching the *Miranda* issue. The majority pretty obviously wanted to get to *Miranda*.

Likewise, whether or not the *Harris* opinion "distorted"[138] *Miranda* and *Walder*, it surely curtailed the former and inflated the latter. The bland, conclusory style of Chief Justice Burger's opinion suggests that no great change was being worked. But blandness of style belied a deep shift in the orientation of the Court.

The Warren Court had recognized, in *Mapp* and *Miranda*, that what happens in one criminal case affects what happens in others. Total devotion to finding the truth in a given case may damage important values—perhaps even the value of finding the truth—in other cases. The Burger Court trivialized these connections as "speculative," and thereby invited the subversion of the suspect's autonomy and equality that the Warren Court had valued. Thus did judicial hypocrisy supply the lubricant that would keep the friction between precedent and policy at manageable levels.

THE PARADOX OF THE UNJUSTIFIED PRECEDENT: *MIRANDA*'S LIFE AFTER DEATH

Once the *Harris* Court took the view that *Miranda* could be violated without violating the Constitution, there would seem to be no way to justify *Miranda*. In federal cases the 1968 Crime Control Bill had repudiated *Miranda* in favor of the voluntariness test. In state cases the court can reverse convictions only on constitutional or federal statutory grounds. Deeply as *Miranda* had entered into public consciousness, good lawyers could well wonder whether *Miranda* was any longer sound law.

For several years after *Harris* the Burger Court relentlessly pursued the strategy of separating the *Miranda* rules from the real Constitution. In *Michigan v. Tucker*[139]—Justice Rehnquist's first major criminal procedure opinion—the Court held that the *Miranda* exclusionary rule did not require excluding the testimony of a witness brought to light by an admission obtained in violation of *Miranda*. Rather than simply balance the deterrent benefits of excluding the fruits of *Miranda* violations against the evidentiary cost, the majority opinion took pains to characterize the *Miranda* rules as "procedural safeguards [that] were not themselves rights protected by the Constitution but were instead measures to insure that the right against compulsory self-incrimination was protected."[140] Justice White took the trouble to file an opinion recording his continued belief that *Miranda* "was ill-conceived and without warrant in the Constitution."[141] Only Justice Douglas dissented, in an opinion that apprehended the logical conclusion of Rehnquist's characterization of *Miranda*. Douglas took the quite conventional view that state action cannot be quasi-unconstitutional or a little unconstitutional.[142] "The Court," wrote Geoffrey Stone, "deprived *Miranda* of a constitutional basis but did not explain what other basis for it there might be. Thus, *Tucker* seems certainly to have laid the groundwork to overrule *Miranda*."[143]

Hard on the heels of *Tucker*, the Court handed down the decision in *Michigan v. Mosley*,[144] which relied on the *Tucker* conception of *Miranda* to justify the renewed questioning of a suspect who invokes the right to silence in response to the required warning. In *Oregon v. Mathiason*[145] the Court held that even stationhouse interrogation is not custodial within the meaning of *Miranda* when the suspect "voluntarily" comes to the station at the "request" of police. *Miranda* was fast becoming more honored in the breach than in the observance.

The turning point for *Miranda* came in 1977, in the strange and terrible case of *Brewer v. Williams*.[146] Williams abducted, raped, and murdered a ten-year-old girl in Des Moines on Christmas Eve of 1968. On the morning of the 26th, Henry McKnight, a local defense lawyer, came to the Des Moines police station and told the officers that Williams would surrender to the Davenport police. Williams did so, and was arrested and given *Miranda* warnings in Davenport.

When Davenport officers telephoned their colleagues in Des Moines, McKnight was still at the station. McKnight spoke with Williams by telephone, and advised him that Des Moines police would drive to Davenport to take custody, and that Williams should say nothing to the officers about the case. McKnight and the police agreed that Detectives Leaming and Nelson would collect Williams, and that they would not question him until after Williams had personally consulted McKnight.

Williams was arraigned in Davenport, and was again advised of his rights. A Davenport lawyer named Kelly was appointed to represent him. Kelly was refused permission to accompany Williams back to Des Moines; like McKnight, he advised Williams to say nothing to the police on the drive. In discussions with the police officers, Kelly insisted that the police honor what Kelly understood to be their agreement with McKnight—that Williams not be questioned during the trip to Des Moines.

In Davenport, Detective Leaming again delivered *Miranda* warnings to Williams. Shortly after setting out, Leaming, who knew that Williams was an escaped mental patient with strong religious convictions, delivered the so-called "Christian Burial Speech":

I want to give you something to think about while we're traveling down the road. . . . Number one, I want you to observe the weather conditions, it's raining, it's sleeting, it's freezing, driving is very treacherous, visibility is poor, it's going to be dark early this evening. They are predicting several inches of snow for tonight, and I feel that you your-self are the only person that knows where this little girl's body is, that you yourself have only been there once, and if you get a snow on top of it you yourself may be unable to find it. And, since we will be going right past the area on the way into Des Moines, I feel that we could stop and locate the body, that the parents of this little girl should be entitled to a Christian burial for the little girl who was snatched away from them on Christmas [E]ve and murdered. And I feel we should stop and locate it on the way in rather than waiting until morning and trying to come back out after a snow storm and possibly not being able to find it at all.[147]

Williams asked Leaming why the detective believed they would drive by the body, and Leaming replied that he knew the body was in the vicinity of Mitchellville. Then Leaming told Williams not to answer, but only to think about it.

A hundred miles out of Davenport, Williams asked the police if they had found the victim's shoes. When they answered in the negative, he directed them to a service station where he had left the shoes, but none were found. Then he asked the police if the blanket had been found; again the answer was negative, and Williams directed the police to a rest area where he had left the blanket. Again, nothing was found. Finally (outside Mitchellville, which shows that Leaming was a shrewd guesser or very lucky) Williams told police the location of the body, which they found.

Williams moved to suppress his statements to the police, and the body, on both *Miranda* and *Massiah* grounds. The trial court overruled the motion, and Williams was convicted and sentenced to life in prison. On review, the case closely divided the judges. The Iowa Supreme Court affirmed, five to four;[148] the Eight Circuit panel that upheld the federal district judge's decision to issue a writ of habeas corpus provoked a sharp dissent from Judge Webster (who would later head the FBI and the CIA);[149] and the Supreme Court likewise decided the case by the margin of one vote.

Justice Stewart, the author of *Massiah*, wrote the majority opinion, which Brennan, Marshall, Powell, and Stevens joined. In Stewart's view, the Sixth Amendment right to counsel had attached when Williams was arraigned in Davenport. Leaming's "Christian Burial Speech" was a successful attempt to "elicit incriminating statements" that was not preceded by any waiver of the right to counsel. *Massiah* therefore required suppression of Williams's statements and the victim's body.

What does this resolution of the case have to do with *Miranda*? The case needs to be understood in both its legal and factual contexts. Legally, *Brewer v. Williams* came to the Court after *Harris*, *Hass*, *Tucker*, and *Mosley*; after, that is, the Court had characterized *Miranda* rules as "procedural safeguards" that might be dishon-ored without violating any provision of the Constitution. Factually, the Court "re-versed the defendant's conviction for the 'savage murder of a small child' even though no Justice denied his guilt, he was warned of his rights no fewer than five times, and any 'interrogation' that might have occurred seemed quite mild."[150]

The Eighth Circuit had placed primary reliance on *Miranda*.[151] Thus, when the case came before the Supreme Court, the issue seemed to be whether a Court that had not yet reversed a conviction or excluded a single item of evidence on *Miranda* grounds could bring itself to free a Christmas Eve child murderer because the police resorted to a nonviolent, nonfraudulent psychological ploy after the suspect had invoked his *Miranda* rights. Surely the smart money was betting that the Court would find some way to avoid this outcome.

The Iowa Supreme Court had ruled that Williams had waived his rights under both *Miranda* and *Massiah*. "It seems clear," the court wrote, "after considering the statement of Captain Leaming about the difficulty in finding the body after a snowfall and the statement of his own attorney that he would have to show where she was, the decision to reveal her whereabouts during the trip was made by his own free will."[152] The logical problem with finding a *Miranda* waiver, however, is that Leaming delivered the Christian Burial Speech *after* Williams said he didn't want to talk to the police until after consulting McKnight in Des Moines, and *before* he made the statements that the Iowa court characterized as a waiver. If the speech violated *Miranda*, its evidentiary success could not work a waiver retroactively.

To square Williams's conviction with *Miranda*, the Court might have characterized the Christian Burial Speech as something other than interrogation,[153] or denied that the speech caused Williams to reveal the body.[154] Both approaches founders on the congruence of the speech with the tactics commended by police interrogation manuals and condemned by *Miranda*:

It is true that *Miranda* contains much talk about "custodial police interrogation," "in-custody interrogation," "questioning initiated by law enforcement officers," and about the warnings that must be given "prior to any questioning." But it also contains strong criticism and apparent condemnation of (1) many standard interrogation techniques that need not take the form of "questions," such as "posit[ing]" "the guilt of the subject as a fact," "minimiz[ing] the moral seriousness of the offense," and "cast[ing] blame on the victim or on society," and (2) various stratagems that do not require any "verbal conduct" on the part of the police at all, such as the "false line-up" and the "reverse line-up."[155]

Justice Stewart decided the case on Sixth Amendment grounds, but nonetheless noted that Leaming "deliberately and designedly set out to elicit information from Williams just as surely as—and perhaps more effectively than—if he had formally interrogated him."[156]

A ruling that Leaming's speech did not constitute interrogation would have eviscerated *Miranda* by enabling the police to resort to that majority of interrogation techniques that do not involve literal questions. The state seemed to accept this, and devoted twenty pages of its brief to the project of persuading the Court to overrule *Miranda*.[157] Twenty-one other states joined an amicus brief urging the same result, and citing *Harris*, *Tucker*, and *Mosley* as having recognized that *Miranda* was wrongly decided.[158]

The justices were unimpressed, perhaps swayed by the opposing brief prepared by Iowa law professor Robert Bartels, which emphasized the empirical research suggesting that *Miranda* had not seriously impaired the ability of the police to obtain confessions.[159] The majority, content to throw out the conviction on *Massiah* grounds, concluded that there was "no need to review in this case the doctrine of *Miranda v. Arizona,* a doctrine designed to secure the constitutional privilege against compulsory self-incrimination, *Michigan v. Tucker.* . . ."[160] Three of the dissenters expressly "agree[d] with the Court that this is not now the case in which that issue need be considered."[161] The fourth dissenter, Chief Justice Burger, made no reference at all to the submission of the states.

If *Brewer v. Williams* was not the case in which to reconsider *Miranda,* what better case was likely to ever reach the Court? Williams had received the warnings on multiple occasions and he had in fact consulted with counsel. The Christian Burial Speech was a ruse, but it was neither a lie nor a threat. If *Miranda* required, as the Eighth Circuit had held, reversing Williams's conviction for an especially odious crime, didn't that make his case the perfect one for overruling *Miranda*?

Perhaps the complications posed by the division of the justices on the right-to-counsel issue prevented the formation of a consensus on modifying or discarding *Miranda.* Subsequent developments suggest, however, that the basic conservatism of the Burger Court had come to *Miranda*'s rescue. Not until the year 2000 (at which point even Chief Justice Rehnquist would vote to uphold *Miranda*) did any of the justices find the right case in which to reconsider *Miranda. Williams* marks the point at which the opportunity for out-and-out counterrevolution effectively had passed.

To be sure, the Burger Court refused to broaden the rights recognized by *Miranda.* In *Fare v. Michael C.*[162] the Court rejected the claim of a juvenile suspect whose request to consult his probation officer, as opposed to a lawyer, was refused by the police during questioning. In *North Carolina v. Butler*[163] the Court reversed the state supreme court's ruling requiring an express waiver of the *Miranda* right to counsel. Once warned, the suspect might make a knowing and voluntary, albeit implied, waiver simply by making a statement.

These rulings, however, were not major blows to *Miranda,* and a surprising turnaround was in store. In *Tague v. Louisiana*[164] the Court summarily reversed the defendant's conviction because the state court had found a valid waiver based on the testimony of an officer who could not, at trial, recall the content of the warning he administered or if he had asked whether the suspect understood whatever rights the officer had read. Under *Miranda,* the state has the "heavy burden" of proving waiver. Only Justice Rehnquist dissented on the merits.

Tague added nothing to the jurisprudence of confessions. Nonetheless, for the first time, the Burger Court had excluded a statement on the authority of *Miranda.* If *Tague* is of itself doctrinally insignificant, the Court's willingness to take the case and reverse summarily reflects a different attitude toward *Miranda,* an attitude that would change the law in the upcoming cases of *Rhode Island v. Innis*[165] and *Edwards v. Arizona.*[166]

Innis adopted a fairly generous definition of interrogation, although the standard was given a narrow interpretation in the instant case. *Edwards* distinguished invocation of the right to counsel from invocation of the right to silence. Under the *Mosley* decision the police could, given some break in the action far short of release from custody, may reapproach the suspect, administer fresh warnings, and obtain a valid waiver. Not so, holds *Edwards*, when the suspect invokes the right to counsel. Subsequent cases have made clear that reinterrogation after invocation of the right to counsel violates *Miranda* even if the suspect has in fact met with counsel and even if the police interrogate about an unrelated crime.[167]

The striking feature of *Innis* and *Edwards* is how sharp critics of *Miranda* took a hand in expounding it. Justice Stewart dissented in *Miranda* but wrote *Innis* and *Williams*. Justice White dissented in *Miranda* but wrote *Edwards*, declaring for the Court that "it is inconsistent with *Miranda* and its progeny for the authorities, at their instance, to reinterrogate an accused in custody if he has clearly asserted his right to counsel."[168] "[W]hen an accused has invoked his right to have counsel present during custodial interrogation, a valid waiver of that right cannot be established by showing only that he responded to further police-initiated custodial interrogation even if he has been advised of his rights."[169]

In his concurring opinion in *Mosley*, Justice White explained the basis of this distinction. The suspect who invokes the right to silence but not to counsel believes himself capable of protecting his interests without a lawyer; his later decision to respond to questions deserves as much respect as the earlier decision not to do so. By contrast, once "the accused [has] expressed his own view that he is not competent to deal with the authorities without legal advice, a later decision at the authorities' insistence to make a statement without counsel's presence may properly be viewed with skepticism."[170] Even Chief Justice Burger, concurring in *Innis*, could bring himself to say that "[t]he meaning of *Miranda* has become reasonably clear and law enforcement practices have adjusted to its strictures; I would neither overrule *Miranda*, disparage it, nor extend it at this late date."[171]

Edwards seemed to breathe new life into *Miranda*, but the Burger Court soon qualified its new rule by holding, in *Oregon v. Bradshaw*,[172] that the protection afforded by *Edwards* evaporates once the suspect initiates a conversation with police about the case—even one as colorless as asking "What is going to happen to me now?" The "*Edwards-Bradshaw* initiation test . . . *at most* demands evidence of a generalized desire or willingness to discuss the investigation."[173] Such a standard "allows officers to recommence interrogation in many situations in which suspects may not have changed their minds."[174] *Edwards* to be sure made initiation a prerequisite of waiver following assertion of the right to counsel, as *Mosley* had not done with respect to the right to silence. But *Bradshaw* made the hurdle of initiation far less daunting than it seemed when *Edwards* was decided.

THE ENDURING INCONSISTENCY IN THE LAW

Edwards, moreover, did not deny the characterization of the *Miranda* rules as "procedural safeguards" rather than "constitutional rights." This characterization would soon resurface in the case of *New York v. Quarles*.[175] When a woman reported to two New York City police officers that the man who had just raped her had entered a supermarket armed with a gun, the officers entered the store and spotted the suspect. He ran toward the back of the store, and the police lost sight of him for a few seconds. They then spotted him again, and ordered him to stop and put his hands over his head. An officer frisked Quarles and discovered that the suspect was wearing an empty shoulder holster.

The officer handcuffed Quarles and then asked "Where's the gun?" Quarles indicated some empty boxes and said "The gun is over there." The police then discovered a loaded. 38 caliber revolver. Only then did the police administer *Miranda* warnings.

Quarles posed an embarrassing case under *Miranda*. Undoubtedly Quarles, who was handcuffed and surrounded by several police officers, was in custody. Just as clearly the police had interrogated him; "Where's the gun?" is an express question. Yet the behavior of the police presented none of the dangers of incommunicado coercion inspiring *Miranda*. The police could not be faulted for immediately asking the suspect about the location of the missing weapon. The fact that they administered the warnings immediately after finding the weapon strongly suggests their complete good faith.

The New York courts took a formalist approach to the custody-interrogation formula and suppressed the evidence. When the Supreme Court took the case, there could be little doubt that a reversal was probable. How that reversal would be arranged, however, was an open question. The United States argued in an *amicus* brief that the Court should recognize an exception to *Miranda* parallel to the Fourth Amendment's search-incident-to-arrest exception to the warrant requirement.[176] In a five-to-four decision, however, the Court adopted what it somewhat unfortunately labeled as "a 'public safety' exception to the requirement that *Miranda* warnings be given before a suspect's answers may be admitted into evidence."[177]

Justice Rehnquist's justification for the exception begins with the proposition that the "prophylactic *Miranda* warnings . . . are 'not themselves rights protected by the Constitution but [are] instead measures to insure that the right against compulsory self-incrimination [is] protected.' "[178] These judge-made procedural safeguards might be justified in some cases, but not in others, by a balance of costs and benefits. In the instant case, "the need for answers to questions in a situation posing a threat to the public safety outweighs the need for the prophylactic rule protecting the Fifth Amendment's privilege against self-incrimination."[179]

The trouble with this analysis is that the "fewer convictions" are a "cost" of *Miranda* primarily because of the damage lost convictions do to the public safety. To appropriate a cliche from another topic: Guns don't kill, people do. When a murderer invokes his rights under *Miranda* and a confession is lost, the public safety is very much endangered. I would feel safer in a community with a lost revolver in it than I would in a community in which a mentally disturbed child-murderer like Robert Williams is at large.

The Court has never held, however, that *Miranda*'s protection vary on account of the seriousness of the offense. Miranda confessed to rape, and Edwards to murder, but the Court threw out their statements. The focus on public security, a value inherently in competition with the privilege against self-incrimination, suggested that the balancing approach taken by the *Quarles* majority might do to *Miranda* what "balancing" had done to the exclusionary rule.

Quarles was an attractive case for the government less because of a heightened governmental interest than because of a diminished individual interest. As the state argued in its brief, the case "exhibits none of the evils which the *Miranda* opinion was designed to eradicate."[180] Prior decisions, however, had applied *Miranda* to custodial questioning that was limited in duration and conducted outside the police station.[181] The turn to a public safety exception is in part explicable because of the equation of custody and arrest.

What if the police had questioned Quarles about the location of a missing weapon back at the station, hours after the arrest? Presumably the "narrow exception"[182] recognized in *Quarles* would not apply, even though the balance of costs and benefits seems unchanged. The lower courts have in fact confined the exception to the immediate aftermath of arrest, and to police questioning justified by an immediate threat.[183] So long as these limitations apply, the *Quarles* exception should be rechristened the "emergency exception."

Quarles has not led to the sort of exceptions to *Miranda* critics might have feared; there is no "homicide exception" or "serial killer exception" or "narcotics kingpin" exception that a balancing process might logically entail. Instead, rather than making further inroads into the *Miranda* rules, the Rehnquist Court has adhered to[184] and even expanded[185] the *Edwards* rule, and held that *Miranda* claims, unlike Fourth Amendment claims, may be reasserted by state prisoners via petitions for federal habeas.[186] As with the Fourth Amendment exclusionary rule, the formal outlines of the *Miranda* doctrine remain; but the Court has abandoned the doctrinal justification for the rules it continues to enforce. The confessions cases are incoherent on their own terms, and only some conception of *stare decisis* can make sense of them.

The Court's recent decision in *Dickerson v. United States*[187] has done more to confirm, than to dispel, the impression that the *Miranda* cases are irreconcilable. The Fourth Circuit Court of Appeals seized on the *Harris-Tucker-Quarles* line of cases to uphold the constitutionality of Title II of the 1968 Crime Control Bill. As the defendant pointed out in a petition for certiorari, the Fourth Circuit's focus on the *Tucker* line necessarily gave no weight to the state *Miranda* cases such as *Edwards* and *Withrow v. Williams*.

When the Court accepted the case for review, there seemed to be only three possible decisions. The justices might have reaffirmed *Miranda* by holding that the state *Miranda* cases repudiate the prophylactic-rule cases. They might have done the opposite, and overruled the state cases on the ground that *Miranda* was not required by the Fifth Amendment. Finally, they might have attempted to reconcile the state *Miranda* decisions and the prophylactic-rules cases by focusing on the specific facts presented in the latter line of decisions.

Although difficult, such a reconciliation is not impossible. In *Harris* and *Tucker* the interrogations took place before *Miranda* was decided, so that the police had acted in good faith when they failed to deliver the warnings. Alternatively, a defendant who takes the stand might be thought to waive the Fifth Amendment objection to impeachment use of prior compelled statements. The haste and uncertainty of a police investigation might justify a relaxed exclusionary rule for fruits of *Miranda* violations, as compared with the strict standard required when testimony is compelled under an immunity grant during a carefully planned grand jury investigation. Such arguments are not inevitable, but they are not impossible either. But making them would have forced the Court to acknowledge the basic inconsistency in its prior opinions.

Given these three choices, the majority chose "none of the above." Chief Justice Rehnquist, hitherto an implacable foe of *Miranda*, wrote the opinion for a seven-justice majority reaffirming *Miranda* and striking down Title II as unconstitutional. The opinion, however, is utterly conclusory. The state *Miranda* cases, according to Chief Justice Rehnquist, clearly show that *Miranda* "announced a constitutional rule."[188] But the prophylactic-rules cases are, apparently, not called into question by this characterization of *Miranda*.

Why not? *Dickerson* repeatedly concludes that *Miranda* is indeed "a constitutional decision,"[189] "of constitutional origin,"[190] and "is constitutionally based."[191] The only "constitutional basis" for *Miranda* is the Fifth Amendment. Why then doesn't a *Miranda* violation trigger the *Portash* ban on impeachment with compelled admissions and the *Kastigar* rule requiring the government to prove an independent source for fruits?

More concretely, on remand, suppose Dickerson testifies at trial inconsistently with his *Miranda*-tainted admissions. Does *Harris* or *Portash* govern the use of his admissions for impeachment? Since the majority cites *Harris* without critique, one must assume that the majority intends for *Harris* to remain the law. But there is no critical discussion of *Portash* either.

The prophylactic-rules cases, the majority opines, "illustrate the principle— not that *Miranda* is not a constitutional rule—but that no constitutional rule is immutable. No court laying down a general rule can possibly foresee the various circumstances in which counsel will seek to apply it, and the sort of modifications represented by these cases are as much a normal part of constitutional law as the original decision."[192] Chief Justice Rehnquist fails to point out that the *Miranda* majority indeed foresaw—and condemned—the use of unwarned statements for impeachment purposes. Nor does he deign to notice the holding in *Portash* barring impeachment use of immunized grand jury testimony. Evidently unexplained and apparently arbitrary distinctions are, for Chief Justice Rehnquist, "a normal part of constitutional law."

The *Dickerson* majority did attempt to explain *Oregon v. Elstad* on the theory that "refusing to apply the traditional 'fruits' doctrine developed in Fourth Amendment cases" "simply recognizes the fact the unreasonable searches under the Fourth Amendment are different from unwarned interrogation under the Fifth Amendment."[193] Chief Justice Rehnquist must know, however, that the Fifth

Amendment exclusionary rule for fruits under *Kastigar* is *stricter*, not laxer, than the Fourth Amendment exclusionary rule.

Chief Justice Rehnquist's decision to join the majority, the absence of concurring opinions, and opinion's greater overall concern for the Court's authority relative to Congress than to the coherence of the law the Court has made all point to a compromise decision. The apparent gist of that compromise is that the *status quo* will be maintained. The existing law, however, is regarded by virtually every informed observer as inconsistent and unprincipled.[194]

Justice Scalia's dissenting opinion, joined by Justice Thomas, can be censured for embracing the naive assumption that admissions obtained in secret and manipulative interrogation of physically restrained and uncounseled suspects are generally voluntary. The dissent, however, accurately targets the majority's refusal to face up to the Court's inconsistent pronouncements about *Miranda*. In a particularly telling salvo, Justice Scalia notes that the *Dickerson* majority seems to give itself the power to declare constitutional rules that go beyond the constitution, when the Court has denied Congress any such power despite the textual authority given to Congress by section five of the Fourteenth Amendment.

"Logic will out," Justice Scalia declares.[195] But the tension between the prophylactic-rules cases and the state *Miranda* cases has existed at least since *Tucker* came down a quarter century ago. Evidently, those of us waiting for neutral principles and candid opinions in criminal procedure cases can expect to wait a while longer. Simultaneously conclusory and inconclusive, the *Dickerson* opinion makes an ideal capstone for contemporary constitutional criminal procedure.

CONCLUSION

I have traversed the history of modern confessions law in such detail to substantiate some of the generalizations made in Chapter 3. Current law is dysfunctional as well as incoherent. The turn to incorporation has meant that even after thirty years of insincere distinctions, professional criminals arrested on probable cause can avoid giving any explanation of their activities without any legally cognizable inference of guilt being drawn from their reticence. Yet the great majority of suspects waive their *Miranda* rights in the very same stationhouse environment the *Miranda* decision persuasively described as inherently coercive. At least a few of those who waive their rights end up confessing to crimes they did not commit. As with criminal procedure doctrine generally, the police are largely unregulated, yet guilt can go unpunished and innocence suffer.

For the most part we still don't know what went on during interrogation, and the due process test has atrophied. Recording requirements, time limits, and the prohibition of particularly *sub dolis* interrogation tactics have proved the road not taken. Instrumental concerns have sapped the life from incorporation, but the Warren Court landmarks still rule us, albeit not quite from the grave. Rather, they persist like the undead of vampire fiction, their rules still followed but their reason repudiated. The next chapter turns to a normative analysis of the law this historical process has bequeathed to us.

5

Evaluating Fundamental Fairness, Selective Incorporation, and Conservative Balancing

The conservative Court's reaction against the Warren Court's selective-incorporation revolution is now largely spent. Criminal procedure to be sure remains furiously controversial, but the battle lines have become jagged and unpredictable. The balances struck by the Burger Court mark the jumping-off point for a new generation of judges, lawyers, and commentators. The prevailing doctrinal regime is the product of an understandable historical process; but it is not, *as a regime*, characterized by the principled consistency required of an enduring body of constitutional law. The Supreme Court can avoid a thorough-going reconsideration of the whole field only at the cost of continuing the process that has brought it to its present state of disarray. That reexamination is bound to occur, later if not sooner. In this chapter, I explain why the three doctrinal approaches thus far attempted—fundamental fairness, selective incorporation, and conservative balancing—should be regarded as failures.

A NOTE ON CONSTITUTIONAL THEORY

Evaluating the three doctrinal frameworks that have thus far commanded majority support on the Supreme Court requires the development of criteria for evaluating such doctrinal regimes. While this might at first blush appear to depend on adopting (or inventing) a comprehensive theory of constitutional interpretation, it turns out that such a move is both unnecessary and indeed self-defeating. Most constitutional theories (and almost all the plausible ones) share a common content-independent respect for a conventionally determined corpus of authoritative legal materials. The constitutional text, the history behind the text, and established precedents all play prominent roles in constitutional rhetoric. A few eccentric academics aside, all theories—positivist or normative, originalist or noninterpretive—accept these sources as authoritative, and pretty much in the order listed.[1]

A doctrinal framework that flouts the conventional constraints on legitimate interpretation therefore fails on all accounts. If those constraints leave room for judicial choice, a doctrinal framework should promote the political and moral values implicated by the criminal process. The inquiry, however, is not, as H.L.A. Hart might have understood it, cleanly bifurcated between an assessment of authoritative constraints followed by an unconstrained legislative assessment of the permissible alternatives.[2] Legitimacy is relative, not absolute. Strong policy considerations can reinforce a position that is relatively weak on grounds of authority, and the reverse is also true. Very strong authoritative support can trump advantages of policy.

This account looks a great deal like Dworkin's vision of adjudication generally,[3] but the disputes in legal theory need not divert us. American constitutional practice conventionally follows this authority-policy dialectic; a Hartian positivist in the particular position of a U.S. judge would decide cases much as would Dworkin's universal Hercules.[4] Perhaps more to the point, no other kind of constitutional rhetoric has much chance of success. Approaches more formalistic on the one hand, or more realistic on the other, would fail to engage—let alone persuade—a pragmatic judiciary.

Constitutional doctrine cannot succeed without securing the support of judges who disagree about many fundamental principles of legal or political theory. A truly innovative constitutional theory, *even if normatively superior to all others on first principles*, could not secure such undertheorized agreement, for by hypothesis a novel comprehensive theory would be one now supported by no one.[5] Conventionalism is all there is, and conventionalism itself reflects the significant but inconclusive importance of both authority and policy.

The previous chapters have laid extensive groundwork for a discussion of the authoritative legal materials—text, history, and precedent. Before evaluating the fundamental fairness, selective incorporation, and conservative balancing frameworks, I turn to develop some nonobvious points about policy considerations in criminal-procedure cases.

THE PRIORITY OF INSTRUMENTAL VALUES

Even those strongly devoted to formal constraints on judicial authority recognize that those constraints leave considerable latitude in constitutional criminal-procedure cases. Indeed, lower court judges, whose decisions may be reversed for inconsistency with established doctrine, often discover either that the import of established doctrine for a case depends on what values doctrine is thought to reflect, or that purely formal analysis leaves the question open to determination by unconstrained policy considerations. This situation confronts the Supreme Court on an even more regular basis.[6]

Thus, the values that criminal procedure serves typically determine the outcomes of cases, even when the constraints on legitimate interpretation are fully honored. Whether articulated as a running conflict between two internally consistent models, as Herbert Packer would have it,[7] or as the necessity of compromise in any system of criminal procedure, as Mirjan Damaska would have it,[8] the seemingly standard dispute in criminal procedure cases pits the truth-finding mission of the process against supposedly competing values such as individual autonomy, privacy, or dignity. I shall argue, however, that prevailing thought greatly exaggerates the conflict between the truth-finding function, properly understood, and the values of individual autonomy, privacy, or dignity.

This exaggeration, I believe, is due to neglect of the possibility that the substantive criminal law has authoritatively ordered the values of punishing wrongdoers and honoring the rights of individuals. The neglect follows in part from the tendency to compartmentalize thinking along the lines of the law-school curriculum, and in part from the tendency to confuse the purposes of the criminal law with the purposes of punishing criminals.[9] Dispelling the analytic confusion offers the best hope of overcoming the intellectual inertia.

Punishment is usually thought of as being justified by some positive purpose or combination of positive purposes, such as retribution, deterrence, and incapacitation. The "general justifying aim" of punishment, however, is limited by side-constraints, such as the values of responsibility, proportionality, and equality.[10]

Legality is sometimes characterized as one such side-constraint,[11] but this is a false step. As the level of penal legislation, and even of interpreting penal legislation, the trade-offs between preventing or denouncing crime and respecting individual autonomy are inevitable and difficult. That there must be penal legislation condemning the conduct to be punished, however, is a limiting principle of an entirely different character. The priority of the legality principle over the general justifying aim of punishment is virtually complete. However harmful, wrongful, or even odious, conduct not proscribed in advance may not be punished.[12]

Before the Solons and the Hammurabis gave laws to humankind, prevailing authority punished wrongdoers. In totalitarian societies today, prevailing authority punishes supposed wrongdoers without law, and so, appropriately enough, without trial. The purpose of criminal law is not identical to the purpose of punishment. Rather, the general justifying aim of the criminal law is to limit punishment, not to enable it.

The effect of substantive criminal law is to prevent the punishment of those who have not violated its strictures. Thus, positive law has the great virtue of enabling individuals to protect themselves from punishment by complying with knowable rules.[13] It also has the yet more profound value of requiring a prospective and general determination that community interests require the imposition of punishment before individual liberty may be curtailed by the criminal sanction.[14] No doubt a commitment to positive law, standing alone, is *insufficient* to prevent the persecution of the harmless but unpopular or the totalitarian extension of government authority. But it is equally beyond doubt that a commitment to positive law is *necessary* if these fundamental political goals are to be met.

The purpose of substantive criminal law, then, is to limit punishment to cases of violation of the law. The substantive law also provides for punishment in instances of violation; but it should be clear from what has been said that preventing the punishment of the innocent has priority over punishing the guilty. Absent this priority, wrongdoers who violate no positive law ought nonetheless to be punished, for deterrent or retributive purposes as one's theory of punishment might require. Perhaps violation of positive law has normative significance, so that whoever violates a law ought to be punished; but this would not secure the lawful wrongdoer against punishment absent the priority of legality over the aims of punishment.

The criminal law could not succeed in its punishment-limiting mission in the absence of two further principles. The first of these is the requirement that violations of the criminal law be convincingly proved at a fair trial before punishment may be imposed. The second of these is that the criminal law must to a very considerable degree monopolize the community's access to the coercive methods of social control. Call the first principle the adjudication requirement, and the second the exclusivity principle. These principles, derived from the substantive criminal law, together provide the foundations for an instrumental theory of criminal procedure.

The legality principle implies the adjudication requirement because legality itself is vulnerable to factual subversion. The clearest illustration is the practice of show trials, such as those that still take place in some totalitarian countries. Complacent Americans might well recall *Frank v. Magnum* and *Moore v. Dempsey*.[15] Even when the trial is more than a sham, honest but common erroneous convictions would nullify the legality principle. If a mere likelihood of guilt sufficed to justify conviction, the security against unjustified punishment would be lost. The authorities could compel undesirables to submit to lottery-like proceedings. Even absent deliberate persecution, simple error would condemn many people who have not broken the law.

When crime is a major source of fear (and when has that, at least in American history, not been so?), the decision to confine, by positive law, state power to punish may seem doubtful. Then, efforts to equate erroneous punishment with the erroneous evasion of punishment may seem attractive precisely because that equation tends in effect to permit the state to punish according to the discretion of its agents. But the case for criminal law, and thus for a distinctive and distinctively biased criminal procedure, remains compelling.

To be sure, the priority of the value of preventing arbitrary, oppressive, or erroneous punishment over the value of enabling justified punishment is extensive, but not complete. All human institutions are fallible. Only the abolition of punishment could preclude unjustified punishment with certainty. The degree of the risk that is justified cannot be specified with arithmetic precision, although Blackstone put the acceptable ratio of false acquittals to false convictions at ten to one.[16] Nonetheless, from both utilitarian and deonotological moral premises, the preference for false acquittal over false conviction is very powerful.

From a utilitarian perspective, a false conviction both imposes the pain of punishment without justification, and also typically permits the escape of the guilty party. Given the apparently permanent scarcity of prison space, false acquittals or undiscovered crimes do not diminish the prison population. Given our inability to predict future criminal behavior,[17] incapacitation suffers little from false acquittals. Who can say that Willie Horton committed graver outrages than would have the felon confined in his place?[18] Moreover, from the standpoint of incapacitation, the hard-core recidivist who escapes conviction on doubtful evidence will soon enough give police and prosecutors another chance to put him away.

As for deterrence, to the extent potential criminals calculate, they count on escaping detection, not on being arrested and then falsely acquitted.[19] It is true that about half of all arrests do not result in a conviction;[20] but it is also true that fewer than half of all offenses are reported to police,[21] and that fewer than half of all reported offenses are cleared by an arrest.[22] Again, the scarcity of prison space means that the factor limiting punishment of the guilty is not the short supply of those convicted, but the short supply of affordable and humane sanctions to impose upon them.

Even if substantially reducing the number of unjust acquittals, at the expense of a slight increase in the number of unjust convictions, would reduce the crime rate measurably, considerations of justice counsel against such a reduction. No doubt the aggregate amount of happiness matters, but the distribution of happiness matters too. We may not go with Rawls and insist that every institution do no injury to the least well-off before we call it justified,[23] but few would deny that individuals suffer a disproportionate share of the costs of crime control when convicted of offenses they did not commit.

If the connection between marginally increasing the risk of punishment run by the guilty and preventing future crimes were clearer than it is, or if a substantial number of crimes that might be prevented involved homicide, rape, or aggravated assault, the victims of unprevented offenses might have a stronger claim upon those whose guilt the evidence suggests but fails to prove. We should nonetheless abjure a causal attitude toward punishing the innocent as too dangerous a political principle to have at large. Consideration of the utility of practices and principles tends to merge with deonotological thinking.[24] From either perspective, thoughtful people would prefer to inhabit a society with a strong commitment to preventing unjust punishment.[25]

Even the assignment of a purely retributive purpose to punishment would not diminish the preference for false acquittals over false convictions. Retributivists generally distinguish the escape of deserved punishment and the infliction of undeserved punishment; indeed it is thought to be a great advantage of retributive theory that, unlike utilitarian accounts, retributivism categorically forbids punishing the innocent.[26] The retributivist might modify this statement by insisting that retributivism categorically forbids only the deliberate punishment of the innocent;[27] but on an institutional level communities deliberately choose the risk of error they will run. A retributivist surely would reject a system that convicted forty innocent persons for every sixty guilty persons, even if the judge and jury in any given case believed that guilt in each instance was more likely than not.

An instrumental theory of criminal procedure therefore differs profoundly from an instrumental theory of civil or administrative procedure. The substantive law of torts or contracts aims to impose liability on those who breach their obligations fully as much as it aims at securing against liability those who uphold their obligations. Administrative entitlement schemes aim both at awarding benefits to the eligible and at denying benefits to the ineligible. Administrative regulatory schemes aim at imposing sanctions on violators as much as they aim at avoiding the imposition of sanctions on the compliant. By contrast, criminal procedure's bias against unjust conviction is virtually built into the substantive criminal law.

The legality principle implies not only the adjudication requirement, but also the exclusivity principle. In its strongest form, the exclusivity principle holds that public authority may resort to the most coercive forms of social control *solely* through the criminal process. In practice, almost all nations recognize some exceptions, such as civil commitment and preventive detention. Both practices have been abused, both in the United States and elsewhere; and in this country both are now hedged by constitutional safeguards that resemble, although they are not fully equivalent to, those attending the criminal process.[28]

Legality, even coupled with the adjudication requirement, would be an empty principle if the government could at its discretion visit serious injury on individuals without invoking the criminal process. A South American republic might have, on paper, a scrupulously fair system of criminal trial; but if death squads murder government foes at will, the substantive criminal law will fail its purpose. The exclusivity principle may survive some grudging exceptions such as civil commitment; but if the substantive law is to succeed in its liability-limiting purpose, public officials may restrain the critical liberties of individuals solely through the criminal process.

The exclusivity principle connects the legality principle with police practices. In the civil law even those facing substantial liabilities respect the authority of official process. The criminal law must cope with a different sort of litigant; and therefore the law enforcement agencies are empowered to arrest, to interrogate, and to search. Unlike the processes of investigation in civil or administrative matters, the methods of investigating crime can themselves work oppressive violations of individual liberty.

Absent the immediate need to prevent crime, the coercive powers of the police are justified by the need to compel unwilling litigants to submit to the process of adjudication. When neither justification is in play—that is, when the police exercise their unique coercive powers absent an incipient offense *or* a justifiable expectation of a formal prosecution—justification cannot be derived from the substantive criminal law. In such cases we are not dealing with criminal procedure at all, but instead with a coercive species of administrative law, like conscription, quarantine, or civil commitment.

Consider the example of arrest. Arrests sometimes initiate criminal prosecutions. When founded on probable cause the arrest is justified by the need to compel the unwilling litigant to submit to adjudication. But very often arrest serves an independent social control function, as in punishing domestic battery or prostitution or public drunkenness, or separating the combatants in a barroom brawl.

If arrest in these latter contexts is to be justified, it must be on the basis of a compelling state interest aside from the enforcement of the criminal law. Very often this might be so; arrest to prevent the probable resumption of a violent quarrel can be thought of as a one-person curfew. Still to ask whether the arrest is supported by strong suspicion of guilt of a crime that will never be charged, let alone end in conviction, mischaracterizes the situation as a criminal procedure problem. If police should have some power to arrest for social control purposes independent of prosecution, those powers should be defined and limited by justifications independent of the criminal law.

A defensible formulation of an instrumental theory of criminal procedure must incorporate both the adjudication requirement and the exclusivity principle. Without these commitments, criminal procedure cannot reflect the substantive criminal law's liability-limiting purpose by favoring false acquittals over false convictions, and by limiting the application of official violence against the law-abiding in the course of investigation. The central meaning of due process—that punishment without trial is forbidden—is more than amenable to encompassing these commitments.

On such an instrumental account, the conflict between discovering the truth and respecting individuals is demoted to a subordinate role. An investigative process in which the burdens on individual liberty bear a fair relation to the expectation of an ultimate conviction, coupled with a trial process calculated to convict only in cases in which guilt is highly probable, secures the values of individual autonomy, privacy, and dignity all due respect. So long as the substantive criminal law provides punishment only for wrongful acts, procedures that convict only when guilt is highly probable ensure to the extent feasible that punishment is deserved, thus treating the accused at least in part as an end-in-himself. Similarly, a procedure biased against conviction minimizes the risk that an innocent person will bear an unjust share of the cost of controlling crime. In such a system, sentences imposed following conviction will impair individual autonomy no more than the substantive law requires.

So long as the burdens imposed by investigation vary in proportion to the likelihood of a conviction, those methods will not unjustifiably offend individualistic values. Such impositions as search and arrest undoubtedly offend freedom and dignity, but when in fact justified by the prospect of invoking the adjudicatory process and securing a conviction, these burdens are justified by the same reasons that justify punishment of those crimes. Again, a procedure that minimizes the visitation of arrest, search, and like restraints on innocent persons secures freedom and dignity to the extent consonant with the justification of punishment.

Arguably, a different answer might be in order when the methods of investigation or adjudication trench upon the freedom or dignity of persons not suspected of crime. When the police search the home of a husband arrested for robbery, the privacy of the wife and children is invaded. When the defense cross-examines the complaining witness in a rape case, her privacy is likewise invaded.

The balance between the intrusiveness of a practice and the likelihood of convicting a genuine criminal, however, is not a matter of waiver. Until the moment of conviction, the suspect is presumed to be as innocent as anyone else, and some persons, even in an ideal system, will be convicted even though they are innocent. The justification for violating freedom and dignity is not because suspicion justifies punishment before trial. Rather, investigative burdens must sometimes fall on the innocent for the same reason that an unjust conviction must sometimes fall on the innocent. If apparent guilt beyond reasonable doubt justifies the imposition of a criminal sentence, substantial suspicion justifies some lesser intrusions, regardless of whether they fall upon the guilty or the innocent.

For example, police may mistakenly identify a man as one for whom a warrant is outstanding. It turns out they are mistaken; the arrested man only resembles the true culprit. The arrest, however, is no less justifiable because it turned out to restrain an innocent person. Indeed, the methods of investigation rarely intrude solely upon the interests of those suspected of crime. Wiretaps monitor conversations between the suspect and plainly innocent callers; searches of multi-resident dwellings commonly invade the privacy of innocent cotenants; even arrest deprives families and employers of their interest in associating with the suspect. So long as these burdens are justified by the expectation that they will lead to the conviction of the guilty, it should not matter that the burden falls on a person who is not suspected of any wrongdoing. Given the substantive law's liability-limiting purpose, proportionately greater burdens may be imposed for the purpose of clearing the innocent of criminal charges.

Some methods of investigation might be so onerous, or so politically dangerous, as to be impermissible even if certain to reveal conclusive evidence of crimes. Torture of an individual who is both certainly guilty and who certainly has knowledge of the guilt of others is one example. After all, cruel and unusual punishments may not be inflicted even upon those adjudicated guilty. To permit the police to inflict a sanction in the investigative process that no court could impose as a sentence would violate the exclusivity principle.

The suggestion that criminal procedure should express respect for autonomy, privacy, or dignity by affording procedural protections beyond those required by the instrumental theory I have described is unconvincing.[29] Formal procedures express respect for persons solely through their instrumental function. Individuals who have no reason to expect to be accused of crime have neither the need nor the desire to address a jury, to consult a defense lawyer, or to cross-examine witnesses.

Process does not express respect for persons; rather, coercion expresses disrespect for persons, a disrespect that process aims to confine to justifiable cases. To be sure, any system that permits widespread arbitrary or erroneous punishment offends freedom and dignity. To the extent that the threat to autonomy, privacy, or dignity flows from the risk of unjustified punishment, however, a theory responsive to the threat is at bottom instrumental. In the context of the adjudication requirement, values such as autonomy, privacy, or dignity have no real role that is not mediated through the substantive criminal law.

The application of the exclusivity principle, however, entails an independent role for the values of individual autonomy, dignity, or privacy in the criminal procedure calculus. Some methods of investigation impose patently onerous burdens on individuals, while some qualify as *de minimis*. No one would say that looking up an individual's number in a telephone directory is the sort of invasion of liberty that must be justified by a strong expectation of an ultimate conviction. Everyone would agree that arresting an individual constitutes just such an invasion.

Between these poles fall a variety of investigative practices, such as the recruitment of informants, or the physical surveillance of a suspect's movements, or the collection of information about his finances, that might be thought to offend the exclusivity principle if undertaken without any expectation of an ultimate conviction. Which investigative tactics qualify as *de minimis*, and which qualify as substantial, invasions of individual liberty is a question about which reasonable minds might differ, based perhaps on their respective perceptions of such values as autonomy, privacy, and dignity.

Moreover, the weight of an individual's interest in freedom from a particular investigative burden might depend on the value attached to privacy or dignity. Should equivalent levels of suspicion be required for all searches—strip searches, home searches, wiretaps, auto searches, and so on? In each case the search must be justified by some expectation of securing a conviction or preventing an incipient offense; but the degree of suspicion required in each instance may depend on the weight attached to autonomy, dignity, or privacy.

This is a far more modest role for the conflict of individual values with the instrumental functions of criminal procedure than is typically presupposed by judges and scholars alike. The instrumental theory connects the justifications for both adjudicatory and investigative procedures to the negative purposes of the criminal law. Adjudicatory procedures that minimize unjust conviction satisfy those negative purposes. Investigative practices that injure individuals can be justified by the positive purposes of the criminal law, but only to the extent that the investigative practice is likely to prevent an imminent or continuing offense or to punish an offense through the adjudication process. *Which* investigative practices implicate the exclusivity principle, and *how likely* they must be of securing a conviction, are important questions that may depend on other values. The instrumental theory, however, has the virtue of framing the issue appropriately.

The instrumental theory encompasses not only due respect for individual dignity, but also due respect for the "checking value" of preventing tyranny.[30] That criminal procedure has an important role to play in a liberal democracy's scheme of checks and balances should be clear. Consider, for example, a law making it a crime to criticize the government. Such a statute obviously violates freedom of speech, and would violate the First Amendment if adopted in the United States.

But suppose that the government simply selected its critics for prosecution on false charges, or, more crudely yet, had them shot "while resisting arrest." Without the exclusivity principle and the adjudication requirement, it would be very difficult to maintain any of the other checks on authoritarianism.

Yet the instrumental theory secures the checking value of criminal procedure. Fair trials and proportionate police practices permit opponents of the government to stay out of trouble with the law. Show trials and death squads are, after all, the paradigm cases the instrumental theory aims to prohibit. Reliable trials and decent police methods can coexist with tyranny, if the substantive criminal law makes opposition to the regime an offense. But the sensible division of labor between criminal procedure and other doctrines of civil liberty is to limit the substantive criminal law according to such substantive principles as freedom of speech and conscience, and to secure those substantive protections against circumvention through an instrumental understanding of criminal procedure. To go further in preventing tyranny by approving procedures calculated to defeat the enforcement of politically oppressive substantive laws runs a very great risk of nullifying perfectly just laws.

The problem of discriminatory enforcement calls for a slightly different analysis. If the legislature creates offenses that are routinely committed by far more people than can possibly be prosecuted, and the executive selects for prosecution only critics of the regime, or members of unpopular groups, the exclusivity principle is arguably violated. Practically speaking, those prosecuted are being punished, not for the offenses of which they are guilty, but on account of status or lawful conduct. Thus the instrumental theory might well satisfy the moral claims of equality, as well as the moral claims of dignity and the prudential concern for the checking value.

The application of the instrumental theory to selective prosecution, however, is somewhat problematic. From the standpoint of legality, guilty defendants have no cause to complain that other guilty defendants go unwhipped of justice. At some extreme global prohibitions discriminatingly enforced could undermine the legality principle (imagine a law forbidding respiration in public, enforced only against blacks, or Jews, or gays). Short of such extremes discriminatory enforcement does not seem to offend legality, and yet still seems to offend the independent value of equality among persons.

Equality quite unproblematically forbids selecting persons for punishment based on race. Moreover, whether based on equality or on legality, any challenge to selective enforcement turns on the motives or reasons for selecting one target rather than another. Antidiscrimination law, both inside and outside the criminal justice system, therefore develops special rules or procedures for testing official motives. Here it is due regard for equality that gives the instrumental theory all it deserves by way of regulating selective enforcement. Thus it is sensible to rely primarily on antidiscrimination law to deal with discrimination. In this country, this implies that equal protection analysis deserves an independent and vigorous role in criminal justice.

There is one important overlap between instrumental procedural concerns and the value of equality. Sometimes the prejudice of police, witnesses, jurors, or judges threatens the reliability of the process. When this occurs, the instrumental theory coincidentally promotes equality, and nondiscrimination law coincidentally promotes reliability, by forbidding alike invidious discrimination that threatens to punish the innocent. To take one prominent example, whether to treat discrimination in jury selection solely as a nondiscrimination matter under the equal protection clause, or to treat it also as a violation of the Sixth Amendment right to an impartial jury or the due process right to a fair trial, depends on an assessment of whether racial discrimination in jury selection undermines the fairness of the trial.

Just as with dignitary values and the checking value, instrumental theory often promotes the value of equality. The instrumental theory makes it difficult to convict or to punish informally innocent members of despised groups. But no conceivable criminal procedure regime could by itself secure all that racial justice requires.

Thus the instrumental theory should not be understood as an alternative to antidiscrimination law in criminal procedure. Subjecting members of all races, classes, and genders to brutal investigations and unreliable trials, however, is at least as unpalatable as proceeding fairly against arbitrarily or invidiously selected targets. To adopt the terms of our Constitution, due process should not be asked to do the work of equal protection, and vice versa.

THE URGENCY OF RULE-OF-LAW VALUES

Courts deciding a case can describe the holding broadly or narrowly. As Cass Sunstein has argued,[31] narrow holdings reflect the important values of judicial restraint. Circumstances may change, the courts may not have the information required for formulating a general policy, and legislatures or lower courts may initiate changes that make a wide ruling unnecessary or undesirable.

Narrow rulings, however, compromise consistency and clarity, two important rule-of-law values. In the criminal procedure context these rule-of-law values have special urgency. In 1998, the most recent year for which statistics are available, there were more than *fifteen million* arrests in the United States.[32] In making these arrest decisions, law enforcement officers need to know the limits of their authority. If they exceed it, not only are the rights of citizens violated, but the sanction may be the exclusion of any evidence thereby discovered. In the millions of these arrests that result in formal charges, prosecutors, defense lawyers, and trial judges need to know both the constitutional limits on the police and the constitutional requirements applicable to the trial process. Narrow, fact-bound rulings leave the actors in the criminal process without the guidance they need.

Treating like cases differently always raises troubling normative questions. Inconsistent results in criminal cases are especially troubling because the consequences are so extreme. A thin distinction between the cases of two civil plaintiffs at worst means that one has been arbitrarily denied damages for tort or contract.

A thin distinction between two criminal defendants may mean the difference between the release of one murderer and the execution of another.

The intellectual separation of the criminal procedure cases from constitutional law at large has some unfortunate consequences. Judges and scholars may lose sight of the fact that in ruling on a suppression motion in a misdemeanor drug case the governing law is indeed constitutional law. Nonetheless, we should not simply assume that criminal procedure cases are just like commerce clause or sexual privacy cases. The unique volume of criminal cases, and the unusual dominance of exclusion and retrial in the remedial scheme, give rule-of-law values more urgency than they deserve in other contexts.

We have now the criteria needed to evaluate competing approaches to constitutional criminal procedure. To the extent permitted by authoritative sources of constitutional law, a doctrinal framework for criminal procedure should institutionalize the instrumental theory of criminal procedure. Unless constrained to do so by constitutional authority, criminal procedure should not place obstacles in the way of punishing the guilty except to the extent that those obstacles protect the innocent. Moreover, doctrine should serve rule-of-law values by expressing the governing law as clearly and comprehensively as circumstances permit. I now apply these criteria to the regimes of fundamental fairness, selective incorporation, and conservative balancing.

THE CRITIQUE OF FUNDAMENTAL FAIRNESS

Tested by the criteria of legitimacy, instrumental reliability, and clarity and consistency, the fundamental fairness regime fares poorly indeed. To begin with legitimacy, one might suppose that the fundamental fairness approach favored by Justice Harlan—who often objected to the Warren Court's doctrinal innovations on the ground of illegitimacy[33]—would have an unquestionable authoritative pedigree. The legitimacy of fundamental fairness, however, has been more frequently assumed than discussed.

Probably the closest thing to a thorough defense of fundamental fairness is Justice Harlan's dissent in *Duncan v. Louisiana*.[34] There Harlan made clear that to him fundamental fairness in criminal cases was but one example of substantive due process. To counter the charge that substantive due process conferred lawless discretion on the justices, Harlan insisted that the Fourteenth Amendment required "intermediate premises" to guide adjudication.[35] He identified the appropriate intermediate premise as American political tradition.

This position, obviously, cannot be any stronger than the general case for substantive due process. The legitimacy of substantive due process has been challenged vigorously, often enough by those sympathetic to fundamental fairness analysis in criminal cases but hostile to such decisions as *Lochner* or *Roe v. Wade*.[36] As I explain in Chapter 6, I am persuaded that the conventional sources of constitutional law can support substantive due process review. Nonetheless the fundamental fairness regime was both illegitimate and unwise.

Three key considerations undermine the legitimacy of fundamental fairness. First, even rudimentary procedural requirements exceeded the appropriate scope of substantive due process review. While the historical materials and the cases support some substantive review under the due process clause, it needs to be recalled that not every unwise or unjust piece of legislation loses the right to call itself law. Antebellum jurists thought that slavery or confiscation might violate substantive due process—pretty extreme injustices. The cases have consistently maintained that only "fundamental" rights can be vindicated by substantive due process. Thus to extend substantive due process analysis to the close regulation of criminal procedure goes well beyond what the legitimate sources of constitutional law can support.

Fundamental fairness cases have recognized a constitutional right to appear at trial in civilian clothes rather than a prison uniform,[37] to not be impeached with the failure to make a statement after receiving the *Miranda* warning,[38] and to introduce hearsay declarations tending to show that a third party committed the charged offense.[39] These are justifiable rules if our focus is preventing miscarriages of justice, but they cannot reasonably be described as "the essence of ordered liberty," on a par with security against chattel slavery or arbitrary confiscations.

In other words, fundamental fairness analysis can be legitimate only within the limits that cabin legitimate substantive due process analysis, and those limits are quite properly exceedingly narrow. Fundamental fairness, therefore, could not legitimately secure the instrumental theory of criminal procedure. The Court never went far enough toward preventing unjust conviction or extra-judicial punishment, yet even the steps the justices were willing to take exceeded the proper limits of substantive due process.

The second key to understanding the illegitimacy of fundamental fairness analysis is that substantive due process doctrine *displaced* procedural due process completely. Early in the twentieth century the Court held that taxpayers and regulated businesses had a due process right to a quasi-judicial trial—including an exclusive record and cross-examination—before the imposition of liabilities by administrative agencies.[40] At the time, a state defendant could receive the death penalty based on arbitrary searches, coerced confessions, and a trial without counsel for the defense.

No one has ever questioned the legitimacy of procedural due process, the right to a fair hearing before conviction. Yet the shift in the criminal cases to substantive due process meant that the judicial restraint, entirely appropriate to that mode of review, produced an easy tolerance of brutal police practices and unreliable trials. Reducing criminal procedure to the proscription of such things as mob-dominated trials and interrogation under torture had the perverse effect of nullifying the clearly legitimate requirement of procedural due process. Procedural due process means a fair hearing before conviction, and hearings can be unfair without evoking the intense moral disapproval required to invalidate a law as a matter of substantive due process. Thus fundamental fairness was doubly illegitimate, because while the theory improperly expanded the scope of substantive due process, it even more improperly contracted the scope of procedural due process.

Finally, even if the Court somehow managed to fit the square peg of criminal procedure into the round hole of substantive due process, the justices never specified the values that determine fundamental fairness, let alone assign them consistent priorities. Instead, the standard of fundamental fairness was "to be tested by an appraisal of the totality of facts in a given case."[41] The combination of so nebulous and normative a standard as "fundamental fairness" with case-by-case adjudication amounted to a constitutional chancellor's foot.

The Court never narrowed the scope of the normative inquiry into fundamental fairness. Fundamental fairness could be a matter of minimizing errors, or of minimizing erroneous convictions, or of preserving individual dignity. Neutral principles could not possibly have emerged from such an open-ended inquiry. Similarly situated defendants would inevitably be treated differently. Law enforcement officers and lower court judges would not have the guidance they need to deal with the steady volume of criminal cases implicating constitutional standards.

A very strong commitment to federalism might be thought to justify the fundamental fairness regime.[42] Nowadays the states are widely thought to possess sufficient political influence to maintain their status without judicial protection against federal encroachment.[43] But political influence cannot protect the states against incursions by the federal courts. Arguably, this respect for state independence justified the deference the Supreme Court showed in applying the test of fundamental fairness.

The federal justification, however, is itself only credible because the legitimacy of fundamental fairness analysis is so tenuous. Individual rights derived from the Fourteenth Amendment *necessarily* constrain state sovereignty. When the Fourteenth Amendment requires state respect for an individual right, the Amendment itself resolves the competition between freedom and federalism. At least since *Brown v. Board of Education of Topeka*, and probably since *Carolene Products*, federalism has not been understood to demand special deference to state decisions implicating freedom of religion, expression, or racial discrimination.

The Court's deference to the states in the criminal procedure field had more to do with doubts about the legitimacy of fundamental fairness than about affirmative concern for state sovereignty. Federalism does not support fundamental fairness; rather, the justices who turned to a vague and value-laden formulation of individual rights were justifiably concerned with the risk of arbitrarily imposing their own, perhaps idiosyncratic, value judgments. Fundamental fairness might have justified deference to the states, but deference to the states could not justify fundamental fairness. Any positive interpretation of due process in criminal cases, based on text, history, and precedent rather than on interpretive despair, must take due account of federalism.[44] But once arrived at, a principled interpretation of the Fourteenth Amendment cannot be countered by an appeal to state sovereignty.

Why not, for instance, require lawyers for all indigent defendants whose names begin with the letters A–M? In half of the cases, the right to a fair trial is honored, and in half the cases, the states may do as they please. No one would defend such an arrangement, but it is not too far from how fundamental fairness actually worked. If anything, the fundamental fairness regime was even worse, because at least the initial letter of the defendant's name can be determined in advance. The vagueness of the fundamental fairness test necessarily required intrusive oversight by the federal courts even in cases the states ultimately won. The federal-state friction surrounding *Brown v. Allen*,[45] and the Fortas brief in *Gideon*,[46] illustrate the point.

The vacuity of the fundamental fairness approach made it as unjust as it was illegitimate. By permitting all values to compete in every case, the fundamental fairness standard neglected the dominant value in criminal procedure—the avoidance of erroneous punishment. At least through midcentury, American criminal process was in many states characterized by arbitrary arrest and search, third-degree interrogation tactics, and unreliable trial procedures.[47] Racism was pervasive.[48] It was unexceptional for an indigent black to be tried without counsel,[49] or by an all-white jury,[50] or convicted on the force of a confession secured by a long bout of secret questioning.[51]

The assumption underlying the Court's approach, however, held that state criminal process worked serious injustice only in rare cases. Had the assumption been true, the Supreme Court could have picked out the few rotten apples from the vast orchard of the criminal justice system, without intruding too deeply into the sphere of the states, neglecting any compelling need for systematic reform, or making arbitrary distinctions among the defendants challenging their convictions. But the assumption was false; and as a result, the Court became ever-more involved in reviewing state convictions, failed to achieve any meaningful reform of the criminal justice system, and could reverse the occasional suspect conviction only by leaving many indistinguishable ones undisturbed.

As a general matter, the state courts found nothing fundamentally unfair unless the Supreme Court had spoken directly to the issue. Because no single fact was dispositive, the case-by-case adjudication of fundamental fairness claims effectively disabled the Supreme Court from requiring essential procedural safeguards in state prosecutions.

Thus, the regime of fundamental fairness described the controlling values at too high a level of generality to secure either the principled decisions demanded by legitimacy or the procedural safeguards demanded by the need to prevent erroneous punishment. I shall illustrate this twofold objection in three contexts: the right to counsel, searches and seizures, and confessions.

Betts v. Brady, which initiated the unfortunate turn to case-by-case adjudication, is an excellent example of what was wrong with fundamental fairness. The Court there unconvincingly distinguished *Powell v. Alabama* and thereby exposed indigent defendants to the risk of unjust conviction that attends the denial of counsel. The Scottsboro Boys had been "ignorant and friendless negro youths, strangers in the community,"[52] facing a capital charge. Smith Betts by contrast was tried for robbery, and the only issue at his trial had been whether the eyewitnesses, one of whom was acquainted with Betts, were more worthy of belief than the alibi witnesses. Betts "was a man forty three years old, of ordinary intelligence, and ability to take care of his own interests on the trial"[53] of the narrow issue of identification. He had, after all, "once before been in a criminal court."[54]

The suggestion that Betts, "a farm hand" of "little education,"[55] could conduct the kind of cross-examination that might shake eyewitness testimony—notoriously as unreliable in fact as it sounds credible to the ear—is naive. Betts could not know, as experienced counsel would know, all of the lines of impeachment available to counter eyewitness testimony. Betts in fact failed to point out some serious weaknesses in the prosecution's case, such as the fact that the victim identified Betts at a show-up rather than a lineup, and that the state never proved that Betts ever had possessed a handkerchief, dark glasses, and overcoat such as those worn by the robber.[56]

Thus, the seemingly dispositive distinction between *Betts* and *Powell v. Alabama* was the absence of the death sentence in *Betts*. From the perspective of due process, this distinction is arbitrary. As Francis Allen put it, "[i]f the rights of counsel are deemed an inherent part of the concept of 'fair hearing,' as has been consistently asserted by the Court since the *Powell* case, the crucial inquiry would seem to be, not so much the penalties imposed on the defendant upon conviction, but the *need* for skilled representation in the proceedings directed to the establishment of guilt."[57] Perhaps the gravity of the penalty plays a role in determining the scope of required procedural safeguards, as the long-standing Sixth Amendment exception for "petty offenses" suggests. But the *Betts* approach might be restated as classifying a life sentence under the rubric of *de minimis non lex curat*.

Indeed, the *Betts* Court did not purport to establish a rule requiring appointment of counsel in capital, but not in noncapital, cases. Rather, "want of counsel in a particular case may result in a conviction lacking in . . . fundamental fairness."[58] Thus a defendant in a noncapital case might demonstrate special circumstances, such as the complexity of the case or the slow-mindedness of the accused, that would compel the appointment of counsel as a constitutional matter.[59]

If, as the *Betts* Court asserted, "there are fair trials without counsel employed for the prisoners,"[60] then there should be no inflexible requirement of counsel in capital cases. If, on the other hand, counsel is indispensable to a fair trial, then special circumstances need not be shown before appointing counsel in felony cases. In the event, the lower courts rarely found special circumstances, and the Supreme Court could not review more than a handful of the contrary decisions.[61] Leaving aside the constraints on the Court's docket, how many unrepresented defendants could press their case to the Supreme Court?[62]

Thus, the generality of the fundamental fairness standard necessarily precluded the development of neutral principles for right-to-counsel law.[63] Neither the distinction between capital and other cases, nor the rule permitting appointment of counsel given special circumstances, rested on any actual difference in the risk of unjust conviction. In practice, moreover, the *Betts* rule ran an unacceptable risk of error in a large number of cases. From the perspectives of legitimacy and of policy, the *Betts* doctrine was a dismal failure.

If fundamental fairness fared poorly in the right-to-counsel context, the doctrine failed even more miserably in the context of police practices. For example, in *Stroble v. California*[64] the Court upheld a confession given only an hour after the suspect was kicked and menaced with a blackjack. Yet in *Haynes v. Washington*[65] the Court threw out a confession because the police refused to permit Haynes to call his wife until he made a statement, even though Haynes had made a spontaneous admission of guilt prior to his arrest.

Between *Stroble* and *Haynes* the cases fall almost randomly, but with a decided preference for admitting confessions. For example, in *Payne v. Arkansas*,[66] the Court threw out a confession given after the chief of police threatened to turn the suspect over to a mob. In *Thomas v. Arizona*,[67] decided the same day, the Court held voluntary a confession given *the day after* the sheriff thwarted an attempt by members of the posse to lynch the defendant at the time of arrest. The Court rejected the possibility that the suspect might have apprehended lynching at some future point, should he lose the favor of his protector, the sheriff. The state trial court apparently found this a quite credible theory, for it admitted an oral confession, given in court in the presence of the sheriff and one deputy, but it threw out two *subsequent* extra-judicial confessions made in the presence of additional deputies as "procured by threat of lynch."[68]

The lower courts could not have followed the Supreme Court's arbitrary course even if they had tried—and many of them did not even try. Left adrift in the vacuum of fundamental fairness, the lower courts typically admitted confessions that were obtained by abusive police tactics.[69] When the Supreme Court tried to clarify the test, the result was *Culombe v. Connecticut*—in which even the justices who agreed with a restatement of the test disagreed about how it applied to the instant facts.[70]

With respect to searches and seizures, the distinction drawn in *Rochin*[71] between unreasonable searches and unreasonable searches that shock the conscience was never substantiated. If what shocked the conscience in *Rochin* was flagrant lawlessness, then the Court should have suppressed the evidence gathered by the warrantless bugging of Irvine's bedroom.[72] If, instead, what was shocking was the extraction of evidence from the body, then the involuntary blood test in *Breithaupt*[73] should have resulted in suppression. The effect of these successive, unconvincing distinctions was to limit freedom from unreasonable searches and seizures to freedom from unreasonable aggravated assault.

The fundamental fairness test described the governing values too generally, compelling *ad hoc* decisions based on inconsistent values. At the level of theory fundamental fairness permitted the judges to throw out almost any conviction they found offensive. At the level of practice, fundamental fairness invited erroneous convictions and punitive police practices. The theory offended the legitimacy criterion; the practice offended the relevant policy considerations.

THE CRITIQUE OF SELECTIVE INCORPORATION

I shall evaluate the Warren Court criminal cases by concentrating on three famous landmarks: *Gideon v. Wainwright, Miranda v. Arizona*, and *Terry v. Ohio*. Others could do as well, but few students of criminal procedure would deny that these cases offer a representative sample of the Warren Court's work, a sample of great importance even in today's jurisprudence. If well-founded objections lie against these decisions, defenders of the Warren Court would be hard-pressed to justify the body of its legacy.

I shall argue that the Warren Court's turn to incorporation presented the justices with a recurring dilemma between the text of the incorporated amendments and the instrumental and rule-of-law values that matter so much in criminal cases. In a nutshell, fidelity to incorporation would have meant betraying instrumental reliability concerns, prompting the Court (as we have seen) to compromise incorporation to the point where the amendments lost most of their distinctive content. Due process values ultimately determined the shape of doctrine; indeed it would be considerably easier to derive *Gideon, Miranda*, and *Terry* from the due process clause than from the Fourth, Fifth, and Sixth Amendments. Incorporation, however, had the effect of *confining* the operation of due process values within the arbitrary confines of the amendments.

From the standpoint of legitimacy, the Warren Court first had to overcome the textual, historical, and precedential obstacles to incorporation itself. The Court then turned about and struggled to square the text, history, and precedent of the incorporated amendments with due process values. Essentially due process was reduced to the amendments, and the amendments were reduced to due process.

This result seems at odds with the text, which after all seems to suppose some differences between due process and the amendments. At the time of the Warren Court transition it was also at odds with prevailing precedent. The historical record on incorporation at the very least leaves room for the position that incorporation was not required by the text and history of the Fourteenth Amendment.

If the authoritative legal materials permit the play of pragmatic considerations, instrumental and rule-of-law values incline against the selective incorporation framework. Incorporation arbitrarily confined the operation of due process values to such categories as "searches and seizures," "the assistance of Counsel," and compelled self-incrimination. Within those categories, the Court managed to accommodate instrumental values only by compromising the supposedly inflexible text of the amendments. Even so, enough of the text survives to create arbitrary escape-hatches for the guilty.

Gideon

Probably no decision in the field of constitutional criminal procedure enjoys anything like the unqualified and unanimous approval judges, scholars, and ordinary citizens express about *Gideon v. Wainwright*. Everyone, myself included, agrees that the constitutional right of indigent defendants to appointed counsel announced in *Gideon* provides a critical safeguard against unjust conviction, and a noble symbol of our commitment to equal justice.[74] Yet *Gideon*, like more controversial precedents, is as written both illegitimate and unwise.

Gideon took the Sixth Amendment rather than the due process approach to the right-to-counsel problem. This turn soon exposed the conflict between the text of the incorporated amendments and the dominant values in criminal procedure. The text of the Sixth Amendment says that "[i]n *all* criminal prosecutions, the accused shall enjoy the right . . . to have the Assistance of Counsel for his defence." The text doesn't say anything about providing indigent defendants with publicly paid representation. From a historical perspective the likely purpose of the provision was to repudiate the English practice of *prohibiting* the defendant from appearing through counsel in certain classes of cases. The text, moreover, says "all" criminal prosecutions, not "some."

Gideon thus took a Procrustean approach to the Sixth Amendment. Where the amendment says the defendant may appear through counsel, *Gideon* stretches the amendment to cover subsidizing counsel for the poor. Where the amendment says "all," *Gideon* reduces the amendment to covering felony cases. Would the Court now or ever uphold a federal statute that forbade a misdemeanor defendant from appearing through privately retained counsel? If not, how can "all" mean "all" when the issue is prohibiting appearance through counsel, but mean "some" when the issue is providing indigent defense?

Defending *Gideon* pretty much requires something like a *Mathews v. Eldridge* procedural due process analysis of the costs and benefits of court-imposed procedural safeguards. But by relying on the Sixth Amendment (albeit in a distorted fashion) the Warren Court deflected attention from instrumental reliability in favor of a formalistic focus on the textually referenced "assistance of counsel." The incorporation approach necessarily failed to describe Gideon's constitutional right with appropriate generality. There is nothing *intrinsically* valuable about lawyers; that is why subsequent cases have developed the idea, if not the reality, that defense counsel's assistance must be *effective*. Instead, counsel is valuable to an accused because counsel is an essential safeguard against unjust conviction. Gideon's right was not to a lawyer, but to a trial that ran no more than some practically irreducible risk of falsely convicting him.

I say the incorporation approach necessarily circumscribes too narrowly this constitutional right because the focus on the specific procedures in the Sixth Amendment leads to the conclusion that *those procedures* are themselves the ultimate value protected by due process—as if people should be lining up to be indicted so that they could enjoy the inestimable privilege of counsel, jury trial, confrontation, or compulsory process. Instead, counsel is constitutionally required because without counsel the risk of unjust conviction rises beyond the irreducible.

This is not to say, as *Betts* announced, that the indigent sometimes can do without counsel. There simply is no felony case where counsel does not massively reduce the chances of a more serious conviction than is warranted by the law and the evidence. But *Gideon*'s selective incorporation foundation privileges the right to counsel because counsel is mentioned in the Sixth Amendment. The Sixth Amendment says nothing about private investigators, expert witnesses, discovery against the prosecution, or any of a number of other safeguards against unjust conviction that may very well be at least as important as counsel in particular cases. The Court has yet to recognize that without these safeguards, a trial can be as wanting in due process as a trial without counsel.[75] The delay in this recognition is at least partly attributable to selective incorporation.

Moreover, *Gideon*'s focus on the constitutionally irrelevant language of the Sixth Amendment has crippled serious scrutiny of *how well* counsel performs the constitutionally relevant function of defending the accused. Defense of the indigent, in many American jurisdictions, falls considerably below the level of effectiveness that what would trigger an electoral revolt if found in the prosecutor's office.[76] Yet because each defendant has "counsel"—no matter how overworked, inexperienced, lazy, or incompetent—the constitutional minima appear to be satisfied.

To be sure, there is a body of ineffective assistance doctrine.[77] But the crucial failures of the defense function occur before the trial. Pretrial investigation and savvy plea bargaining are the hallmarks of a competent defense. Their absence leaves the accused vulnerable to a one-sided and sometimes unnecessary trial. But so long as counsel plays the losing hand well at the trial, there will be no finding of ineffectiveness.

If incorporation has deflected attention from what counsel must do to fulfill the constitutional minima of a criminal *trial*, reliance on the Sixth Amendment's language has led to requiring counsel *before* trial on an arbitrary and sometimes perverse basis. For example, a Court less obsessed with selective incorporation would not have looked to the right to counsel as the principal security against erroneous eyewitness identifications. Principled concern for the risk of unjust conviction might have led to substantive safeguards against misidentification. Instead, the Warren Court reflexively focussed on the Sixth Amendment right to counsel, without recognizing that absent some substantive right against suggestive procedures, counsel could make at most a limited contribution to preventing a miscarriage of justice. When Justice Stewart finally persuaded a majority of the justices to recognize the right to counsel only from the moment of formal accusation,[78] constitutional scrutiny of identification procedures became a virtual dead letter.

Ordinarily, counsel consults with the accused at the first appearance after arrest, before the prosecutor has the opportunity to make a formal charging decision. But when the suspect remains at large for a sustained period of time following the crime, or when the suspect is identified only after a protracted investigation, formal charges may be filed before the arrest. *Massiah*[79] held that in these cases, statements obtained by undercover operatives in the absence of counsel are inadmissible. Thus, evidence obtained without brutality that would be welcomed if secured prior to indictment becomes tainted by an event of which the suspect and the investigators are equally ignorant.

Considered as a whole, right-to-counsel doctrine is dysfunctional. During the investigation, counsel may be required so that the disclosure of probative evidence of guilt is nullified, but is not required to develop probative evidence of innocence. Focus on whether the accused has a right to counsel during the investigation has deflected attention from other potential procedural safeguards that might do far more than counsel can to prevent a miscarriage of justice. After the investigation is closed, so long as counsel puts on a show of advocacy, the Sixth Amendment, like the judicial conscience, is satisfied.

Miranda

The most difficult challenge to any critic of *Miranda* is to overcome all the bad arguments other critics have made against that decision. From the *Miranda* dissenting opinions to Justice Scalia's dissent in *Dickerson*, *Miranda*'s critics have done little more than point out that unrestrained police questioning can extract probative evidence of vicious crimes. Undoubtedly this point is true, but those who make it never face up to the contradiction, implicit or explicit, in squaring the objection with the Constitution.

Not one critic of *Miranda* claims that individuals, in custody or not, have no right to remain silent in response to official inquiry.[80] No one questions the defendant's right to stand silent in court. For more than a century the Supreme Court has upheld the right of a witness before the grand jury to refuse to answer questions that might incriminate. Where are the critics of the Fuller Court, who handcuffed the law enforcement team back in *Counselman v. Hitchcock*?[81]

But if the critics of *Miranda* fail to reconcile the desire for evidence with the right to remain silent, the authors and defenders of *Miranda* also entertain these same inconsistent value judgments. If *Miranda*'s critics inexplicably support the Fifth Amendment, *Miranda* itself inexplicably allows the accused to make a "knowing, intelligent, and voluntary waiver" of the right to silence under the very same pressures that are thought to constitute compulsion in the first place. Waiver is common, indeed so common that empirical studies consistently show that *Miranda* has not diminished significantly the effectiveness of police interrogation.[82] That finding, in turn, provides powerful evidence that interrogation is compulsion.

The judicial ambivalence about police interrogation betrays the doctrinal illegitimacy that infects *Miranda*'s roots in the Fifth Amendment privilege. If due process unequivocally protected the right to contumaciously refuse to answer nonviolent questions, the Court would not permit waiver without consultation with counsel. Certainly the accused is not permitted to plead guilty without such consultation. We can only imagine the judicial reaction to the suggestion that the accused be "permitted" to enter a guilty plea after arrest, but before presentment.

The reasoning in *Miranda* runs as follows. The due process clause incorporates the Fifth Amendment privilege; police interrogation amounts to compulsion within the meaning of the Fifth Amendment; but the warning and offer of counsel dispel that compulsion, enabling the suspect to make an uncompelled waiver. The premise rested on the then-newly minted decision in *Malloy v. Hogan*,[83] in which the Court announced that the Fourteenth Amendment incorporated the Fifth. *Malloy* suffers all the liabilities of selective incorporation generally. Even among the incorporation decisions, *Malloy* deserves the booby-prize for legitimacy, inasmuch as the justices there overruled two, rather than one, of their own precedents.[84]

Thus, the first of *Miranda*'s three justifications was at best dubiously legitimate, and the remaining two contradict one another. Like the decision in *Gideon*, the focus on incorporation diverts attention from the heart of the matter. In *Gideon* the heart of the matter is what kind of defense representation is essential to prevent unjust conviction; in *Miranda* the central question is how to prevent police brutality without giving up confessions. Some sort of compromise is inevitable. It would, however, be much easier to justify a *Miranda*-style compromise from the due process clause than from the privilege against self-incrimination.[85] Due process values surely regulate the quest for truth through potentially cruel or unreliable questioning. Nothing in the text of the due process clause or the values it reflects demands the same doublethink required by the *Miranda* waiver doctrine.

Moreover, the reliance on the self-incrimination privilege rather than due process seriously curtails the range of possible compromises, whether judicial or legislative. *Miranda* leaves interrogation in the hands of the police, because once the accused is represented by counsel the privilege will defeat interrogation ever after. The police continue to have an incentive to extract confessions through violence, intimidation, manipulation, and deception.

As with *Gideon*, incorporation confined the operation of due process values. There is nothing in the self-incrimination privilege from which judges might derive recording requirements or bright-line time limits. Yet the incorporated privilege bars in-court questioning when the suspect has the assistance of counsel, which might well secure more evidence with less cruelty than police interrogation. As *Dickerson* recognizes, *Miranda* may now be too deeply embedded in police and popular culture to be disturbed. All the more reason, then, to regret the due process road not taken.

Terry

Terry v. Ohio[86] arose from an incident in Cleveland on Halloween of 1963, a little more than two years after *Mapp*. Officer McFadden was on patrol for pickpockets and shoplifters in a section of downtown Cleveland. His attention focused on two men, Terry and Chilton. One of the two left the other and walked past some stores, paused in front of one of them, and then walked back to the other. Then the second man walked down the same block, looking inside the store window, and then rejoining his partner. The two repeated this behavior for ten minutes, making twelve sorties between them. During this period, they were briefly joined by a third man, Katz, who spoke with them briefly and then left, heading west on Euclid Avenue.

Terry and Chilton eventually followed the path taken by Katz. McFadden followed them; and when they rejoined Katz in front of another store, McFadden identified himself as a police officer and demanded the names of the three. One of the suspects mumbled, and McFadden grabbed Terry and patted down Terry's overcoat. McFadden felt a pistol in one of the pockets.

The policeman then ordered all three suspects into the store, and lined them against a wall with their hands up. A further frisk discovered another pistol in Chilton's coat, but none on the person of Katz. Terry was charged with carrying a concealed weapon, and moved to suppress the evidence as the fruit of an illegal search.

The prosecution defended the search as incident to a lawful arrest. The Ohio courts rejected this approach, holding that McFadden did not have probable cause to arrest Terry until after the frisk. Nonetheless, the Ohio courts reasoned that McFadden's actions had been reasonable.[87] The trio's suspicious behavior called for further investigation.[88] If McFadden had the right to stop and question them, his own safety required a frisk for weapons.[89]

The Supreme Court affirmed, in an opinion by Chief Justice Warren. Warren began by sketching the policy debate about street encounters, in which the police "need [for] an escalating set of flexible responses, graduated in relation to the amount of information they possess" competed with the risk of "substantial interference with liberty and personal security."[90] The exclusionary rule, Warren wrote, although concerned with "the imperative of judicial integrity," is primarily a deterrent, and the rule "is powerless to deter invasions of constitutionally guaranteed rights where the police either have no interest in prosecuting or are willing to forgo successful prosecution in the interest of serving some other goal."[91]

Warren was certainly candid to lead with policy arguments. His subsequent discussion of the legal question is predetermined by the policy premises; so adroit is his handling of the Fourth Amendment question that that Amendment poses no obstacle at all to reaching the desired result.

Arguably, Ohio should prevail because Terry had not been "seized" or "searched," only "stopped" and "frisked." The majority "emphatically reject[ed] this notion."[92] "It must be recognized," the Court wrote, "that whenever a police officer accosts an individual and restrains his freedom to walk away, he has 'seized' that person."[93] And to say that a frisk of the person for weapons is not a search would be "nothing less than sheer torture of the English language."[94] " 'Search' and 'seizure' are not talismans."[95]

The danger attending this textual argument is that it proves too much. The language of the Fourth Amendment seems to imply that searches and seizures are "reasonable" only when supported by probable cause. Otherwise, as Justice Douglas pointed out in dissent, "the police have greater authority to make a 'seizure' and conduct a 'search' than a judge has to authorize such action."[96]

Not even Douglas denied that exigency justified an exception to the warrant requirement. But how much evidence of crime did the police require before stopping a person for investigation?

The *Terry* opinion is evasive on this question. Warren wrote that "[i]t would have been poor police work"[97] for McFadden to have done nothing. The "crux of this case, however, is not the propriety of Officer McFadden's taking steps to investigate petitioner's suspicious behavior, but rather, whether there was justification for McFadden's invasion of Terry's personal security by searching him for weapons in the course of that investigation."[98] The Court held that the lesser intrusion of a frisk could be justified by something short of probable cause.[99]

Concurring, Justice Harlan argued that the Court had put the cart before the horse by putting the frisk before the stop.[100] If McFadden was "reasonable" in demanding to know what Terry was up to, then the officer's safety made it reasonable to conduct the frisk for weapons. "There is no reason why an officer, rightfully but forcibly confronting a person suspected of a serious crime, should have to ask one question and take the risk that the answer might be a bullet."[101]

In *Terry*'s two companion cases, the justices again dealt only obliquely with the degree of suspicion an officer must entertain before stopping an individual for investigation. In one case, *Sibron v. New York*, Officer Martin observed Sibron converse with known narcotics addicts on several occasions over a period of several hours. Ultimately, Martin escorted Sibron out of a restaurant, and said "[y]ou know what I am after." When Sibron responded by reaching a hand into a pocket, Martin reached in and pulled out heroin.

The Court held that the heroin should have been excluded. "The inference that persons who talk to narcotics addicts are engaged in the criminal traffic in narcotics is simply not the sort of reasonable inference required to support an intrusion by the police upon an individual's personal security."[102] As for the officer's safety, Martin had no reason to believe that Sibron was either armed or violent; and in any event the search he conducted was not the pat-down for weapons but a search for narcotics that bypassed the pat-down stage.[103]

In the final case, *Peters v. New York*, Samuel Lasky, an off-duty police officer, heard a noise in the hallway of his apartment building. He saw two men whom he had not seen before in twelve years as a tenant, tip-toeing down the hallway in a furtive matter. After calling the police, Lasky stepped into the hallway and slammed the door; at this, the two suspects fled. Lasky caught up with Peters; a pat-down of the person indicated a hard object that might have been a knife. When Lasky pulled it from Peter's pocket, it turned out to be a plastic envelope containing burglar's tools. The Court upheld the admission of the burglar's tools on the theory that Lasky had probable cause to arrest Peters, so that a warrantless search was justified as incident to a lawful arrest.[104]

Now the three cases, read together, make a great deal of sense from a policy standpoint. But it is virtually impossible to accept *Terry* without admitting that there are some "searches" that are constitutionally permitted based on "reasonable grounds" falling short of probable cause. In *Sibron* the majority admitted as much: "If Patrolman Martin lacked probable cause for an arrest, however, his seizure and search of Sibron might still have been justified at the outset if he had reasonable grounds to believe that Sibron was armed and dangerous."[105]

The majority's insistence on treating *Peters* simply as a case of a traditional arrest reveals some hesitancy in accepting this new standard of Fourth Amendment reasonableness. Why hesitate? Presumably the justices shared the concern of Douglas that reducing the Fourth Amendment to an inquiry into "reasonableness," unconstrained by any implications from the Warrant Clause about what makes searches "reasonable," was both illegitimate and a threat to individual liberty.

Harlan was willing to acknowledge openly what the majority hesitated to admit—that some police intrusions require justification, but not the traditional showing of probable cause. For Harlan the cases raised questions about the scope of the protections "afforded by the Fourth *and* Fourteenth Amendments."[106] Measuring the degree of justification by the magnitude of the intrusion was a familiar feature of due process adjudication, to which Harlan remained committed. But to square the stop-and-frisk rules with selective incorporation is a daunting challenge. In subsequent cases the Court has adopted the Harlan view. Settled doctrine now authorizes the police to detain forcibly suspicious persons for a brief period of investigation, when there are articulable facts amounting to more than mere suspicion but less than probable cause. When similar facts support an inference that the suspect might be armed and dangerous, a protective frisk is likewise authorized to protect the police during the stop-for-investigation.

Although I approve of the Court's decision in *Terry*,[107] I believe that case reveals as much about the defects of the Warren Court's selective incorporation decisions as any other. Forced to hammer the square peg of state police practices into the round hole of the Fourth Amendment's language, the *Terry* Court pretty much disincorporated the Fourth Amendment. "Searches and seizures are not talismans," and police who search and seize may "lack probable cause" yet have "reasonable grounds."

If the Court had adhered to selective incorporation, it would have been hard pressed to deny that Officer McFadden had violated the Fourth Amendment—despite the apparent reasonableness of his actions.[108] Terry had been both seized and searched; exigent circumstances could have excused the failure to obtain a warrant, but not the absence of probable cause. By reducing the Fourth Amendment to an inquiry into reasonableness, uninformed by the dictates of the warrant clause, the *Terry* Court admitted that the incorporation of the Fourth Amendment had failed.

What was unique about *Terry* is that the Court did not revert to *Betts*-style case-by-case adjudication. Rather, the Court candidly consulted the competing policy considerations, and then issued a general standard—the reasonable suspicion standard—that could guide police and lower courts. Like the decision in *Miranda*, *Terry* recognized that the Court could impose standards of general applicability in the course of deciding constitutional cases. Unlike *Miranda*, however, the *Terry* decision was not beset by an internal contradiction.

The generality of the Fourth Amendment's language enabled this approach. *Terry* succeeded in accommodating selective incorporation with sensible policy considerations only because the language of the Fourth Amendment's first clause so greatly resembles the language of due process analysis. *Terry* illustrates two vital points: that selective incorporation bears only an arbitrary relation to the relevant values in criminal procedure, and that the courts can articulate workable standards derived from more general constitutional language. Given the dubious legitimacy of selective incorporation, the first point is a dispositive one against that approach. And, given that interpretive desperation inspired the *Betts* doctrine of case-by-case adjudication, the second point is a dispositive one against fundamental fairness. In short, fundamental fairness described the governing values too generally; selective incorporation described those values too particularly.

THE CRITIQUE OF CONSERVATIVE BALANCING

The Warren Court precedents presented the conservative majority that emerged in the seventies with a dilemma that continues to trouble the Court. The conservatives were unwilling either to perpetuate the status quo, or to overrule landmark decisions. As we have seen, they responded to this dilemma by adopting a stock rhetorical strategy. At the first stage, the conservatives would characterize the outcome of the case as uncertain, either because the constitutional right was not self-defining or because the appropriate remedy for a conceded violation was a matter of judicial discretion. At the second stage, the justices resolved the uncertainty by balancing the rights of the suspect against the interests of society. With rare exceptions, the Court would conclude that the latter outweighed the former.

At one level, this approach is a reversion to fundamental fairness. The balancing process permits any value to compete with any other. Nonetheless, the Burger Court did not revert to case-by-case fundamental fairness analysis. Like the Warren Court in *Terry* and *Miranda*, the Burger Court balanced on a wholesale rather than a retail basis. For example, in curtailing the exclusionary rule the Court did not return to the *Wolf-Rochin-Breithaupt* doctrine of discretionary exclusion in individual cases. Instead, the Court crafted categorical exceptions, allowing the use of tainted evidence before grand juries,[109] to impeach the defendant,[110] in collateral civil proceedings,[111] and so on.

Within the constraints of legitimate interpretation, any regime of constitutional criminal procedure should devote itself openly to the competing values. And unless those values are articulated in general standards, lower courts and law enforcement agencies will be unable to conform to them; and similarly situated suspects and defendants will be differentiated arbitrarily.

That said, I am constrained to say that the modern balancing approach combines the worst aspects, respectively, of fundamental fairness and selective incorporation. The interests of the suspect are seen through the narrow lens of the Bill of Rights, while the interests of the government are as wide as the horizon of a sympathetic judiciary. Typically, the Burger and Rehnquist Courts balanced the government's interest in proving guilt against the suspect's interests in a way that would not have permitted the decision of the precedent invoked by the defendant. The resulting body of law is neither legitimate nor tailored to promote the appropriate values.

After twenty years of conservative balancing, constitutional criminal procedure is shot through with arbitrary distinctions. A statement obtained without a waiver from a suspect in custody is inadmissible under *Miranda*, but, under *Harris*, will be heard by the jury if the defendant takes the stand.[112] Questioning in violation of *Miranda* can be justified by public safety under *Quarles*,[113] but not if the connection to public safety stems from the need to convict the suspect, such as those in *Edwards*[114] and *Minnick*[115] who had committed murder. Under *Edwards* a suspect who invokes the right to counsel is immune to further questioning, while a suspect who invokes the right to silence may be reinterrogated under *Mosley*.[116] If the police stage a conversation to play on a suspect's better motives, they may not, under *Innis*,[117] be found to have interrogated the suspect; but if the suspect, under *Bradshaw*, asks "what is going to happen to me now?" then he has initiated a conversation about the case and exposed himself to further questioning.[118]

Tapping a suspect's telephone is a search, but not if the caller happens to be an undercover agent.[119] If, however, the suspect has been formally charged, then the agent has violated the Sixth Amendment, even if neither the agent nor the suspect knows an indictment is outstanding.[120] Under *Acevedo* the police need a warrant if they execute a search of the suspect's bag on his driveway, but not if they wait until he has actually entered his automobile.[121] Under *Hicks* the police need a warrant before checking the serial numbers of possibly stolen stereo components,[122] but under *Watson* they need no warrant for the vastly greater intrusion of an arrest.[123] And, under *Hoffa*,[124] *Smith*,[125] and *Miller*[126] they need neither warrant nor probable cause to plant a spy in the suspect's intimate circle, to record his correspondents whether by mail or telephone, or to examine his bank records.

Under *Strickland* the accused has the right to the effective assistance of counsel,[127] but under *Cronic* ineffectiveness cannot be inferred without proof in a record made by a lawyer who is plainly unqualified to try the case. The government must prove guilt beyond reasonable doubt under *Winship*[128] and *Mullaney*,[129] but the defendant must prove self-defense beyond reasonable doubt under *Martin*.[130] Under *Chambers v. Mississippi*[131] the accused has the right to introduce probative exculpatory evidence, but under *Arizona v. Youngblood*[132] the government has no obligation to preserve evidence that is potentially conclusive of innocence.

Strained arguments can be offered to justify each of these distinctions, but at some point critics of the Court are entitled to resort to Occam's razor. The case law abounds with unconvincing distinctions because the Burger and Rehnquist Courts were unwilling either to follow or to overrule Warren Court cases.

Distinctions such as these do not rest on neutral principles, unless naked precedent counts as a "reason quite transcending the result in the case at hand."

Naked precedent does not supply such a reason, whether one believes in a strong or a weak account of precedent's authority.[133] On a strong account, the conservative justices should have adhered to Warren Court precedents honestly. They should have recognized that precedents are more than judgments associated with facts; they are judgments associated with facts by a normative justification. Good lawyers can almost always express that justification at many different levels of generality; nonetheless the former decision must remain justifiable if the latter is to be squared with precedent. A Court that was truly bound by *Miranda* would not have decided *Harris, Mosley,* and *Quarles.*

Dickerson offers an excellent example of how the Court has struggled with the problem of the illegitimate precedent. The prophylactic-rules cases rejected *Miranda*'s deep justification in factually indistinguishable cases. This turn left *Miranda* itself eligible for overruling, but in the state *Miranda* cases different majorities proceeded in accordance with *Miranda*'s original justification. Now the Court has reaffirmed *Miranda* without explicitly questioning the prophylactic-rules cases.

Dickerson makes no attempt to distinguish, or repudiate, *Tucker.* Chief Justice Rehnquist wrote both *Tucker* and *Dickerson.*[134] *Dickerson* purports to distinguish *Elstad* but the attempt is patently unconvincing.[135] Justice Stevens dissented in *Elstad* but joined the majority in *Dickerson.*[136] Legal minds as formidable as these cannot possibly subscribe to the *Dickerson* opinion's feeble attempt to distinguish *Elstad.* Just as in a famous scene from *The Wizard of Oz,* we are solemnly enjoined to *pay no attention to those cases behind the curtain!*

True, the precise issue before the Court was whether government agents are constitutionally obliged to give the warnings, not the scope of the exclusionary remedy. The steady flow of criminal cases, however, means that there is no easy way to avoid decision. For example, there was a fruits issue resolved against Dickerson by the district court.[137]

Simultaneously with the decision in *Dickerson* the Court denied certiorari in a circuit court case denying qualified immunity to police who question suspects who invoke their *Miranda* rights, a practice that apparently had become common due to the admissibility of derivative evidence and of tainted statements to impeach.[138] Now the lower courts must grapple with these issues in the light of a *Miranda* opinion that secured the agreement of both Rehnquist and Stevens, who have hitherto expressed incompatible views.

The Court's opinion might have taken a more scrupulous attitude toward *stare decisis,* either by articulating some genuine distinctions between the impeachment or fruits cases and *Miranda,* or by expressly disapproving prior decisions that cannot be reconciled with *Miranda*'s reaffirmed constitutional stature. There *are* plausible arguments for reconciling the prophylactic-rules cases with the state *Miranda* cases. Professor Weisselberg has pointed out that in *Harris, Tucker,* and *Elstad* the police violated *Miranda* in good faith.[139] The impeachment exception might be justified on other theories, such as the idea that the accused who takes the stand waives the privilege against self-incrimination.[140] Likewise the fruits cases might be reconciled with *Kastigar* by focusing on the comparative haste and uncertainty of police investigations relative to grand jury investigations, and the corresponding difficulty of proving independent source or inevitable discovery in the *Miranda* context.[141] Alternatively, the *Dickerson* opinion could have directly repudiated the prophylactic-rules cases. Instead the Court clings obstinately to the two lines of cases that were inconsistent enough to require granting certiorari in *Dickerson* in the first place.

Chapter 6 develops a principled yet pragmatic approach to *stare decisis* in criminal procedure cases, an approach that calls for faithful adherence to the justifying logic of prior decisions by individual justice but that also calls for an open willingness to overrule prior cases when they have lost the support of a current majority. For now it should suffice to say that conservative balancing offended important rule-of-law values by departing from precedent without either principled reasons for distinguishing precedents or a forthright willingness to repudiate them.

If, as I have argued, the Warren Court's selective incorporation doctrine had illegitimately focused on the Bill of Rights, rather than on the values served by the instrumental theory of criminal procedure, some realignment of doctrine with those values was in order. But the conservative justices never recognized that innocent people can be punished in the investigation process even if they are never charged. Nor did they honor the preference for false negatives over false positives in the process of adjudication. The legacy of the Burger and Rehnquist Courts is an unprincipled body of law that fails to serve the appropriate policy considerations. Consider, by way of examples, the exclusionary rule cases, the confession cases, and the fair-trial cases.

In *Calandra*, the Court correctly ascribed a deterrent purpose to the exclusionary rule.[142] But it then characterized the marginal deterrent effect of suppression in grand jury proceedings as "speculative" and thus outweighed by the cost to the truth-finding mission of the criminal process.[143] The Court's approach is illegitimate and unwise.

The balancing process in this instance is illegitimate because it counts violations of the Constitution as desirable. If the police had complied with constitutional standards, the evidence subject to suppression would never have been discovered.[144] To view the "loss" of the evidence as a "cost" treats the acquisition of the evidence as a gain.

The Court's logic reached an embarrassing conclusion in the *Leon* case. The text of the Fourth Amendment provides that "no warrants shall issue, but upon probable cause." The Court held that when a warrant issues without probable cause, the evidence is nonetheless admissible if the police acted in good faith. Because good-faith reliance on an illegal warrant also immunizes the police from damage actions,[145] the Court in effect eliminated all remedies for a conceded violation of the Constitution.[146] The costs of the warrant process may make the exclusionary rule redundant in the warrant context;[147] but the elevation of a policy preference for evidence over a constitutional preference for privacy is clearly illegitimate.

There are situations in which the exclusionary rule causes the loss of evidence that the police might have obtained without violating the Constitution. The police may have had probable cause but failed to seek a warrant when one was required; or they may have lacked probable cause but could have established it with some additional investigation. In these cases the "criminal is to go free because the constable has blundered."[148] But the Court never even made an effort to distinguish evidence that was beyond the constitutional power of the government and evidence that might have been lawfully seized given better police work.

In any event, pecking away at the exclusionary rule is a mistake from the standpoint of policy. The Burger Court's exclusionary rule cases express skepticism about whether the exclusionary rule actually deters.[149] This agnosticism is hard to explain; the evidence supporting the rule's deterrent effect is overwhelming.

In the immediate aftermath of *Mapp*, warrant use skyrocketed and police-training programs began to focus on the Fourth Amendment.[150] While two early studies found that suppression in the city of Chicago was so common as to call into question the rule's effectiveness,[151] subsequent studies of multiple locations have consistently found that exclusion is quite rare[152]—indicating that the rule in fact deters. Police departments demonstrably respond to changes in Fourth Amendment law.[153] Experienced law-enforcement officials confirm that the rule influences their behavior.[154]

The process of recognizing categorical exceptions, in all probability, dilutes the rule's deterrent effect. The Court has created these exceptions one at a time, never asking whether their cumulative effect might threaten deterrence. There are now a great many uses for illegal evidence; the exclusionary rule will only bite if (1) the suspect does not either plead guilty or win a dismissal prior to the ruling on the suppression motion; (2) the suspect does not take the stand in his own defense; (3) the evidence would not have been discovered eventually anyway; (4) the tainted evidence does not lead to admissible derivative evidence that is as probative of guilt as the lost evidence. Obviously, the Court has increased the incentives to search illegally.

True, no empirical study documents the reduced deterrence attributable to the exceptions. The Court is therefore correct in a sense when it describes the marginal deterrent benefits of the rule in particular contexts as "speculative." But we do not need empirical evidence to justify the belief that increasing the incentives for behavior will cause more of that behavior.

The justices do not doubt that the criminal law deters the commission of crimes, even crimes of recklessness or negligence. They do not doubt that the tort system deters corporations from marketing dangerous products or employing negligent agents. The Supreme Court itself promulgated Federal Rule of Evidence 407, which excludes evidence of subsequent remedial measures in tort suits out of the fear that admissibility would deter defendants from undertaking the needed repairs.[155] The supposition that the exceptions to the exclusionary rule will not dilute its deterrent effect flies in the face of the legal system's working assumptions about incentives and behavior.

In *United States v. Payner*[156] the government deliberately took advantage of the standing doctrine by burglarizing the motel room of the suspect's accountant to obtain the records needed to prove tax evasion. The Court approved the admission of the evidence, even though it was quite clear that the standing doctrine had invited a deliberate violation of the Constitution. The case illustrates that exceptions to the exclusionary rule in fact weaken deterrence, and that the Court's hostility is ultimately directed less to the exclusionary remedy than to the constitutional right.

The Court's approach to *Miranda* reflects the same false fidelity to precedent, and the same indifference to police overreaching, as the exclusionary rule cases. On the one hand, in *Harris, Tucker, Mosley,* and *Quarles* the Court described the rights conferred by *Miranda* as "not themselves rights protected by the Constitution"[157] but rather required only by a "prophylactic rule."[158] On the other hand, in *Edwards, Roberson,* and *Minnick* the Court excluded statements solely because the police had not ceased questioning in the face of a request for counsel. If the *Harris* line of cases is correct, then the Court has no authority to reverse the state convictions in the *Edwards* line. If the *Edwards* line of cases is correct, then the Court is subverting constitutional rights in the *Harris* line.[159]

Like the exclusionary rule cases, the *Harris* line gives the police considerable incentive to violate *Miranda*. The suspect's invocation may be seen by the court as equivocal; a subsequent statement may be seen as initiated by the suspect. Even if the courts deem the statement tainted under *Miranda*, the government might still use it if the suspect testifies. Since the police cannot expect to obtain a statement after defense counsel enters the case, they have nothing to lose by disregarding *Miranda*.

The police therefore have the incentive to question until they get the answer they desire.[160] At worst, it will provide them with leads and the prosecutor with impeachment material. Those hostile to the privilege against self-incrimination may see this result as desirable. It should be remembered, however, that police interrogation is not a deposition. It is, as the case may be, manipulative, confrontational, or fraudulent. Some innocent persons confess under its pressures;[161] many more are needlessly subjected to them.

The modern Court has claimed that *Miranda* was illegitimate. Yet the justices have refused to overrule that landmark decision. Instead, they have at times limited *Miranda* for reasons inconsistent with any justification it might have, and at times applied *Miranda* at least as vigorously as the Warren Court intended. As a result, professional criminals enjoy an escape-hatch from any questioning, however gentle, while people who may not be guilty are subjected to a degrading process that can in extreme cases lead to an unjust conviction. Whether from the standpoint of legitimacy or policy, the confessions this process extracts from the guilty fail to justify its contradictions and its cruelties.

Parallel defects have marred the Court's approach to the criminal trial. Never questioning *Duncan v. Louisiana*,[162] the Court has held that a jury can be composed of six persons,[163] and that the jurors need not be unanimous to convict.[164] Without questioning *Pointer v. Texas*,[165] the Court has held that any long-standing hearsay exception—however unreliable the evidence may be in a particular case—satisfies constitutional confrontation requirements.[166] Without questioning *In re Winship*,[167] the Court has held that the burden of proof on affirmative defenses can be shifted to the defense.[168]

Consider, finally, the right-to-counsel cases. On the one hand, the Court continues to subscribe to *Gideon*. On the other hand, counsel will not be deemed ineffective unless a discrete, negligent error, or series of discrete negligent errors, resulted in demonstrable prejudice to the defendant. In principle, the *Strickland* test asks the right question, by concentrating on the fairness of the trial rather than on the mere presence of a licensed lawyer. In practice, however, the requirement that the defendant demonstrate the likelihood of a different result on the basis of a record prepared by incompetent counsel in practice nullifies the supposed right.

The accused has not so much the right to counsel, but the right to defense representation that does not cause a complete "breakdown in the adversary process."[169] As a result, an unknowable number of individuals will be convicted of crimes they did not commit. No one can say how their cases might have come out if first-class lawyers had represented the defense. Those who agree that the prevention of false convictions deserves priority over the prevention of false acquittals cannot regard the absence of a "breakdown" in the proceedings with equanimity.

In each instance, the justification for the later decision undermines the justification for the precedent that the Court purports to respect. In each instance, the risk of unjust conviction or punitive police practices is needlessly increased. The Court repeatedly has balanced values not affirmed by the Constitution against values affirmed by the Constitution. Typically, the extra-constitutional values have prevailed over the constitutional values. The Constitution, moreover, *justifiably* exalts security against false conviction and arbitrary restraint over the discovery of evidence of guilt. The Court's narrow focus on the value of proving guilt at trial has meant that the wrong values have enjoyed priority in the balancing process.

6

Criminal Procedure Through the Lens of the Fourteenth Amendment

The first four chapters of this study traced the history of constitutional criminal procedure through its basic phases—fundamental fairness, selective incorporation, and conservative balancing. Chapter 5 set forth a critique of each of these regimes according to criteria set by a conventionalist theory of constitutional interpretation and an instrumental theory of criminal procedure. The instrumental theory in turn has two primary components, the exclusivity principle and the adjudication requirement. Although the instrumental theory largely incorporates independent values such as individual privacy and dignity, it cannot capture the value of equality among persons, which accordingly deserves independent respect and analysis.

This chapter develops an alternative model of constitutional criminal procedure, a theory based directly on the Fourteenth Amendment. Although the model includes a vigorous role for the equal protection clause, the heart of the theory is the connection between the traditional meaning of due process and the instrumental theory of procedure. Substantively, due process always has meant that the government must *justify* physical restraint of individuals. Procedurally, due process always has meant that individuals charged with crime be given the opportunity of a fair trial before punishment.

The theory defended here applies these ancient principles to modern conditions. Substantively, the theory holds that the police may not deprive individuals of their liberty in the name of law enforcement unless the severity of the deprivation bears a reasonable relationship to the prospect of preventing or punishing an offense. Procedurally, the theory holds that those accused of crime be given the opportunity for an instrumentally reliable trial. The Supreme Court's general procedural due process test—the three-factor test announced in *Mathews v. Eldridge*—properly frames the inquiry into instrumental reliability. Procedural due process also regulates police investigations, because the reliability of the trial often turns on the reliability of the antecedent investigation.

It might seem that insisting on justifications for liberty-limiting methods of investigation, fair trials to ascertain guilt and innocence, and racial fairness in criminal justice follow naturally from the text and history of the Fourteenth Amendment's first section. Yet as we have seen, the modern law has marginalized the due process and equal protection clauses in criminal cases. The aim of this chapter is to persuade you that a doctrinal focus on the Fourteenth Amendment could do more than current law to secure the appropriate values within the limits of legitimate adjudication. Before defending the theory's interpretation of due process, or turning to the equal protection clause, I would like to explain it, placing special emphasis on the difference between substantive and procedural due process.

PROCEDURAL VERSUS SUBSTANTIVE DUE PROCESS

As the *Hurtado* opinion recognizes,[1] imposing due process as a limit on the legislature in a republican government presents a troubling dilemma. If the government's obligation to follow the law is satisfied by compliance with a statute, then the legislature is effectively unregulated by the constitutional provision. On the other hand, if legislation in a republic is not "the law of the land," then what else counts as higher law with the power to trump the expressed will of the polity?

Understood as a limit on executive, administrative, and judicial decisions, due process does not present any such daunting challenge. To be sure it is necessary to define "life, liberty and property" independently of legislative classification, but this is natural enough with respect to life and liberty, and a theory of property based on custom and expectation can achieve a legislation-independent constitutional definition of "property."[2]

Thus a great divide separates substantive from procedural due process. Substantive due process can be classified as a limit on legislative decisions to impose obligations on private parties. Procedural due process can be classified as the official obligation to provide a fair hearing to an aggrieved individual whenever the government claims the positive law authorizes injuring that individual. Of course procedural due process restrains the legislature *with respect to procedure.*[3] Trial by ordeal, or official fact-finding by state-employed psychics, would not be saved from constitutional attack by legislative authorization. But procedural due process does not speak to the constitutionality of legislative decisions to regulate the primary conduct of individuals—to impose duties or liabilities when legislatively defined facts are present.

Procedural due process, however, does entail a substantive constitutional right against arbitrary physical injury or restraint. Suppose the legislature passed a statute providing that John Smith shall serve ten years in prison, or that all Jews shall be gassed. Scrupulously fair trials to determine whether the defendant really is John Smith, or really is Jewish, would not insulate the statute from a due process challenge.

That may be why the Barons at Runnymeade did not insist solely on modes of procedure but insisted also that punishment be authorized by the law of the land.[4] In their day the law of the land was customary, feudal law, as distinct from the royal prerogative. The basic idea that legislative or executive designation, standing alone, does not qualify as cause for physical restraint, nonetheless is a permanent and essential feature of due process.

As articulated by the modern Supreme Court, individuals have a substantive due process right to personal liberty that can be abridged by the government only upon a showing that the restraints imposed are narrowly tailored to serve a compelling state interest.[5] The cases in which the Court has approved detention other than as punishment for crime—quarantine laws,[6] preventive detention,[7] and civil commitment[8]—can all be squared with this demanding test. Call this right to freedom from physical injury or restraint absent compelling justification "minimal substantive due process."

Soon after the *Hurtado* decision, the Court went far beyond minimal substantive due process and began to treat Fourteenth Amendment due process as a limitation on the police power of the state legislatures.[9] This development is not as illegitimate or illogical as often suggested. The basic arguments against substantive due process are: (1) that the text of the due process clause refers to procedure, not to substance;[10] (2) that the framers understood due process as a requirement for judicial procedure in criminal cases, not as a substantive limit on legislation;[11] and (3) that substantive due process would authorize standardless judicial review of legislation, contrary to the democratic process set up by the rest of the Constitution.[12] Each of these arguments is plausible, but none is conclusive.

Textually, it begs the question to say that "due process of *law*" refers to substance rather than procedure. If the law of the land is customary or natural law, then there is nothing contradictory or illogical about the proposition that a statute contrary to fundamental principles of justice violates the law of the land. There is more wit than wisdom in Dean Ely's equation of substantive due process with "green pastel redness."[13] "Midnight blue" would sound like a nonsense phrase to someone armed with a dictionary but without experience in common English usage. Nineteenth-century lawyers often thought of "law" as customary or natural law,[14] and on that understanding it is perfectly logical to say that a statute contrary to fundamental principles of justice is not law.

Antebellum state cases involving "law of the land" clauses, with some exceptions,[15] did not endorse substantive due process review. But these cases have less bearing on the Fourteenth Amendment than antebellum Supreme Court cases. If we look to the Supreme Court decisions, we find that *Murray's Lessee* indeed took a procedural view of due process.[16] Nothing in *Murray's Lessee*, however, denies the existence of substantive due process. Indeed, the Court there specifically noted that the due process clause restrains the legislature with respect to procedure.[17] In other cases, the Supreme Court gave the Fifth Amendment due process clause a distinctly substantive content.

Bloomer v. McQuewan, decided in 1853, arose after a licensee purchased some machines and a license to use them from the holder of the patent on the machine.[18] The license ran for the duration of the patent, but the patent was extended by a private bill in Congress. The issue was whether the licensee's right to use the machines previously purchased was extended along with the life of the patent. The Court held that it did, and added that any other construction of the law would call its constitutionality into question under the Fifth Amendment. A special act of Congress terminating the purchaser's right to use the machines before the original patent had run out, the Court said, "certainly could not be regarded as due process of law."[19]

Bloomer might be written off as an obscure patent-law case, but there is nothing obscure about the next substantive due process case in the Supreme Court. In *Dred Scott v. Sandford*,[20] the Court struck down the Missouri Compromise as unconstitutional. Chief Justice Taney's opinion rests the unconstitutionality of the legislation on the Fifth Amendment's due process clause.[21] In Taney's view, if slaves became free in the territories by the force of federal legislation, then Congress would have deprived the slaveholders of their property. Taney did not rely on the takings clause, which would have left the door open for abolition coupled with the payment of compensation. By holding that any federal destruction of a property interest in slavery violated the due process clause, his opinion aimed to immunize slavery from any congressional regulation.

Corwin[22] and Ely[23] have dismissed the Taney opinion as erroneous, clearly refuted by the dissent of Justice Curtis. Curtis does have the better of Taney, but Curtis did not deny that the Fifth Amendment due process clause might invalidate unjust statutes. Instead, he argued that because slavery is "contrary to natural right" the courts would enforce slavery only when commanded to do so by positive law.[24] This position was entirely orthodox, but it would be unnecessary unless the Fifth Amendment due process clause contained some substantive limits based on natural law. If Congress were *not* constrained by natural law, Congress could ban slavery in the territories even if slavery were consistent with "natural right." The Curtis dissent does more to confirm than to refute the claim that antebellum lawyers thought of due process in substantive, natural law terms.[25]

The opponents of slavery were just as willing as Taney to find their positions in the substantive content of Fifth Amendment due process. As many recent writers have stressed, the antislavery wing of the Republican party had insisted that the Fifth Amendment due process clause forbade congressional legislation authorizing slavery in the territories.[26] Abolitionist theorists went so far as to claim that the Fifth Amendment due process clause forbade slavery in the states, *Barron v. Baltimore*, the three-fifths clause, and the importation clause notwithstanding.[27] These Republicans were wrong about *Barron*, which they could not overturn retroactively. But prospectively they could not be wrong about their own intentions, and the Fifth Amendment due process clause could have banned slavery only if due process has a substantive component.

The Fourteenth Amendment repeals Dred Scott's citizenship holding by express terms. Nothing in the amendment subtracts from the content of due process.[28] It is hard to believe that the drafters of this amendment to protect the freed slaves would have forgotten the substantive uses to which the due process language was put during the controversy over slavery. Indeed, Bingham said that due process had been violated by slavery, and that the Fourteenth Amendment finally would make due process enforceable against the southern states.[29]

While the amendment was pending before the states, John Norton Pomeroy wrote of the Fifth Amendment due process clause that "[o]f course it forbids any act of legislature or of executive which takes one person's property and gives it to another; or which would imprison or otherwise punish a person without any of the forms of judicial procedure."[30] At the same time Judge Cooley opines that due process or law-of-the-land clauses impose substantive limits on legislative power.[31] He says that sumptuary laws[32] and laws barring public employment on account of party affiliation[33] should be held void under state "law of the land" provisions. His acceptance of the cases upholding the prohibition of liquor and pornography[34] as valid exercises of the police power does more to confirm than to qualify his view that *some* state laws are unconstitutional because they violate the unwritten "law of the land."

Less than four years after the ratification of the amendment, the Supreme Court again asserted that due process had a substantive component. *Osborn v. Nicholson* was a suit on a note given in consideration for the purchase of a slave who was liberated by Union forces before the note was due.[35] The purchaser of the slave defended on the ground that emancipation had made his end of the bargain worthless. Holding that the note was enforceable against the purchaser of the slave, Justice Swayne, a Lincoln appointee who would later dissent in the *Slaughter-House Cases*, wrote that nullifying the contract would "take away one man's property and give it to another. And the deprivation would be 'without due process of law.' This is forbidden by the fundamental principles of the social compact, and is beyond the sphere of the legislative authority both of the States and the Nation."[36] The supporting footnote does not cite, as a modern lawyer would expect, the Fifth and Fourteenth Amendments. Instead the citation is to state substantive due process cases, including *Wynehammer v. People*. A decade later comes *Hurtado*, which has been with us ever since.

Substantive due process is neither a contradiction nor alien to the legal thought of those who framed the Fourteenth Amendment. It should be remembered, however, that only extreme legislative acts did not qualify as law in the minds of the framers. The slavery controversy is illustrative. Abolitionists thought that statutes upholding chattel slavery violated due process, while Chief Justice Taney thought the same about arbitrary expropriations—taking from A and giving to B, as it was often put.[37] It is a long way from these examples to *Lochner* or *Roe v. Wade*.[38]

With respect to Fourteenth Amendment due process, the privileges-or-immunities clause was plainly intended to impose some limits on state legislation. The clause explicitly forbids the making, as well as the enforcement, of law abridging privileges or immunities. Its purposes at least included authorizing congressional protection of the rights to hold and convey property, sue and be sued, and the other elements in the 1866 Civil Rights Act.[39] The constitutional text, however, does not enumerate these rights as among the "privileges or immunities of citizens of the United States." If "privileges or immunities" meant that the states could now deny to no one the rights they could not restrict to residents under Article IV, *Corfield v. Coryell* seems to say that the intention was to protect "fundamental" rights. Substantive due process might thus be a more-or-less legitimate stand-in for privileges or immunities.[40]

Whatever substantive due process lacks in textual and historical support is by now made up by sheer force of precedent. The selective incorporation decisions[41] and the privacy decisions[42] openly rest on substantive due process, as do several other decisions[43] that are in no danger of imminent overruling. If these substantive due process cases have a legitimacy deficit with respect to text and history, their defenders can point to the acceptance, by generations of justices and by the country at large, of the Court's authority to vindicate unenumerated rights.

Why, then, the juristic skepticism about substantive due process? I think the underlying problem is not that substantive due process completely lacks authority in the conventional sources of constitutional law. It is, rather, that there are no accessible standards for judges to consult in identifying "the law of the land." This concern drove the Court to nullify the privileges-or-immunities clause. That purported originalists do not extend their theory to the privileges-or-immunities clause makes it pretty obvious that the problem is less legitimacy than determinacy. Words like "fundamental" don't cabin discretion very much; tradition can be read in many ways and at many levels of generality.[44] One could hardly look for a better illustration than the conflicting views of Fifth Amendment due process espoused during the slavery controversy. In the end opposition to substantive due process adjudication has less to do with faith in legislatures than with fear of judges.

So substantive due process is a part, but a suspect part, of our constitutional tradition. Even on its own terms, a conventionalist argument for substantive due process must acknowledge that only the violation of the very most important moral or natural rights might bring legislation into conflict with the substantive force of the due process clause. Even when the doctrine is expressed in that guarded way, history teaches that the courts have been neither very principled nor very wise in their selection of the fundamental rights that deserve substantive due process protection. It follows that while substantive due process adjudication is not beyond the pale, it is quite properly regarded as a doctrine of last resort.

There is, however, no cloud over minimal substantive due process, the substantive constitutional right to stay out of jails, prisons, asylums, and so on absent a compelling state interest. Without this substantive baseline, the universally accepted constitutional guarantee of fair procedure would be nugatory. To read the due process clause even as narrowly as a guarantee of fair procedure in criminal cases entails at least this much of a substantive entitlement to physical liberty.

Now a peculiar feature of minimal substantive due process is that despite the general requirement that official detention policies be narrowly tailored to serve compelling state interests, the content of the criminal code is left, within the widest limits, to legislative discretion.[45] A criminal defendant charged under an arguably unjust or unwise law—a gambling, weapons, drug, or sex charge, say—will not be heard to argue that the criminal code is not narrowly tailored to promote a compelling state interest. Instead, the courts simply conclude that the state has a compelling interest in enforcing its criminal code, whatever its contents. If a law styled as penal imposes liability for mere status,[46] or imposes a penalty insanely out of proportion to the offense,[47] the Court will strike down a criminal statute as unconstitutional. So long, however, as a law prospectively provides for punishing conduct, the legislature's decision to declare the conduct criminal suffices to overcome challenge on minimal due process grounds.

When the legislature resorts to physical restraint independently of the criminal code, a much stricter inquiry into compelling interests and narrow tailoring follows.[48] This poses some problems for a due process theory of criminal procedure, because some police practices might be justified either as means to enforce the criminal code and/or as independent social control policies. The Supreme Court's *Schall*[49] and *Salerno*[50] opinions characterize preventive detention as an independent social control policy; it might be better to treat preventive detention as part of the criminal process. On the other hand, arrest is theoretically justified by the need to initiate the criminal process against reluctant litigants, yet practically the police make many arrests with far more interest in immediate social control than in ultimate prosecution.[51]

If all this is well taken, a few important implications follow. First, procedural due process analysis is entirely legitimate, and as a necessary corollary of procedural due process, minimal substantive due process is likewise legitimate. Second, general, as distinct from minimal, substantive due process, because of its theoretically narrow legitimate scope but practically boundless potential application, should be a doctrine of last resort. Finally, in conducting substantive due process analysis, the more closely the judges can align their reasoning with widely accepted features of our constitutional tradition, the better.

The next section explores how criminal procedure doctrine, early and late, has confused substantive with procedural due process. I propose to base constitutional criminal procedure primarily on procedural due process and its minimal substantive due process counterpart. Such a move would advance the relevant policy considerations while freeing constitutional doctrine from the liabilities that attend generalized substantive due process analysis.

SUBSTANTIVE DUE PROCESS RIGHTS TO FAIR PROCEDURE: THE ENDURING CONSTITUTIONAL CONFUSION

The confusion of substantive and procedural due process has its roots in Magna Charta itself. Modern American readers have been tempted to read "by a judgment of peers and according to the law of the land" conjunctively, with a right to judgment of peers protecting procedural fairness and the law of the land protecting substantive justice.[52] But this reading is less plausible than a disjunctive reading, in which the King pledges *either* a judgment of peers or a judgment according to the law of the land.[53] Certainly a judgment of peers did not immediately supersede the familiar medieval procedures of battle, compurgation, and ordeal.

Nonetheless Chapter 39 aimed to regulate both procedure and substance. A judgment of peers was not to rubber-stamp the royal prerogative, but to apply the customary substantive law. And the law of the land not only limited the royal prerogative substantively, but also required traditional procedures, i.e., battle, compurgation, or ordeal.[54]

So it is perhaps understandable that the Supreme Court's opinion in *Hurtado v. California* adopted the view that the Fourteenth Amendment requires procedural safeguards in state criminal cases only to the extent that those *procedural* safeguards satisfied the test of *substantive* due process.[55] Is grand jury presentment, the *Hurtado* Court asked, one of those "fundamental principles of liberty and justice that lie at the base of all our civil and political institutions?" This basic confusion of substantive and procedural due process has become an enduring legacy.

The "fundamental fairness" regime repeatedly asked this same question. The selective incorporation cases asked it too, answering that most of the procedural safeguards in the Bill of Rights are indeed "fundamental." The Burger and Rehnquist Courts have not questioned the incorporation decisions, but have very much narrowed the meaning of the Bill of Rights provisions.

In response, one might have anticipated that litigants would bring due process challenges to circumvent the prevailing conservative interpretation of the incorporated amendments. The Court, however, has taken the view that the incorporated amendments define due process in criminal cases, and that freestanding due process claims are to be rather skeptically received.

For example, excessive force claims against the police practically cry out for due process analysis, for in such cases the suspect's claim is that the police have bypassed the trial and imposed their own brand of unofficial punishment.[56] But the Court has insisted on analyzing excessive force and even excessive deadly force cases under the Fourth Amendment,[57] preferring to say that a suspect shot to death by the police has been "seized" rather than "deprived of life."[58] While the Court's opinions contain dicta suggesting the substantive due process might prohibit police practices that fall outside the scope of "searches and seizures,"[59] neither the Burger nor the Rehnquist Court has ever reversed a conviction because the police practices were shocking or fundamentally unfair.

Thus the conservative Court practically has banned due process analysis from police practices cases, leaving the field regulated solely by the Fourth, Fifth, and Sixth Amendments. This is a grave disservice to innocent suspects. Pretrial procedure can leave the criminal defendant facing erroneous but now entrenched identification testimony, without the benefit of exculpatory physical evidence the police neglected to collect or preserve, defended by an overworked lawyer with no time to conduct a new investigation. This can (and does) happen, without any unreasonable searches, without any compelled testimony, and without any denial of counsel. The distinction between investigation and adjudication is far less palpable than current doctrine admits.

When defendants have challenged clearly adjudicatory procedures on procedural due process grounds, the modern Court has continued the basic confusion of substantive and procedural due process. After some early willingness to apply the administrative due process balancing test of *Mathews v. Eldridge*[60] in criminal cases,[61] in *Medina v. California*[62] the Court, as we have seen, took the view that instrumental considerations are secondary to historical ones in the criminal context.

The various attitudes brought together by the *Medina* opinion make a good deal of sense so long as questions about criminal procedure are asked in substantive due process terms. Substantive due process has a questionable textual warrant, an unsavory history, and lies at the center of the violent arguments about *Roe v. Wade*. So the justices are naturally a little ginger about substantive due process, and they look to history and tradition to constrain the exercise of their constitutional chancellor's foot.

But there is another way of asking criminal procedure questions, in terms of procedural due process. In a generalized substantive due process analysis, the question is: Does the state's procedure violate the unenumerated limits on the state's police power, by offending fundamental rights validated by tradition? In a procedural due process analysis, the question is: Does the state's procedure subject the individual to an unacceptably high risk of an erroneous decision? The minimal substantive due process counterpart to this question is: Did the methods of investigation deprive the individual of liberty without a proportionate expectation of preventing or punishing crime? On purely normative grounds, these latter two questions are the ones we should be asking in criminal procedure cases, at least if the argument in Chapter 5 is accepted. If procedural due process enjoys a major legitimacy advantage over substantive due process, then a strong case can be made doctrinally, as well as morally, for moving to a procedural due process regime in constitutional criminal procedure.

Indeed, hidden within the *Medina* opinion is the ghost of procedural due process, struggling to be heard. If we strip away the references to fundamental fairness, what the *Medina* Court actually did was to recognize two ways for a defendant to challenge a state rule on procedural due process grounds. One approach is historical; if a founding-era consensus against the state's procedure can be shown, the state loses. The other approach is instrumental, i.e., whether the procedure is unfair "in operation." Despite all the language in *Medina* about history, it seems pretty clear that the historical avenue is illusory, leaving in practice only the instrumental test.

Suppose a criminal defendant shows a complete common-law consensus to the effect that a perfectly reliable type of evidence should be excluded. For example, a child abuse defendant moves to bar the victim, now six years old, from testifying. At common law, this would have been the usual result, on the ground that a child of tender years cannot understand the oath and its potentially eternal consequences.[63] Would any court do anything but laugh at the defendant's due process argument, despite its impeccable historical pedigree?

On the other hand, suppose the state excludes reliable defense evidence that would not have been admissible at common law. For example, suppose a state procedural rule has the effect of preventing the defendant herself from testifying. At common law, the defendant could not be sworn as a witness (again on the theory that this made damnation too likely).[64] Could the state justify its rule on the basis of common-law history? Suppose instead that a state barred coconspirators from testifying on one another's behalf,[65] or prohibited a defendant from cross-examining a witness who gives testimony favorable to the state after being called by the defense.[66] These cases actually reached the Supreme Court, and in each the Court struck down the state rules, history notwithstanding.[67]

In other words, once the "fundamental fairness" language gets put in perspective, and once the historical analysis is understood as pretty much beside the point, *Medina* holds that the bottom-line inquiry in a criminal-side procedural due process case is instrumental. A great many other cases rely on instrumental considerations, without regard for historical practice.[68] Procedural due process cases recognize, under appropriate circumstances, constitutional rights to a change of venue to avoid local prejudice;[69] to the disclosure of exculpatory evidence during the discovery process;[70] to rules of evidence that exclude unreliable prosecution evidence[71] and that admit reliable exculpatory evidence;[72] against knowing use of perjured testimony by the prosecution;[73] to appear at trial in civilian clothes, not prison issue;[74] to limiting closing argument by the prosecutor;[75] and to the reasonable doubt standard of proof respecting elements of the charged offense.[76]

In each instance, the Court's inquiry has been instrumental; in each case, history has not been dispositive; and in each case, the state practices held inconsistent with due process do not shock the conscience. Implicit in these due process cases is the appropriate standard for judging due process challenges to adjudicatory procedures, which is whether the challenged practice creates a significant and avoidable risk of unjust conviction. This standard resembles the *Mathews* standard, but it takes account of the distinctively weighty individual interest against erroneous "termination" of one's liberty from criminal conviction.

In these criminal-procedure due process cases the Court does not follow the *Betts v. Brady*[77] case-by-case approach. Instead, modern due process cases establish principles that apply in categorical terms to future cases. For example, under *Brady v. Maryland* the government must turn over relevant, exculpatory evidence on request, *in every case*. Under *Winship* the government must prove the elements of the charge beyond reasonable doubt *in every case*. Sometimes doctrine is stated in such fact-specific terms that the standard requires case-by-case adjudication, as with questions about changes of venue to counter pretrial publicity.

In the main, however, the Court has applied the painfully learned lessons about regulating police investigation to the regulation of trial procedure. Due process, no less than the Fourth or Fifth Amendments, can be translated into generally applicable rules.

Certainly this methodology is consistent with *Mathews v. Eldridge*. Just as in the administrative due process cases, the trade-offs between instrumental reliability and cost are more a matter of judgment than computation.[78] They likewise depend on some rough-and-ready assessments of the risk of error and how far that risk might be reduced by additional procedural safeguards. The resulting judgment about the overall fairness of the procedure in both administrative and criminal cases is articulated with as much generality and precision as the subject admits, generally in the form of rule-like declarations that certain categories of cases require certain procedural safeguards.[79]

The observation that *Mathews* is insufficiently determinate is not a sound objection. Of course *Mathews* sets a standard for inquiry rather than a rule that can be mechanically applied. The three-factor test asks the courts "how much can society afford to pay for safeguards against erroneous decisions?" The judges will answer that question, as they answer many others, under the influence of their own values and experience. The important point is that this is the right question to ask. The usual objection to the instrumental inquiry mandated by *Mathews* is that this approach slights dignitary values.[80] Chapter 5 set forth reasons for believing that instrumental considerations incorporate due regard for dignitary ones in criminal procedure. The prominence of dignitary due process theories in the administrative law literature, however, offers strong evidence that the general due process standard matters but is necessarily highly general. If the standard didn't matter, why the fuss over dignitary versus instrumental values? And if "dignity" supplies a sufficiently determinate index of acceptable procedures in specific contexts, surely instrumental reliability can provide at least that much guidance.

What I argue for in this book is a general move away from the current focus on the Bill of Rights in favor of procedural due process analysis. Following the four *Medina* dissenters, the Court should return to the practice of openly consulting the *Mathews* factors in criminal cases. Although the *Medina* majority recognized a major role for instrumental analysis in criminal cases, the "fundamentally unfair in operation" language too readily tolerates the denial of affordable procedural safeguards that might prevent miscarriages of justice.[81] The concerns with founding-era common-law practice and the delicate attitude toward state prerogatives are entirely appropriate in general substantive due process analysis, but they are quite inapposite in procedural due process analysis. If criminal procedure should be about correctly determining guilt and innocence, constitutional doctrine should speak the language of procedural due process.

Indeed, there is really a much stronger case for applying *Mathews* in criminal cases than in administrative cases. Legislatures create the administrative entitlements, and face political incentives that encourage rational trade-offs between funding benefits and funding procedural safeguards against erroneous terminations. But legislatures have no discretionary power to create or to destroy constitutional liberty. The clash of interest groups over entitlements is far more evenly matched than the one-sided politics of law and order. Neither greater-includes-the-lesser logic, nor considerations of institutional competence, counsel judicial deference to legislative decisions in criminal cases.

Ake v. Oklahoma[82] exemplifies the approach I have in mind. There, applying the *Mathews* test prior to the *Medina* opinion, the Court held that defendants have a procedural due process right to court-appointed expert witnesses to rebut expert testimony on behalf of the prosecution. The *Ake* Court described the appropriate inquiry as whether the defense had access to "the basic tools" of an effective defense. This test has not been generously interpreted by the lower courts. Nonetheless, it is an illuminating comment on the power of doctrine that even a conservative majority could be moved to order the expenditure of public funds when faced with the prospect that a criminal trial ran a gratuitous risk of error, despite compliance with every specific safeguard in the Bill of Rights.

PROCEDURAL DUE PROCESS: THE THEORY EXPLAINED

The text of the due process clause derives from Magna Charta's Chapter 39, so that the instrumental theory is firmly rooted in both the constitutional text and in legal history. Indeed, the instrumental theory is clearly included by the most famous early American expositions of the clause. While *Murray's Lessee* equated due process with common-law procedure, and Webster and Story thought of due process as requiring regular procedure in courts of law, all agreed that due process requires, in Webster's phrase, "a law that hears before it condemns."[83] Nor is there any shortage of Supreme Court decisions declaring that due process requires a fair trial before punishment for crime.[84] The selective incorporation of the Sixth Amendment procedural safeguards hold that those safeguards are essential to the fair trial guaranteed by the due process clause. In short, the equation of the instrumental theory with Fourteenth Amendment due process enjoys very strong support in the conventional sources of constitutional law.

This seemingly banal interpretation has more power than might at first appear. The methods of police investigation, such as search, arrest, and interrogation, frequently "deprive" individuals of their "liberty," deprivations that can be justified by the state's interest in enforcing the criminal law only to the extent that these deprivations have some prospect of resulting in a just conviction. Moreover, because the outcome of trials depends so heavily on the evidence gathered during the police investigation, police practices can undermine the fairness of the trial. Thus police practices, which might at first seem quite outside the concerns of procedural due process, implicate both the exclusivity principle and the adjudication requirement. If, as I claim, the Fourteenth Amendment embraces the exclusivity principle and the adjudication requirement, due process has the potential to generate a comprehensive and rational scheme of limits on police practices. In this section, I explain the theory by contrasting it with the three previous regimes—fundamental fairness, selective incorporation, and conservative balancing.

The regime I envision differs from the "fundamental fairness" approach to due process in three important respects. First, fundamental fairness analysis confused substantive and procedural due process. The fundamental fairness cases followed a substantive due process methodology—is the claimed procedural safeguard "fundamental" to our system of ordered liberty?—but consistently concluded that only a demonstrably *unreliable* trial violated fundamental rights. The confusion has not been much noticed by scholars, because of the professional divide between specialists in criminal procedure and constitutional law generally. But the confusion is there, and if criminal procedure doctrine has any hope for coherence that confusion needs to be clarified.

Oddly, it is consensus rather than controversy that makes the confusion so intractable. Almost everybody agrees that the states have constitutional power to punish crimes, and very broad discretion in defining offenses. Almost everybody recognizes that other than the criminal law, there are a very few constitutionally permissible occasions for incarcerating people—civil commitment, quarantine, and conscription heading the list. What I have termed minimal substantive due process properly governs constitutional challenges to corporeal restraints, with the understanding that enforcing the criminal law (regardless of its particular content) qualifies as a compelling state interest.

Once the state has adopted positive law defining a category of persons who may, consistent with substantive due process, be stigmatized or confined, procedural due process governs the fairness of the process by which the state identifies persons who fall within the legal category. Fundamental fairness analysis simply continued the substantive due process methodology by asking whether, for example, appointed counsel for indigent defendants was "fundamental." Obviously nobody has a preexisting desire for a criminal defense lawyer; people are not lined up outside the state's attorney's office demanding to be charged for the purpose of triggering their rights to counsel, jury trial, and so on. At a theoretical level then the theory defended here differs from fundamental fairness by focusing clearly and openly on procedural due process.

With respect to adjudicatory procedure this focus is easy to maintain, but complications arise when procedural due process analysis confronts police investigations. Individuals have a liberty interest in freedom from punishment; in the criminal cases there is no agonizing over whether text and history recognize a "protected interest" against conviction on a criminal charge. Due process therefore requires a fair trial before conviction. Deprivations of liberty less onerous than conviction may be imposed incident to the investigation and prosecution of offenses, but if search, arrest, interrogations, and so on fall on individuals without a reasonable expectation of preventing an offense or of ultimately securing a conviction, then the deprivations of liberty are *not* incident to the criminal process.

But such burdens might still be constitutional, defended by the state as free-standing social control strategies along the lines of curfew laws and civil commitment. For example, what about police arrest decisions, which frequently are motivated by immediate concerns for social control rather than by the expectation of a prosecution? For a law professor's hypothetical, surely it must be constitutional for the police to arrest a lunatic or a diplomat immediately before or after a homicide or a robbery, even though the insanity defense or diplomatic immunity will preclude prosecution.

The theory defended here has no difficulty justifying an arrest for the purpose of preventing an incipient offense. If the officers reasonably believe the boyfriend will continue to beat the girlfriend as soon as the officers have gone, then an arrest is the only way to prevent an imminent crime. By contrast, if the parties do not cohabitate, the girlfriend has gone home, and the police have no reason to doubt the appearance of the boyfriend on a citation, the arrest has become detached from the adjudicatory process and now serves as an executive-imposed deterrent penalty.

On the other side of the coin there are many official practices that can produce evidence of crime that are not motivated by the desire to do so. Firefighters discover evidence of arson; social workers discover evidence of child abuse; regulators discover evidence of corporate crimes. In a nutshell the waters are muddied by the possibility that the police may be engaged in freestanding social control practices rather than criminal law enforcement, and that civil agencies of the government may be engaged in criminal law enforcement.

If we recall the basic structure of the "liberty" protected by the due process clauses, however, we have some hope of sorting out even this residual confusion. Restraints on individual liberty require justification. The enforcement of the criminal law is one such justification, and there are a few others. When the state justifies the intrusion on the ground of criminal law enforcement (including the prevention of incipient offenses), the question is a procedural due process question: Is the intrusion justified by the prospect of preventing and/or prosecuting criminal offenses? When the state justifies the intrusion as a freestanding social control measure, the issue is framed by minimal substantive due process: Is the restraint narrowly tailored to serve a compelling state interest?

This understanding of due process clearly conflicts with the Court's recent decision to uphold custodial arrests for minor traffic offenses.[85] Looking at the issue through the lens of the Fourth Amendment, a five-justice majority concluded that founding-era practice did not clearly prohibit arrests for petty offenses, and that the desirability of a clear rule made all arrests based on probable cause, no matter how minor the offense or how remote the risk of nonappearance, "reasonable." If the Court had asked the right question—can the government justify so major a restraint of individual liberty?—it might have given a better answer. Custodial arrests for misdemeanors can be justified by the government's interest in criminal law enforcement only if the individual poses some risk of nonappearance or continued offending. Requiring *Terry*-type suspicion of nonappearance or continued offending would involve no more uncertainty than attends reasonable suspicion or probable cause decisions generally.

The distinction between substantive and procedural due process leads to a second major difference between the proposed approach and fundamental fairness. A procedural due process regime, although obviously general, would be far more determinate, far more sharply focused, than the inquiry into fundamental fairness. In a police practices case, the issue would be whether the police (a) deprived the suspect of liberty without a sufficient expectation of exposing or preventing crime, or (b) conducted the investigation in a way that prevented the suspect from having a fair trial. In an adjudication case, the issue would be simply whether the state procedure exposed the defendant to an unnecessary risk of false conviction.

Admittedly, there is room for reasonable jurists to disagree about when a police intrusion amounts to a deprivation of "liberty," about when the expectation of a valid prosecution is great enough to justify particular invasions of liberty, and about when the risk of a miscarriage of justice is necessary. But these are far more specific than the invitation to strike down anything that is "fundamentally unfair." The administrative due process cases call for parallel judgments, and although they are controversial, they can hardly be described as lawless.

Third, the regime I defend would not proceed on a case-by-case basis. Instead, following the Supreme Court's example in *Miranda*, *Terry v. Ohio*,[86] and *New York v. Belton*,[87] the general requirements of procedural due process would be translated into constitutional doctrine as general rules. *Terry* holds that reasonable suspicion is required to detain for investigation; *Miranda* requires a standard warning before custodial interrogation; *Belton* authorizes a search of the passenger compartment, but not the trunk, of an automobile incident to the arrest of the driver or a passenger.

Each of these constitutional rules requires interpretation at its margins, but unquestionably each has been a success from the standpoint of guiding police and lower courts. As developed more fully later in this chapter, *better* rules may be conceivable, but it is not conceivable that more general standards, whatever their spirit, could improve on doctrine in these areas. Not only do general standards, as experience with fundamental fairness proved, make it difficult for police and state courts to comply with federal law, with the concomitant risk that vague standards of due process will be self-defeating. They also promote the disparate treatment of similarly situated individuals, and they create needless friction between the state and federal court systems.

Selective incorporation suffers from the same confusion of substantive and procedural due process as fundamental fairness. Where fundamental fairness said "because your trial was fair your fundamental rights weren't violated," selective incorporation said "your trial wasn't fair because you didn't have the benefit of the Bill of Rights safeguards." Sometimes this was true—a fair trial without counsel, confrontation, and compulsory process is an oxymoron—but often it was not, as with the privilege against self-incrimination or the double-jeopardy clause.

Procedural due process speaks directly to the fairness of criminal trials. To the extent that the Bill of Rights provisions promote fair trial, they would coincide with the dictates of procedural due process. To the extent that those provisions frustrate the ends of justice without protecting the innocent against false conviction, they should not be enforceable against the states under the Fourteenth Amendment. Due process analysis, however, might well lead to the imposition of many new standards on the criminal justice system, both state and federal. For example, due process might provide the predicate for at long last imposing some sensible regulations on the process of developing eyewitness identification evidence. The direct focus of procedural due process on reasonable police methods and fair trials, unmediated by preoccupation with the Bill of Rights, sharply distinguishes this approach from selective incorporation.

Nonetheless there is at least one continuity between selective incorporation and procedural due process. Both approaches aim to formulate doctrine as intelligible general rules, rather than as a normative standard like "fundamental fairness." What the procedural due process theory recognizes, however, is that the work of translating general constitutional provisions into doctrinal rules requires a mediating layer of judge-made law.[88] Sometimes a Bill of Rights provision might play this role, but this is an unlikely scenario. Typically the Bill of Rights itself stands in need of intermediate, judge-made rules (the Fourth Amendment comes to mind), and when the Bill of Rights text is narrow the language leads the judges away, rather than toward, a focus on fair trials. For instance, focus on the text of the confrontation clause has led to a constitutional preference for receiving hearsay testimony rather than hearing the declarant's own words by closed-circuit television or videotape.[89] The Court's turn to the Sixth Amendment right to counsel as a remedy for unreliable identification procedures offers another good example of how focus on the Bill of Rights deflects attention from the appropriate instrumental concerns. So while procedural due process acknowledges the soundness of the move away from case-by-case constitutional formulation of criminal procedure doctrine, it insists that the correct focus is on due process rather than the Bill of Rights.

As we have seen, the modern Court's approach puts primary emphasis on the Bill of Rights criminal procedure provisions, narrowly construed. If a challenge to state criminal processes fails under the Bill of Rights, a due process challenge can be made, subject to a historical test, under *Patterson v. New York*. If that challenge also fails, the *Medina* opinion and a long line of precedents recognize the possibility that a state procedure might be unfair "in operation" nonetheless. The *Medina* opinion makes clear that the inquiry into unfairness-in-operation is very similar to the instrumental inquiry defended here. Procedural due process analysis therefore has some support in current law.

The proposed theory departs from the *Medina* Court's approach in two critical respects. First, the *Medina* opinion makes the unfortunate feedback from incorporation explicit: Due process is to function as a gap-filler, a doctrine consulted only in those rare cases in which the Bill of Rights provisions do not cover the ground of dispute. By contrast, because procedural due process analysis is logically independent of the incorporated amendments, and because procedural due process analysis precisely captures the relevant policy considerations, our thinking about criminal procedure analysis should begin, not end, with procedural due process.

If the individual can show that his trial ran a needless risk of false conviction, or that the police investigation punished him independently of any conviction, the state should not be heard to plead compliance with the Bill of Rights as an excuse. If, by contrast, the individual fails to show anything unfair about his trial, or any unjustified restraint or violence during the investigation, the Bill of Rights should not be converted into a loophole.

On a conventionalist theory of interpretation, the incorporation precedents of course deserve some respect. A heavy presumption weighs against overruling them. In some cases that presumption can be overcome. The Fifth Amendment privilege against self-incrimination and double-jeopardy clauses do very little to secure decent police methods and fair trials, and a strong case can be made for overruling *Malloy v. Hogan*[90] and *Benton v. Maryland*.[91] Leaving these provisions aside, however, the incorporation decisions can be squared with procedural due process analysis.

Once the post-incorporation Court focused on reasonableness rather than on warrants, the Fourth Amendment lost its independent content. Fourth Amendment analysis now is indistinguishable from an instrumental due process inquiry, except that the restrictive definitions of "searches and seizures" open the door to unreasonable, yet constitutional, police investigations.[92] Due process analysis could fill this unfortunate gap, while any "search" or "seizure" that is "reasonable" under the Fourth Amendment should satisfy procedural due process standards as well.

While the Fifth Amendment privilege against self-incrimination prohibits nonviolent official questioning in public proceedings, the Court has construed the privilege to permit secret interrogation by the police out of court. Rational regulation of police questioning—recording requirements, time limits, and so on—could be imposed on procedural due process grounds. So in the interrogation area the procedural due process regime would work a major change, but it would be a change for the better.

As for double jeopardy, repeated litigation of the same charge implicates both the adjudication requirement (for a weak case, tried often enough, may be accepted by one of the many juries to whom it is offered) and the exclusivity principle (for even if each of several successive juries acquits, the expense and travail of repeatedly standing trial can become punishment in its own right). The double-jeopardy clause, however, does not protect finality effectively, because most criminal behavior give rise to many different legal offenses. Each, so far as the clause is concerned, can be tried separately.[93] Although the Court adopted a collateral estoppel rule in *Ashe v. Swenson*,[94] it did so more despite rather than because of the specific text of the double-jeopardy clause.[95] Even the *Ashe* rule provides limited protection against repetitive litigation, because if a general verdict of acquittal reasonably can be construed as compatible with a subsequent charge there will be no estoppel.[96] For offenses separated by time and space, or general verdicts of acquittal that might be based on many different factual predicates, the *Ashe* rule provides no protection against relitigation.[97]

The rigid bar on government appeals tolerates clear errors by juries. A due process finality rule, requiring mandatory joinder of offenses arising out of the same transaction absent good cause shown,[98] but permitting one retrial at the behest of the state in cases of gross error, could advance the legitimate interests of both the state and the defendant.

A due process approach, as Justice Harlan pointed out in his *Gideon* concurrence, can support a right to appointed counsel in felony cases. Due process, however, focuses on the reliability of the proceedings, so that due process analysis can justify expert witnesses and investigators as well as lawyers for the indigent. Moreover, due process analysis extends to any point at which the reliability of the outcome might be undermined, so that the arbitrary distinctions between pre- and post-indictment lineups and interrogations could be put to rest.

Of course, lawyers are not necessarily the best safeguard against misidentification. Due process could justify some simple rules that could do far more to reduce that risk than the *Wade* and *Gilbert* doctrines. For example, there is typically no reason why the lineup or show-up needs to be administered by a police officer who knows which of the subjects is the suspect.[99] With lineups, unlike show-ups, there is typically no reason why the defense could not be permitted to supply one of the foils. There is no reason why witnesses cannot be first given a blank lineup or photo array.

Just as due process analysis could free the courts from relying on the right to counsel as the only available procedural safeguard, due process analysis could also greatly reduce judicial hostility to involving defense lawyers in the investigation process. The current, Bill-of-Rights based system depends on waivers of the Fifth Amendment privilege as absolutely necessary to obtain information from the suspect. Lawyers obviously impair the ability of the police to obtain *Miranda* waivers. The bottom-line reason for not recognizing the right to counsel until the commencement of formal proceedings is that the Fifth Amendment privilege means that the only practical window for interrogation is the period following arrest but preceding the appointment of counsel.

Once the suspect's rights are defined in terms of instrumental procedural considerations—that is, calculated to protect the innocent but not to shield the guilty—the fear of lawyers would abate. If a suspect can be questioned on the record, with an inference guilt from silence available to the jury, why not have a defense lawyer represent the suspect from the moment of arrest? Few other reforms are more in keeping with the legality and regularity promoted by due process.

The incorporation of the Sixth Amendment jury trial guarantee is a complex story. From a procedural due process perspective, jury trial gives the defense an important option against trial by the court. However attractive professional adjudication along the European model may be, the alternative to trial by jury in our state systems is less attractive. Practically considered, *Duncan v. Louisiana*[100] is perfectly defensible on procedural due process grounds, especially so because the Court has approved nonunanimous verdicts.[101] Certainly no strong case to overrule the jury-trial precedents can be made now.

Moreover, from the standpoint of *prospective jurors*, as opposed to defendants, a case can be made for incorporating jury trial as a matter of substantive due process. From the prospective juror standpoint, jury trial is substantive, not procedural; it provides members of the community with the practical power to nullify unpopular laws. It therefore plays an important role in preventing a potential tyranny. *Duncan*, certainly defensible on procedural due process grounds, thus draws added strength from substantive due process.

Primary concern for due process, however, might support a defense right to trial by the court in appropriate cases. The Supreme Court has rejected any right to a bench trial on demand,[102] and for the most part the government is happy to have trial by the court. Nonetheless in particularly notorious or complex cases jury trial might not be fair trial, and the defense should have the right, in such unusual cases, to trial by the court.

The Court has read the Sixth Amendment confrontation and compulsory process clauses quite narrowly, albeit more broadly than their framers may have intended. What the Court has groped for in these provisions is a defense right to exclude evidence that does more to undermine than to promote the reliability of the trial, and a defense right to introduce evidence that does more to promote than to undermine that same reliability. Procedural due process could support these rights directly, without the complications posed by the precise language of the confrontation and compulsory process clauses. From the standpoint of due process, there is at least as much reason for constitutional scrutiny of declarants as of witnesses, and at least as much reason for concern with limits on the admissibility of a defense witness's testimony as with compulsory process to secure that witness's presence. There is no need to rethink the incorporation of these Sixth Amendment rights, but it might be necessary to go beyond them in a procedural due process regime. The recognition of a constitutional law of criminal evidence, founded on due process, might in turn help to rationalize interpretation of the confrontation and compulsory process clauses.

A procedural due process regime, then, would reverse the priority that now governs criminal-procedure analysis. The Bill of Rights would remain in force whenever its terms are consistent with due process, but the primary focus would be on the instrumental reliability of the investigation and the trial.

The second major difference between a procedural due process regime and the current conservative balancing has to do with the degree of deference paid by courts to legislatures. The current regime, following received wisdom about the doubtful legitimacy of substantive due process, takes a narrow view of federal court responsibility in criminal-procedure cases. This deference is surely appropriate in unconstrained substantive due process adjudication such as *Roe* or *Lochner*. It is equally inappropriate in procedural due process analysis.

There is no trace of illegitimacy attached to procedural due process analysis. The framers clearly intended due process to govern procedure, and the cases have always found in the due process clause a right to fair procedures. True, there has been much dispute about what fair procedure is; but about the legitimacy of procedural due process analysis there is no doubt.

So too, what I have called minimal substantive due process is of unquestionable legitimacy. "Liberty" in the due process clause means at least what it meant to Blackstone: the right of locomotion, to go about as one pleases unless the government can justify restraint.[103] The precedents have never questioned this core meaning of "liberty," although they have often found confinement justified by imperative government interests.

Instrumental analysis, moreover, is more determinate than unconstrained substantive due process analysis. Whether a particular procedure is conducive to false convictions, or a particular police practice unlikely to prevent or discover crime, is not an easy question. But these are questions that do not depend on their answer on the judge's personal moral or political convictions.

The conservative Court's deference to legislatures in the criminal-procedure field is a hangover from substantive due process adjudication. Once the focus shifts to procedural due process, the legitimacy deficit disappears. To be sure courts never purport to strike down legislation just because they disagree with it. But to the extent that the Court's caution in criminal due process cases reflects skepticism about the legitimacy or determinacy of substantive due process analysis, that caution has no place in procedural due process analysis.

Indeed, procedural due process analysis could recognize that legislative work in the criminal-procedure field deserves more distrust than deference. The legislative record on preventing false convictions and police abuse is embarrassing. Legislatures have not adopted even minimal regulations of identification procedures, have not provided anything like adequate support for indigent defense, and have, in the great majority of jurisdictions, even now not yet required the recording of interrogations or consent searches. Yet legislatures have repeatedly conferred broader powers on police, and, by constantly increasing already severe penalties, have given prosecutors enormous discretionary power.

Such a consistent pattern is not an accident. Legislative indifference to convicting, let alone hassling, the innocent reflects elementary public choice theory.[104] The losers from broader law enforcement powers are overwhelmingly young, overwhelmingly male, and disproportionately black. Women generally, and white males over forty, have little to fear from police excesses or self-fulfilling investigations. They have a lot to lose from predatory crime.[105]

In short, pro-government criminal-procedure legislation injures members of groups with relatively little political power, and it benefits groups with relatively strong political power. Legislatures have repeatedly demonstrated their sensitivity to these incentives. Instead of deferring to legislative choices made against this background, the federal courts should, consistently with the *Carolene Products* footnote and the representation-reinforcing theory of judicial review, face up to reality. If the federal courts tolerate unreliable trial procedures or police abuse, nobody else is going to stop it.

This points up one important contrast between the criminal-procedure cases and *Mathews v. Eldridge*. In the administrative entitlement context, legislatures define both the substantive entitlement and the procedures that determine its termination. There is no reason to suppose that legislatures creating benefits are hostile to the class of beneficiaries. There is accordingly some reason for judicial deference to legislative decisions about allocating scarce resources between transfer payments and eligibility procedures. By contrast, in the criminal context, the underlying entitlement to liberty is founded directly on the Constitution, and there are good reasons, confirmed by long experience, to doubt legislative judgments about the adequacy of the procedures for terminating the individual's liberty interest. Legislative support for indigent defense is a painfully obvious, and painfully illustrative, example.

In at least one respect a procedural due process regime, even one applied with rigorous scrutiny by the federal courts, would greatly strengthen the structure of federalism. A procedural due process regime could free the states from those Bill of Rights provisions that do nothing to prevent unfair trials or police excesses. This would restore a considerable degree of state autonomy over criminal procedure. Fair trials and proportionate police practices can take different forms. As it stands, criminal-procedure law is now a monolith.

A due process approach's contribution to federalism has an intensely practical dimension. The increasing role of the federal government in criminal justice threatens to swamp the federal courts and to displace the traditional state responsibility for enforcing the criminal law.[106] A great deal of the federal enforcement effort targets crimes that are not in any meaningful way distinct from garden-variety state offenses. Car-jacking and drug prosecutions come to mind. These crimes can be enforced by the states; whether rural or urban most street crime doesn't cross state lines. Instead, the federal role has expanded because the federal government has the money and the political will to assume responsibility for an increasing spectrum of criminal prosecutions.

A procedural due process regime's willingness to disincorporate some of the Bill of Rights provisions, such as the privilege against self-incrimination and the double-jeopardy clause, would give states willing to adopt appropriate statutory reforms a considerable advantage in law enforcement *vis a vis* the federal government. It would then make strategic sense for state police and state courts to handle as much of the crime problem as possible. That practical incentive might be enough to arrest, and ultimately reverse, the current drift toward the nationalization of law enforcement.

THE THEORY DEFENDED, OR, *HURTADO* REVISITED

How does the procedural due process approach respond to the interpretive challenges identified back in *Hurtado v. California*?[107] The *Hurtado* Court took the substantive due process route out of interpretive desperation; the justices could see no other escape from the positivist trap. The procedural due process theory, however, takes the positivist trap *en passant*. No one can be punished except according to positive law, although the precise content of the substantive criminal law is not restricted by procedural due process. The only limit on state positive law the procedural due process theory insists on is that criminal liability be imposed prospectively, for conduct not status (what I have called "minimal substantive due process"). Thus the theory reads due process as requiring legality in positive, not natural law, terms.

This interpretation steers a middle course between the indeterminacy objection and the constitutional straight-jacket. The procedures required by due process are determined by consulting the instrumental theory of criminal procedure—has the government violated either the exclusivity principle or the adjudication requirement? These inquiries obviously are not self-executing, but equally obviously they are intelligible and bounded. They very much depend on contemporary circumstances, so that interrogation rules quite properly should have changed to account for the creation of modern municipal police forces, just as rules of evidence must keep up with advances in forensic science.

The difficult challenges for the procedural due process theory are the Bill of Rights problem and the parade of horribles. If the Bill of Rights provisions are *not* incorporated, couldn't a state ban trial by jury? Permit endless relitigation by the government? Permit trial by affidavit, without an opportunity for cross-examination? And if incorporation is wrong, what about protecting freedom of speech, press, and conscience against repression by the states?

The answers to these questions are bound together, in an approach to the incorporation question that distinguishes substantive and procedural guarantees in the Bill of Rights. I suggest that the Fourteenth Amendment, under either the rubric of substantive due process or privileges-or-immunities clause, protects some unenumerated rights against the states. I suggest further that one very sensible way to cabin the dangerous judicial power to recognize such rights is by incorporating the substantive provisions of the Bill of Rights—the first three amendments and the takings clause, and the Eighth Amendment. The Sixth Amendment right to jury trial could be incorporated either on procedural due process grounds (an alternative to trial by the court promotes the instrumental reliability of the process) or substantive due process grounds (the right of citizens to participate in the administration of justice, and to nullify oppressive laws, is deeply rooted in our political tradition). Claims to unenumerated substantive rights not protected by the Bill of Rights should be received with utmost caution, although the text and history of the Fourteenth Amendment clearly approve at least some such rights. But with respect to the procedural provisions in the Bill of Rights, I suggest incorporating only those that coincide with what procedural due process analysis would independently require.

"How convenient!" I hear you say. Criminal procedure is saved from incorporation, but civil liberties at large go undisturbed. Very clever. And the authoritative support for it?

There is, perhaps surprisingly, very strong authoritative support for just this reading. With respect to unenumerated rights generally, everyone involved in framing and ratifying the Fourteenth Amendment agreed that sections one and five conferred power on Congress to adopt the Civil Rights Act—which protects rights nowhere explicitly enumerated in section one. When pressed as to just what rights section one did protect, proponents of the Amendment typically responded by saying "fundamental rights."

The generation that adopted the Fourteenth Amendment also engaged in a great debate about criminal procedure. Bentham's vitriol had done much to discredit common-law procedures and rules of evidence. Prior to the adoption of the amendment, several states had dispensed with grand jury presentment. Contemporaneous with the amendment, states began to allow defendants to give sworn testimony, over the objection that the right to testify would have the effect of compelling testimony from defendants who dared not risk the jury's inference from silence. Municipal police forces were in their infancy, and police interrogation began to replace judicial examination by the committing magistrate.

A spirit of reform and innovation ran through these developments. In 1871 Judge Cooley wrote that "[t]he innovations which have been made in criminal procedure in modern times have been so great that a trial on a charge of crime now bears as little resemblance to one in the time of the Stuarts, as the service in a Christian church does to the heathen sacrifice to idols."[108] Justice Mathews's opinion in *Hurtado* celebrated the changes of a "quick and active age" and stressed the need to accommodate legal reforms and the Constitution.

When good lawyers did line the proposed Fourteenth Amendment up against the changing pattern of criminal procedure in the states, they did not envision incorporation of the Bill of Rights provisions. For example, John Norton Pomeroy criticized the rule of *Barron v. Baltimore*, and saw in the then-pending Fourteenth Amendment a critical safeguard against the exclusion of blacks from the protections of the Bills of Rights in the several states.[109] In the very same pages, however, he speculated about American states moving to the continental inquisitorial system of criminal procedure,[110] and was especially confident that the states would do away with the privilege against self-incrimination.[111] "The provision that no person shall be compelled to be a witness against himself can only be supported by that intense reverence for the past which is so difficult to be overcome."[112] The Fourteenth Amendment, apparently, was no barrier to Benthamite reform.

Early cases and commentary rejecting the enforcement of the Bill of Rights against the states typically involved procedural provisions, not substantive ones. In the Supreme Court, for example, the *Twitchell* case rejected enforcement of the Fifth and Sixth Amendment provisions on fair notice of the charge in an indictment; *Walker v. Sauvinet* rejected enforcement of the Seventh Amendment civil jury trial guarantee; *Spies* and *Twining* rejected enforcing the Fifth Amendment privilege against self-incrimination; *Hurtado* and *Maxwell* rejected the grand jury requirement in the Fifth Amendment. Not until 1922 did the Supreme

Court say, in *dictum*, that the First Amendment doesn't apply to the states[113]—a *dictum* disavowed only three years later.[114]

The historical record is not unanimous, for the Court did reject the claim that the Fourteenth Amendment incorporated the Eighth Amendment in the 1890s.[115] A perfect synthesis, however, is impossible, because at least some of the conventional authorities flatly contradict one another. After all, Bingham and Howard both endorsed *total* incorporation (on quite different theories), a view overwhelmingly rejected by contemporary judges and commentators.[116]

The real burden of my argument is not to show that the Fourteenth Amendment protects some unenumerated substantive rights, and that these include those protected against federal incursion by the First and Eighth Amendments and the Fifth Amendment's takings clause. Those conclusions have at least some support in text and history, and are overwhelmingly confirmed by precedent. The burden of my argument, rather, is to show that procedural rights not dictated by procedural due process are not candidates for incorporation through the back door of substantive due process.

If, as I have argued, substantive due process legitimately may be invoked to invalidate extreme injustices such as slavery and arbitrary confiscations, there is little risk that grand jury presentment, the rigid bar on reprosecution, or a privilege against adverse inferences from the failure to respond to orderly, recorded questioning, might be sustained on substantive due process grounds. Fully granting the open-textured quality of the adjective in the "fundamental rights" formulation, a criminal defendant tried by reliable procedures, without brutality, simply has not been denied any fundamental rights.

What procedural safeguard that does *not* protect innocent people ought to count as a fundamental right? If the argument developed in Chapter 5 is sound, dignitary theories of procedure add little to instrumental considerations. If that is so, once a court rejects a procedure, such as grand jury presentment, on instrumental, procedural due process grounds, there is no reason to reconsider the question on substantive due process grounds. The historical evidence, while not dispositive of a substantive due process claim, is surely relevant, and it reinforces the normative position just taken.

The framers' support for "fundamental rights" was typically general; when lawyers, judges, and commentators got down to the procedural requirements in the Bill of Rights, only a few thought of them as among the rights protected by the privileges-or-immunities clause. Lawyers, judges, and commentators did recognize the potential application of the due process clause to criminal procedure. Respected jurists, with few exceptions, however, rejected incorporation of the procedural elements in the Bill of Rights.[117] In contrast, the takings clause was the first item in the Bill incorporated by the Supreme Court, followed by the First Amendment.

A distinction between substance and procedure draws additional support from considerations of institutional competence. An instrumental inquiry into fair procedures is far more determinate than any inquiry into "fundamental fairness."

There is a correspondingly diminished risk that judicial decisions will turn on purely personal moral or political judgments. By contrast, substantive due process analysis runs the greatest risk of judicial lawlessness. The substantive items in the Bill of Rights offer useful guidance about the content of substantive due process. It makes sense to say that, if we are to have substantive due process at all, freedom of speech, security of private property, and the proscription of cruel punishments rank among—and may come close to exhausting—the substantive rights protected by the Fourteenth Amendment.

RULES VERSUS STANDARDS

Prior to *Betts v. Brady*[118] the Supreme Court had defined due process in criminal cases by defining principles applicable to categories of cases. *Powell v. Alabama*[119] dealt only with a capital case, but the language in the opinion looked very much in the direction of requiring counsel, on due process grounds, in all serious cases. *Brown v. Mississippi*[120] declared torture a violation of due process with no suggestion that any exception should ever be recognized. *Betts* departed from the prior formulation of doctrine in rule-like terms in favor of considering the totality of the circumstances in each and every case.

The Warren Court's return to the announcement of generally applicable doctrine provoked some criticism of what was seen as judicial legislation. The *Miranda* rules became a common target of this argument. Yet the practice of announcing rules in the course of deciding cases both antedated and survived the Warren Court. Pre-*Betts* due process cases were couched in terms of prospectively applicable standards. Moreover, in federal cases under the Fourth Amendment the Court quite freely articulated the basis for decision in particular cases in a rule-like manner.

The *Weeks* case held that illegally seized evidence generally must be excluded,[121] while the *Agnello* case held,[122] among other things, that only the search victim could suppress tainted evidence. The *Carroll*[123] case recognized a categorical exception to the warrant requirement for automobile searches, and the *Olmstead*[124] case ruled that absent a physical trespass electronic eavesdropping did not constitute a search. Thus the definition of searches and seizures, the warrant requirement and the exceptions thereto, and the remedy for Fourth Amendment violations, were all defined in rule-like terms in the federal cases decided during the fundamental fairness regime. On some issues, notably the permissible scope of a warrantless search incident to arrest, the Court in this period disdained rule-formulation in favor of case-by-case adjudication, with predictably confusing and arbitrary results.[125]

The Burger and Rehnquist Courts have continued the tradition of defining doctrine in rule-like terms. The *Belton*[126] rule permits search of the passenger compartment of an automobile incident to the arrest of the driver even if their driver is wanted for nothing more violent than tax evasion, and is handcuffed in the sealed back seat of a patrol car while the search takes place. The *Ross*[127] interpretation of the automobile exception applies even when the vehicle to be searched is parked for an indefinite period next door to a courthouse teeming with judges with authority to issue warrants. *Edwards v. Arizona*[128] added a bright-line rule to the basic structure of *Miranda*, holding that under no circumstances may the police continue the interrogation of a suspect in custody who requests a lawyer.

In these cases and many others (including the adminsitrative due process cases setting out constitutional procedural requirements on a wholesale basis) the Court simply publishes the reasoning for the decision in the instant case. If the justices in the majority find certain facts necessary and sufficient to determine the result, and the opinion describes those facts, then the Court's opinion will announce a generally applicable rule. Of course the justices may not anticipate the future perfectly; it may turn out that some unforeseen case comes before them, in which the facts previously thought dispositive are trumped by the unexpected. Put another way, litigants can always attempt to distinguish precedent, and ask the Court to recognize an exception to a general rule previously declared.

Objections to this process are wholly unconvincing. We want the Court to explain its decisions, and the better the explanation, the more likely it is that we can know what result to expect in future cases. The suggestion that Article III's case-and-controversy requirement bars the recognition of rules in judicial opinions[129] is groundless. The only constitutional requirements under Article III are that litigants face actual injury and that the controversy not be feigned or moot. Criminal defendants clearly satisfy these requirements. If the Court on occasion allows a criminal defendant to argue for a general rule on the ground that it may protect other persons in the future, a prudential analysis of third-party standing might be appropriate. But there is no hard and fast Article III prohibition of third-party standing.[130]

On policy grounds the case for general rules governing criminal procedure is overwhelming.[131] The volume of cases presenting constitutional issues, and the need to supply police and lower courts with reliable guidance, weigh strongly in the direction of rule-like opinions.[132] If police and lower courts can't tell what the law is, illegal searches, interrogations, and trial practices will take place needlessly, followed by the equally needless reversal of convictions so obtained. If ever there was a context for rules as opposed to standards, that context is criminal procedure.

The case for clear rules to govern distinct categories of cases was made most prominently by Anthony Amsterdam and Wayne LaFave.[133] Professor LaFave has articulated the following sensible principles to evaluate a proposed bright-line rule:

(1) Does it have clear and certain boundaries, so that it in fact makes unnecessary case-by-case evaluation and adjudication? (2) Does it produce results approximating those which would be obtained *if* accurate case-by-case application of the underlying principle were possible? (3) Is it responsible to a genuine need to forego case-by-case application

of a principle because that approach has proved unworkable? (4) Is it not readily subject to manipulation and abuse?[134]

The case for bright-line rules has been challenged by Albert Alschuler, Craig Bradley, and Chris Slobogin.[135] In one way or another, each questions the feasibility, rather than the desirability, of the LaFave criteria. The skeptics make some important points, but I believe the case for bright-line rules remains powerfully convincing.

Professor Alschuler argues that the Fourth Amendment posits a negligence-type standard that is largely irreducible, so that "[a]bandoning the judging of categories, courts should resume the judging of cases."[136] Whenever possible reasonableness should be determined *ex ante* by neutral judges, but when Fourth Amendment claims are litigated *ex post* the courts should aim to inculcate the basic Fourth Amendment norms, parable style, by case-specific rulings. On Alschuler's account, a comprehensive code of criminal procedure would be a disaster, even if written by legislatures or the police themselves, because the cases involve too many variables to be categorized coherently.

Professor Bradley makes the more modest claim that *the Supreme Court* is incapable of formulating comprehensive and comprehensible rules. He vigorously defends rules, but insists that only an administrative agency could succeed in drafting them.

Professor Slobogin takes the Alschuler view, but with an important, and in my view, critical shift in emphasis. Slobogin emphasizes the indeterminacy of the probable cause and reasonable suspicion standards, fairly noting that these amorphous criteria are not rules at all but rather standards that are applied with something less than consistency.[137] Slobogin himself, however, seems to favor rules that specify the quantum of suspicion required to justify particular categories of intrusions on individual liberty.[138]

We need to carefully distinguish the judicial capability to formulate clear rules from the content of those rules. Obviously a vague standard is better than a rule that clearly requires the wrong result in every case. Leaving the merits of the particular doctrines aside, I think the Supreme Court's decisions in *Miranda*, *Belton*, and *Terry* illustrate both the potential and the limit for formulating bright-line rules in criminal-procedure cases.

Professor Bradley concedes that *Miranda* stands as an example of the Court formulating the sorts of rules he favors.[139] Now *Miranda* was an exceptional case, a self-conscious exercise in judicial lawmaking, based on long experience with the confessions problem, and illuminated by the facts of several cases, state and federal, taken from across the country. The Court should do more of that; *Belton* and *Ross* should have been considered together, and given the furious litigation of container-search cases it should have been easy enough to grant certiorari in a couple of search-incident cases and a couple of probable cause cases. Better bright-line rules might have come from such a process than the ones the Court actually produced. If the issue is stated as the *capacity* of the Court to formulate general rules that provide clear guidance to police, however, *Miranda* offers a powerful example of that very capacity.[140]

Perhaps *Miranda*'s success reflects the relative homogeneity of interrogation cases, in contrast to the more various and more dynamic context of Fourth Amendment issues. *Belton* therefore offers an illuminating illustration. Few of those enamored of *Miranda* favor *Belton*, and vice versa, but both cases announced rules that can (and are) followed in the vast bulk of actual cases.

Critics of *Belton*, beginning with Justice Brennan's dissent, and including both Professor Alschuler and Professor LaFave, have pointed out that the *Belton* rule left some uncertainties about the scope of search incident to the arrest of a vehicle occupant.[141] All rules leave some uncertainties (what H.L.A. Hart called the area of "open texture").[142] As Professor Alschuler pointed out, *Belton* does not determine the scope of a search incident to an arrest on board a cabin cruiser.[143] This is not a point that has caused much consternation among police or trial judges, because arrests on cabin cruisers are quite rare.

Experience has shown that the early critics overstated the residual uncertainties of the *Belton* rule. Apparently unanimous judicial authority holds that the search permitted under *Belton* extends to the areas of hatchbacks, campers, and so on that are accessible without leaving the passenger compartment of the vehicle, and to the glove compartment, whether locked or unlocked.[144] The cases are equally uniform in prohibiting, absent probable cause, search of an automobile trunk that can be accessed only by leaving the vehicle.[145] Respecting the time frame for executing the *Belton* search, Professor LaFave sensibly points out that "the fact that in almost all cases the search will be undertaken at the place of arrest is, as a practical matter, likely to overcome any problems as to temporal proximity."[146] *Belton* is overbroad and invites arrests made for the ulterior purpose of searching a car, but in the main it has provided a reasonably determinate rule.[147] Other rules might have been better and at least as clear, but *Belton* no less than *Miranda* illustrates the Court's capacity for formulating rules.

Terry marks the limit of the desirability of doctrinal rules. As Professor Slobogin pointed out, the difficulty of articulating precise rules is much greater with respect to the quantum of suspicion required to justify a police intrusion than with respect to when the police need a warrant or are required to administer the *Miranda* warning. Here the factual variations between cases become so pronounced that efforts at categorization, of the sort attempted in *Spinelli*, are essentially counterfactual. Every datum known to the police alters the *ex ante* probability that a proposed search or arrest is justified, which makes standards preferable to rules in this context. *Terry* recognized as much, and held that in all cases falling within a definite category of police behavior—the stop for investigation—the police must satisfy a general standard. Like Professor Stuntz,[148] I am less skeptical about the determinacy of the probable cause and reasonable suspicion standards than Professor Slobogin; but no one would classify "probable cause" or "reasonable suspicion" as a rule rather than a standard.

The approach I defend takes what we have learned about the formal qualities of criminal-procedure doctrine from Fourth and Fifth Amendment cases like *Miranda*, *Terry*, and *Belton*, and applies that learning to procedural due process. There scarcely could be a greater contrast between due process analysis under *Betts v. Brady* and the approach I defend. Under *Betts*, the judges asked whether the totality of the circumstances in each case indicated a denial of fundamental fairness. The standard was conclusory and its application deliberately idiosyncratic. By contrast, a procedural due process regime, mediated by the development through cases of generally applicable rules, would involve the application of a meaningful standard applied on a general basis, and might generate comprehensive and comprehensible rules that produce justifiable results in recurring categories of cases.

SCRUPULOUS *STARE DECISIS* IN CRIMINAL-PROCEDURE CASES[149]

The case for relatively clear rules in criminal procedure has important implications for the degree of respect deserved by precedent. Given the volume of criminal cases and the cost of remedying mistakes by police and trial judges, inconsistencies in the case law of the sort bred by conservative balancing is disturbing from a pragmatic, as well as a principled, perspective.

Granted, the decisions of a collective body are liable to inconsistency in a way that individual decisions are not. Collective decision theory's impossibility theorem teaches that no unrigged collective decision process can secure completely transitive results.[150] Thus there will be at least some occasions when a committee in a sequence of cases prefers outcome *A* to outcome *B*, outcome *B* to outcome *C*, and outcome *C* to outcome *A*.

Social choice theory does not, however, prove that intransitive collective preferences need be common, practically important, or unexplained by individual members of the committee. Indeed with respect to both courts and legislatures the most interesting question would appear to be why, given Arrow's theorem, republican institutions do not produce manifestly incoherent decisions more often than they do.

With respect to courts, Professor Stearn has argued that legal conventions such as standing and *stare decisis* operate to reduce the predicted intransitivity of collective decisions.[151] It may turn out that institutional criticism of the Court as a body is justifiable, but that issue can be left unresolved for purposes of my present argument. Even if collective decision theory supplied an excuse for the court as a body, it cannot immunize individual justices from the charge of inconsistency. The argument that follows suggests that individual justices should adopt a more rigorous approach to *stare decisis* in criminal procedure cases. Such an approach, it is submitted, would minimize both the frequency, and the consequences, of the sort of unjustified distinctions drawn in the *Miranda* cases.[152]

Typically a majority that agrees on a decision inconsistent with a prior decision will be composed of two factions. The first faction includes the dissenters from the prior decision, who continue to believe the first decision mistaken. Although in the minority in case 1, the former dissenters are now reinforced by the vote or votes of those who believe that case 2 is really distinguishable from case 1. If case 1 was decided by a narrow majority, it can well be that in case 2 seven or eight justices agree that cases 1 and 2 should reach the same result, but the Court concludes that the two cases are distinguishable.

Let us label the two factions the "idiosyncratic center" and "the unrepentant dissenters." Thus in *Dickerson*, for practical reasons, a majority did not want to return to case-by-case adjudication. Nonetheless, at least Chief Justice Rehnquist presumably still disagrees with *Miranda*'s original justification. If at least two other justices in the *Dickerson* majority (as sheer speculation, say O'Connor and Kennedy) reject *Miranda*'s original justification but refuse to overrule *Miranda* itself because of *stare decisis*, no more than four justices would support *Miranda*'s original justification.

The situation is likely to get even messier, because Justice Scalia announced in dissent that he will continue to vote his conscience in future *Miranda* cases.[153] If Justice Thomas, who joined Scalia's dissent, follows suit, there will be two votes for the government in every *Miranda* case. One supposes that they will often enjoy the support of the Chief Justice, whose majority opinion labors so hard to avoid repudiating the prophylactic-rules cases. Only two more justices would be needed to rule in favor of admitting a disputed statement. We may thus see cases in which distinct majorities of the justices agree that the suspect was in custody, that the suspect was interrogated, that the suspect did not make a valid waiver, that *Miranda* remains good law, and that the confession is nonetheless admissible.

Given the need for broad rulings in criminal-procedure cases, it is especially important for justices to accept the justification of precedents with which they disagree. There is no way to prevent one or two justices from sincerely but implausibly seeing a distinction between similar cases. Scrupulous *stare decisis*, however, could avoid writing idiosyncratic distinctions into actual law. Unrepentant dissenters should confine themselves to critique, and wait for the day when their views persuade a majority. Justice Harlan's opinion in *Orozco v. Texas* takes the correct approach; his vote to join the majority in *Harris* does not.

Consider, in this context, the fruits and impeachment cases. Surely not every justice in the majorities in *Harris*, *Tucker*, *Hass*, and *Elstad* believed that those decisions were really consistent with *Miranda*. While it may never be proved, it is likely that at least some of the justices in those majorities understood their votes as laying the groundwork for an eventual overruling of *Miranda*.[154] As a result, we now deal with major inconsistencies between the *Miranda* cases and the formal-compulsion Fifth Amendment cases, a tension that went far enough as to persuade one Court of Appeals that *Miranda* itself was no longer good law. If Chief Justice Burger, and Justices Rehnquist, Blackmun, White, Stewart, and Harlan had followed *Miranda*'s doctrinal logic, they would have prevented the inconsistent development of the case law in the first place. A great deal of the criticism of the existing law therefore falls to prior votes by justices accepting the prophylactic-rules characterization in prior cases.

The obligation of individual justices to follow precedents with which they disagree is supported by constitutional principle as well as by criminal justice pragmatism. A powerful argument can be made that individual justices who continue to vote on the premise that prior decisions were wrong is engaging in civil disobedience rather than adjudication. The special institutional challenges in the criminal cases gives this jurisprudential claim a special pragmatic urgency, but it a strong claim in its own right.

In its dealings with officials of the state governments and of the other branches of the national government, the Supreme Court has maintained that the Court's decisions are the supreme law of the land. The claim that a single official, sincerely disagreeing with the Court's interpretation, may disregard that interpretation in favor of his own, was precisely the claim that Governor Faubus made in *Cooper v. Aaron*.[155] The Court rejected that claim unanimously, and has not since called *Cooper* into question.[156] The *Dickerson* majority rejected the claim that the Congress, a coordinate branch of the federal government, might disregard the Court's interpretation of the Constitution.[157] Indeed, the Court has rejected that claim even when Congress acts pursuant to its textually granted power under section five of the Fourteenth Amendment.[158]

The broad principle announced in *Cooper* is of course intensely controversial.[159] A strong tradition in both political history and contemporary scholarship defends the right of presidents and legislators to act on their independent interpretations of the Constitution, even when their interpretations conflict with established Supreme Court precedent.[160] On the other hand, the practical need for some final authority on constitutional interpretation, and the institutional advantages of the judiciary in playing that role, support the expansive position taken by the Court in *Cooper*.[161]

In any given case the Supreme Court may be wrong (legally and/or morally) and the other official right (again legally and/or morally). As Professors Schauer and Alexander have pointed out, if the law is to fulfill the settlement function, there must be a decision rule to govern such conflicts.[162] The location of interpretive finality can only be guided by institutional predictors of right decisions. This side of heaven, these predictors will sometimes assign interpretive finality to an institution entertaining a mistaken view. Realistically the decision rule can only minimize, not eliminate, constitutional mistakes.

The argument for the content-independent authority of Supreme Court precedents *vis a vis* individual justices is stronger than the argument for judicial supremacy generally. In the first place, individual justices who agree with the *Cooper* principle cannot reject the authority of precedents without unreasonable inconsistency. Whatever the theory on which the doctrine of judicial supremacy rests, no justice can consistently maintain judicial supremacy while regarding herself as unobligated by decisions of the Court.[163]

This is not to say that civil disobedience is never justified. Von Stauffenberg was a hero, not a wrongdoer. Justice Brennan signed the opinion in *Cooper*, but he might have concluded that other obligations had priority over his obligation to treat *Gregg* as the law.[164] Judicial civil disobedience, however, is especially hard to defend. Judges, unlike ordinary citizens, swear an oath to uphold the law. Unlike ordinary citizens, they claim the obedience of others to their decisions on the basis of a general obligation to obey the law. They have the options of recusal, resignation, and concurrence-with-critique. One wonders how Justice Brennan would have dealt with lower court judges who subverted the Court's rulings in *Miranda* or *Roe v. Wade* by saying "Here I draw the line."

Alternatively, a justice might reject *Cooper* and agree that all officials in all branches owe allegiance to the Constitution as each interprets it. Justice Scalia may well take this very view,[165] in which case his promised defiance of *Miranda* and *Dickerson* would not be a manifest inconsistency. My claim here, however, is that whatever the merits of the larger debate over *Cooper*, individual justices in criminal-procedure cases ought to follow in good-faith precedents they believe mistaken. This narrow claim draws its strength from the heightened importance of the settlement function with respect to judges, and the special importance of the settlement function in criminal-procedure cases.

Consider, first, the difference between individual Article III judges, including Supreme Court justices, and other public officials. Presidents and members of Congress have their own constitutional responsibilities, which sometimes call for constitutional interpretation. The case for coordinate review is strongest when officials in the political branches find it necessary to interpret the Constitution in the exercise of their own constitutional duties. Thus a legislator is thought free to vote against a bill she regards as unconstitutional, even though Supreme Court precedent holds that such a bill is constitutional. A president is thought to have a right to veto a bill under similar circumstances.

A plausible rejoinder might be made to the effect that voting against legislation that would promote the general welfare because of reservations about formal legality the courts have rejected is both practically unheard of and gratuitously costly.[166] However that argument might be resolved, judges play a different role than the president and members of Congress. Judges act on the basis of debatable constitutional interpretations all the time. Indeed, unlike other officials, they do very little *except* make debatable legal interpretations. A Supreme Court justice who views *Cooper* as inapplicable to herself logically takes the same view regarding lower court judges as well. How can a justice ask an appellate or district court judge to violate a solemn oath to uphold the Constitution?

Suppose a justice is sitting by designation on a circuit court panel. The case is governed by a Supreme Court decision from which this justice dissented. Is the justice free to disregard the precedent? If yes, are not her colleagues on the circuit court panel equally entitled to do so? If not, why is the justice obliged to follow precedent on circuit but not on the Supreme Court?

The settlement function of law is generally thought to require adherence to precedent by lower court judges. Interpretive autonomy could not be regulated by the threat of reversal. Trial judges can bend factual findings to reach the results each thinks constitutionally required in ways that are immune to appellate scrutiny. Appellate judges know the limits on the Supreme Court's docket very well. Interpretive anarchy in the judiciary would lead to something approaching genuine anarchy. Not only would similar cases be resolved differently, forum-shopping become imperative, and uncertainty make reliance problematic. Many of the constitutional interpretations that would be allowed to flourish would be quite wrong as well.

Whatever the merits of the case for judicial supremacy generally, the case of an individual justice is closer to that of a lower court judge than it is to that of the president or a senator. Moreover, the settlement function of law is magnified by the institutional context of criminal procedure. If my analysis of the institutional context of criminal procedure is correct, individual justices should follow precedent *even if precedent is indeed erroneous*. Better a second-best rule consistently applied than a second-best rule erratically applied.

This account of scrupulous *stare decisis* is not in service to any particular ideological cause. The individual justices who refused to follow *Gregg v. Georgia*[167] may well be right that the death penalty is immoral. They were certainly within their rights to criticize *Gregg* in the hope that a majority of their colleagues would one day hold capital punishment unconstitutional *per se*. But they were no more authorized by law to dissent from the imposition of the death penalty in a case free from error under *Gregg* and its progeny than a condemned prisoner was authorized by law to escape. Imagine the reception the convict would receive when he cites the opinions of Brennan, Marshall, and Blackmun as authority for a jailbreak.

Perhaps capital punishment is a special case, unique in its moral gravity. If this is so, however, the correct approach for a justice unwilling to have blood on her hands is to recuse herself from capital cases. Let justices capable of following the law decide the case.[168] That, at least, seems to have been the Court's message to those judges on the *lower* federal courts who blocked executions on less than compelling legal grounds.[169] It is also the message the Court consistently has sent to mere citizens called for jury duty who honestly express implacable moral opposition to a penalty the Court has found constitutional.[170]

The death penalty example is a telling one, because just as in the *Miranda* context the unrepentant dissenters enabled the formation of majorities upholding inconsistent results. With two votes against the imposition of the death penalty under any circumstances, the defendant needed to convince only three of the seven remaining justices that the challenged sentence ran afoul of *Gregg* and its progeny. As a result, state capital punishment statutes were struck down both because they allowed too little, and because they allowed too much, discretion.[171]

The death penalty example is telling in another way as well. Continued dissent has been the exception, not the rule. Many prominent criminal-procedure examples might be cited, including Justices White's majority opinion in *Edwards v. Arizona* and Justice Harlan's concurring opinion in *Orozco v. Texas*, both applying *Miranda*. Chief Justice Rehnquist's *Dickerson* opinion reflects the same respect for authority, although *Miranda* predates the Chief Justice's tenure on the Court. That only a few justices have felt the need for repeated dissent in the especially troubling moral context of capital punishment does more to bolster than to weaken the argument for scrupulous *stare decisis*.[172]

If we add the need for broad rulings in the criminal context to the powerful case for treating majority decisions as binding individual justices, we have a compelling warrant against the Marshall/Brennan/Blackmun practice in the death cases and against the promised Scalia/Thomas practice in future *Miranda* cases. The clarity of the needed rules will be compromised, and like cases will be treated differently. The general duty of officers of the republic to obey the Constitution as construed by the Court is given special urgency in the criminal context.

My claim is distinct from any claim that criminal-procedure precedents deserve special deference from future Supreme Court *majorities*. Quite the reverse; given the volume of constitutional litigation involving criminal-procedure questions, Supreme Court majorities should feel at least as free to overrule precedent in these cases as in others. The larger the corpus of precedents the more likely that inconsistent outliers will emerge over time. For that reason the Court should have a clear conscience about periodically cleaning house.

Views about the weight of the content-independent respect constitutional precedents deserve from succeeding majorities of the Supreme Court vary. Justice Brandeis famously argued that because constitutional decisions could not be changed by ordinary legislation, the Court should feel more willing to reconsider constitutional precedents than decisions that Congress or the states could modify by statute.[173] By now equally famous is the view of the plurality in *Planned Parenthood of Southeastern Pennsylvania v. Casey*,[174] to the effect that especially prominent decisions inviting extensive reliance should not be overruled in the face of criticism that might be understood as an attack on the independence of the Court.

The criminal-procedure context generally calls for following the Brandeis approach. The Supreme Court makes a vast amount of quite quotidian law regulating the police and the criminal trial process. A few landmarks stand out, *Gideon* and *Miranda* most prominently. But in the main the Court has, by the default of legislatures and the textual commands of the Constitution, become the most important source of criminal-procedure law. Given this institutional context, when a Supreme Court precedent loses majority support, conflicts with other decisions that retain majority support, and a case presenting the question comes properly before the Court, there should be a willingness to overrule openly rather than to put on the fig leaf of unconvincing distinctions.

There is a sense that the incorporation regime is too well-settled to be reconsidered.[175] When asked about overruling the incorporation decisions, for example, Justice Scalia is reported to have replied "I'm a serious constitutional scholar, not a nut."[176] Yet a justice who favors a due process approach to criminal-procedure cases need not depart from the judicial mainstream. Such a justice could begin by concurring in decisions based on the current paradigm but suggesting a due process approach in separate opinions. If a majority of the justices came round to such a view, the Court could reinvigorate independent due process analysis by discarding the artificial limits set by the *Medina* and *Lewis* decisions. Once due process regained its independent potency, a majority might be willing to at least modify incorporation along the lines suggested by Justices Harlan and Powell. The states, for example, might be allowed to require pretrial in-court questioning of the accused subject to an adverse influence at trial from the failure to answer questions. Substituting, in state cases, due process analysis for analysis based on the procedural provisions in the Bill of Rights would be the end, rather than the beginning, of a long process of reform. So long as individual justices adhered to incorporation precedents until a majority was prepared to depart from them, the law would not be distorted by competing paradigms. If the prospects of success look bleak, they are surely more promising than those confronting Justice Black in the 1940s, when he began his ultimately successful struggle on behalf of the incorporation approach.

CONSTITUTIONAL REMEDIES

A shift in emphasis away from the Bill of Rights and toward procedural due process analysis will not by itself extricate us from the difficulties of identifying the appropriate remedy for constitutional violations. When the police violate the exclusivity principle by abridging individual liberty during the course of investigation, the remedial issue differs little if at all from the current Fourth Amendment context. The courts can either exclude the evidence, or leave the search victim to pursue an illusory tort remedy.

Since *Mapp* the Supreme Court has made this choice in favor of exclusion, but in an ever-more half-hearted way. The proliferation of exceptions to exclusion manifest the Supreme Court's hostility to the exclusionary rule, even if the rule's persistence reflects just how skeptical even conservative jurists are of the tort remedy.[177] Trial court judges can't change the law, but they do find the facts and apply the law. Judges ruling on suppression motions frequently credit implausible police testimony,[178] and favor the government when deciding borderline cases under the probable cause or reasonable suspicion standard.[179] Especially in state court systems with elected judges, a system that depends on the willingness of judges to throw out cases against palpably guilty criminals quite simply asks too much.[180] This is not to say that the exclusionary rule is a total failure or should be abolished. But it does point to the key defect in the exclusionary rule, which is that by excluding discovered evidence we are "rubbing our noses"[181] in the price we pay for the Constitution. Prudence recommends a different remedy—if one can be found.

If the exclusionary rule's inherent defect is that only the guilty can call it into play, the key difficulty with the tort remedy is the intractable unwillingness of

legislatures to provide a tort system that really deters unconstitutional police behavior.[182] Minimum damages, set high enough to deter without regard to the
quantum of actual damage sustained by the victim, plus attorneys' fees, payable
by the police department or the municipality, would indeed deter. They might
deter so well that police would refrain from much lawful activity and so cost us
more in the way of lost evidence than the exclusionary rule. They have thus far
certainly deterred legislatures from imposing any such system.

When the police undermine the adjudication by collecting evidence in a needlessly unreliable manner, an even more painful remedial dilemma arises. When
the police stage a needlessly suggestive lineup, or fail to preserve physical evidence that might have been tested later by, for example, the DNA technique, the
courts confront what may be called the problem of second-best evidence. Ideally
the police should have staged an unsuggestive lineup, or preserved the physical
evidence for testing. But judges no more than other human beings have power to
change the past. And in these cases the proof the government does have is not, in
the usual sense, unreliable. It just isn't as reliable as it should have been.

If the courts exclude the evidence the government *does* have, the jury is denied relevant evidence in the hope that this sanction will deter future failures to
develop the case in the most reliable way. Next time around, the police will conduct a better lineup, or preserve the physical evidence as the case may be. This is
a high price to demand for deterrence of slipshod investigations, a price the
Supreme Court has refused to pay.

In the identification cases the Court now requires exclusion only when the
identification was tainted by unnecessary suggestion *and* this suggestion caused
a substantial risk of mistaken identification.[183] Even then a subsequent courtroom
identification typically will be received as "independent" of the pretrial identification.[184] In the physical evidence context, the Court concluded that the police
have incentives of their own to preserve evidence, and so there was no need for
enforcing a constitutional requirement to that effect.[185]

Despite the furious controversy over the exclusionary rule, there is a good deal
of common ground. It is generally agreed that tort remedies, as presently arranged,
are ineffective, and that they could be made effective only by curtailing the immunity defenses, imposing entity liability, and setting minimum damages at a
level high enough to deter.[186] Exclusion, by contrast, solves the representation
problem and the evaluation problem. The criminal defendant, after *Gideon*, will
have a lawyer,[187] and suppression comes close to setting the sanction equal to the
anticipated gain from the violation.[188] On the other hand, the disadvantages of
exclusion are equally well known. Exclusion does nothing for the innocent, in
rare cases costs the community convictions that might have been obtained with
better police work, and can be self-defeating to the extent that the judges tilt their
rulings to avoid releasing the obviously guilty.

What I want to suggest here is that judges have the power to enter, and ought
to begin experimenting with, orders suppressing evidence unless the police department or the city pays a sum set by the court to the victim of the constitutional

infraction.[189] The theory is that current law empowers the suppression of the illegally obtained evidence, so that the contingent suppression order does not involve any usurpation of power. The judge is cutting the government a break, not imposing any new obligation. If the city doesn't like the number set by the judge, the city can just refuse to pay and let the chips fall where they may when the case proceeds without the evidence subject to the suppression order.

In reality, however, this practice opens up some exciting new possibilities. From the standpoint of law enforcement, the community would no longer be stuck with the loss of a conviction that might have been obtained with better police work. From the standpoint of civil liberties, judges would be far more willing to reject police perjury and to apply the probable cause and reasonable suspicion standards even-handedly knowing that there is an alternative other than tolerance of either private crime or public lawlessness.

Defendants would still have powerful incentives to litigate their claims. As things stand many defense lawyers have learned not to waste time on suppression motions. The contingent suppression ruling greatly increases the probability that a motion will be granted. Even in contingent form, a successful motion would benefit the defendant. Better prison and ten thousand dollars than prison, period. Moreover, the prospect of weighty damage awards can cause prosecutors to strike a generous plea bargain in exchange for release from liability.

Would a contingent suppression order comply with *Mapp v. Ohio*? Once the Warren Court refused to apply *Mapp* retroactively, it became obvious that *Mapp* rested on deterrence, not on self-incrimination or judicial integrity. *Calandra* and its progeny have reinforced that message. If *Mapp*, as I believe, held that some effective remedy is constitutionally required and that experience had proved that judicially mandated exclusion was the only thing that worked, then *Mapp* does not preclude a remedial innovation that deters as effectively as exclusion.

Would a contingent order deter as effectively as exclusion? A simplistic answer would be no, on the theory that the prosecution can always elect the least painful alternative, so that a contingent suppression order might reduce, but cannot increase, the penalty for constitutional violations. This view is simplistic, because it depends on the assumption that the outcome of the suppression motion is independent of the remedy. The defense is far more likely to win a motion that leaves ultimate responsibility for the release of the guilty on the prosecution, the police, or the city.

The contingent order might further deterrence in another way. Once in place, the contingent suppression motion would sap the vitality of the exceptions to the exclusionary rule. If the government turns down the damages option, the impeachment, attenuation, inevitable discovery, and standing exceptions might be reconsidered. After all, the government did violate constitutional rights; if the government won't pay the damages, why should it be allowed to benefit from its wrongdoing? This might not happen right away, but in the long run severing the exclusionary rule from the necessary loss of the evidence could reinforce the judicial willingness to apply the exclusionary rule so as to restore the *status quo ante* as an alternative to payment of damages.

Of course, if the court sets damages too low, deterrence could suffer dramatically. One great advantage of the exclusionary rule is that it approximates an equation of the government's expected gain from the violation and the expected cost of the sanction. The equation is not perfect, for a variety of reasons. Sometimes the government is not interested in prosecution, only in seizing contraband. And to the extent that the exclusionary rule reduces the probability of a defense victory on the suppression motion, the loss in certainty of the sanction may more than undermine the theoretically correct severity of exclusion.

In a damages-only regime, everything depends on setting the damages correctly. Too high, and the police will refrain from lawful investigations. Too low, and the police will be invited to buy their way around the Constitution. The contingent suppression remedy eliminates the risk of setting damages too high; the government can decide not to pay and at worst lose the case. The real danger attending a mixed exclusion/damages regime is therefore that the damages will be set too low, inviting the police to purchase exemptions from the exclusionary rule.

Ultimately the minimum damages for categories of violations—illegal stops, illegal frisks, illegal auto searches, illegal home searches, and so on—would be set by the federal courts as a matter of constitutional law. They could be adjusted in light of changes in circumstances, economic and otherwise. A certain amount of initial experimentation would be highly informative. If the government typically refuses to pay the damages and accepts exclusion instead, then pretty plainly the damages would be too high. If, on the other hand, the government always agreed to pay the damages and never accepted exclusion, then even more clearly the damages would be too low.

I have previously suggested, quite casually, $10,000 for an illegal stop, $25,000 for an illegal search, and $50,000 for an illegal home invasion.[190] Those numbers might sound draconian in light of police officer salaries, but it must be remembered that under the proposed remedy, the courts can totally bypass individual liability and impose entity liability, without immunity. Just as with the exclusionary rule, the city and the police department will get the message across to individual officers.

If law enforcement agents deliberately violate constitutional limits, expecting to pay the prevailing damages as a cost of doing business, the courts could either increase the amount necessary to stave off exclusion or simply impose a noncontingent suppression order. Another complication concerns illegal interrogations; to the extent that the Fifth Amendment forbids *using*, as well as *obtaining*, admissions from the defendant, the Constitution would not permit the purchase of license to violate its terms. With that caveat, I submit that the contingent suppression order would mark a promising improvement on the remedial approaches hitherto attempted.

In particular, the contingent suppression order has great appeal in the context of second-best evidence. If the government stages an unnecessarily suggestive lineup, the court could exclude the lineup evidence and bar any in-court identification, unless the government pays a substantial penalty for making the trial record less trustworthy than it easily could have been. Likewise with the failure to collect or preserve potentially exculpatory evidence, the court could exclude state evidence that might have been contradicted by the lost evidence, subject to the payment of a substantial penalty. Without throwing out second-best evidence, the courts could give the police powerful incentives to prepare a better record in subsequent cases.

A NOTE ON EQUAL PROTECTION

The due process theory I have defended would make some important contributions to reducing racial discrimination in criminal justice. Requiring more-reliable, less-intrusive investigations and more rigorous trials *for everybody* would do more to protect blacks than whites, because blacks are more likely than whites to be targeted for crimes they didn't commit, and to lack the resources to prove their innocence through the aid of highly paid defense lawyers. But just as obviously, an instrumental theory of procedure doesn't do enough to combat discrimination. Any such theory leaves open the possibility that laws violated by both blacks and whites will be enforced disportionately when violated by blacks.

This possibility is all too real. Although black and white usage rates for marijuana and cocaine are similar, blacks are four or five times more likely to be prosecuted for these offenses.[191] In some of our states there are more young black men in prison, on probation, or awaiting trial than are enrolled in institutions of higher education.[192] A third of the nation's young black men are under the control of the criminal justice system; a quarter of the black male population will serve prison time if present trends continue.[193] The available empirical evidence strongly suggests that the police use the power to stop for investigation under *Terry* against a disproprionate number of blacks and Hispanics.[194]

These facts cry out for equal protection analysis. Conventional equal protection doctrine requires proof of invidious intent to establish a constitutional violation.[195] Intent, in this context, means hostility toward members of a suspect class; mere knowledge that a policy will have even grossly disproportionate effects will not suffice.[196] Intent can be proved by direct evidence of what state actors did and said, or inferred from overwhelming statistical disparities.[197] A showing of something less than catastrophic disparities will not, in the constitutional context, trigger the burden-shifting analysis applied in the Title VII cases. When, however, the individual can show that state actors were motivated in significant part by racial animus, the government will lose unless it can prove that the individual would not have been treated any differently had she belonged to a different race.[198]

The incorporation model, however, has stunted equal protection doctrine in much the same way that it has stunted independent due process doctrine. The Fourth Amendment cases have banished official motivation from the considerations that make searches or seizures reasonable or unreasonable. For example, in *Whren v. United States*, the Court upheld a traffic stop made by vice squad officers because the vehicle containing the young black suspects had indeed been driven in violation of some traffic laws.[199]

The Supreme Court has *never* reached the merits of an equal protection challenge to the exercise of police enforcement discretion. There are only a handful of cases in the federal courts of appeals.[200] If legal consciousness began to think of criminal procedure in Fourteenth Amendment terms, more equal protection challenges would be brought, and they might be more sympathetically received.

Batson illustrates that even conservative justices may take an aggressive approach to equal protection cases. At least three special features of jury selection cases help to explain the Court's willingness to intervene in *Batson*. First, reversing convictions on jury selection grounds does not ordinarily free the guilty. It only requires a retrial with a properly selected jury; if the state has a strong case, the chances are that the defendant will be convicted on remand. In effect, the remedy for jury selection errors is a deterrent monetary penalty, not nullification of valid charges.

By contrast, when the requested relief is the release of the guilty, judicial sympathy will be limited. Because most crime is intraracial, the judge who quashes the prosecution of a black suspect on equal protection grounds is doing no favor to the community.[201] The real evil in such a case is not the prosecution of the defendant, but the failure of the system to target for investigation equally guilty white offenders. The courts have the power to nullify the prosecution of blacks, but they have had no such power to compel the investigation of whites.

Second, because the jurors are not suspects, the government in a jury selection case can make no use of the fact that strong sociological evidence shows that blacks as a class, especially young black men, are more likely than others to commit the common street crimes.[202] Regardless of the reasons for this disparity, when suspects raise equal protection challenges there is the standing risk that courts will view an inference of suspicion from racial status as rational. The jury selection pool is drawn from all ages and genders; the same judges who might tolerate an inference of suspicion on the street based on race, age, and gender might well recoil from any inference of unfitness for jury duty based on race alone.

Third, overwhelming empirical evidence indicated that prosecutors had abused the *Swain* rule by systematically purging juries of blacks in cases against black defendants. The corrosive effects of this practice had become notorious.

When these conditions have not obtained, the Court has reverted to a grudging view of inferring invidious intent from disparate impact. In *United States v. Armstrong*, the Court rejected a defense request for discovery of prosecuturial decisions in drug cases against white suspects.[203] Only if the defendants could show "some evidence" of discrimination in charging decisions would the majority have allowed discovery. The ruling has a Khafkaesque quality; to show discrimination you must show disparate treatment in other cases, but you cannot discover the treatment in other cases without first proving discrimination.[204]

The *Armstrong* litigation differed from *Batson* along all three lines previously discussed. The individuals were not prospective jurors, but apparently guilty criminals seeking to escape their just deserts. Even if disparate impact were shown, that might only reflect higher rates of black offending—and if it were the case, perhaps it might as well go unsaid, disposed of as a technical matter of pretrial discovery. Finally, the United States Attorney's offices enjoy a strong reputation for integrity; there is no long empirical record of federal discrimination in charge selection as there was a long record of discrimination in the exercise of peremptory challenges.

If police decisions in selecting black individuals for investigations were challenged on equal protection grounds with the contingent exclusionary rule as the expected relief, the matrix of decision would change dramatically. A decision for the defense would not necessarily free the guilty. Instead, just as reversal in jury selection cases does, the contingent order would impose a monetary penalty for the government's improper motives, without nullifying a search or arrest that, but for the tainted motive, was entirely justified.

Moreover, there is strong, and growing, empirical evidence that police targeting decisions are discriminatory. The available studies show a serious disparate impact from police decisions to stop for investigation or for traffic enforcement.[205] A swelling chorus of "anecdotal" evidence testifies to the frequency with which law-abiding young black and Hispanic men are detained for investigation by the police, and to the corrosive effect on public confidence in the administration of justice these confrontations produce.[206]

The remaining difference between jury selection and police practices cases is the willingness to infer criminality from racial status. In the context of Fourth Amendment challenges to immigration enforcement the Supreme Court has expressed some tolerance for considering apparent Hispanic ethnicity as one reason for stopping vehicles to investigate illegal immigration.[207] Standard equal protection law is to the contrary; if race is a factor in the decision, the government has the burden of proving that the decision would have been the same even if the individual had been white instead of black.[208]

The tolerance of race-based decision making found in some of the Fourth Amendment cases has no place in equal protection analysis. What the Fourth Amendment cases strikingly neglect is the injustice of selecting persons for deprivations of liberty and dignity because they happen to be black. That more of them turn out to be guilty than would be true in an equally large sample of persons drawn from other races is irrelevant. Not only are a great many *innocent* people detained, frisked, searched, and generally ill-used by the police on account of their race.[209] Even the guilty have the right to be treated as individuals. Randall Kennedy makes a devastating, unanswerable point: If color blindness is a principle important enough to call into question affirmative action programs designed *for the benefit* of the one racial group our society reduced to slavery, surely it is a principle important enough to trump some marginal efficiencies in policing.[210]

Imagine a government office that refused to hire blacks because sociological evidence shows that blacks are more likely than whites to commit theft. Suppose that a sports franchise segregated the stadium seating arrangements to concentrate security guards in the black sections, or that a public school required black, but not white, students to pass through metal detectors or to submit to urinalysis to test for drug abuse.

Each of these examples rests on an inference of criminality based on collective character. The equal protection clause forbids that inference even when it seems rational in light of empirical evidence. It could go without saying that stopping blacks but not whites to investigate a specific crime in which the witnesses or informants described the perpetrator as black is a different matter.[211]

The offensiveness of the previous examples, I think, shows that the real basis for current doctrine is the unwillingness to free the guilty for the sake of equality. The contingent exclusionary rule has the potential to cut this albatross from the neck of equal protection analysis. In effect, a contingent suppression order replicates the consequences of retrials in jury-selection cases. The government pays a monetary penalty for impure motives, but does not forfeit the prosecution of a guilty defendant.

Satisfying these conditions could lead to at least three doctrinal reforms. First, prevailing equal-protection mixed-motive doctrine should trump the Fourth Amendment's objective tests.[212] Officers who select suspects for investigation based in part on race would be called upon to prove that white suspects would have been treated identically. At the intersection of race and crime equal protection scrutiny should reach its zenith, not its nadir. Once the remedy does not automatically free the guilty, the laxer standard in the Fourth Amendment cases would become indefensible.

Second, the Court might resort to the *Batson* burden-shifting analysis on a wider basis.[213] Surely municipal police are less deserving of a presumption of regularity than the United States Attorney's office, which was the locus of alleged discrimination in the *Armstrong* case. A growing empirical record documents the disproportionate impact of street-level policing on blacks and Hispanics. In the police-practices context *Batson* might be understood to authorize discovery of the arresting officers' track records, and a Title VII type rebuttable inference of animus from even a limited record of disparate impact.

Third, absent the consequence of wholesale nullification, the Court might reconsider the distinction between intent and knowledge. The *Feeney* case establishing the distinction involved a state statute that provided a preference for veterans in state hiring decisions. Ninety-eight percent of veterans in the state were male. The law thus had a foreseeable impact on women, but the Court held that knowledge without hostility failed to make out an equal protection violation.

The *Feeney* decision did not involve race and it did not involve crime. Racial classifications, are subject to strict scrutiny, unlike gender classifications, which are subject to intermediate scrutiny. Criminal liabilities are the most onerous the government can impose. When police and prosecutors determine strategic enforcement priorities, knowing that these decisions will have an overwhelmingly disparate impact on blacks, the distinction between invidious intent and "malign neglect" seems untenable.[214]

In short, the contingent exclusionary rule offers the judges the opportunity to impose a kind of tax on state action that subjects blacks, but not similarly situated whites, to the burdens of investigation, prosecution, and imprisonment. Whether, in a conservative political period, the judges would take that opportunity is problematic. What I would claim is that by offering a remedy that does not automatically free the guilty, and by redirecting attention from the Bill of Rights to the Fourteenth Amendment, the approach I defend would greatly enhance the prospects for more rigorous equal protection scrutiny of criminal law enforcement. The statistics with which we started make that an urgent project.

CONCLUSION

The Fourteenth Amendment model of constitutional criminal procedure cases is now complete. According to the model, procedural due process prohibits unnecessary risks of erroneous convictions at trial, and requires that, if burdens on individual liberty are to be justified by the government's interest in criminal law enforcement, those burdens must be proportionate to the expectation that crime will thereby be prevented or exposed. The urgency of rule-of-law values in the criminal-procedure context calls for applying these principles by formulating doctrinal rules. These same rule-of-law values call on individual justices to follow the justifying logic of precedents they do not approve; rule-of-law values likewise call for Supreme Court majorities to overrule freely and candidly precedents that have lost contemporary majority support.

As a matter of constitutional law and political necessity, the federal courts have an obligation to develop effective remedies for self-executing constitutional provisions. In the spirit of *Mapp*, this obligation might be met by a mixed regime of damages and exclusion, in which the payment of damages as an alternative to suppression permits the courts to develop a schedule of minimum damages, impose entity liability, and cut through immunity defenses. Such a remedial scheme in turn would greatly facilitate the development of more rigorous equal protection analysis in criminal cases. The final chapter turns to how this general regime might be applied to some illustrative problems in criminal procedure.

7

Applications

Thus far I have argued for a new constitutional regime in criminal procedure, a regime based in state cases directly on the Fourteenth Amendment rather than on the Bill of Rights. The previous chapter explained how such a regime would be more consonant both with the legitimate sources of constitutional law and with the instrumental values that ought to control when authoritative sources leave room for reasonable disagreement. This chapter describes some illustrative applications of the proposed regime. In the process I hope to emphasize its advantages over its doctrinal competitors.

PROTECTING THE INNOCENT

Due Process Limitations on Police Investigations— Identification Evidence

The once-prevailing view held that almost all criminal defendants are guilty.[1] Attributing to municipal police forces competence exceeding that of, say, NASA seems improbable, and a growing body of evidence suggests good reason for skepticism about the reliability of police investigations. A continuing stream of high-profile cases of wrongful conviction floods the newspapers.[2] More systematic evidence comes from the results of DNA tests performed at the request of police. In a nationwide sample of more than twenty thousand such tests, a quarter of the conclusive results exonerated the suspect.[3] There is little reason to think that the police do better in cases without DNA evidence.

Of course there's the trial process to backstop the police investigation. But a fair trial is no substitute for a fair investigation. A celestial dream-team of Cicero, Lincoln, and Darrow couldn't call an alibi witness who was never identified, obtain a laboratory test on physical evidence that was never collected, or shake the testimony of an eyewitness prompted into certitude by the police. Recognizing the continuity of the investigation and the trial is the first step toward realizing procedural due process in the investigation.

The leading cause of false convictions is erroneous eyewitness testimony.[4] Constitutional doctrine regulating identification procedures is virtually nonexistent. There is a right to counsel at post-indictment lineups[5] but the government can avoid this requirement simply by delaying indictment until after the lineup.[6] In any event the right to counsel does not apply to photographic arrays,[7] which are at least as common as lineups.

There is a vestigial due process test that authorizes exclusion of a pretrial identification only when unnecessary suggestiveness viewed in the totality of the circumstances shows a high probability of mistaken identification.[8] The test is rarely met.[9] The current due process test, moreover, like the fundamental fairness cases whence it derives, gives the police no guidance on how identifications ought to be conducted.

Application of an instrumental procedural due process test modeled on *Mathews v. Eldridge* could improve the situation. To a degree the problem is irreducible. Perception and memory are not very good, especially under stress.[10] The available empirical evidence suggests that eyewitnesses do a passable job of identifying the perpetrator *when the perpetrator* is in the lineup or the photo array.[11] The problem is that the witnesses tend to pick *someone* even when the perpetrator is *not* in the lineup. Not surprisingly they tend to select the individual in the array or the lineup who most closely resembles the perpetrator.

Two straightforward, *Miranda*-style rules suggest themselves as a matter of procedural due process. First, the foils in the lineup or the array should bear a reasonable resemblance to the description of the perpetrator given by the witnesses before any confrontation with the suspect. Second, the identification procedure should be administered by officers who are ignorant of the suspect's identity.

The reasonable-resemblance requirement reduces the risk that the suspect will be chosen merely because of a resemblance to the perpetrator. With foils who could not have committed the crime (police officers or those who were in jail at the time of the offense, photographs of deceased persons, etc.) but who resemble the described perpetrator, this risk would be reduced to its practical minimum. "Reasonable resemblance" is obviously a standard rather than a rule, but just as with "probable cause" there will be clear cases where the standard is and is not met.[12] In clear cases of violation suppression would be appropriate on reliability grounds; in less clear cases a contingent suppression order might be justified solely by deterrence considerations.

The second rule, when complied with, would eliminate the risk of official suggestion. An officer who does not know which of the subjects is the suspect cannot point the witness at the suspect. One possibility would be to have the crime lab administer identification proceedings; but the important point is that whoever is in charge of administering the proceeding not know the identity of the suspect.

Given that the empirical evidence seems to show that witnesses do as well with photographs as with corporeal lineups,[13] administrative and security considerations seem farfetched.

The *Mathews* factors are dramatically illuminating here. The risk of error is, as half a century of research has shown, high. The consequence of error is criminal conviction, often of a serious felony. The cost of these safeguards, especially if implemented with photo arrays, are low. How much more work would it be to choose photos that resemble the descriptions, give the deck of pictures to an officer who doesn't know which is the suspect's, and then conduct the same process as is done now?

Neither selective incorporation's futile reliance on the right to counsel, nor the crabbed fundamental fairness understanding of due process, has done anything to reduce the greatest single risk of erroneous conviction. Applying familiar principles of procedural due process to police investigations, and issuing categorical rules to implement those principles, could go a long way to reduce this very risk.

Due Process Limits on Police Investigations—Informants

In the years between *Mapp* and *Katz* the Supreme Court refused to categorize the use of informants as a "search" under the Fourth Amendment. Following the reorientation of Fourth Amendment law to protect privacy rather than property, the Court characterized *Hoffa* as holding that there is no reasonable expectation of privacy in information trusted to another person absent a legally enforceable privilege.[14] This analysis is as odious as it is counterfactual, denying as it does the common experience that people in trouble can trust their friends and that this trust is one of the things that makes friendship valuable.

Informants are wholly unregulated by the Fourth Amendment, and freestanding due process claims are analyzed as a matter of shocking the conscience. The lower courts have approved police schemes to involve the suspect in a love affair with a prostitute-turned-informant,[15] and cash payments to children to betray their parents.[16] As one might expect, police reliance on informants has become pervasive. Almost all search warrant applications now include some reference to a confidential informant, and a disturbing percentage of them include nothing else.[17] Informants work on a contingent fee basis, receiving a share of forfeiture proceeds, direct cash payments, or forgiveness of their own crimes. These incentives can involve hundreds of thousands of dollars and decades of time behind bars.

These incentives lead to at least two highly undesirable results. First, many innocent people have their trust exploited by government spies.[18] Second, informants may manufacture or misrepresent evidence against other individuals.[19]

Katz notwithstanding, the text of the Fourth Amendment poses an obstacle to equating spying with searching. The two practices bear the same relation as robbery and embezzlement. A long line of cases has taken this view of the text.[20] Bringing informants under the Fourth Amendment therefore poses something of an uphill struggle.[21]

By contrast, informants might well be subjected to both substantive and procedural due process analysis. As a matter of what I have termed minimal substantive due process, official deprivations of "liberty" can be justified by law enforcement, but only to the extent that the degree of the intrusion is proportioned to the probability of a successful prosecution. Current law permits the police to recruit spies from a citizen's intimate circle, or to insinuate a professional informant into that circle, without a trace of suspicion. If such targeting were understood as a deprivation of liberty—of one's freedom of association, if not of a more general "right to be let alone"—then it would have to be justified by at least the *Terry* showing of reasonable suspicion.

As a matter of procedural due process, informants are actually much worse than hidden microphones and wiretaps. Machines can't lie for money or to escape punishment. Informants can and frequently do.[22] Worst of all, in this context, is the jailhouse snitch, who shows up on the last day of the government's case when things haven't gone so well for the prosecution.

Here a *Mathews* analysis could yield another simple and sensible rule. Absent exigent circumstances, informant testimony about a suspect's statements should be admissible only when corroborated by a recording. The cost of recording equipment is quite modest and it has become impressively inconspicuous.[23] Inside jails, there is no reason why informants should not wear a wire when security permits; and when it does not the cells themselves can be monitored electronically. Outside of institutions, undercover police officers wear wires routinely. If informants had to produce corroborating recordings to receive their "earnings," in all but extreme cases they would find a way to do so. The *Mathews* factors are again illuminating. The risk of error from uncorroborated informant testimony is great, the individual's interest in avoiding error is great, and the cost of the proposed procedural safeguard is modest.

The contrast with selective incorporation is instructive. In an incorporation regime the chief safeguard on informant testimony, as with identification evidence, is the right to counsel. Prior to indictment, the right to counsel does not apply at all, so that there is no check on manufactured or distorted informant testimony. After indictment, *Massiah* flatly bars any "elicitation" by the informant. Of course informants willing to make up confessions will be equally willing to testify that these confessions were "spontaneous."[24] The incorporation approach is as likely to exclude reliable evidence as it is to admit unreliable evidence. By contrast, a procedural due process approach could support a recording requirement that would unequivocally advance instrumental reliability.

Procedural Due Process in Adjudication: Rethinking the Effective Assistance of Counsel

Case studies on false convictions typically show that more than one thing went wrong with the process. One of the things that often goes wrong in these cases is the performance of the defense function.[25] A vigorous defense based on a thorough investigation makes false conviction extremely difficult. Unfortunately, the state of indigent defense is parlous in most jurisdictions, and scandalous in the others.[26]

In contract or appointment indigent defense systems fees are often capped at Khafkaesque levels—twenty or thirty dollars an hour, a few hundred dollars per case, and so on.[27] Public defenders' offices face overwhelming caseloads with staffs that are neither as well paid nor as well supported as their counterparts in the prosecutor's office.[28] In Minnesota—a far cry from Mississippi or Arkansas—desperate public defenders recently voted to join the Teamsters Union.[29]

Ineffective assistance doctrine under *Strickland v. Washington* does next to nothing to address the problem. The *ex post* inquiry into negligence and prejudice mandated by *Strickland* requires reviewing courts to assess the performance of counsel on a record made by counsel. The worse the pretrial investigation was, the harder it is to prove that the investigation prejudiced the defendant at trial.

The appropriate inquiry should ask *before trial* whether the defense can contest the issue with the prosecution on a roughly equal basis. Roughly speaking, indigent defenders should have qualifications, compensation, and caseloads comparable to their counterparts in the prosecutor's office. Any *ex post* analysis, even one as rigorous as Judge Bazelon defended in *Decoster*, would still confront appellate courts with apparently guilty defendants demanding a second trial in a system in which most defendants get no trial at all. By contrast, *ex ante* challenges would permit judicial intervention without overturning convictions. There are procedural obstacles to such challenges, but none that are insurmountable.[30]

Unlike some of the previous examples, a *Mathews* analysis here is not unequivocal. Although the risk and consequence of error due to ineffective assistance are great, the cost of improving the defense function is significant. Here we need to remember the strong priority preventing erroneous convictions deserves over enabling justified convictions. Not only is unjust conviction a profoundly unfair burden on the individual, but a system that runs unnecessary risks of error is politically dangerous.

The cost of procedural safeguards against false conviction should be understood as part of the cost of criminal law enforcement, not as a freestanding claim on public funds. The public is willing to pay billions for prisons, police, and prosecutors that might well be spent on education, health care, or what not. Indigent defense should be thought of as entailed by the priority of law enforcement, in the same way that we would never think of drafting young men for police work at submarket wages, or of building prisons with slave labor to save money.[31]

The parity standard for indigent defense nicely captures this understanding of the cost issue. The adversary system promotes reliability only when the adversaries are evenly matched. Parity, however, could be achieved by reducing the resources available to the prosecution. Indeed, a high degree of parity could be achieved by integrating the prosecution and indigent defense functions in the same office, as was long done in the military justice system. The parity approach offers a way to improve reliability without forcing an expenditure of funds, although that would be the likely result of parity analysis. What the parity standard insists on, though, is that the public view the cost of procedural safeguards against unjust conviction as part and parcel of the cost of the criminal justice system.

A selective incorporation regime could lead to the parity standard on Sixth Amendment grounds. There is, however, an important difference in emphasis between the Sixth Amendment right to "the assistance of counsel" and the procedural due process right to a fair trial. A respirating body with a law degree satisfies the text of the Sixth Amendment; indeed, the *Strickland* Court invoked the language of the amendment as support for a harsh standard of ineffective assistance.[32] A focus on the fairness of the trial would make it easier to see how caseloads, qualifications, and compensation can make the process unreliable, the nominal assistance of counsel notwithstanding. Procedural due process, by contrast, focuses on the fairness of the trial, which would make it easier to cut through appearances.

CONVICTING THE GUILTY

About half of all arrests do not end in conviction.[33] Some arrests don't end in prosecution because the police never intended to initiate the criminal process. The arrest was made for immediate social control purposes, such as breaking up a fight or getting a drunk off the streets on a cold night. Nonetheless it is easy to believe that among those arrests that don't end in conviction are a substantial number of guilty persons who escape their just deserts.

A substantial body of research on these "lost arrests" confirms that many meritorious cases result in dismissal before trial.[34] Contrary to some law-and-order rhetoric, however, the lost arrest research shows that the constitutional exclusionary rules do not result in the release of large numbers of dangerous criminals. It is reliably estimated, for instance, that the exclusion of evidence on account of unconstitutional police conduct results in the dismissal of charges against less than 1% of those arrested, typically in less serious cases.[35]

The single biggest cause of lost but meritorious prosecutions is the failure of witnesses to give evidence.[36] This can occur from fear, loyalty, or alienation. Here the Constitution, as presently construed, plays a role, albeit one quite unsuspected by conservative critics of modern doctrine.

The hearsay rule and its constitutional counterpart forbid convicting the accused on the basis of police accounts of what the eyewitnesses said out of court. Even without a confrontation clause, procedural due process would forbid trial by affidavit or by dossier.[37] The conventional piety about jury ability to evaluate demeanor appears to be utterly baseless,[38] but there is considerable force to the system's commitment to cross-examination as "the greatest legal engine ever invented for the discovery of truth."[39]

The obvious way to reduce witness noncooperation, as Professor Graham observed more than a decade ago, is to take admissible statements from the witnesses as quickly as possible, preferably in the very wake of the crime.[40] The equally obvious obstacle to this approach is that meaningful cross-examination depends on the availability of counsel with notice of the charge, and both the filing of charges and the appointment of counsel are now systematically delayed following arrest.

The reason for the delay is the felt necessity of some window of opportunity for police interrogation. Given the privilege against self-incrimination, any opportunity for questioning the suspect will be lost with the appearance of defense counsel. The Supreme Court has imposed a presumptive 48-hour limit on this window,[41] and maintained the *Miranda* rules to regulate how the police exploit it. The critical point remains that *because of the privilege against self-incrimination*, there is a gap—a window of virtual lawlessness—between the arrest and the filing of charges.

Suppose, however, that the suspect could be questioned, either in court or by the police, in the presence of defense counsel? Proposals for in-court interrogation of the suspect have been around for most of this century.[42] Their common prerequisite is the legal, as well as the informal, power of the trial court to draw an inference of guilt from the refusal to answer. So long as *Griffin v. California*[43] remains the law, the suspect who refuses to answer may never face the jury because no jury could convict without the (presently illegal) inference of guilt from silence.

Any thoughtful reader who compares *Malloy v. Hogan*[44] with Bentham's devastating send-up of the privilege[45] will realize that the incorporation of the Fifth Amendment privilege as a matter of substantive due process is something less than inevitable.[46] This is especially so for those who recall that the state in *Malloy* conceded the incorporation question, so that no contrary argument was before the Court—notwithstanding *two* considered precedents holding that the privilege was not incorporated.[47]

I have long argued for disincorporating the privilege,[48] but even a more modest step might suffice to close the gap. Following Justice Harlan, Justice Powell took the position that incorporated criminal procedure provisions need not apply to the states in precisely the same way that they apply to the federal government.[49] If the Court were to allow the states a little leeway with the privilege, as it allows them a little leeway with the jury trial guarantee in the Sixth Amendment, it would be possible to arrange for pretrial questioning subject to an inference of guilt from the failure to answer.

Griffin rests on two considerations. First, an innocent defendant may refuse to testify at trial because of the fear of impeachment with prior convictions.[50] Second, following a *Boyd*-vintage statutory ruling in a federal prosecution, the *Griffin* majority expressed concern for the innocent but ineffective witness—who by reason of slow-mindedness or inarticulateness does more harm than good to a meritorious defense.[51]

Suppose a state provided for questioning those arrested on probable cause, in the presence of defense counsel, with the right to refuse to answer questions subject to a permissive adverse inference at trial. Suppose further that the *defense* had the right to introduce this pretrial testimony *without* opening the door to impeachment with prior convictions.

The ban on impeachment with priors would undercut the most important of *Griffin*'s supports. As for the ineffective witness scenario, taking the testimony *before* trial radically changes the picture. If the accused makes a misstep out of confusion or ignorance, there is time to take corrective action. For example, a motion might be made to exclude the pretrial statement as unreliable, or to re-open the pretrial proceeding so the defendant could put in additional clarifying testimony.

Compared to the present system of police interrogation, based on lies, manipu-lation, and intimidation, such a system would greatly reduce the risk of innocent suspects falsely incriminating themselves. It would end the ability of sophisti-cated offenders to permanently insulate themselves from humane questioning. Even under *Griffin* such a system might be sustainable. If the compelling criti-cism of the privilege itself is thought to furnish even a warrant for taking the Harlan/Powell view of the incorporated amendments in state cases, such a sys-tem would easily pass constitutional scrutiny.

From the standpoint of convicting the guilty such a system has obvious bene-fits, particularly with respect to sophisticated offenders. But the real opportunity for the prosecution such a system would create is by closing the gap between the arrest and the process of formal adjudication. If the suspect could be questioned *after* defense counsel enters the case, the right to counsel could be extended to the moment of arrest. The government could afford to file charges promptly. And with the filing of charges and the appearance of counsel, it would become possi-ble to take prompt, cross-examined, videotaped depositions from the witnesses.

The Federal Rules of Evidence, which are widely followed in the state courts as well, would admit such deposition testimony at trial if the witness is either un-available or gives trial testimony inconsistent with the deposition.[52] Current con-frontation clause law permits use of the pretrial testimony in both situations.[53] Once the depositions are in hand, however, the prosecution is in a strong posi-tion. If the witness testifies consistently with the deposition, the prosecution is satisfied. If the witness testifies inconsistently with the deposition, the deposition would be admissible as substantive evidence, not just to impeach. And if the wit-ness refuses to testify or fails to appear under subpoena, the witness is unavail-able and the deposition could come in on its own.

The taking of prompt, pretrial testimony from the witnesses is not a panacea. Organized gangs would still have motive to retaliate against witnesses, although criminal liability for witness intimidation creates a counterincentive.[54] Both direct and cross-examination may be difficult early in the case, when the facts and issues are not as clear as at trial. Professor Graham makes an important sug-gestion: Deposition testimony elicited on cross by defense counsel should not be admissible against the defense.[55] Otherwise, counsel, who may have little knowl-edge of the case at the time of the deposition, will be inhibited from the kind of thorough cross that warrants admitting the deposition at trial.

Ironically, video depositions might have more confrontation clause problems under current law than the cold transcript of a preliminary hearing. Justice Scalia, who along with Justice Thomas believes that the confrontation clause does not apply to hearsay declarants as distinct from "witnesses,"[56] nonetheless induced the Court to recognize a right to physically confront those witnesses who testify at the trial.[57] This may be a historically plausible reading of the confrontation clause, although a majority of the court, per Chief Justice Rehnquist, has clearly rejected it.[58]

It is cross-examination, not physical confrontation, that is the strongest guarantee of reliability. We would laugh at any system in which the witnesses must face the accused but not answer questions put by defense counsel. Empirical studies show that juries pay close attention to videotaped testimony[59] and that ordinary people do not accurately evaluate witness demeanor.[60] As a matter of procedural due process, the gain to reliability from face-to-face confrontation is marginal and the cost can be high.

This is especially so given that the face-to-face requirement has never been applied to hearsay declarants. Thus trial judges are tempted to admit hearsay statements that were not sworn, cross-examined, or even reliably recorded when witnesses fail to testify at trial. Prompt depositions would surely be more reliable than much of the casual hearsay that is now admitted as "excited utterances" or to show "state of mind." If the Sixth Amendment ever were read to favor excited utterances or statements against interest over recorded, sworn, and cross-examined pretrial testimony, it would only reconfirm the need to shift the constitutional focus from incorporation to due process.

In short, the incorporation of the Fifth Amendment privilege has made the window of lawlessness a practical necessity. A turn to due process would free the states to close that gap, by creating prompt formal processes for questioning both the suspect and the witnesses under circumstances reliable enough to justify admitting the resulting statements at trial. Such a turn would do vastly more to bring the guilty to justice than would the repeal of all the constitutional exclusionary rules combined. At the same time it would enable the right to counsel to extend to the moment of custody. And what could be more in keeping with the legality and regularity due process enshrines than insisting that the criminal justice process be open to counsel for the citizen from beginning to end?

REDUCING RACIAL UNFAIRNESS: WHAT EQUAL PROTECTION CAN, AND CANNOT, ACHIEVE

Given a contingent exclusionary remedy, strong empirical evidence of disproportionate impact, and a firm rejection of inferences of criminality based on group characteristics, there is a good chance that the courts would adopt something like the *Batson* approach in police practices cases. Freed from the burden of allowing the guilty to escape, the courts would be free to infer invidious intent from disparate impact.

When this disparate impact is reflected in a long historical record and strong evidence of contemporary persistence, as with the disparate impact on blacks of the exercise of police discretion, the courts would be justified in shifting the burden of proof on the intent issue along the lines of the Title VII cases. In other words, once the defendant proves that he is black and was targeted for investigation by the police, the government would have to come forward with a race-neutral explanation, which would in turn shift the burden to the defense to prove that the explanation is pretextual. Against the argument that *Batson* does not trigger burden-shifting so automatically, it should be remembered that a prosecutorial peremptory challenge of the sole black on a venire can trigger the government's burden of coming forward with a race-neutral explanation.[61]

In typical cases the government can easily supply a race-neutral explanation. Probable cause or reasonable suspicion provide race-neutral explanations—unless the defense can show that white citizens in similar situations are not stopped or arrested as was the defendant. The burden-shifting approach, however, has considerable power.

Peremptory challenges can be, and typically are, motivated by stereotypes and hunches. All *Batson* did was remove race from the otherwise boundless universe of reasons for exercising a peremptory. Prosecutors can readily point to arbitrary, but nonracial, reasons for their strikes.[62] Decisions to detain, search, or arrest suspects are less susceptible to pretextual justifications.

A case like *Whren*, for example, might come out quite differently in a burden-shifting regime. Once Whren proved that he was black and had been stopped for traffic offenses by the drug squad, the government would be hard pressed to come forward with a nonpretextual reason for the stop. Would white citizens have been stopped by the drug squad for minor traffic violations? How many white citizens had these vice officers cited for traffic violations in the last year?

Even if all burden-shifting accomplished was to force the police to lie successfully about the role of race in their decisions, some good would come of it. There seems to be a significant residuum of old-fashioned, bare-knuckles racism among the police. Mark Furhman, Rodney King, Abner Louima—these are names from the 1990s, not the 1890s. An Ohio police department settled a 1993 lawsuit after admitting that some of its officers referred to their unit as the SNAT team—SNAT being an acronym for "Special Nigger Arrest Team."[63]

At a minimum, burden-shifting analysis would drive the crudest manifestations of police racism underground. Even if this is all burden-shifting accomplished, it would be an improvement. What begins as hypocrisy can turn into orthodoxy. Police culture will never internalize a race-neutral norm so long as the courts approve of decisions based on race. Driving the crudest forms of racism underground is a step toward stigmatizing racial stereotypes, like brutal interrogation tactics, as unprofessional as well as immoral.[64] After all, in the equal protection context it is the *reason* for official action, not the action itself, that violates the Constitution.

While those who see an urgent need to reduce the extreme racial disparities in criminal law enforcement should welcome more vigorous equal protection doctrine, they should fight for stricter scrutiny of police practices with a sober sense of the limits of court-ordered reforms. Ultimately racial fairness requires either decriminalizing recreational drug use or enforcing the drug laws against white

Americans far more vigorously. The courts face major institutional limitations in pursuing either strategy. The need for judicial prudence should not be minimized; efforts at what the courts cannot achieve may very well get in the way of the things that they can achieve. The contingent exclusionary remedy would open the door to burden-shifting analysis in police practices cases, and thereby reduce the enduring insult felt by so many law-abiding black Americans who are, innocence notwithstanding, targeted by the police for degrading confrontations. But no foreseeable judicial innovation could force elected officials to enforce the drug laws against the white majority with anything like the ferocious enthusiasm with which they are enforced against the black minority.

REDUCING RACIAL UNFAIRNESS—DUE PROCESS CLAIMS

One consequence of more rigorous equal protection scrutiny in criminal cases would be an increasing reticence on the part of police and prosecutors to admit that race influences their decisions. This is a regrettable but inevitable consequence of tightening equal protection scrutiny, but it also points up an important interface between equal protection and due process. Discrimination can operate only within the sphere of discretionary authority. Police discretion to stop for investigation, to frisk for weapons, to "ask" for consent, and so on make targeting blacks for investigation effective. The more that discretion is cabined by constitutional rules that limit police authority over citizens generally, regardless of race, the less scope there will be for discriminatory enforcement.

Due process has always supplied the remedy for lawless discretion. As a matter of procedural due process, for example, a very powerful case can be made for requiring the taping of interrogations, including the administration of the *Miranda* warnings and the suspect's waiver. Likewise, before a suspect is "deprived" of the "liberty" interest in freedom from search, a warning of the right to refuse, and, absent exigency, recording the consent given, might be required on procedural due process grounds.[65] An honest recognition of how coercive the "request" for consent is in the real world[66] could lead to a reasonable-suspicion requirement before the request can lawfully be made, which would curtail the practice of using traffic enforcement as the predicate for drug investigations.

A secondary consequence of such requirements would be raising the cost of coercive investigative encounters. Singling people out for coercive, stigmatizing public encounters is cheaper and easier than working undercovers and informants to support warrant applications.[67] Reducing the difference between the cost to the police of these various approaches would have a beneficial spillover effect on evenhanded law enforcement. The comparative cost advantage of stop-and-frisk over informants might increase if the courts, as suggested earlier, began to regulate the use of informants. The correct doctrinal move in the interests of equality is not to give the police lawless discretion to mount investigations with a disproportionate impact on whites, but to subject all police practices that threaten individual "liberty" to legal regulation and judicial review.

FEDERAL CASES

The Fourteenth Amendment regime I have defended clearly has no place in federal cases, save to the extent that the Fifth Amendment is construed to include an equal protection component. The Bill of Rights criminal procedure terms plainly apply in federal cases, so that departures from the self-incrimination privilege, the double-jeopardy clause, the confrontation clause, and so on could not be countenanced in federal cases.

This is as it should be. The framers' concern with the new federal government was the fear of tyranny. All the provisions in the Bill of Rights aim at least in part at checking the emergence of a federal Leviathan. The incorporation revolution had an effect that Justice Harlan predicted—federal constitutional standards were diluted in response to the pressures of policy in state cases. With the increasing willingness of Congress to federalize the criminal law and fund its enforcement, we have witnessed in our own time something the framers would have condemned—routine federal prosecutions of garden-variety felonies under relaxed constitutional standards.

Any direct opposition to this trend—under the commerce clause, say—seems highly unlikely to stem the tide. What could stem the tide is a return to federalism in criminal procedure. We need not bring back *Boyd* in all its aspects to reestablish a state advantage in criminal law enforcement. Were we to do so, legislators would see a practical incentive in keeping criminal law enforcement where it belongs. At the same time, in the political cases the federal docket will always include, a more robust reading of the Bill of Rights would serve the checking function the framers thought so important.

To take but one example, the privilege against self-incrimination has known its finest hours in resisting political prosecutions. A vigorous enforcement of the privilege—including, for example, bringing back a measure of *Boyd*'s regard for private papers—might be a welcome check on government overreaching during some new period of political pathology. So long as murder, rape, and robbery remain the province of state courts, the price of such broad protections in federal cases could be borne in good conscience.

CONCLUSION

Anyone who reads the newspapers can tell that our criminal justice system punishes too many innocent people, permits the escape of too many guilty people, and has an unconscionably disproportionate impact on blacks. The Fourteenth Amendment clearly speaks to these challenges—due process demands reliable procedures, and equal protection prohibits invidious discrimination. As this chapter has shown, due process and equal protection could generate some practical constitutional rules that would do far more than existing law to protect the innocent, enable the conviction of the guilty, and reduce racial unfairness in the administration of justice.

That reforms such as these can be plausibly grounded on the Fourteenth Amendment does not of course guarantee that conservative judges will adopt them. We should not forget, however, that the modern Supreme Court's most enlightened criminal-procedure decisions were *Ake v. Oklahoma*, a freestanding procedural due process decision, and *Batson v. Kentucky*, a freestanding equal protection decision. A turn to due process and equal protection doctrine would not only enable, but invite and encourage, reforms directed at improving reliability and reducing racial unfairness.

Moreover, judicial ideology runs in cycles. In time the Supreme Court will again assume a more active role in national life. The Warren Court went astray by invoking the Bill of Rights, which deflected attention from reliability and equality. The turn to incorporation was, to say the least, not compelled by the legitimate sources of constitutional law. When different justices return to the challenge of more fully honoring both our values and our Constitution in criminal justice, the Fourteenth Amendment, not the Bill of Rights, should mark the point of their departure.

Epilogue

Claims about law or politics typically can be challenged by raising the level of generality in the debate. In law, for instance, arguments from policy can typically be challenged by formalists as illegitimate, while arguments from authority can typically be challenged by realists as ingenuous, disingenuous, or both. Formalist readers may be puzzled by how much attention I have devoted to empirical evidence and policy arguments, while realists may find all my talk about legitimacy and history rather beside the point.

I've tried to ground a synthesis of doctrine and values as deeply as I can. To those who (no doubt with considerable justice) demand a deeper defense, all I can say is that at least I am quite aware of the controversial traditions of legal positivism and political liberalism in which I stand. Perhaps the best way to reflect that awareness is by restating my ambition in terms of a compliment Hart paid to Bentham—appropriately enough, in the context of discussing Bentham's views on the privilege against self-incrimination. Of Bentham, Hart wrote that even where he "fails to persuade, he still forces us to think."[1] If I have achieved that much, this study will have succeeded beyond my fondest hopes.

Notes

INTRODUCTION

1. See, e.g., Yale Kamisar et al., *Modern Criminal Procedure* 25 (West, 8th ed. 1994).

2. See Edward Connors et al., *Convicted by Juries, Exonerated by Science: Case Studies in the Use of DNA Evidence to Establish Innocence After Trial* 20 (U.S. Dept. of Justice, 1996).

3. See Michael Tonry, *Malign Neglect* 109–111 (Oxford U. Press, 1995); National Criminal Justice Commission, *The Real War on Crime* 115 (Steven Donziger ed. 1996).

4. *Cf.* Marvin Frankel, *From Private Rights to Public Justice*, 51 N.Y.U. L. Rev. 516, 526 (1976) (*Miranda* is a "tense, temporary, ragged truce between combatants."). Less the "temporary," that description remains precise.

5. 424 U.S. 319 (1976).

6. 476 U.S. 79 (1986).

7. 470 U.S. 68 (1985).

CHAPTER 1

1. See *Hurtado v. California*, 110 U.S. 516, 518 (1884). The killing was motivated by Stuardo's affair with Hurtado's wife, but Hurtado evidently acted in cold blood. The victim was shot twice, once in the back as he attempted to flee. See Richard Cortner, *The Supreme Court and the Second Bill of Rights* 12 (U. Wisconsin Press, 1981).

2. *Hurtado*, Brief for Plaintiff in Error at 5–6.

3. In *Twitchell v. Pennsylvania*, 74 U.S. 321 (1869), the petitioner complained that his indictment for murder, by failing to specify the murder weapon, violated the Sixth Amendment by failing to inform him of the nature of the charge. Although the case came to the Court after the Fourteenth Amendment became effective, neither counsel nor the unanimous Court discussed the Constitution's new provision. The Court refused a writ of error on the ground that the Sixth Amendment does not apply to the states.

4. *Hurtado*, Brief for Plaintiff in Error at 26–38; Brief for Defendant in Error at 5–10.

5. 110 U.S. at 528–32.

6. 110 U.S. at 531.

7. Joseph Story, 3 *Commentaries on the Constitution of the United States* § 1783 at 661 (Hilliard, Gray, 1833) ("this clause in effect affirms the right of trial according to the process and proceedings of the common law") (footnote omitted).

8. *Murray's Lessee v. Hoboken Land and Improvement Co.*, 59 U.S. (18 How.) 272 (1855).

9. *Dartmouth College v. Woodward*, 17 U.S. (4 Wheat.) 518, 581 (1819).

10. Id.

11. Thomas Cooley, *Treatise on the Constitutional Limitations* 356 (Little, Brown, and Co., 1868). ("The principles, then, upon which the process is based are to determine whether it is 'due process' or not, and not any consideration of mere form. Administrative and remedial process may change from time to time, but only with due regard to the old landmarks established for the protection of the citizen.")

12. See Edward S. Corwin, *The Doctrine of Due Process of Law Before the Civil War*, 24 Harv. L. Rev. 460, 466–76 (1911); Robert E. Riggs, *Substantive Due Process in 1791*, 1990 Wis. L. Rev. 941, 977–84.

13. See *Scott v. Sandford*, 60 U.S. (19 How.) 393, 450–53 (1857).

14. See Michael Kent Curtis, *No State Shall Abridge* 46–47 (Duke U. Press, 1986).

15. See *Arnett v. Kennedy*, 416 U.S. 134 (1974) (plurality opinion); *Bishop v. Wood*, 426 U.S. 341 (1976); *Bailey v. Richardson*, 182 F.2d 46 (D.C. Cir. 1950), aff'd by an equally divided court, 341 U.S. 918 (1951).

16. See Frank Easterbrook, *Substance and Due Process*, 1982 Sup. Ct. Rev. 85.

17. In *Frank v. Mangum*, 237 U.S. 309 (1915), discussed *infra*, the Court affirmed a conviction rendered at a mob-dominated trial because the state appellate court had found that the trial was not in fact influenced by the mob. See id. at 335–36 ("a determination of the facts as was thus made by the court of last resort of Georgia . . . must be taken as setting forth the truth of the matter, certainly until some reasonable ground is shown for an inference that the court which rendered it either was wanting in jurisdiction, or at least erred in the exercise of its jurisdiction[.]"). Taken seriously, the *Frank* rationale would all but nullify habeas corpus review in the federal courts. The essence of the Court's argument is that a formal judgment of conviction is weighty evidence of the conviction's constitutionality, i.e., that the defendant is guilty because the state says so.

18. Brief for Plaintiff in Error at 38, *Hurtado v. California*, 110 U.S. 516 (1884).

19. Id. at 39.

20. What sacred right is it [Hurtado] is contending for? The right to have had nineteen lawful citizens sit in solemn secrecy to hear his cause from his prosecutors *ex parte*, and to return in Court "a true bill" against him. No one, it seems to me, familiar with the manner of investigations by grand juries would complain because he had been deprived of a hearing before a secret tribunal, constituted and constructed as this is. No one who appreciated life or liberty would clamor after a hearing before a grand jury when he had the privilege of going before a committing magistrate, in open day, be confronted by his accusers at the threshold of his cause, see them and hear them and be prepared to meet their accusations, and if he desires, put in his defense.

This, unless it is inhibited by the Constitution to the states, will ere long take the place of the grand jury, because it commends itself to those interested. For the people the grand jury may be the better method of procedure; but what accused would exchange an open examination before a committing magistrate for a secret inquisition into his offenses?

Brief for Defendant in Error, at 20. "Today, approximately 26 states fall in this information-state category. An additional five states require prosecution by indictment for only capital offenses or capital and life imprisonment offenses." Wayne R. LaFave & Jerold H. Israel, 2 *Criminal Procedure* § 15.1(b) at 279 (West, 1984) (footnotes omitted).

21. *Hurtado*, 110 U.S. at 529.

22. Id. at 535 (emphasis added).

23. Id.

24. Id. at 535–36.

25. Id. at 537.

26. Id. at 536.

27. Professor Israel notes that the *Hurtado* opinion recognized at least three distinct limitations on due process review of state convictions. First, *Hurtado* accepted historical practice as a constitutional safe harbor. Second, the opinion appears to recognize only basic notice and an opportunity to be heard as fundamental. Third, as the next section of the text discusses, the opinion concludes that due process is exclusive, rather than inclusive, of the specific procedures required by the Bill of Rights. See Jerold H. Israel, *Free-Standing Due Process and Criminal Procedure: The Supreme Court's Search for Interpretive Guidelines*, 45 St. L. U. L.J. 303, 346–50 (2001). As Professor Israel points out, however, "[i]n subsequent years, the Court became more and more willing to assume the position of ultimate arbiter and gradually chipped away at the limiting principles of *Hurtado*." Id. at 350.

28. 83 U.S. (16 Wall.) 36 (1873).

29. *Hurtado*, 110 U.S. at 534–35.

30. Id. at 547–49 (Harlan, J., dissenting).

31. In *Gitlow v. New York*, 268 U.S. 652 (1925), the Supreme Court assumed that freedom of speech and press "are among the fundamental personal rights and 'liberties' protected by the due process clause of the Fourteenth Amendment from impairment by the States." Id. at 666. The Court expressly rejected a dictum to the contrary contained in *Prudential Insurance Co. v. Cheek*, 259 U.S. 530, 543 (1922). The Court supported this rejection with footnote nine, citing *Patterson v. Colorado*, 205 U.S. 454, 462 (1907) (a case in which the Court had also assumed, without so holding, that due process includes freedom of expression); *Twining v. New Jersey*, 211 U.S. 78, 108 (1908) (a criminal procedure case applying the "fundamental" liberty test to deny that due process prohibits double jeopardy); *Coppage v. Kansas*, 236 U.S. 1, 17 (1915) (a notorious substantive due process case invalidating a state law prohibiting "yellow dog" contracts); *Fox v. Washington*, 236 U.S. 273, 276 (1915) (holding that a colorable federal constitutional question was raised by a state court decision, the opinion in which declared that the federal constitution protects the freedom of speech); *Schaefer v. United States*, 251 U.S. 466, 474 (1920) (a federal prosecution of the publishers of a German-language newspaper for interfering with the war effort during World War I; opinion contains this dictum: "That freedom of speech and of the press are elements of liberty all will acclaim."); *Gilbert v. Minnesota*, 254 U.S. 325, 338 (1920) (another case in which the court assumed, without deciding, that the federal constitution protects freedom of speech); and *Meyer v. Nebraska*, 262 U.S. 390, 399 (1923) (a substantive due process decision striking down a state law that forbade the teaching of foreign languages). The specific page citations in footnote nine are confusing, bordering on random; but there can be no doubt that to the *Gitlow* Court freedom of expression was nothing but another species of the "liberty" protected by substantive due process. This same "liberty" included the right to freedom of

contract, the constitutional value animating *Coppage* and *Lochner v. New York*, 198 U.S. 45 (1905).

The assumption made in *Gitlow* became settled law. In *Stromberg v. California*, 283 U.S. 359, 368 (1931), Chief Justice Hughes could declare that "[i]t has been determined that the conception of liberty under the due process clause of the Fourteenth Amendment embraces the right of free speech." *Gitlow* is the oldest case in the citations that follow. This same equation with the "liberty" protected by substantive due process provided the support for the inclusion of religious liberty and freedom of the institutional press within the Fourteenth Amendment due process clause. See *Cantwell v. Connecticut*, 310 U.S. 296, 303 (1940); *Near v. Minnesota*, 283 U.S. 697, 707 (1931).

32. *Chicago, Burlington & Quincy R.R. Co. v. Chicago*, 166 U.S. 226 (1897).

33. Id. at 234–35.

34. Id. at 237 ("[n]o court . . . would hesitate to adjudge void any statute declaring that 'the homestead now owned by A should no longer be his, but should henceforth be the property of B.' ").

35. Id. at 238.

36. 211 U.S. 78 (1908).

37. Id. at 99.

38. Id. at 110.

39. Id. at 106–14.

40. *Gitlow* was decided in 1925. The Court did not reverse a state court judgment for conflict with a Bill of Rights freedom incorporated in the Fourteenth Amendment until *Stromberg v. California*, 283 U.S. 359 (1931).

41. In *Powell v. Alabama*, 287 U.S. 45 (1932), the Supreme Court reversed the state court convictions because the defendants had not been afforded meaningful assistance of counsel in a capital case. But *Betts v. Brady*, 316 U.S. 455 (1942), made clear that the Sixth Amendment right to counsel did not apply to the states. In *Wolf v. Colorado*, 338 U.S. 25 (1949), the Court held that the Fourth Amendment's prohibition of unreasonable searches and seizures applied to the States. Even then, the Court refused to impose the exclusionary rule on the states in cases in which state officers violated due process by searching or seizing unreasonably.

42. 83 U.S. 36 (1873).

43. Id. at 74–80.

44. See id. at 96 (Field, J., dissenting) ("If this inhibition has no reference to privileges and immunities of this character, but only refers, as held by the majority of the court in their opinion, to such privileges and immunities as were before its adoption specifically designated in the Constitution or necessarily implied as belonging to citizens of the United States, it was a vain and idle enactment, which accomplished nothing, and most unnecessarily excited Congress and the people on its passage."); id. at 129 (Swayne, J., dissenting) ("The construction adopted by the majority . . . turns, as it were, what was meant for bread into a stone.").

45. 83 U.S. at 78 ("such a construction followed by the reversal of the judgment of the Supreme Court of Louisiana in these cases, would constitute this court a perpetual censor upon all legislation of the States, on the civil rights of their own citizens, with authority to nullify such as it did not approve as consistent with those rights, as they existed at the time of the adoption of this amendment.").

46. For example, John Norton Pomeroy wrote that

The decision made in the Slaughter-House Case can hardly be regarded as final in giving a construction to the fourteenth amendment. When the court is so evenly divided, and when the dissenting minority support their position by such powerful reasoning, and especially when the course of argument pursued by the majority is not absolutely essential to the correctness of the actual conclusion reached by them, the case cannot be considered as a very strong and weighty precedent.

An Introduction to the Constitutional Law of the United States § 256e at 178 (Hurd and Houghton, 9th ed. 1886). See also William Royall, *The Fourteenth Amendment: The Slaughter-House Cases*, 4 Southern L. Rev. (New Series) 558 (1879). After reviewing the debates in Congress, Royall offered this pungent critique of *Slaughter-House*:

And when it is considered, as every one acquainted with the history of the times knows, that the entire purpose of this amendment, and of the other two adopted about the same time, was to put the negroes upon a footing, before the law, of perfect equality with the whites, how can it be doubted that it was intended the words should have their natural meaning? Is it credible that they intended to say the negroes shall not be prohibited by the Southern states from petitioning Congress, or from sailing from New York to Havre, but they may be prevented by the states from suing in the courts to recover wages they have earned; they may be prevented by the states from acquiring title to property they have paid for; they may be prohibited by the states from assembling together to deliberate peacefully upon the measures best calculated to advance the interests and prosperity of their race; they may be restrained of their liberty, when, under the Constitution of the United States, they have done all that the law requires them to do in order to be set at liberty?

Id. at 575–76. The accompanying, equally rhetorical footnote concludes with this shot: "What would Mr. Thadeous Stevens have thought, if he had been told that the constitutional amendments accomplished no more for the negro than this?"

47. 92 U.S. 90 (1875).

48. *Walker v. Sauvinet*, Brief for Defendant in Error at 5:

In the Slaughter-House cases, the question of what constituted the privileges and immunities of citizens was discussed *in extenso*. But so far, no case has been found in which a trial by jury in a State court, was considered one of the rights, privileges or immunities of citizens of the United States.

49. *Walker*, 92 U.S. at 92.

50. 123 U.S. 131 (1887). It was not entirely clear whether the defendants were "citizens of the United States" as referred to in the clause, but the Court proceeded on the assumption that the clause applied.

51. For a sketch of Tucker, see Paul D. Carrington, *The Twenty-First Wisdom*, 52 Wash. & Lee L. Rev. 333, 333–36 (1995).

52. See 123 U.S. at 151:

The position I take is this: Though originally the first ten Amendments were adopted as limitations on Federal power, yet in so far as they secure and recognize fundamental rights—common law rights—of the man, they make them privileges and immunities of the man as citizen of the United States, and cannot now be abridged by a State under the Fourteenth Amendment. In other words, while the ten Amendments, as limitations on power, only apply to the Federal government, and not to the States, yet in so far as they declare or recognize rights of persons, these rights are theirs, as citizens of the United States, and the Fourteenth Amendment as to such rights limits state power, as the ten Amendments had limited Federal power.

53. See id. at 152:

This conclusion is confirmed by the consideration that the propounders of the Fourteenth Amendment were looking to the protection of the freedmen from the peril of legislation in the South against those fundamental rights of free speech; of freedom from unreasonable searches; of double jeopardy; of self-accusation; of not being confronted with witnesses and having benefit of counsel and the like;

and if these are construed as the privileges and immunities of citizens of the United States, the Fourteenth Amendment secures them; otherwise not. The fundamental nature of these rights, as common law rights, which were recognized at the time of the Revolution as the inherited rights of all the States may be seen by reference to [Blackstone and Story]. As to searches, self-accusation, etc., see [Story, *May's Constitutional History of England*, and "especially" *Boyd v. United States*].

54. See Curtis, *No State Shall Abridge* at 215–16 (cited in note 14); Akhil Reed Amar, *The Bill of Rights and the Fourteenth Amendment*, 101 Yale L.J. 1193 (1992).

55. See Cong. Globe, 39th Cong., 1st Sess. 2542 (1866) (Statement of Rep. Bingham); Richard Aynes, *On Misreading John Bingham and the Fourteenth Amendment*, 103 Yale L.J. 57 (1993).

56. Cong. Globe, 39th Cong., 1st Sess. 2765–66 (1866) (statement of Sen. Howard).

57. See Aynes, 103 Yale L.J. at 83–94 (cited in note 54).

58. See 83 U.S. at 118–19 (Bradley, J., dissenting).

59. See 123 U.S. at 151.

60. Id. at 148–49.

61. See id. at 166.

62. 74 U.S. 321 (1869), cited in *Spies*, 123 U.S. at 166.

63. See 123 U.S. at 166–67.

64. Id. at 167–80.

65. Id. at 181.

66. Id. at 180. For the proposition, rejected in the text, that the *Spies* case "was disposed of on other grounds," see *Twining v. New Jersey*, 211 U.S. 78, 92 (1908); Stanley Morrison, *Does the Fourteenth Amendment Incorporate the Bill of Rights? The Judicial Interpretation*, 2 Stan. L. Rev. 140, 147–48 (1949). Neither Morrison nor the *Twining* opinion explains this conclusion.

67. *O'Neil v. Vermont*, 144 U.S. 323, 332 (1892); see id. at 361 (Field, J., dissenting).

68. See *Maxwell v. Dow*, 176 U.S. 581 (1900), Brief for Plaintiff in Error at 10–12.

69. *Maxwell*, 176 U.S. at 601:

Counsel for the plaintiff in error has cited from the speech of one of the Senators of the United States, made in the Senate when the proposed Fourteenth Amendment was under consideration by that body, wherein he stated that among the privileges and immunities which the committee having the amendment in charge sought to protect against invasion or abridgment by the States, were includes those set forth in the first eight amendments to the Constitution, and counsel has argued that this court should, therefore, give that construction to the amendment which was contended for by the Senator in his speech.

What speeches were made by other Senators, and by Representatives in the House, upon this subject is not stated by counsel, nor does he state what construction was given to it, if any, by other members of Congress. It is clear that what is said in Congress upon such an occasion may or may not express the views of the majority of those who favor the adoption of the measure which may be before that body, and the question whether the proposed amendment itself expresses the meaning which those who spoke in its favor may have assumed that it did, is one to be determined by the language actually therein used and not by the speeches made regarding it.

What individual Senators or Representatives may have urged in debate, in regard to the meaning to be given to a proposed constitutional amendment, or bill or resolution, does not furnish a firm ground for its proper construction, nor is it important as explanatory of the grounds upon which the members voted in adopting it.

In the case of a constitutional amendment it is of less materiality than in that of an ordinary bill or resolution. A constitutional amendment must be agreed to, not only by Senators and Representatives, but it must be ratified by the legislatures, or by conventions, in three fourths of the States before such amendment can take effect. The safe way is to read its language in connection with the known condition of affairs out of which the occasion for its adoption may have arisen, and then to construe it, if there be therein any doubtful expressions, in a way so far as is reasonably possible, to forward the known purpose or object for which the amendment was adopted.

(citations omitted).

70. John Randolph Tucker, 2 *The Constitution of the United States* 854 (Henry St. George Tucker ed., Chicago, Callaghan & Co. 1899) (footnote omitted).

71. See, e.g., Randall Kennedy, *Race, Crime and the Law* chs. 1–5 (Pantheon, 1997).

72. See id. at 42–44.

73. 118 U.S. 356 (1886).

74. 100 U.S. 303 (1879).

75. See *Batson v. Kentucky*, 476 U.S. 79, 84–88 (1986).

76. 103 U.S. 370 (1880).

77. For an eye-opening account of black jury participation, see Gilbert Stephenson, *Race Distinctions in American Law* 247–72 (D. Appleton, 1910).

78. *Swain v. Alabama*, 380 U.S. 202 (1965).

79. On this point the *Neal* Court followed the earlier decision in *Virginia v. Rives*, 100 U.S. 313 (1879).

80. See Kennedy, *Race, Crime and the Law* at 175–76 (cited in note 71); Benno C. Schmidt, *Juries, Jurisdiction, and Race Discrimination: The Lost Promise of* Strauder v. West Virginia, 61 Tex. L. Rev. 1401, 1462–72 (1983).

81. *Andrews v. Swartz*, 156 U.S. 272, 275–76 (1895).

82. See Jeffrey S. Brand, *The Supreme Court, Equal Protection, and Jury Selection: Denying That Race Still Matters*, 1994 Wis. L. Rev. 511, 544–49.

83. See Schmidt, 61 Tex. L. Rev. at 1461 (cited in note 80) ("In any event, it was not only short-sightedness that produced the jurisdictional structure in which jury discrimination was permitted to flourish. The structure reflected the Court's commitment to a vision of federalism stated in extreme form by Justice Field, but shared in its essence by all of the Justices.").

84. 294 U.S. 587, 592–93 (1935).

85. See Schmidt, 61 Tex. L. Rev. at 1479 (cited in note 80).

86. See *Frank v. Mangum*, 237 U.S. 309, 335–36 (1915) (mob domination of a trial does not violate due process so long as state appellate review, untainted by improper influences, finds allegation of mob action unfounded); *Twining v. New Jersey*, 211 U.S. 78, 111–13 (1908) (due process does not include privilege against self-incrimination); *West v. Louisiana*, 194 U.S. 258, 263–64 (1904) (due process does not include Sixth Amendment right of confrontation); *Maxwell v. Dow*, 176 U.S. 581, 584–85 (1900) (reaffirming constitutionality of information prosecution against due process and privileges-and-immunities attack); *Brown v. New Jersey*, 175 U.S. 172, 175–76 (1899) (struck jury does not violate due process); *Hodgson v. Vermont*, 168 U.S. 262, 272 (1897) (information in instant case provided adequate notice of crime charged; *Hurtado* reaffirmed); *Duncan v. Missouri*, 152 U.S. 377, 382–83 (1894) (change in organization of state appellate courts does not violate due process); *Hallinger v. Davis*, 146 U.S. 314, 324 (1892) (due process does not prevent court from accepting guilty plea in capital case); *Leeper v. Texas*, 139 U.S. 462, 468 (1891) (various errors of state law alleged; no due process violation); *In re Converse*, 137 U.S. 624, 631–32 (1891) (alleged error state law did not amount to due process violation); *Caldwell v. Texas*, 137 U.S. 692, 698–99 (1891) (form of indictment immaterial to due process); *In re Kemmler*, 136 U.S. 436, 449 (1890) (due process does not forbid execution of convicted murderer by electrocution).

    The Supreme Court did vacate a state death sentence in *In re Medley*, 134 U.S. 160 (1890), not because of a due process violation, but because the state had replaced the murder statute in effect at the time of the crime with a statute providing for solitary confinement pending execution. The Court found that this violated the *ex post facto* law clause of Article I, section 10. Id. at 173. Leaving to the state courts the determination of whether the new statute left the state for a time without any murder statute at all, the Court directed that the warden release the prisoner, but that the state attorney general be informed precisely when and where this was to be done. Id. at 174.

    87. Cases invalidating state statutes for violation of the Fourteenth Amendment are collected in Felix Frankfurter, *Mr. Justice Holmes and the Supreme Court* app. 1 (Harvard U. Press, 1938). A glance at this compilation confirms that the justices were not reluctant to apply their natural law theory of due process to strike down state statutes for confiscating private property or interfering with contractual liberty. The record is not, as sometimes caricatured, that of a reactionary Court subservient to business interests. See Melvin Urofsky, *Myth and Reality: The Supreme Court and Protective Legislation in the Progressive Era*, 1983 Y.B. of the Supreme Court Historical Society 53, 53–55. Nonetheless, the Court struck down enough commercial regulation to disqualify judicial diffidence about applying the Fourteenth Amendment as an explanation for the dormancy of due process in criminal litigation during the period discussed.

    88. 116 U.S. 616, 633–35 (1886).

    89. 19 Howell's St. Tr. 1029 (1765).

    90. *Boyd*, 116 U.S. at 630.

    91. See id. at 624.

    92. Id. at 633.

    93. 192 U.S. 585 (1904).

    94. *Weeks v. United States*, 232 U.S. 383 (1914).

    95. See id. at 396.

    96. Id.

    97. On the basic incompatibility of *Adams* and *Weeks*, see *Flagg v. United States*, 233 F. 481, 486–87 (2d Cir. 1916) (Veeder, J., concurring).

    98. *Weeks*, 232 U.S. at 398 (citing *Boyd* and *Twining v. New Jersey*, 211 U.S. 78 (1908)).

    99. 251 U.S. 385 (1920).

    100. See *Hale v. Henkel*, 201 U.S. 43 (1906).

    101. 269 U.S. 20 (1925).

    102. Id. at 35.

    103. 255 U.S. 298 (1921).

    104. Id. at 309.

    105. *Weeks v. United States*, 232 U.S. 383, 393 (1914).

    106. 267 U.S. 132 (1925).

    107. Id. at 153.

    108. 277 U.S. 438 (1928).

    109. "There is no room in the present case for applying the Fifth Amendment unless the Fourth Amendment was first violated. There was no evidence of compulsion to induce the defendants to talk over their many telephones." Id. at 462.

    110. Id. at 464.

    111. Id. at 469–70 (Holmes, J., dissenting) (even "apart from the Constitution the Government ought not to use evidence obtained and only obtainable by a criminal act").

112. In one of the most celebrated passages in all of constitutional law, Brandeis wrote:

The makers of our Constitution undertook to secure conditions favorable to the pursuit of happiness. They recognized the significance of man's spiritual nature, of his feelings and of his intellect. They knew that only a part of the pain, pleasure and satisfactions of life are to be found in material things. They sought to protect Americans in their beliefs, their thoughts, their emotions and their sensations. They conferred, as against the Government, the right to be let alone—the most comprehensive of rights and the right most valued by civilized men. To protect that right, every unjustifiable intrusion by the Government upon the privacy of the individual, whatever the means employed, must be deemed a violation of the Fourth Amendment. And the use, as evidence in a criminal proceeding, of facts ascertained by such intrusion must be deemed a violation of the Fifth.

Id. at 478–79 (Brandeis, J., dissenting).

113. 142 U.S. 547 (1892).

114. See id. at 562 ("It is impossible that the meaning of the constitutional provision can only be, that a person shall not be compelled to be a witness against himself in a criminal prosecution against himself.").

115. See *Wilson v. United States*, 162 U.S. 613 (1896); *Pierce v. United States*, 160 U.S. 355 (1896); *Sparf & Hansen v. United States*, 156 U.S. 51 (1895); *Hopt v. Utah*, 110 U.S. 574 (1884).

116. 168 U.S. 532 (1897).

117. 384 U.S. 436 (1966).

118. Bram made the incriminating statements while in custody, after being stripped and searched. Cf. *Stein v. New York*, 346 U.S. 156, 179–88 (1953) (detention incommunicado and marathon questioning; confession held voluntary); *Stroble v. California*, 343 U.S. 181, 185, 190–91 (1952) (defendant kicked and threatened with blackjack one hour before questioning; confession held voluntary); *Lisenba v. California*, 314 U.S. 219, 238–40 (1941) (twelve days of detention incommunicado, including slapping of defendant; confession held voluntary).

119. See John Wigmore, 3 *Evidence* § 823 (3d ed. 1940). Of *Bram* Wigmore wrote that it, "by reason of its exalted source, must be specifically repudiated." Id. at 250 n.5.

120. As held in the two opinions in *Mattox v. United States*, 156 U.S. 237, 244–50 (1895) & 146 U.S. 140 (1892).

121. 174 U.S. 47 (1899).

122. See Francis Wharton, *A Treatise on Criminal Pleading and Practice* §§ 558 & 559 (Kay and Brother, Philadelphia; 9th ed. 1889); P.W. Viesselman, *Abbott's Criminal Trial Practice* §§ 14 & 16 (Lawyer's Co-Operative Publishing Co., Rochester, N.Y.: 4th ed. 1939); W.L. Clark, *Handbook on Criminal Procedure* § 157 (West Publishing, St. Paul, Minn.: 1895). My review of the West American Digest, Century Edition (criminal law, section 1500), covering the years 1658 to 1896, and the West Decennial Digest for 1897–1906 and 1907–1916 (criminal law keynote 641(3)) disclosed no federal cases involving the appointment of counsel for indigent defendants. In all probability, this reflects the prevalence of appointing counsel for the indigent. See *Johnson v. Zerbst*, 304 U.S. 458 (1938), Brief for Petitioner at 12. In their study of criminal justice in Alameda County, California, during the period 1870 to 1910, Lawrence Friedman and Robert Percival report that counsel was not only available in felony cases as a matter of law, but that 85% of felony defendants were represented by retained or appointed counsel, and that most of the unrepresented pleaded guilty. Lawrence Friedman & Robert Percival, *The Roots of Justice* 170–73 (U. North Carolina Press, 1981). Even in felonies, however, there was no right to *appointed* counsel at the pretrial examination. See id. at 154.

In police court, which handled most cases, lawyers were neither available at state expense nor frequently employed. See id. at 124. But if the police court imposed a sentence in excess of a $35 fine or seventeen days in jail, the case could be retried *de novo* in superior court. Id. at 118. Whether Alameda County provides representative data is an open question. The treatise writers, however, seem to take the appointment of trial counsel for the indigent for granted; it would seem to follow that at least for serious cases, the Friedman & Percival data reflect what was believed to be the norm by contemporary authorities. What did not typically occur was the appointment of counsel for indigent defendants who pleaded guilty rather than stand trial.

123. 304 U.S. 458 (1937).

124. See Friedman & Percival, *The Roots of Justice* at 36–38, 134 (cited in note 122).

125. For the suggestion, see, e.g., Akhil Reed Amar, *Fourth Amendment First Principles*, 107 Harv. L. Rev. 757, 788 (1994).

126. 199 U.S. 372 (1905).

127. 201 U.S. 43 (1906).

128. Id. at 74–76.

129. See Morgan Cloud, *The Fourth Amendment During the* Lochner *Era: Privacy, Property, and Liberty in Constitutional Theory*, 48 Stan. L. Rev. 555, 600–601 (1996); William Stuntz, *The Substantive Origins of Criminal Procedure*, 105 Yale L.J. 393, 431–32 (1995).

130. 160 U.S. 469 (1895).

131. *Hicks v. United States*, 150 U.S. 442 (1893).

132. William Duker, *The Fuller Court and State Criminal Process: Threshold of Modern Limitations on Government*, 1980 B.Y.U. L. Rev. 275, 276 notes "that this application of federalism and equal treatment [in the Fuller Court criminal cases], like the application of all 'neutral' principle, was not truly neutral, but this should not cast a shadow on the motives of the Court. Its conception of the judicial role, like that of the Warren and Burger Courts, was merely a reflection of its understanding of contemporary constitutional and normative values."

133. 237 U.S. 309 (1915).

134. See William Duker, *A Constitutional History of Habeas Corpus* 12–63 (Greenwood Press, 1980); Wayne R. LaFave & Jerold H. Israel, 3 *Criminal Procedure* § 27.1 (West, 1984). Strictly speaking the writ originated as a device by which the common-law courts could compel the attendance of persons for any purpose, including punishment; but in "the mid-fourteenth century . . . it came to be used as an independent proceeding designed to challenge illegal detention." Id. at 285.

135. Indeed, in the very passage that rendered "per legem terrae" into "due process of law," Coke described habeas corpus as one remedy for imprisonment contrary to law. See Edward Coke, *Second Institute* (1642), reprinted in Roscoe Pound, *The Development of Constitutional Guarantees of Liberty* 148, 159 (Yale U. Press, 1957).

136. The modern statute is 28 U.S.C. § 2254. The statute provides that the federal court may issue the writ "in behalf of a person in custody pursuant to the judgment of a State court" when the state prisoner "is in custody in violation of the Constitution or laws or treaties of the United States."

137. Probably the most commonly-repeated statement about habeas corpus, from judges and commentators, during the late nineteenth and early twentieth centuries was to the effect that the writ could not be used as a writ of error. See, e.g., William Church, *A Treatise on the Writ of Habeas Corpus* § 363 at 502–503 (Bancroft-Whitney, 1893).

138. See *Ex Parte Watkins*, 28 U.S. (3 Pet.) 193 (1830) (per Marshall, C.J.).

139. The seminal case is *Ex Parte Lange*, 85 U.S. 163 (1877), holding that when the petitioner has been twice convicted for the same offense, the court imposing the second conviction, in violation of the Constitution, lacks jurisdiction so that the second judgment is void. See also *Ex Parte Wilson*, 114 U.S. 417 (1885); *Ex Parte Bigelow*, 113 U.S. 328 (1885); *In re Nielsen*, 131 U.S. 176 (1889). The double-punishment cases might not of themselves have led to the equation of constitutional and jurisdictional defects, for whether as a matter of due process or double jeopardy constitutional finality rules aim in part at preventing a second trial from occurring at all. The critical impulse down the slippery slope came in *Ex Parte Siebold*, 100 U.S. 371 (1879), holding that a conviction for violating an unconstitutional statute was void for want of jurisdiction and thus no bar to issuing the writ. Nonetheless the courts rejected many petitions because the alleged errors did not meet the jurisdictional threshold. See, e.g., *Riddle v. Dyche*, 262 U.S. 333 (1923); *Ex Parte Harding*, 120 U.S. 782 (1887); *Felts v. Murphy*, 201 U.S. 123 (1906).

140. *Frank v. Mangum*, 237 U.S. 309, 327–35 (1915).

141. On the Frank case, see Francis Busch, *Guilty or Not Guilty?* 1–74 (Bobbs-Merrill, 1952). Evidence that has since come to light establishes Frank's innocence beyond reasonable doubt. The state of Georgia pardoned Frank posthumously in 1986. See *Georgia Pardons Victim 70 Years After Lynching*, N.Y. Times A16 (March 12, 1986).

142. 261 U.S. 86 (1923).

143. Id. at 91. Professor Klarman points out that there is language in *Moore* criticizing the adequacy of the state corrective process, so that technically *Moore* might be consistent with *Frank*. He concludes, however, that "[w]hile the decisions may be technically consistent, it seems more likely that the Justices in *Moore* simply were more solicitous of the defendant's rights." Michael Klarman, *The Racial Origins of Modern Criminal Procedure*, 99 Mich. L. Rev. 48, 59 (2000).

144. *Frank*, 261 U.S. at 92.

145. See generally Francis Allen, *The Supreme Court and State Criminal Justice*, 4 Wayne L. Rev. 191 (1958). Professor Allen observes, at 195:

Perhaps the remarkable thing about the history of the due process clause in the state criminal cases is not that doctrine has burgeoned and proliferated in the last quarter-century. Rather, it may be more surprising that for over half a century the due process clause was permitted to lie virtually dormant in these cases. For, if one puts aside a series of decisions in which criminal provisions of a state anti-trust statute were declared void for uncertainty, it is substantially accurate to say that not until 1923 and the decision of *Moore v. Dempsey* . . . does the due process clause become an effective device for the regulation of state criminal process. Not until *Powell v. Alabama* decided in 1932, almost sixty-five years after the adoption of the Fourteenth Amendment, does the modern law of the area really commence.

(footnotes omitted).

146. 287 U.S. 45 (1932).

147. For a superb history, see James Goodman, *Stories of Scottsboro* (Pantheon, 1994).

148. *Powell*, 287 U.S. at 51.

149. Id. at 71. "To hold otherwise," the Court's next sentence reads, "would be to ignore the fundamental postulate, already adverted to, 'that there are certain immutable principles of justice which inhere in the very idea of free government which no member of the Union may disregard' " (quoting *Holden v. Hardy*, 169 U.S. 366, 389 (1898)). The actual marriage of fundamental fairness and selective incorporation was yet some time away, but this passage certainly signaled the engagement.

150. 297 U.S. 278 (1936).

151. Id. at 284. The state supreme court rejected Brown's state claim as procedurally defaulted, and rejected his federal constitutional claim as barred by *Twining*. See *Brown v. State*, 158 So. 339, 341–42 (Miss. 1935); Klarman, 99 Mich. L. Rev. at 68 (cited in note 143).

152. Id. at 286.

153. 309 U.S. 227 (1940).

154. The point is well made in Yale Kamisar, *What is an "Involuntary" Confession?*, in *Police Interrogations and Confessions: Essays in Law and Policy* 1–25 (1980).

155. 314 U.S. 219, 236 (1941) ("As applied to a criminal trial, denial of due process is the failure to observe that fundamental fairness essential to the very concept of justice."). Fine words, but what do they mean?

156. Lisenba murdered his wife for insurance money, and evidently entered into marriage with that very purpose, having once before committed a similar murder. In the initial attempt to kill his wife, he bound her and induced rattlesnakes to bite her; but the venom did not kill, only causing ugly swelling. The victim was thereafter drowned in a pond. See id. at 223–25.

157. 316 U.S. 455 (1942).

158. Id. at 462 (footnote omitted).

159. As Allen, 4 Wayne L. Rev. 191 at 192 (cited in note 145), says of *Powell v. Alabama*, the opinion "provides the full and considered discussion of the issues appropriate to the importance and significance of the interests at stake. At the same time, the actual holding of the case is expressly predicated upon and limited by the particular facts of the record."

CHAPTER 2

1. 316 U.S. 455, 474 n.1 (1942) (Black, J., dissenting).

2. 332 U.S. 46, 68–92 (1947) (Black, J., dissenting).

3. 83 U.S. 36 (1873).

4. 92 U.S. 542 (1876).

5. 211 U.S. 78 (1908).

6. 302 U.S. 319, 324–28 (1937).

7. *Adamson*, 332 U.S. at 70 (Black, J., dissenting).

8. Id. at 84–85 (Black, J., dissenting).

9. Id. at 74–75. See id. at 92–123 (Appendix to Black's dissent).

10. Id. at 90–92.

11. See Cong. Globe, 39th Cong., 1st Sess. 1089–90 (1866) (statement of Rep. Bingham); Richard Aynes, *On Misreading John Bingham and the Fourteenth Amendment*, 103 Yale L.J. 57, 71–74 (1993).

12. See Cong. Globe, 39th Cong., 1st Sess. at 1290–92 (1866) (statement of Rep. Bingham).

13. Cong. Globe, 42d Cong., 1st Sess. app. 84 (1871) (statement of Rep. Bingham).

14. Cong. Globe, 39th Cong., 1st Sess. 2765–66 (1866) (statement of Sen. Howard).

15. Howard quoted *Corfield*'s enumeration of private-law rights and the privilege of habeas corpus, and then said: "To these privileges and immunities, whatever they may be—for they are not and cannot be fully defined in their entire extent and precise nature— to these should be added the personal rights guarantied and secured by the first eight amendments . . . . " Id. at 2765.

16. See, e.g., Cong. Globe, 39th Cong., 1st Sess. at 2462–63 (statement of Rep. Garfield); id. at 2498 (statement of Rep. Eliot); David P. Currie, *The Constitution in the Supreme Court* 347 (U. Chicago Press, 1985) ("Speaker after speaker proclaimed that it was this statute for which the fourteenth amendment would provide an unassailable constitutional base.") (footnote omitted); William Nelson, *The Fourteenth Amendment* 115 (Harvard U. Press, 1988) ("At the very least, section one was understood to remove all doubts about the constitutionality of the 1866 Civil Rights Act and thus to give Congress legislative power in reference to basic rights of contract, property, and personal security.").

17. Black's biographer quotes him as follows: "If I didn't find that [i.e., incorporation] was their [i.e., the framers'] view, my career on the Court would have been entirely different. I would not have gone with due process and I'd be considered the most reactionary judge on the Court." Roger K. Newman, *Hugo Black* 353 (Pantheon Books, 1994).

18. Charles Fairman, *Does the Fourteenth Amendment Incorporate the Bill of Rights? The Original Understanding*, 2 Stan. L. Rev. 5, 134, 139 (1949).

19. Id. at 68–134.

20. Id. at 101 (Kansas abandoned grand jury presentment in 1868); id. at 110 (Wisconsin abandoned grand jury presentment in 1870); id. at 115–16 (Michigan abandoned grand jury presentment in 1859).

21. Id. at 137.

22. William Winslow Crosskey, *Charles Fairman, "Legislative History," and the Constitutional Limits on State Authority*, 22 U. Chi. L. Rev. 1 (1954).

23. For the history of the controversy, see Richard L. Aynes, *Charles Fairman, Felix Frankfurter, and the Fourteenth Amendment*, 70 Chi.-Kent L. Rev. 1197 (1995).

24. Charles Fairman, *History of the Supreme Court of the United States—Reconstruction and Reunion, Part One* 1207–1300 (Macmillan, 1974).

25. See Michael Kent Curtis, *No State Shall Abridge* (Duke U. Press, 1986); Robert Kaczorowski, *The Politics of Judicial Interpretation: The Federal Courts, Department of Justice and Civil Rights, 1866–1876* (Oceana Publications, 1985); Earl Maltz, *Civil Rights, the Constitution, and Congress, 1863–1869* (U. Press of Kansas, 1990); Akhil Reed Amar, *The Bill of Rights and the Fourteenth Amendment*, 101 Yale L.J. 1193 (1992). Fairman's position is supported against Curtis in Raoul Berger, *The Fourteenth Amendment and the Bill of Rights* (U. Oklahoma Press, 1989); James E. Bond, *No Easy Walk to Freedom: Reconstruction and the Ratification of the Fourteenth Amendment* 261–63 (Praeger, 1997). Professor Thomas has recently brought out a substantial challenge to the incorporation theory. See George C. Thomas III, *When Constitutional Worlds Collide: Resurrecting the Framers' Bill of Rights and Criminal Procedure*, 100 Mich. L. Rev. 145 (2001). I am indebted to Professor Thomas for calling Dean Bond's book to my attention. Otherwise we have worked quite independently, and indeed largely with separate sources. That we could do so may be some evidence in itself of the strength of the anti-incorporation position.

26. On this point, Fairman and the proponents of incorporation find common ground. See Horace Edgar Flack, *The Adoption of the Fourteenth Amendment* 153–54 (The Johns Hopkins Press, 1908); Amar, 101 Yale L.J. at 1249–51 (cited in note 25).

27. See Nelson, *The Fourteenth Amendment* at 118–19 (cited in note 16):

Understanding section one as an instrument for the equal rather than absolute protection of rights resolves the contradiction in the evidence that has so puzzled historians. American states in the mid-nineteenth century did, in fact, provide their citizens with most of the protections contained in the Bill of Rights, including those mentioned by Jacob Howard in his presentation of the Fourteenth Amendment to the Senate. But the eleven states to which Bingham referred, together with a few other states, had failed to give the rights to their black citizens. By virtue of its guarantee of equality, section one would authorize Congress to rectify that failure and thus enable Bingham to declare that Congress would have power to enforce the Bill of Rights. But at the same time the amendment would have no impact in a state that allowed the institution of criminal proceedings by information rather than indictment: a state would be free to disregard entirely a provision of the Bill of Rights such as the guarantee of grand jury indictment, and Congress would have no power to intervene.

See also John Harrison, *Reconstructing the Privileges or Immunities Clause*, 101 Yale L.J. 1385, 1465 (1992).

28. In *United States v. Hall*, 26 F. Cas. 701 (C.C.S.D.Al. 1871) (no. 15,282), the court rejected a demurrer to an indictment under the Enforcement Act of 1870 against Klansmen who had broken up a Republican political meeting and murdered two of those in attendance. The court held that First Amendment rights, along with the other rights protected in the first eight amendments, were privileges or immunities of national citizenship; and that when the states failed to protect the exercise of these rights, the federal government could proceed directly against private persons for interfering with them. Id. at 81–82.

In *United States v. Crosby*, 25 F. Cas. 701, 704 (C.C.D.S.C. 1871), the court dismissed a count in an indictment under the Enforcement and Ku Klux Klan acts, which charged a conspiracy to interfere with the exercise of the right to freedom from unreasonable search and seizure because the Fourth Amendment did not apply to the states.

29. 74 U.S. 321 (1869). David Currie has characterized *Twitchell* as a "pre-fourteenth amendment" [*sic*] case. *The Constitution in the Supreme Court: Limitations on State Power, 1865–1873*, 51 U. Chi. L. Rev. 329, 360 n.186 (1984). The Fourteenth Amendment had been declared effective by Congress and the secretary of state in July 1868. See John E. Nowak, Ronald Rotunda, & J. Nelson Young, 3 *Treatise on Constitutional Law* 679 (West, 1986). There can be no doubt that the new amendment applied to Twitchell's case, as he challenged the constitutionality of his indictment, which was filed in December of 1868. *Twitchell*, 74 U.S. at 322. In any event the murder took place on November 22, 1868, well after the effective date of the amendment. See John D. Lawson, *The Trial of George S. Twitchell for the Murder of Mary E. Hill*, in 6 Am. St. Tr. 1 (1916).

30. See *Twitchell*, 74 U.S. at 323 (argument in support of the petition). There are no briefs for the case, presumably because the Court refused to grant Twitchell's petition for a writ of error, which would have brought the case to the Court for plenary consideration. Oral argument on the petition took place only a few days before Twitchell's scheduled execution. The report of the argument, however, makes clear that Twitchell primarily relied on the Sixth Amendment notice claim, and that his invocation of the Fifth Amendment was aimed at Pennsylvania's departure from common-law practice in the form of indictments. See id. at 323–24.

31. Id. at 325–26.

32. Professor Amar explains *Twitchell* as a case of judicial incompetence. He argues that Twitchell also raised a due process claim, that the justices must have known that the Fourteenth Amendment included a due process clause, and so the case teaches nothing about the Fourteenth Amendment. See Amar, 101 Yale L.J. at 1255 (cited in note 25). This is not a terribly compelling account; we should not presume incompetence from all nine justices, plus defense counsel, if a reasonable alternative explanation exists.

There is just such an explanation. Twitchell's due process claim was dependent on his Fifth and Sixth Amendment claims. He argued that the defects in the indictment made the conviction void, so that "the warrant of the Governor for the execution was, therefore, not a 'due process' of law." *Twitchell*, 74 U.S. at 324. He did not argue that the indictment itself violated due process. The nullity of the conviction was the premise, not the conclusion, of Twitchell's invocation of due process. There was thus no need for the Court to undertake any due process analysis once it disposed of the Fifth Amendment grand jury and Sixth Amendment notice claims. The Court, in short, unanimously agreed that the Fourteenth Amendment gave no help to Twitchell's Bill of Rights claims, and that *Barron v. Baltimore* remained good law after the adoption of the amendment.

33. James Kent, 1 *Commentaries on American Law* 456 n.1 (Little, Brown, and Co., Oliver Wendell Holmes, Jr. ed. 1873). Kent, of course, could not have discussed the Fourteenth Amendment, and Holmes's decision not to discuss the new amendment is therefore not surprising. But if Holmes thought that the Fourteenth Amendment cast a cloud over *Barron*, he would not have inserted the citation to *Twitchell* without a caveat.

34. Thomas Cooley, *Treatise on the Constitutional Limitations* 19 & n.1 (Little, Brown, and Co., 1868) ("And it is to be observed as a settled rule of construction of the national Constitution, that the limitations it imposes upon the powers of government are in all cases to be understood as limitations upon the government of the Union only, except where the States are expressly mentioned.").

35. Thomas Cooley, *Treatise on the Constitutional Limitations* *19 n.1 (Little, Brown, and Co., 2d ed. 1871). The language stating the "settled rule of construction of the national Constitution" does not change, but now the footnote picks up *Twitchell*.

36. Id. at *397. In this passage Cooley moves directly from the "privileges or immunities" language in the Fourteenth Amendment to discuss the case law, including *Corfield*, that had developed concerning "privileges and immunities" under Article IV.

37. Id. at *397:

It was not within the power of the States before the adoption of the fourteenth amendment, to deprive citizens of the equal protection of the laws; but there were servile classes not thus shielded, and when these were made freemen, there were some who disputed their claim to citizenship, and some State laws were in force which established discriminations against them. To settle doubts and preclude all such laws, the fourteenth amendment was adopted; and the same securities which one citizen may demand, all others are now entitled to.

See also id. at *294:

The most important clause in the fourteenth amendment is that part of section 1 which declares that all persons born or naturalized in the United States, and subject to the jurisdiction thereof, are citizens of the United States of the State wherein they reside. This provision very properly puts an end to any question of the title of the freedmen and others of their race to the rights of citizenship; but it may be doubtful whether the further provisions of the same section surround the citizen with any protections additional to those before possessed under the State constitutions; but as a principle of State constitutional law has now been made a part of the Constitution of the United States, the effect will be to make the Supreme Court of the United States the final arbiter of cases in which a violation of this principle by State laws is complained of, inasmuch as the decisions of the State courts upon laws which are supposed to violate it will be subject to review in that court on appeal.

(footnotes omitted).

38. Id. at *19 n.1. This sentence asserting state power to abolish jury trial, even in criminal cases, did not appear in the first, 1868, edition. Cooley's decision to make this assertion after ratification suggests how alien the incorporation theory was to him.

39. Joseph Story, II *Commentaries on the Constitution of the United States* §§ 1931–34 (Little, Brown, and Co., Thomas Cooley ed. 1873).

40. Id. at § 1943.

41.

The States, in the enforcement of their own laws for the preservation of peace and order, may dispense with the grand jury if the legislature shall so provide; and they may make all State offences triable before a single judge, instead of by jury, if that mode of trial shall be thought most politic or most conducive to justice. And no more under the fourteenth article than previously can the federal government interfere with the mode prescribed for the trial of State offences: whatever is established will be due process of law, so that it be general and impartial in operation, and disregard no provision of federal or State constitution.

Id., § 1947 at 666.

42. *Weimer v. Bunbury*, 30 Mich. *201 (1874).

43. Id. at *208.

44. *State v. Schumpert*, 1 S.C. 85 (1869) (30 West's S.C. Reports 40 (Nov./Dec. 1868)) (three-judge court unanimously rejects claim that Fifth Amendment presentment clause bars initiation of prosecution by arrest warrant, citing *Barron*).

45. *Prescott v. Ohio*, 19 Ohio St. 184, 187 (1870) (five judges unanimously reject Fifth Amendment challenge to juvenile court process, citing *Twitchell*).

46. *State v. Jackson*, 21 La. Ann. 574, 575 (August 1869) (five-judge court unanimously rejects Fifth Amendment challenge to information procedure, citing *Barron*).

47. *State v. Wells*, 46 Iowa 662, 663 (1877) (five-judge court unanimously rejects defendant's Fifth Amendment presentment clause claim, citing *Barron*).

48. *Kalloch v. Superior Court*, 56 Cal. 229, 237–41 (1880) (en banc) (seven-judge court unanimously rejects both due process and privileges-or-immunities challenges to information procedure under Fourteenth Amendment).

49. *Rowan v. State*, 30 Wis. 129, 148–50 (1872). The conviction was reversed, however, because the jurors were permitted to go home for the night during deliberations.

50. See Gerhard O.W. Mueller, *Crime, Law and the Scholars* 35–45 (Heinemann Educational, 1969). Mueller opines that Bishop "proceeded with a remarkable scholarly care and an unprecedented meticulousness," id. at 37, and that Wharton "was not only a first-rate lawyer, especially in the criminal field, but also a man of universal interests extending over all spheres of political endeavor," id. at 42.

51. Joel Prentiss Bishop, 1 *Commentaries on the Law of Criminal Procedure* § 608 at 433–34 (Little, Brown, and Co., 1866) (citing *Noles v. State*, 24 Ala. 672 (1854)).

52. Joel Prentiss Bishop, 1 *Commentaries on the Law of Criminal Procedure* § 99 at 60 (Little, Brown, and Co., 2d ed. 1872).

53. Id. at 60 n.4.

54. Joel Prentiss Bishop, 1 *Commentaries on the Law of Criminal Procedure* § 145 at 81 (Little, Brown, and Co., 3d ed. 1880).

55. Id.

56. Id.

57. Joel Prentiss Bishop, 1 *New Criminal Procedure* § 145 at 85 (T.H. Flood, 4th ed. 1895) (citations omitted).

58. Francis Wharton, 1 *A Treatise on the Criminal Law of the United States, Pleading and Evidence*, § 213 at 151 n.j (Kay and Bro., 6th ed. 1868) (citing *State v. Keyes*, 8 Vt. 57 (1836)).

59. Francis Wharton, 1 *A Treatise on the Criminal Law of the United States, Principles, Pleading, and Evidence* § 213 at 209 (Kay and Bro., 7th ed. 1874).

60. Francis Wharton, *A Treatise on Criminal Pleading and Practice* § 88 at 65 (Kay and Bro., 8th ed. 1880). At this point the pleading-and-practice volume has become independent but is still numbered as an eighth edition.

61. Francis Wharton, *A Treatise on Criminal Pleading and Practice* § 88 at 63 (Little, Brown, and Co., 9th ed. 1889).

62. See 83 U.S. 36, 118–19 (Bradley, J., dissenting). Justice Bradley, however, did not agree with Justice Black, for he thought that the privilege or immunities of citizens of the United States included the right to operate a slaughterhouse, a privilege not mentioned in the Bill of Rights. Id. at 119. Justice Swayne endorsed both Bradley's opinion and Field's. See id. at 124 (Swayne, J., dissenting). It is difficult to tell what he thought about incorporation, however, because Field's opinion does not endorse incorporation, relying rather on the fundamental-rights approach of *Corfield v. Coryell.*

63. Justice Harlan defended the total incorporation theory in his dissenting opinion in *Maxwell v. Dow*, 176 U.S. 581, 611–613 (1900) (Harlan, J., dissenting). Why total incorporation became plausible only thirty-two years after the ratification of the amendment is a mystery. Eight years later, in *Twining v. New Jersey*, 211 U.S. 78, 123 (1908) (Harlan, J., dissenting), Justice Harlan seemed to rely on a selective rather than a total incorporation approach.

64. *Chicago, Burlington & Quincy R.R. Co. v. Chicago*, 166 U.S. 226, 241 (1897).

65. 176 U.S. 581, 611–13 (1900).

66. Tinsley E. Yarbrough, *Judicial Enigma* 185 (Oxford U. Press, 1995).

67. I certainly have not waded through the mass of public debate over the Amendment during the 1866 election campaigns and during the ratification debates. Those who have, such as Fairman and Flack, agree that the incorporation question was not discussed. I will quote Flack, a proponent of incorporation, on this point:

The declarations and statements of newspapers, writers and speakers, which have been given, show very clearly, it seems, the general opinion held in the North. That opinion, briefly stated, was that the Amendment embodied the Civil Rights Bill and gave Congress the power to define and secure the privileges of citizens of the United States. There does not seem to have been any statement at all as to whether the first eight Amendments were to be made applicable to the States or not, whether the privileges guaranteed by those Amendments were to be considered as privileges secured by the Amendment, but it may be inferred that this was recognized to be the logical result by those who thought that the freedom of speech and of the press as well as due process of law, including a jury trial, were secured by it.

Flack, *Adoption of the Fourteenth Amendment* at 153 (cited in note 26). Somewhat later, however, Flack discusses Bingham's 1871 assertion that the Amendment incorporated the Bill of Rights. In reply to Bingham,

Mr. Storm, of Pennsylvania, said that little attention was given the first section when the Amendment was before the House, because the attention of the country was called to the question of changing the basis of representation. He furthermore declared that if the views now announced by those advocating the bill had been uttered when the Amendment was before Congress, it would never have been ratified, and added: "If the monstrous doctrine now set up as resulting from the provisions of the Fourteenth Amendment had ever been hinted at that Amendment would have received an emphatic rejection at the hands of the people." He also stated that the first section was but a reenactment of the Civil Rights Bill through superabundant caution. Mr. Storm seems to have stated the question fairly, and no doubt he was right in saying that had the people been informed of what was intended by the Amendment, they would have rejected. But it is equally true that there were statements made by men in Congress at the time to show something of what was really meant by it, but these statements seem to have been lost sight of on account of the more stirring and exciting political questions of the time.

Id. at 236–37 (citation omitted). More recently, Dean Bond's impressive study of the ratification contest in the South concludes not only that incorporation was not considered during the ratification process, but that the opponents of the proposed amendment had a great deal to gain from alleging that incorporation would be the effect of ratification. See

Bond, *No Easy Walk to Freedom* at 252–55 (cited in note 25). Especially in light of popular hostility to the prospect of black jurors judging white litigants, Dean Bond's point is a strong one in favor of interpreting silence about incorporation as evidence that incorporation wasn't on the political radar screen.

68. See Nelson, *The Fourteenth Amendment* at 118–19 (cited in note 16).

69. See Aynes, 103 Yale L.J. at 83–94 (cited in note 11) (discussing views or Timothy Farrar, George Pashchal, and John Norton Pomeroy).

70. See *United States v. Hall*, 26. Cas. 79 (C.C.S.D.Al. 1871) (No. 15,282).

71. John Norton Pomeroy, *An Introduction to the Constitutional Law of the United States* (Hurd and Houghton, 1868).

72. Id. §§ 235 & 237.

73. Id. § 242, at 154–55.

74. This is the gist of Nelson's persuasive account. See Nelson, *The Fourteenth Amendment* at 110–47 (cited in note 16).

75. See William Blackstone, 1 *Commentaries* *129 (1765).

76. See, e.g., Nelson, *The Fourteenth Amendment*, at 115 (cited in note 16) ("At the very least, section one was understood to remove all doubts about the constitutionality of the 1866 Civil Rights Act and thus to give Congress legislative power in reference to basic rights of contract, property, and personal security."); Bond, *No Easy Walk to Freedom* at 9 & 261 (cited in note 25).

77. 6 F. Cas. 546, 551–52 (C.C.E.D. Pa. 1823) (No. 3230).

78. See *Slaughter-House*, 83 U.S. 36, 78 (1872).

79. 347 U.S. 497 (1954).

80. Writing for the majority in *Adamson*, Justice Reed powerfully summarized the case against exhuming the privileges-and-immunities clause:

After declaring that state and national citizenship coexist in the same person, the Fourteenth Amendment forbids a state from abridging the privileges and immunities of citizens of the United States. As a matter of words, this leaves a state free to abridge, within the limits of the due process clause, the privileges and immunities flowing from state citizenship. This reading of the Federal Constitution has heretofore found favor with the majority of this Court as a natural and logical interpretation. It accords with the constitutional doctrine of federalism by leaving to the states the responsibility of dealing with the privileges and immunities of their citizens except those inherent in national citizenship. It is the construction placed upon the amendment by justices whose own experience had given them contemporaneous knowledge of the purposes that led to the adoption of the Fourteenth Amendment. This construction has become embedded in our federal system as a functioning element in preserving the balance between national and state power.

332 U.S. at 52–53 (footnotes omitted).

81.

The short answer to the suggestion that the provision of the Fourteenth Amendment, which ordains "nor shall any State deprive any person of life, liberty, or property, without due process of law," was a way of saying that every State must thereafter initiate prosecutions through indictment by a grand jury, must have a trial by a jury of twelve in criminal cases, and must have trial by such a jury in common law suits where the amount in controversy exceeds twenty dollars, is that it is a strange way of saying it.

Adamson, 332 U.S. at 63 (Frankfurter, J., concurring).

82. See *Duncan v. Louisiana*, 391 U.S. 145, 166 n.1 (1968) (Black, J., concurring).

83. See *Wolf v. People*, 187 P.2d 926 (Colo. 1947).

84. Brief for Petitioner, at 13–14.

85. *Wolf v. Colorado*, 338 U.S. 25, 28 (1949).

86. Id.

87. Id. at 33.

88. Id. at 39–40 (Black, J., concurring).

89. Id. at 47 (Rutledge, J., dissenting). More than half a century later, that pithy statement remains the beginning of wisdom about the exclusionary rule.

90. 342 U.S. 165 (1952).

91. See id. at 166.

92. Id. at 172.

93. Read together, *Wolf* and *Rochin* might have meant that only shocking Fourth Amendment violations offend due process, not that due process forbids all Fourth Amendment violations but requires exclusion only for shocking violations. See Yale Kamisar, Wolf *and* Lustig *Ten Years Later: Illegal State Evidence in State and Federal Courts*, 43 Minn. L. Rev. 1083, 1101 (1959). But it made far more sense to take the Court at face value and read *Wolf* as incorporating the Fourth Amendment but not the exclusionary rule. See id. at 1101–1108; Francis Allen, *Federalism and the Fourth Amendment: A Requiem for* Wolf, 1961 Sup. Ct. Rev. 1, 3–5.

94. See *Irvine v. California*, 347 U.S. 128, 145 (1954) (Frankfurter, J., dissenting).

95. Id. at 132.

96. Id. at 133.

97. Id. at 134.

98. Id. at 152 (Douglas, J., dissenting) ("If unreasonable searches and seizures that violate the privacy which the Fourth Amendment protects are to be outlawed, this is the time and the occasion to do it.").

99. Id. at 142, 148 (Frankfurter, J., dissenting).

100. Id. at 138 (Clark, J., concurring).

101. Id. at 139.

102. An FBI investigation into the case "revealed some significant facts which did not appear in the records or the opinion of the Supreme Court and were apparently unknown to the Court at the time of its review of the case . . . . " Note, *State Police, Unconstitutionally Obtained Evidence and Section 242 of the Civil Rights Statute*, 7 Stanford L. Rev. 76, 94 n.75 (1955) (quoting Letter of February 15, 1955 from Assistant Attorney General Warren Olney III). One of these facts was that the officers "were acting under orders of the Chief of Police, who in turn was acting with the full knowledge of the local District Attorney." Id.

103. *People v. Gonzales*, 124 P.2d 44 (1942).

104. 282 P.2d 905 (1955).

105. Roger Traynor, Mapp v. Ohio *at Large in the Fifty States*, 1962 Duke L.J. 319, 321–22.

106. E.g., *Watts v. Indiana*, 338 U.S. 49 (1949).

107. *Stein v. New York*, 346 U.S. 156 (1953).

108. *Stroble v. California*, 343 U.S. 181 (1952).

109. See *Watts*, 339 U.S. at 57 (Douglas, J., dissenting).

110. *Mallory v. United States*, 354 U.S. 449 (1957).

111. *Fikes v. Alabama*, 352 U.S. 191, 199 n.1 (1957) (Frankfurter, J., concurring) ("Flouting of the requirement of prompt arraignment prevailing in most States is in and of itself not a denial of due process.").

112. *Crooker v. California*, 357 U.S. 433 (1958); *Cicenia v. LaGay*, 357 U.S. 504 (1958).

113. *Crooker*, 357 U.S. at 448 (Douglas, J., dissenting) (footnote omitted).
114. *Crooker*, 357 U.S. 441 n.6.
115. Id. at 441.
116. *Cicenia*, 357 U.S. at 505.
117. Id. at 508.
118. Id. at 510.
119. One can understand the reluctance of federal judges to reconsider on habeas the claim that a federal district court, subject to review in a federal court of appeals, erroneously had rejected the petitioner's search-and-seizure or coerced confession claim. See *Fowler v. Hunter*, 164 F.2d 668, 669–70 (10th Cir. 1947); *Eury v. Huff*, 146 F.2d 17, 17–18 (D.C. Cir. 1944); *Bozel v. Hudspeth*, 126 F.2d 585, 587 (10th Cir. 1942); *Price v. Johnston*, 125 F.2d 806, 809–11 (9th Cir. 1942).
120. 297 U.S. 278 (1936) (statement obtained by whipping defendant inadmissible).
121. *Bowen v. Johnston*, 306 U.S. 19, 23–24 (1939).
122. *Waley v. Johnston*, 316 U.S. 98, 104–105 (1942).
123. 344 U.S. 443 (1953).
124. See id. at 482–87.
125. The majority rejected all three habeas petitions, but only after reaching the merits and rejecting, on substantive grounds, the petitioners' claims of coerced confessions and racial discrimination in jury selection. The majority opinion of Justice Reed never specifically addressed the relationship between jurisdictional and constitutional defects. One must scan the opinion of Justice Jackson to discover the standard the majority did not disavow: "It really has become necessary to plead nothing more than that the prisoner is in jail, wants to get out, and thinks it is illegal to hold him." 344 U.S. at 540–41 (footnote omitted). See Henry Hart, *Foreword: The Time Chart of the Justices*, 73 Harv. L. Rev. 84, 106 (1959); Paul Bator, *Finality in Criminal Law and Federal Habeas Corpus for State Prisoners*, 76 Harv. L. Rev. 441, 500 (1963):

The Supreme Court . . . affirmed the convictions . . . not on the basis of *Frank v. Mangum*, that the state had provided adequate corrective process, but by reaching and rejecting on the merits the federal claims presented which had been previously adjudicated by the state courts. The Court did so without any explicit discussion of the question of jurisdiction or any apparent understanding of how radical this step was: with only Mr. Justice Jackson disagreeing, eight of nine Justices assumed that on habeas corpus federal district courts must provide review of the merits of constitutional claims fully litigated in the state-court system.

126. *Brown*, 344 U.S. at 463–64. Formally speaking, the federal forum has no reason to defer to state court findings that, if erroneous, deprive the state court of jurisdiction; a void judgment is just that, void.
127. One who believed that introduction of evidence obtained by police misconduct that fell short of shocking the conscience did not violate due process could quite comfortably maintain an expansive view of the federal habeas jurisdiction. See *Rochin v. California*, 342 U.S. 165 (1952) (per Frankfurter, J.).
128. E.g., *Wesberry v. Sanders*, 376 U.S. 1 (1964).
129. Compare *Williamson v. Lee Optical of Oklahoma, Inc.*, 348 U.S. 483, 489 (1955) with *McLaughlin v. Florida*, 379 U.S. 184 (1964). See generally Ronald D. Rotunda, John E. Nowak & J. Nelson Young, 2 *Treatise on Constitutional Law* § 18.3 (West, 1986) (providing background on standards of review under the equal protection clause).
130. See *Reed v. Reed*, 404 U.S. 71 (1971); *Craig v. Boren*, 429 U.S. 190 (1976).

131. 351 U.S. 12 (1956).

132. Id. at 17.

133. Id. at 24 (Frankfurter, J., concurring in the judgment).

134. *McKane v. Durston*, 153 U.S. 684, 687–88 (1894).

135. See Bator, 76 Harv. L. Rev. at 473 (cited in note 125).

136. *Dowd v. Cook*, 340 U.S. 206, 209–10 (1951); *Cochran v. Kansas*, 316 U.S. 255, 257–58 (1942).

137. 334 U.S. 1 (1948).

138. See Mark V. Tushnet, *Dia-Tribe*, 78 Mich. L. Rev. 694, 696–97 (1980).

139. See Marc M. Arkin, *Rethinking the Constitutional Right to a Criminal Appeal*, 39 U.C.L.A. L. Rev. 503 (1992).

140. 372 U.S. 335 (1963).

141. 372 U.S. 353 (1963).

142. See *Mayer v. Chicago*, 404 U.S. 189 (1971). The Court has not completely refused to require free services to the indigent for use at trial as an equal protection matter, but the services the Court has required only highlight the irony. See *Roberts v. LaVallee*, 389 U.S. 40 (1967) (indigent defendant has right under the Equal Protection Clause to free transcript of preliminary hearing, for use at the trial). Doubtless the transcript would be useful, but scarcely as useful as the best lawyer, or even the best private investigator or expert witness, that money can buy.

CHAPTER 3

1. *Strickland v. Washington*, 466 U.S. 668, 687 (1984).

2. 367 U.S. 643 (1961).

3. 373 U.S. 427 (1963).

4. 385 U.S. 293 (1966).

5. 385 U.S. 206 (1966).

6. *Linkletter v. Walker*, 381 U.S. 618 (1965).

7. *Alderman v. United States*, 394 U.S. 165 (1969).

8. *Kaufman v. United States*, 394 U.S. 217, 238 (1969) (Black, J., dissenting).

9. *Camara v. Municipal Court*, 387 S. 523 (1967).

10. See id. at 538 ("Having concluded that the area inspection is a 'reasonable' search of private property within the meaning of the Fourth Amendment, it is obvious that 'probable cause' to issue a warrant to inspect must exist if reasonable legislative or administrative standards for conducting an area inspection are satisfied with respect to a particular dwelling.").

11. See Caleb Foote, *Vagrancy-Type Law and its Administration*, 104 U. Pa. L. Rev. 603 (1956).

12. 392 U.S. 1 (1968).

13. The Court abandoned the mere evidence rule in *Warden v. Hayden*, 387 U.S. 294 (1967).

14. *Katz v. United States*, 389 U.S. 347 (1967).

15. 401 U.S. 745 (1971) (plurality opinion).

16. *United States v. Miller*, 425 U.S. 435 (1976).

17. *California v. Greenwood*, 486 U.S. 35 (1988).

18. *Veronia School Dist. 47J v. Acton*, 515 U.S. 646 (1995).

19. In *United States v. Chadwick*, 423 U.S. 411 (1976), which involved the warrantless search of a footlocker that was in the process of being loaded into the trunk of a car departing a train station, the Department of Justice urged limiting the warrant requirement to "core privacy interests" such as "homes, offices, or private communications." *Chadwick* (No. 75–721), Brief for Petitioner at 12. The government's brief, which was authored by, among others, Robert Bork and Frank Easterbrook, was unanimously rejected by the justices. Justice Blackmun and Justice Brennan each wrote separately for the purpose of castigating the government for taking such a radical position. After *New York v. Belton*, 453 U.S. 454 (1981), *United States v. Ross*, 456 U. S. 798 (1982), and *California v. Acevedo*, 500 U.S. 565 (1991), however, the Bork-Easterbrook view has become the governing law. Given probable cause, an individual in public can be arrested without warrant and his person minutely searched incident to the arrest. See *United States v. Watson*, 423 U.S. 411 (1976); *United States v. Robinson*, 414 U.S. 218 (1973). If the individual is arrested in a vehicle, not only his person, but the entire passenger compartment and all containers therein, may be searched incident to the arrest under *Belton*. Given probable cause to search for evidence, under *Ross* not only vehicles but any container that might hold the suspected evidence found within the vehicle may be searched without warrant, and this is so, under *Acevedo*, even if the police strategically delay the search of the container until it is coincidentally within a vehicle. Outside of "homes, offices, and private communications" warrants are therefore now only required in the exotic case of a pedestrian who is the innocent custodian of incriminating evidence and so not subject to warrantless arrest.

20. Tainted evidence may now be used (1) in civil proceedings other than forfeiture actions, *United States v. Janis*, 428 U.S. 433 (1976); (2) in pretrial proceedings, *United States v. Calandra*, 414 U.S. 338 (1974); (3) in the government's case at trial, against anyone other than a victim of the illegal search, *Rawlings v. Kentucky*, 448 U.S. 98 (1980); *Rakas v. Illinois*, 439 U.S. 128 (1978); *United States v. Payner*, 447 U.S. 727 (1980); (4) in the government's case at trial, against victims of the illegal search, if the police acted in good-faith reliance on a search warrant, *United States v. Leon*, 468 U.S. 897 (1984), or a statute, *Illinois v. Krull*, 480 U.S. 340 (1987); (5) in the government's case at trial, if the prosecution can show that the evidence probably would have been discovered even absent the illegality, *Nix v. Williams*, 467 U.S. 431 (1984); (6) to impeach the testimony of the defendant, even though the testimony to be impeached was elicited by the government on cross-examination, *United States v. Havens*, 446 U.S. 620 (1980).

Since the introduction of the balancing test in *Calandra* in 1974, the defense has won only one exclusionary rule case in the Supreme Court. See *James v. Illinois*, 493 U.S. 307 (1990) (impeachment exception does not extend to use of tainted evidence to impeach nonparty witness for the defense).

In addition to all these evidentiary uses of tainted evidence, illegally seized drugs are not returned to their possessors, and thus an often considerable loss is inflicted on drug dealers. Illegal searches may also generate useful leads about other offenses. Rational police officers have an incentive to conduct searches lawfully when it is convenient to do so, but they do not face powerful disincentives to search illegally when there is no legal way to secure the suspected evidence or contraband.

21. *Griffin v. Wisconsin*, 483 U.S. 868 (1987).

22. *Malley v. Briggs*, 475 U.S. 335 (1986) (good-faith immunity for seeking warrant unless well-trained officer would have known that probable cause was lacking).

23. *Illinois v. Gates*, 462 U.S. 213 (1983) (test of probable cause is whether, in totality of circumstances, there is a fair probability that contraband or evidence will be found in place to be searched).

24. See my paper, *Living With Leon*, 95 Yale L.J. 906 (1986).

25. See Mark Curriden, *The Informant Trap: Secret Threat to Justice*, N.L.J. A1, A30 (Feb. 20, 1995) (study of federal search warrants in Atlanta, Boston, Cleveland, and San Diego in 1980, 1988, and 1993 shows that in 1980 46% of warrants were based at least in part on confidential informants, but by 1993 proportion had risen to 92%; in 1980 24% of warrants were based on representations of a single confidential informant, but in 1993 this figure had risen to 71%); Lawrence A. Benner & Charles T. Samarkos, *Searching for Narcotics in San Diego: Preliminary Findings From the San Diego Search Warrant Project*, 36 Cal. West. L. Rev. 221, 239 (2000) (confidential informant provided primary basis of probable cause in 36.1% of warrant applications in sample).

26. *Florida v. Bostick*, 501 U.S. 429 (1991). The Supreme Court of Florida, no bastion for bleeding hearts, struck down the bus sweeps but conceded that "Nazi Germany, Soviet Russia, and Communist Cuba have demonstrated all too tellingly the effectiveness of such methods." *Bostick v. State*, 554 So.2d 1153, 1159 (Fla. 1989).

27. *Greenwood*, 686 U.S. 35 (1988).

28. 378 U.S. 1 (1964).

29. 380 U.S. 609 (1965).

30. *Wilson v. United States*, 149 U.S. 60 (1893). Technically, *Wilson* rested on statutory, rather than constitutional ground, but it seems highly unlikely that the *Wilson* Court would have come out differently had the issue been presented under the Fifth Amendment rather than the statute.

31. See Harry Kalven, Jr. & Hans Zeisel, *The American Jury* 161 (U. Chicago Press, Phoenix ed. 1971) (in cases in which the jury learned that the defendant had no prior record, the conviction rate fell from 42% to 25%).

32. 384 U.S. 757 (1966).

33. *Warden v. Hayden*, 387 U.S. 294 (1967).

34. *Couch v. United States*, 409 U.S. 322 (1973) (accountant cannot invoke client's Fifth Amendment privilege to resist subpoena of private papers); *Fisher v. United States*, 425 U.S. 391 (1976) (although attorney-client privilege effectively transfers client's Fifth Amendment rights to lawyer, lawyer cannot resist subpoena for client's private papers prepared by client's accountant because client was not compelled to utter the documents); *United States v. Doe*, 465 U.S. 605 (1984) (taxpayer cannot resist subpoena for preexisting private papers on Fifth Amendment grounds unless compliance with subpoena would admit the existence, authenticity, or possession of the documents).

35. See Robert Mosteller, *Taking the Fifth Amendment Seriously*, 73 Va. L. Rev. 1, 35–36 (1987) (describing generous and demanding approaches to foregone conclusion doctrine). When interpreted rigorously, the foregone conclusion doctrine allows the government to make a showing of the sort that would support a use-immunity order, without actually granting immunity, thus avoiding the prospect of litigating derivative evidence questions at trial. The Supreme Court has recently endorsed a rigorous view of the doctrine, holding that when the government has no independent knowledge that the documents exist prior to issuing the subpoena, the act of production is testimonial and incriminating. *United States v. Hubbell*, 530 U.S. 27 (2000).

36. *Kastigar v. United States*, 406 U.S. 441 (1972).

37. 142 U.S. 547 (1892).

38. *Olmstead v. United States*, 277 U.S. 438, 474 (1928) (Brandeis, J., dissenting).

39. 372 U.S. 335 (1963).

40. *Gideon* (No. 155), Brief for the Petitioner at 33 ("*Betts v. Brady* has engendered conflict between the federal and state courts because of the case by case review it entails and because it does not prescribe a clearcut standard which the state courts can follow.").

41. *Gideon*, 372 U.S. at 349 (Harlan, J., concurring).

42. 377 U.S. 201 (1964).

43. 378 U.S. 478 (1964).

44. See Liva Baker, Miranda: *Crime, Law, and Politics* 28–29 (Atheneum, 1983).

45. Under *Johnson v. Zerbst*, 304 U.S. 458 (1938), the pre-*Gideon* federal practice required offering indigent defendants appointed counsel in court, and required a knowing and intelligent waiver of counsel before the accused could proceed *pro se*. *Zerbst* itself may have been on shaky historical ground, because the Sixth Amendment's basic purpose had been to repudiate English practice that *forbade* defendants in capital cases to proceed without counsel even though the defendant had retained counsel with his own money. Moreover, while the Sixth Amendment was still pending, the first Congress passed a statute providing for appointed counsel in capital cases, a statute that would have been both unnecessary in capital cases and unconstitutional in other cases if the Sixth Amendment were soon to require appointed counsel in all cases. Nonetheless as a matter of practice indigent defendants in noncapital felony cases typically enjoyed free legal services. On all these points, see William M. Beaney, *Right to Counsel* chs. 1–3 (U. Michigan Press, 1955); Alexander Holtzoff, *The Right of Counsel Under the Sixth Amendment*, 20 N.Y.U. L. Rev. 1 (1944).

But whatever the *scope* of the Sixth Amendment right to counsel, it could not be waived simply by showing up at the courthouse without counsel, in the same way that the Fifth Amendment privilege traditionally has been waived simply by answering an incriminating question.

46. See *Diggs v. Welch*, 148 F.2d 667 (D.C. Cir. 1945). The reaction against *Zerbst* foreshadowed the later reaction against the Warren Court revolution. Once *Zerbst* recognized appointed counsel as a constitutional right, not a matter of practice, convicted defendants had strong incentives to allege ineffective assistance, which would frequently be plausible but difficult to establish conclusively. Lacking the resources to guarantee first-rate lawyers on retrial, Judge Arnold looked to the current fundamental fairness cases (*Moore v. Dempsey, Powell v. Alabama*, and *Brown v. Mississippi*) to supply the test for ineffective assistance. Thus *Zerbst* granted indigent federal defendants the right to a lawyer, but only if the lawyer was so bad that the trial was on a par with the kangaroo court in *Dempsey* or the interrogation-by-torture in *Brown* would there be a new trial.

47. See *Trapnell v. United States*, 725 F.2d 149, 151 (2d Cir. 1983) ("By 1962, nine of the eleven circuits were applying the *Diggs* 'farce and mockery' standard. The two remaining circuits adopted the 'farce and mockery' standard in 1965 and 1970, respectively.") (citations omitted).

48. See *Chambers v. Maroney*, 399 U.S. 42 (1970) (rejecting claim that ineffective assistance led to waiver of suppression motion on ground the suppression motion was without merit under Fourth Amendment); *McMann v. Richardson*, 397 U.S. 759, 770–71 (1970) ("Whether a plea of guilty is unintelligent and therefore vulnerable when motivated by a confession erroneously thought admissible in evidence depends as an initial matter, not on whether a court would retrospectively consider counsel's advice to be right or wrong, but

on whether that advice was within the range of competence demanded of attorneys in criminal cases.") The opinion did not elaborate on "the range of competence demanded of attorneys in criminal cases."

49. See *Geders v. United States*, 425 U.S. 80 (1976) (trial court refused consultation between lawyer and defendant during overnight recess); *Herring v. New York*, 422 U.S. 853 (1975) (state statute authorized judge to dispense with closing argument at bench trial); *Brooks v. Tennessee*, 406 U.S. 605 (1972) (state statute requiring defendant testify first, or not at all, during defense case).

50. On the competing approaches, see Bruce Andrew Green, *A Functional Analysis of the Effective Assistance of Counsel*, 80 Colum. L. Rev. 1053 (1980); Philip H. Newman, *Ineffective Assistance of Counsel: The Lingering Debate*, 65 Cornell L. Rev. 659 (1980).

51. *Kirby v. Illinois*, 406 U.S. 682 (1972) (plurality opinion).

52. *Brewer v. Williams*, 430 U.S. 387 (1977).

53. *United States v. Wade*, 388 U.S. 218 (1967).

54. *United States v. Ash*, 413 U.S. 300 (1973).

55. 466 U.S. 668 (1984).

56. Id. at 687.

57. See my paper, *Ineffective Assistance of Counsel: The Case for an* Ex Ante *Parity Standard*, 88 J. Crim. L. & Criminology 242 (1997).

58. *Pointer v. Texas*, 380 U.S. 400 (1965).

59. 399 U.S. 149 (1970).

60. *White v. Illinois*, 502 U.S. 346 (1992) (government may introduce statements for purposes of medical treatment without showing either declarant's unavailability or specific indicia of reliability); *United States v. Inadi*, 475 U.S. 387 (1986) (government may introduce co-conspirator statements without showing declarant's unavailability or specific indicia of reliability).

61. 352 U.S. 432 (1957). *Breithaupt* involved blood drawn from an unconscious accident victim after police smelled liquor on his breath. After *Schmerber* this conduct would not violate either the Fourth Amendment or the Fifth, but in 1957 Breithaupt had a strong argument under *Boyd* that the seizure of his blood violated the Fifth Amendment, and a strong argument under *Gouled* that his blood was mere evidence and so not subject to seizure under the Fourth Amendment. The issue was therefore whether the Fourth Amendment violation required exclusion in a state case, although the *Breithaupt* opinion, as well as the dissents of Warren and Douglas, read *Rochin* as a substantive test of due process rights. Schmerber's counsel, understandably, relied on Warren's dissent, which may help explain the Court's casual adoption of *Rochin*'s language as the test of substantive due process. See *Schmerber*, 384 U.S. 757 (1966) (No. 658), Brief for Petitioner, at 6–8.

62. *Poe v. Ullman*, 367 U.S. 497, 543 (1961) (Harlan, J., dissenting).

63. *Tennessee v. Garner*, 471 U.S. 1 (1985).

64. *Graham v. Connor*, 490 U.S. 386 (1989). The Second Circuit test was announced in *Johnson v. Glick*, 481 F.2d 1028 (2d Cir. 1973) (per Friendly, J.). Chief Justice Rehnquist's opinion in *Graham* went out of the way to cut off substantive due process analysis in future cases:

Today we make explicit what was implicit in *Garner*'s analysis, and hold that *all* claims that law enforcement officers have used excessive force—deadly or not—in the course of an arrest, investigatory stop, or other "seizure" of a free citizen should be analyzed under the Fourth Amendment and its "reasonableness" standard, rather than under a "substantive due process" approach. Because the Fourth Amendment provides an explicit textual source of constitutional protection against this sort of physically intrusive governmental conduct, that Amendment, not the more generalized notion of "substantive due process" must be the guide for analyzing these claims.

490 U.S. at 395 (footnote omitted). This passage reveals how deeply incorporation has entered prevailing legal thought. The chief justice of the United States seems to think that the Fourth Amendment *in terms* applies to the Charlotte, North Carolina, police, and to support this view cites *Garner*'s view of fatal shootings as unreasonable seizures rather than deprivations of life.

65. In *Poe*, Harlan quoted *Rochin*'s language about the need for judges to avoid indulging purely personal value judgments in due process adjudication. See 367 U.S. at 544–45 (Harlan, J., dissenting) (quoting *Rochin*, 342 U.S. at 170–71). At least some of the cases Harlan's *Poe* dissent cites with approval—*Meyer v. Nebraska, Pierce v. Society of Sisters*, and *West Virginia State Board of Education v. Barnette*—would be very hard to justify under a shock-the-conscience test.

66. 397 U.S. 358 (1970).

67. 432 U.S. 197 (1977).

68. *Martin v. Ohio*, 480 U.S. 228 (1987).

69. 424 U.S. 319 (1976).

70. See Henry J. Friendly, *Some Kind of Hearing*, 123 U. Pa. L. Rev. 1267 (1975).

71. 470 U.S. 68 (1985).

72. See *Arizona v. Youngblood*, 488 U.S. 51 (1988) (no due process right to preservation of potentially exculpatory evidence absent bad faith on part of police); *Manson v. Brathwaite*, 432 U.S. 98 (1977) (due process requires exclusion of identification evidence only when pretrial identification procedure was unnecessarily suggestive and created a substantial and irreparable risk of misidentification); David A. Harris, *The Constitution and Truth Seeking: A New Theory on Expert Services for Indigent Defendants*, 83 J. Crim. L. & Crimin. 469 (1992) (*Ake*'s "basic tools" test generally interpreted to require showing expert testimony absolutely necessary, rather than potentially decisive, before appointing expert at state expense); *Patton v. Yount*, 467 U.S. 1025 (1984) (trial court's denial of motion for change of venue on account of prejudicial pretrial publicity can be overturned only for "manifest error").

73. 505 U.S. at 443–46 (citations and all internal quotations marks omitted).

74. Id. at 446.

75. Id. at 448.

76. Id. at 451.

77. See, e.g., *Goss v. Lopez*, 419 U.S. 565 (1975) (minimal hearing required before suspension from public school); *Cleveland Board of Education v. Loudermill*, 470 U.S. 532 (1985) (due process permits minimal pretermination hearing for tenured public employee prior to discharge, provided full adversary hearing is made available after discharge).

78. 100 U.S. 303 (1879).

79. 351 U.S. 12 (1956).

80. 103 U.S. 370 (1880).

81. 294 U.S. 587 (1935).

82. 380 U.S. 202 (1965).

83. Id. at 223.

84. See id. at 246 (Goldberg, J., dissenting) ("By adding to the present heavy burden of proof required of defendants in these cases, the Court creates additional barriers to the elimination of practices which have operated in many communities throughout the Nation

to nullify the command of the Equal Protection Clause in this important area in the administration of justice.").

85. See *Batson v. Kentucky*, 476 U.S. 79, 103–04 (1986) (Marshall, J., concurring) (reviewing statistics in reported cases and quoting prosecutorial jury selection manuals); *Developments in the Law—Race and the Criminal Process*, 101 Harv. L. Rev. 1472, 1565 n.58 (1988) (citing studies); James O. Pearson, Jr., Annotation, *Use of Peremptory Challenge to Exclude from Jury Persons Belonging to a Class or Race*, 79 A.L.R.3d 14 (1977) (collecting cases).

86. "Twenty years later, there are no reported cases in which a court has determined that invidious discrimination under *Swain* has been demonstrated." Sheri Lynn Johnson, *Black Innocence and the White Jury*, 83 Mich. L. Rev. 1611, 1658 (1985) (footnote omitted).

87. *Taylor v. Louisiana*, 419 U.S. 522 (1975); *Duren v. Missouri*, 439 U.S. 357 (1979).

88. In *Duren v. Missouri*, the Court set out the following test, without citation:

In order to establish a prima facie violation of the fair-cross-section requirement, the defendant must show (1) that the group alleged to be excluded is a "distinctive" group in the community; (2) that the representation of this group in venires from which juries are selected is not fair and reasonable in relation to the number of such persons in the community; and (3) that this underrepresentation is due to systematic exclusion of the group in the jury-selection process.

439 U.S. at 364. By itself, representation "not fair and reasonable" in proportion to population, would not make out an equal protection claim under *Yick Wo v. Hopkins, Neal v. Delaware*, or *Norris v. Alabama*.

89. For a review of the attack on *Swain*, see Randall Kennedy, *Race, Crime and the Law* 197–204 (Pantheon, 1997).

90. *People v. Wheeler*, 583 P.2d 748 (1978) (state constitutional right to jury trial includes cross-section requirement that applies to panel as well as venire).

91. *Commonwealth v. Soares*, 387 N.E.2d 499 (1979) (same).

92. *McCray v. Abrams*, 750 F.2d 1113 (2d Cir. 1984).

93. 476 U.S. 79 (1986).

94. *Holland v. Illinois*, 493 U.S. 474 (1990).

95. A point important enough for Justice Goldberg to close his *Swain* dissent with. See 380 U.S. at 247.

96. 517 U.S. 456 (1996).

97. Armstrong indeed came forward with powerful evidence of disparate impact. The Court's ruling raises barriers to discriminatory prosecution claims every bit as high as *Swain* raised against discriminatory jury-selection claims. See, e.g., David Cole, *No Equal Justice* 158–61 (New Press, 1999).

98. *Purkett v. Elem*, 514 U.S. 765 (1995).

99. Kenneth J. Melilli, Batson *in Practice: What We Have Learned About* Batson *and Peremptory Challenges*, 71 Notre Dame L. Rev. 447, 465 (1996).

100. See Jean Montoya, *The Future of the Post-*Batson *Peremptory Challenge: Voir Dire by Questionnaire and the "Blind" Peremptory*, 29 U. Mich. J. L. Ref. 981, 1008–09 (1996); Shari Seidman Diamond et al., *Realistic Responses to the Limitations of* Batson v. Kentucky, 7 Cornell J. L. & Pub. Pol'y 77, 81 (1997).

101. 372 U.S. 353 (1963). *Douglas*, as companion case to *Gideon*, held that indigent defendants had an equal protection, rather than a Sixth Amendment, right to appointed counsel on an appeal of right following a conviction in state courts.

102. *Ross v. Moffitt*, 417 U.S. 600 (1974) (no right to appointed counsel when seeking discretionary review in state supreme court); *Pennsylvania v. Finley*, 481 U.S. 551 (1987) (no right to appointed counsel in state collateral attack proceedings). Illuminatingly, *Ake*, which dealt with indigent defense services *at trial*, rested on due process rather than equal protection.

103. See, e.g., *McKane v. Durston*, 153 U.S. 684 (1894).

104. See Marc M. Arkin, *Rethinking the Criminal Defendant's Right to a Criminal Appeal*, 39 U.C.L.A. L. Rev. 503 (1992).

105. See Chapter 1, section 4.

106. 344 U.S. 443 (1953).

107. See Joseph L. Hoffman & William J. Stuntz, *Habeas After the Revolution*, 1993 Sup. Ct. Rev. 65, 77–85.

108. *Brown v. Allen*, 344 U.S. at 458; id. at 507–08 (opinion of Frankfurter, J.).

109. Id. at 463–64; *Townsend v. Sain*, 372 U.S. 293 (1963) (evidentiary hearing always optional, but sometimes mandatory, on federal habeas petition).

110. *Fay v. Noia*, 372 U.S. 391 (1963).

111. *Gregg v. Georgia*, 428 U.S. 153 (1976).

112. 344 U.S. at 458.

113. 372 U.S. 391 (1963).

114. See, e.g., Paul M. Bator, *Finality in Criminal Law and Federal Habeas Corpus for State Prisoners*, 76 Harv. L. Rev. 441 (1963) (federalist approach); Paul J. Mishkin, *Foreword: The High Court, the Great Writ, and the Due Process of Time and Law*, 79 Harv. L. Rev. 56 (1965); Henry J. Friendly, *Is Innocence Irrelevant? Collateral Attack on Criminal Judgments*, 38 U. Chi. L. Rev. 142 (1970) (instrumental approach).

115. 433 U.S. 72 (1977).

116. 489 U.S. 288 (1989) (plurality opinion).

117. Criticism of *Teague* has been sharp, and, in my view, cogent. See James S. Liebman, *More than "Slightly Retro:" The Rehnquist Court's Rout of Habeas Corpus Jurisdiction in* Teague v. Lane, 18 N.Y.U. Rev. L. & Soc. Change 537 (1990–91); Linda Meyer, *"Nothing We Say Matters"*: Teague *and New Rules*, 61 U. Chi. L. Rev. 423 (1994); Robert Weisberg, *A Great Writ While it Lasted*, 81 J. Crim. L. & Criminology 9 (1990).

118. See *Murray v. Carrier*, 477 U.S. 478 (1986); *Smith v. Murray*, 477 U.S. 527 (1986).

119. See *Teague*, 489 U.S. at 312–14 (plurality opinion).

120. See *Report on Habeas Corpus in Capital Cases*, 45 Crim. L. Rep. 3239 (Sept. 27, 1989).

121. Anti-Terrorism and Effective Death Penalty Act of 1996, Pub. L. No. 104–132, 110 Stat. 1214 (1996). The Act amends 28 U.S.C. § 2254 to provide that the state-court ruling on the petitioner's claim may not be set aside by the federal habeas court unless the state-court ruling "was contrary to, or involved an unreasonable application of, clearly established Federal law, as determined by the Supreme Court of the United States[,]" or "was based on an unreasonable determination of the facts in light of the evidence presented in the State court proceeding." 28 U.S.C. §§ 2254(d)(1) & (2). The revised 28 U.S.C. § 2254(e) recognizes a presumption that state-court factual findings are correct, and provides, consistently with *Sykes*, that a claim not developed in state court may be heard in federal court only if the claim relies on "a new rule of constitutional law" made fully retroactive by the Supreme Court, or "a factual predicate that could not have been previously discovered through the exercise of due diligence." Even when one of these

criteria is met, the petitioner must also make a heightened showing of prejudice, i.e., a showing that "the facts underlying the claim would be sufficient to establish by clear and convincing evidence that but for constitutional error, no reasonable factfinder would have found the applicant guilty of the underlying offense."

The Act also adds a special section on death-row petitions, providing that states that choose to provide appointed counsel for convicts sentenced to death can avail themselves of a six month limitations period on habeas petitions, and on a bar against successive petitions (a bar that can be overcome by a showing of good cause and actual innocence). 28 U.S.C. § 2261–2264 & 2244(b).

For explanations of the 1996 amendments, see Wayne R. LaFave & Jerold H. Israel, *Criminal Procedure* §§ 28.4–28.7 (West, 2d ed. 1992 & 1997 pocket part); Evan Tsen Lee, *Section 2254(d) of the New Habeas Statute: An (Opinionated) User's Manual*, 51 Vand. L. Rev. 103 (1998).

122. *Felker v. Turpin*, 518 U.S. 651 (1996).

CHAPTER 4

1. Wilfred J. Ritz, *Twenty-Five Years of State Criminal Confession Cases in the U.S. Supreme Court*, 19 Wash. & Lee L. Rev. 35, 35–36 (1962).

2. *Rogers v. Richmond*, 365 U.S. 534, 540 (1961).

3. See *Stroble v. California*, 343 U.S. 181 (1952) (defendant kicked and threatened with blackjack one hour before questioning held to have confessed voluntarily).

4. See Comment, *The Coerced Confession Cases in Search of a Rationale*, 31 U. Chi. L. Rev. 313, 320 (1964) ("As the law now stands the police have little to lose from interrogation. They can apply increasingly greater pressure until the suspect confesses. If the confession is admissible, well and good. If it is not, no harm has been done since police wouldn't have been able to get the confession unless they had applied the pressure.") (footnotes omitted).

5. 367 U.S. 568 (1961).

6. Id. at 620 (opinion of Frankfurter, J.) (footnote omitted).

7. Id. at 609.

8. Id. at 634.

9. Id. at 636 (Warren, C.J., concurring).

10. 357 U.S. 433 (1958).

11. Id. at 441.

12. 367 U.S. at 642 (Harlan, J., dissenting).

13. Id. at 636 (Warren, C.J., concurring):

The opinion was unquestionably written with the intention of clarifying these problems of establishing a set of principles which could be easily applied in any coerced-confession situation. However, it is doubtful that such will be the result, for while three members of the Court agree to the general principles enunciated by the opinion, they construe those principles as requiring a result in this case exactly the opposite from that reached by the author of the opinion. This being true, it cannot be assumed that the lower courts and law enforcement agencies will receive better guidance from the treatise for which this case seems to have provided a vehicle.

14. See *Gallegos v. Nebraska*, 342 U.S. 55, 63–64 (1951) (plurality opinion). *Gallegos*, however, is another accident of constitutional history. It would have been anomalous for the Court, but two years after *Wolf v. Colorado*, to announce that illegal detention

mandated exclusion of a confession, when any physical evidence produced by search incident to an illegal arrest would nonetheless be received in evidence at a state trial.

15. 211 U.S. 78 (1908).

16. 332 U.S. 46 (1947).

17. *Gideon v. Wainwright*, 372 U.S. 335 (1963).

18. See *McNabb v. United States*, 318 U.S. 332 (1943); *Mallory v. United States*, 354
U.S. 449 (1957). In these cases the Supreme Court, speaking through Justice Frankfurter
on both occasions, excluded statements obtained by government agents during a period of
"unnecessary delay" between arrest and the production of the person arrested before a
court. The ground of decision in both cases was the Court's "supervisory power" over the
administration of justice in the federal courts, however, and not the Fourth Amendment.
Nonetheless, "many hoped (and many others feared) that some day the Court would apply
the rule to the states as a matter of fourteenth amendment due process." Yale Kamisar,
et al., *Modern Criminal Procedure* 458 (West, 9th ed. 1999).

19. 377 U.S. 201 (1964).

20. Speaking through Justice Stewart, the *Massiah* majority adopted the position taken
by four concurring justices in *Spano v. New York*, 360 U.S. 315 (1959). Spano had been
indicted and then, after he surrendered, questioned extensively by the police. Spano's requests to see counsel were refused; and a police officer friendly with Spano ultimately induced a confession. The *Spano* majority reversed his murder conviction on the ground
that the confession was involuntary; but Stewart, Douglas, Brennan, and Black voted to
reverse on right-to-counsel grounds.

21. See *Spano*, 360 U.S. at 327 (Stewart, J., concurring) ("Our Constitution guarantees
the assistance of counsel to a man on trial for his life in an orderly courtroom, presided
over by a judge, open to the public, and protected by all the procedural safeguards of the
law. Surely a Constitution which promises that much can vouchsafe no less to the same
man under midnight inquisition in the squad room of a police station.").

22. See 377 U.S. at 206.

23. Id. at 204.

24. 378 U.S. 478 (1964).

25. How did Escobedo come to have a lawyer? Liva Baker reports that Wolfson previously had represented Escobedo in a civil suit against the Chicago Transit Authority. See
Liva Baker, Miranda: *Crime, Law, and Politics* 28–29 (Atheneum, 1983).

26. *People v. Escobedo*, 190 N.E.2d 825 (1963).

27. 190 N.E.2d at 829.

28. Id. at 831.

29. 378 U.S. at 485.

30. Id. at 492.

31. 369 U.S. 506, 513 (1962).

32. Brief for the Respondent, *Escobedo v. Illinois* (No. 615) at 39.

33. *Watts v. Indiana*, 338 U.S. 49, 59 (1949) (Jackson, J., concurring).

34. 378 U.S. at 495 (White, J., dissenting).

35. Id. at 487.

36. Id. at 488 (citations omitted).

37. Id. at 488–89 (footnotes omitted).

38. Compare, for example, Arnold N. Enker & Sheldon H. Elsen, *Counsel for the Suspect*: Massiah v. United States *and* Escobedo v. Illinois, 49 Minn. L. Rev. 47, 85 (1964)
("The solution offered by *Massiah* and *Escobedo* is to require the presence of counsel

during the interrogation. No doubt this would provide a credible witness to the proceedings. It would also eliminate the defendant's fear of indefinite detention . . . But . . . it may also eliminate proper questioning.") with Stanley Milledge, Escobedo—*Toward Eliminating Coerced Confessions*, 19 U. Miami L. Rev. 415, 420 (1965) ("[C]ounsel at the police interrogation is a formidable barrier to confessions for the obvious reason that secret police interrogations produce coerced confessions.").

39. See Louis Michael Seidman, Brown *and* Miranda, 80 Cal. L. Rev. 673, 744 (1992) ("*Escobedo, Massiah,* and *Culombe* had already created all the rights any defendant needed. The problem that *Miranda* addressed was how to curb these sweeping protections so as not to interfere with the preservation of interrogation as an effective weapon in the police crime-fighting arsenal.").

40. See Brief for Petitioner at 5–8, *Malloy v. Hogan,* 378 U.S. 1 (No. 110) (1964).

41. See Brief for Respondent at 7–13, *Malloy v. Hogan* (No. 110).

42. Id. at 7.

43. Brief of National District Attorneys' Association, Amicus Curiae, *Malloy v. Hogan* (No. 110). The NDAA was concerned by the holding in *Feldman v. United States,* 322 U.S. 487 (1944), permitting the use in federal court of testimony compelled under a grant of immunity by state authorities. The states had no power to confer immunity from federal prosecution, so if the federal privilege became binding on the states' witnesses might have been able to claim the privilege even after a state immunity order; the witness would still be in jeopardy of federal prosecution based on the answers compelled in state proceedings. In *Murphy v. Waterfront Commission,* 378 U.S. 52 (1964), decided the same day as *Malloy,* the Court agreed with the NDAA and overruled *Feldman.* See 378 U.S. at 77–78.

44. The coerced confession cases are progeny of *Brown v. Mississippi,* 297 U.S. 278 (1936). In *Brown,* the state relied on *Twining,* but the Court held that "the question of the right of the State to withdraw the privilege against self-incrimination is not here involved. . . . Compulsion by torture to extort a confession is a different matter." 297 U.S. at 285. None of the subsequent cases invoked the Fifth Amendment as authority, although references to the privilege in pre-*Escobedo* cases occur in some of the dissenting opinions. See Walter V. Schaefer, *The Suspect and Society,* 15 n.41 (Northwestern U. Press, 1967).

45. *Malloy* invoked the "great case of *Boyd v. United States,*" which has since been overruled. See *United States v. Doe,* 465 U.S. 605 (1984); *Fisher v. United States,* 425 U.S. 391 (1976). Any connection between the Fifth Amendment privilege and the rule excluding the fruits of illegal searches dissolves as soon as the privilege is limited to testimonial evidence—a limitation the Supreme Court was to recognize less than two years later in *Schmerber v. California,* 384 U.S. 757 (1966). See *Bivens v. Six Unknown Named Agents of the Federal Bureau of Narcotics,* 403 U.S. 388, 414–15 (1971) (Burger, C.J., dissenting); Yale Kamisar, Wolf *and* Lustig *Ten Years Later: Illegal State Evidence in State and Federal Courts,* 43 Minn. L. Rev. 1083, 1088–90 n.16 (1959). Justice Brennan himself derived the Fourth Amendment exclusionary rule from the Fourth Amendment, not the Fifth. See *United States v. Leon,* 468 U.S. 897, 933 (1984) (Brennan, J., dissenting).

46. *Malloy,* 378 U.S. at 9 n.7 (quoting Erwin Griswold, *The Fifth Amendment Today* 7 (Harvard U. Press, 1955)).

47. See, e.g., *United States v. Cone,* 354 F.2d 119, 123–27 (2d Cir. 1965) (en banc); *Anderson v. State,* 205 A.2d 281, 285 (Md. 1964); *Commonwealth v. Coyle,* 203 A.2d 782, 794 (Pa. 1964) (stating that the absence of request is "not controlling" but "substantially

distinguishes" the case from *Escobedo*); *People v. Hartgraves*, 202 N.E.2d 33, 35–36 (Ill. 1964); *State v. Smith*, 202 A.2d 669, 678 (N.J. 1964).

48. See *People v. Dorado*, 398 P.2d 361, 367–71 (Cal. 1965); *State v. Dufour*, 206 A.2d 82, 85 (R.I. 1965); *Cooper v. Commonwealth*, 140 S.E.2d 688, 694 (Va. 1965) (holding that no request by the suspect is required when the suspect "was not experienced in criminal procedure, his intellectual endowment was 'at the lower limits of normal,' and his ability to function under stress was 'in a corresponding range.' ").

49. See *Wright v. Dickson*, 336 F.2d 878, 882–84 (9th Cir. 1964); United States ex rel *Russo v. New Jersey*, 351 F.2d 429, 437–40 (3d Cir. 1965) (collecting cases).

50. For a summary of the agitation over *Escobedo*, see Liva Baker, *Crime, Law, and Politics* at 156–61 (cited in note 25).

51. American Law Institute, *Model Code of Pre-Arraignment Procedure*, Tentative Draft No. 1 (March 1, 1966).

52. Fred P. Graham, *The Self-Inflicted Wound* 173 (Macmillan, 1970).

53. *Model Code* § 3.08 (cited in note 51).

54. Id. § 4.04. The code authorized a further period of detention for investigation when the suspected offense was a serious felony, but provided that interrogation could not take place during this extended screening period without the presence, or the consent, of counsel. See id. § 4.05.

55. Id. § 5.04(b).

56. Id. § 5.07(a).

57. Id., Commentary to § 5.07, at p. 48.

58. Id., Commentary to § 5.07, at p. 49:

As legal aid succeeds in equalizing the access of arrested person to counsel at the early stage of their detention, we shall gain experience that thus far has been wanting as to whether the viability of our system of enforcement depends on the absence of attorneys at this early state. If that experience should show that the availability of counsel at the stationhouse puts a stop to questioning and effective screening, and that law enforcement suffers unacceptably as a consequence, our society will have to face more fundamental questions of procedure, such as whether the privilege against self-incrimination should be modified, and if so, how.

59. Baker, *Crime, Law, and Politics* at 103 (cited in note 25).

60. *Miranda v. Arizona*, 384 U.S. 436 (1966) (No. 759), Brief for Petitioner at 31–35.

61. *Westover v. United States* (No. 761), Brief for Petitioner at 21–31.

62. *Vignera v. New York* (No. 760), Brief for Petitioner at 9 & 28.

63. *Miranda v. Arizona* (Nos. 584, 759, 760, 761 and 762), Brief of the American Civil Liberties Union as *Amicus Curiae*, at 5–31.

64. Id. at 13–20.

65. Id. at 22–31.

66. *Westover* (No. 761), Brief for Respondent at 38–42.

67. Id. at 42.

68. Id. at 28–38.

69. Id. at 44.

70. Id. at 45.

71. *Miranda v. Arizona* (Nos. 584, 759, 760, & 762), Brief of the State of New York, et al., as *Amici Curiae*, at 35–39.

72. *Miranda* (Nos. 584, 759, 760 & 762), Brief of the National District Attorneys Association, as *Amicus Curiae*, 21–26.

73. *Miranda* (No. 759), Brief for Respondent at 18–25.

74. The second justice to interrupt John Flynn's argument for *Miranda* was Potter Stewart. This colloquy occurred:

MR. JUSTICE STEWART: What do you think is the result of the adversary process coming into being when this focusing takes place? What follows from that? Is there, then, a right to a lawyer?

MR. FLYNN: I think that the man at that time has the right to exercise, if he knows, and under the present state of the law in Arizona, if he is rich enough, and if he's educated enough to assert his Fifth Amendment right, and if he recognizes that he has a Fifth Amendment right to request counsel. But I simply say that at that state of the proceeding, under the facts and circumstances in *Miranda* of a man of limited education, of a man who certainly is mentally abnormal, who is certainly an indigent, that when that adversary process came into being that the police, at the very least, had an obligation to extend to this man not only his clear Fifth Amendment right, but to accord him the right of counsel.

MR. JUSTICE STEWART: I suppose, if you really mean what you say or what you gather from what the *Escobedo* decision says, the adversary process starts at that point, and every single protection of the Constitution then comes into being, does it not? You have to bring a jury in there, I suppose?

MR. FLYNN: No, Your Honor, I wouldn't bring a jury in. I simply would extend to the man those constitutional rights which the police, at that time, took away from him.

MR. JUSTICE STEWART: That's begging the question. My question is, what are those rights when the focusing begins? Are these all the panoply of rights guaranteed to the defendant in a criminal trial?

MR. FLYNN: I think the first right is the Fifth Amendment right: the right not to incriminate oneself; the right to know you have that right; and the right to consult with counsel, at the very least, *in order that you can exercise the right*, Your Honor.

Transcript of Oral Argument in *Miranda v. Arizona*, in 63 *Landmark Briefs and Arguments of the Supreme Court* 849 (U. Publications of America, Phillip B. Kurland & Gerhard Casper eds., 1975) (emphasis added).

75. 384 U.S. at 461 (footnote omitted).

76. Id. at 457 n.26 (quoting Arthur E. Sutherland, Jr., *Crime and Confession*, 79 Harv. L. Rev. 21, 37 (1965)).

77. Id. at 457.

78. Id. at 468.

79. Id. at 469.

80. Id. at 469–70 (citations omitted).

81. Id. at 470–71.

82. Id. at 472–73.

83. ACLU Brief at 22 (cited in note 63).

84. 384 U.S. at 475.

85. Id.

86. Id.

87. Id.

88. Id. at 479.

89. Id. at 481.

90. Id. at 483–86.

91. Id. at 486.

92. Id. at 499 (Clark, J., dissenting).

93. Id. at 516 (Harlan, J., dissenting).

94. Id. at 508 (Harlan, J., dissenting).

95. Id. at 490.

96. Id.

97. See id. at 506 (Harlan, J., dissenting) (due process test offers "a workable and effective means of dealing with confessions in a judicial manner"); id. at 503 (Clark, J., dissenting).

98. See id. at 539–43 (White, J., dissenting); 384 U.S. at 516–17 (Harlan, J., dissenting).

99. The President's Commission on Law Enforcement and Administration of Justice, *The Challenge of Crime in a Free Society* (U.S. Government Printing Office, 1967).

100. See id. at 303–07.

101. For a history of the bill that ultimately became the Omnibus Crime Control and Safe Streets Act of 1968, see Adam Carlyle Breckenridge, *Congress Against the Court* 39–94 (U. Nebraska Press, 1970); Yale Kamisar, *Can (Did) Congress "Overrule" Miranda?*, 85 Cornell L. Rev. 883, 887–909 (2000).

102. See Breckendridge, *Congress Against the Court* at 69–72 (cited in note 101).

103. Id.

104. The Nixon paper is reprinted in 90 Cong. Rec. 12,937 (1968).

105. 90 Cong. Rec. 14,177 (1968).

106. 90 Cong. Rec. 14,183 (1968).

107. 90 Cong. Rec. 14,184–86 (1968).

108. 90 Cong. Rec.16,299–300 (1968).

109. See, for example, the statements of Senator McClellan quoted by Breckenridge, *Congress Against the Court* at 66 (cited in note 101).

110. 65 Mich. L. Rev. 59 (1966).

111. Welsh S. White, *Defending* Miranda: *A Reply to Professor Caplan*, 39 Vand. L. Rev. 1, 11 (1986).

112. Stephen J. Schulhofer, *Confessions and the Court*, 79 Mich. L. Rev. 865, 869 (1981).

113. Joseph D. Grano, *Voluntariness, Free Will and the Law of Confessions*, 65 Va. L. Rev. 859 (1979). Grano did not defend the old test, but rather urged a standard excluding confessions produced by pressures that would cause a person of ordinary firmness to confess under similar circumstances.

114. Special Project, *Interrogations in New Haven: The Impact of* Miranda, 76 Yale L.J. 1519 (1967).

115. Richard J. Medalie et al., *Custodial Police Interrogation in Our Nation's Capital: The Attempt to Implement* Miranda, 66 Mich. L. Rev. 1347 (1968).

116. Richard H. Seeburger & R. Stanton Wettick, Jr., Miranda *in Pittsburgh: A Statistical Study*, 29 U. Pitt. L. Rev. 1 (1967).

117. See White, 39 Vand. L. Rev. at 19 n.99 (cited in note 111).

The two contemporary empirical studies of police interrogation both found that about 80% of suspects waive their *Miranda* rights, a figure consistent with the results of the early *Miranda* studies. See Paul G. Cassel & Bret S. Hayman, *Police Interrogation in the 1990s: An Empirical Study of the Effects of* Miranda, 43 U.C.LA. L. Rev. 839, 859–60 (1996); Richard A. Leo, *Inside the Interrogation Room*, 86 J. Crim. L. & Criminology 266, 286 (1996). Suspects who waive under *Miranda* might not make a statement even without the warnings, and in many cases the police do not need a confession to make a case.

Professor Cassell's efforts to show a major adverse impact of *Miranda* based on confessions rates or clearance rates strike me as unpersuasive. Confession rates resist objective measurements today just as they did in the aftermath of *Miranda*. Is a false exculpatory story a "confession"? What about an admission that the suspect was present but a denial of any involvement in the crime? To extract percentages of successful interrogations based on such judgment calls is not a very reliable approach to testing *Miranda*'s practical effect. See George C. Thomas III, *Plain Talk About the* Miranda *Empirical Debate: A "Steady-State" Theory of Confessions*, 43 U.C.L.A. L. Rev. 933, 948 (1996). In any event the crude comparison of confession rates in the 1960s with present results cannot account for the possibility that fewer suspects confess today for reasons that have nothing to do with *Miranda*. The waiver rate is a far more objective, and a far more accurate, measure of *Miranda*'s consequences.

Clearance rates tell us very little about *Miranda*'s effects because the warnings are given only after the crime is cleared by arrest. So Cassell is talking about the possibility that *Miranda* causes suspects not to confess to crimes that the police would like to list as "cleared" but are unlikely to charge out, crimes that the suspect might confess without being guilty. Curtailing this sort of dubious accounting practice does not seem like a serious social cost. Moreover, it appears that the rate at which police clear offenses, measured on a per officer basis, has gone steadily up since even before *Miranda*. It is hard to see how *Miranda* could have reduced the clearance rate without having reversed this trend. See Stephen J. Schulhofer, Miranda *and Clearance Rates*, 91 Nw. L. Rev. 278, 286 (1996).

Finally, *even Professor Cassell* estimates *Miranda*'s social cost as the loss of convictions in 3.8% of all arrests. See Paul G. Cassell & Richard Fowles, *Handcuffing the Cops? A Thirty-Year Perspective on* Miranda'*s Harmful Effects on Law Enforcement*, 50 Stan. L. Rev. 1055, 1061 (1998). This estimate is based on the assumptions that *Miranda* caused a 16% drop in the number of cases in which the suspect confesses, and that a confession is necessary to obtain a conviction in 24% of these cases. This in turn assumes, among other things, that (1) all persons who refuse to make an incriminating statement because of *Miranda* are in fact guilty; (2) that *Miranda* causes the loss of confessions randomly, i.e., that the police do not work more successfully to obtain waivers and statements in cases in which these appear to be necessary, or to work harder to obtain evidence other than a confession when it is known that the suspect has invoked; (3) that the confession rate can be consistently estimated by different researchers at different times; (4) that police and suspects would return to 1965 behavior patterns despite three decades of *Miranda*. In my view each of these assumptions is false.

But even the 3.8% estimate, questionable as it is, is not the kind of cataclysm that was expected by the critics of *Miranda*, who predicted that the sky would fall. Perhaps a few acorns did, but that has not caused even a conservative Court, or the police themselves, to advocate overruling *Miranda*.

118. Commentators with quite different views about whether *Miranda* goes too far or not far enough agree that the waiver doctrine is inconsistent with the inherent compulsion thesis. Compare H. Richard Uviller, *Tempered Zeal* 194–96 (Contemporary Books, 1980) with Charles J. Ogletree, *Are Confessions Really Good for the Soul? A Proposal to Mirandize* Miranda, 100 Harv. L. Rev. 1826, 1838 (1987).

119. *Harris v. New York*, 401 U.S. 222 (1971).

120. 221 N.E.2d 541 (1966).

121. 347 U.S. 62 (1954).

122. Id. at 63.

123. See 347 U.S. at 66. This feature of the case "sharply contrasted" with the case of *Agnello v. United States*, 269 U.S. 20 (1925), in which the prosecution asked the defendant whether he had ever seen narcotics, and then "impeached" the defendant's denial with the illegally seized drugs.

124. See 347 U.S. at 65 (the accused "must be free to deny all the elements of the case against him without thereby giving leave to the Government to introduce by way of rebuttal evidence illegally secured by it, and therefore not available for its case in chief.").

125. Id. at 65.

126. *Miranda*, 384 U.S. at 477 ("In fact, statements merely intended to be exculpatory by the defendant are often used to impeach his testimony at trial or to demonstrate untruths in the statement given under interrogation and thus to prove guilt by implication. These statements are incriminating in any meaningful sense of the word and may not be used without the full warnings and effective waiver required for any other statement.")

127. 401 U.S. at 224.

128. See Geoffrey R. Stone, *The Miranda Doctrine in the Burger Court*, 1977 Sup. Ct. Rev. 99, 107–08.

129. 401 U.S. at 225.

130. 401 U.S. at 226. See also id. at 225 n.2:

If, for example, an accused confessed fully to a homicide and led the police to the body of the victim under circumstances making his confession inadmissible, the petitioner would have us allow that accused to take the stand and blandly deny every fact disclosed to the police or discovered as a "fruit" of his confession, free from confrontation with his prior statements and acts.

131. 437 U.S. 385 (1978).

132. 440 U.S. 450 (1979).

133. Blackmun, joined by Chief Justice Burger, dissented on a procedural ground. After the trial court refused to grant Portash's motion to forbid impeachment with the immunized testimony, Portash elected not to testify. In Blackmun's view, the failure to testify deprived the reviewing courts of a concrete factual context in which to examine the effect of impeachment with previously compelled testimony. See 440 U.S. at 463–71 (Blackmun, J., dissenting). But neither of these two members of the *Harris* majority hinted that the *Portash* Court had reached the wrong result.

134. The incentives to violate *Miranda* created by *Harris* are well illustrated by the subsequent decision in *Oregon v. Hass*, 420 U.S. 714 (1975). After receiving *Miranda* warnings, Hass asked for a lawyer. The police, however, continued questioning, and the answers Hass gave were admitted at his trial to impeach his testimony. Hass, unlike Harris, actually asserted his right to terminate questioning under *Miranda*. In such a case, the police have nothing to lose by questioning illegally; the impeachment exception gives them a positive incentive to do so. Nonetheless, in *Hass* the Burger Court again dismissed this incentive effect as "speculative" and permitted the impeachment. 420 U.S. at 723.

135. Alan M. Dershowitz & John Hart Ely, Harris v. New York: *Some Anxious Observations on the Candor and Logic of the Emerging Nixon Majority*, 80 Yale L.J. 1198, 1199 (1971).

136. At trial, defense counsel objected to the state's proposed impeachment with Harris's custodial statement by stating that the prosecutor "has to show it was voluntarily made, under the law, *and* in conformity with the requirements as set up in *Miranda v. Arizona.*

Harris v. New York (No. 206), Appendix at 57 (emphasis added). The petition for certiorari clearly raises the claim that Harris should have given a hearing to contest voluntariness. See *Harris v. New York* (No. 206), Petition for Certiorari at 10. Dershowitz and Ely also quote the transcript of oral argument before the Supreme Court, from which it appears that the voluntariness claim was preserved by counsel for Harris. See 80 Yale L.J. at 1203–04 (cited in note 135).

137. 378 U.S. 368 (1964).
138. Dershowitz & Ely, 80 Yale L.J. at 1218 (cited in note 135).
139. 417 U.S. 433 (1974).
140. Id. at 444.
141. Id. at 460 (White, J., concurring).
142. See id. at 462–63 (Douglas, J., dissenting):

I cannot agree when the Court says that the interrogation here "did not abridge respondent's constitutional privilege against compulsory self-incrimination, but departed only from the prophylactic standards later laid down by this Court in *Miranda* to safeguard that privilege." [citing the majority opinion] The Court is not free to prescribe preferred modes of interrogation absent a constitutional basis. We held the "requirement of warnings and waiver of rights [to be] fundamental with respect to the Fifth Amendment privilege," [citing *Miranda*] and without so holding we would have been powerless to reverse Miranda's conviction. While *Miranda* recognized that police need not mouth the precise words contained in the Court's opinion, such warnings were held necessary "unless other fully effective means are adopted to notify the person" of his rights [citing *Miranda*].

143. Stone, 1977 Sup. Ct. Rev. at 123 (cited in note 128) (footnote omitted).
144. 423 U.S. 96 (1975).
145. 429 U.S. 492 (1977).
146. 430 U.S. 387 (1977). Many of the facts in the case were disputed by one party or the other; the account given here is taken from the majority opinion in the Supreme Court, except where otherwise noted.
147. Id. at 392–93.
148. *State v. Williams*, 182 N.W.2d 396 (Iowa 1970).
149. *Williams v. Brewer*, 509 F.2d 227, 234–37 (8th Cir. 1974).
150. Yale Kamisar, *Foreword*: Brewer v. Williams—*A Hard Look at a Discomfiting Record*, 66 Geo. L.J. 209, 210 (1977) (footnotes omitted).
151. See 509 F.2d at 233–34.
152. 182 N.W.2d at 405.
153. This was the position taken by the dissenting justices. See 430 U.S. at 439–40 (Blackmun, J., dissenting); 430 U.S. at 419–20 (Burger, C.J., dissenting).
154. See id. at 433 (White, J., dissenting).
155. Yale Kamisar, Brewer v. Williams, Massiah, *and* Miranda: What Is *"Interrogation"? When Does It Matter?*, 67 Geo. L.J. 1, 17 (1978) (brackets in original; footnote omitted).
156. 430 U.S. at 399.
157. *Brewer v. Williams* (No. 74–1263), Brief for Petitioner at 14–35. The state's brief resonates with Nixonian law-and-order rhetoric. See, e.g., id. at 35. ("Let's find some substitute for excluding relevant and persuasive evidence. Let's take the handcuffs off the police and put them on the criminals.")
158. *Brewer v. Williams* (No. 74–1263), Brief Amicus Curiae of Americans for Effective Law Enforcement et al. at 10.
159. *Brewer v. Williams* (No. 74–1263), Brief for Respondent at 44–45.
160. 430 U.S. at 397.

161. Id. at 438 (Blackmun, J., dissenting) (footnote omitted). Rehnquist and White joined Blackmun's opinion.

162. 442 U.S. 707 (1979).

163. 441 U.S. 369 (1979).

164. 444 U.S. 469 (1980) (per curiam).

165. 446 U.S. 291 (1980). While the *Innis* case was pending, but before *Tague* was decided, Joseph Grano wrote that a decision in favor of Rhode Island "seems certain given both the room for principled disagreement and the Court's failure in this decade to hold any evidence inadmissible solely on *Miranda* grounds." Joseph D. Grano, Rhode Island v. Innis: *A Need to Reconsider the Constitutional Premises Underlying the Law of Confessions*, 17 Am. Crim. L. Rev. 1, 3 (1979) (footnote omitted). Grano turned out to be right about the result in *Innis*; but in the process of reversing the Rhode Island Supreme Court, the majority adopted a surprisingly generous definition of interrogation.

166. 451 U.S. 477 (1981).

167. *Arizona v. Roberson*, 486 U.S. 675 (1988) (unrelated crimes); *Minnick v. Mississippi*, 498 U.S. 1465 (1990) (post-invocation waiver invalid even though suspect consulted counsel after invocation and before purported waiver).

168. 451 U.S. at 485.

169. 451 U.S. at 484 (footnote omitted).

170. 423 U.S. at 110 n.2 (White, J., concurring).

171. 446 U.S. at 304 (Burger, C.J., concurring).

172. 462 U.S. 1039 (1983).

173. James J. Tomkovicz, *Standards for Invocation and Waiver of Counsel in Confession Contexts*, 71 Iowa L. Rev. 975, 1033 (1986) (emphasis added).

174. Id. at 1033–34 (footnote omitted).

175. 467 U.S. 649 (1984).

176. *New York v. Quarles* (No. 82–1213), Brief for the United States as Amicus Curiae at 7–13.

177. 467 U.S. at 655.

178. Id. at 654 (citation omitted).

179. Id. at 657.

180. *Quarles* (No. 82–1213), Brief for the Petitioner at 10.

181. See *Orozco v. Texas*, 394 U.S. 324 (1969) (suspect surrounded and questioned by armed officers in his bedroom at 4:00 in the morning entitled to *Miranda* warnings); *Rhode Island v. Innis*, 446 U.S. 291 (1980) (suspect under arrest and in police vehicle en route to station may not be interrogated absent warnings).

182. 467 U.S. at 658.

183. For representative cases, see *United States v. Lawrence*, 952 F.2d 1034 (8th Cir. 1992); *United States v. Brady*, 819 F.2d 884 (9th Cir. 1987); *Fleming v. Collins*, 954 F.2d 1109 (5th Cir. 1992) (en banc).

184. *Arizona v. Roberson*, 486 U.S. 675 (1988).

185. *Minnick v. Mississippi*, 498 U.S. 146 (1990) (holding that a suspect who has invoked the right to counsel and then consults with counsel may not be subsequently interrogated absent initiation of dialogue by the suspect).

186. *Withrow v. Williams*, 507 U.S. 680 (1993).

187. 530 U.S. 428 (2000). *Dickerson* has evoked extensive commentary, notably the symposium, Miranda *after* Dickerson: *The Future of Confession Law*, 99 Mich. L. Rev. 879–1247 (2001).

188. Id. at 444.
189. Id. at 432.
190. Id. at 439 n.3.
191. Id. at 440.
192. Id. at 441.
193. Id. at 461 (Scalia, J., dissenting).
194. See, e.g., Paul G. Cassell, *The Paths Not Taken: The Supreme Court's Failures in Dickerson*, 99 Mich. L. Rev. 898, 899–900 (2001) ("The description of *Miranda* as a 'constitutional rule' was sufficient to achieve the Court's apparent twin aims: striking down § 3501 while leaving in place its various decisions crafting exceptions to *Miranda*. But this result-oriented 'success' came at the great cost of any pretense of consistency in the Court's doctrine."); Susan R. Klein, *Identifying and (Re)Formulating Prophylactic Rules, Safe Harbors, and Incidental Rights in Constitutional Criminal Procedure*, 99 Mich. L. Rev. 1030, 1071 (2001) (*Dickerson* Court "breached its duty to provide a justification for *Miranda* or *Dickerson* and squandered an opportunity to rationalize contradictory case law regarding *Miranda*'s exceptions."). Professor Strauss appears to dissent from the prevailing view that *Dickerson* failed to resolve the inconsistency between *Miranda* and the prophylactic-rules cases. See David A. Strauss, Miranda, *The Constitution, and Congress*, 99 Mich. L. Rev. 958, 966–69 (2001) (arguing that the Constitution commonly requires the Court to formulate rules based on a balance of costs and benefits and that the balance may have been different in *Elstad* than it was in *Miranda*). The *Dickerson* majority's willful refusal *to explain* why the balance differs across the *Miranda* and the Fifth Amendment case law, however, powerfully suggests that little can be said to support such a distinction.
195. 530 U.S. at 461 (Scalia, J., dissenting).

CHAPTER 5

1. As Professor Tribe has written:

From the mid 1930's to the present, with the exception of flourishes manifestly designed to call attention to their authors as iconoclasts before delivering an almost always tame bottom line, virtually all who interpret the Constitution or criticize its interpreters come to the task with much the same kit of tools. All claim to be construing the text in light of its language, its structure and its history, giving due weight to precedent and context. Commentators differ as to just how determinate or manipulable the enterprise is, and they differ as to matters of empahsisis—with some insisting that a stress on history is the best way to tame and constrain the process of judgment, and others believing that historical claims often obscure the choices that are being made. But searching for the real differences at this level seems to me a fundamental error.

Laurence H. Tribe, *Contrasting Constitutional Visions: Of Real and Unreal Differences*, 22 Harv. C.R.-C.L. L. Rev. 95, 98–99 (1987).

Despite this overlapping consensus on what counts as constitutional authority, the literature on constitutional theory is vast and continually growing. For an excellent sample of views, see Antonin Scalia, *A Matter of Interpretation* (Princeton U. Press, 1997) (Justice Scalia defends originalism, and a distinguished panel, including Professor Tribe, comments.). If compelled to adopt a fully described constitutional theory, I would apply positivist jurisprudence to American legal practice, and end up with something very similar to the conventionalist approaches of David Strauss or Richard Fallon. See David A. Strauss,

Common Law Constitutional Interpretation, 63 U. Chi. L. Rev. 877 (1996); Richard H. Fallon, Jr., *Stare Decisis and the Constitution: An Essay on Constitutional Methodology*, 76 N.Y.U. L. Rev. 570 (2001); Richard H. Fallon, Jr., *A Constructivist Coherence Theory of Constitutional Interpretation*, 100 Harv. L. Rev. 1189 (1987).

2. See H.L.A. Hart, *The Concept of Law* 132 (Clarendon Press, 1961) ("Here at the margin of rules and in the fields left open by the theory of precedents, the courts perform a rule-producing function which administrative bodies perform centrally in the elaboration of variable standards.").

3. See generally Ronald Dworkin, *Law's Empire* ch. 4 (Belknap Press, 1986).

4. See David Lyons, *Principles, Positivism, and Legal Theory*, 87 Yale L.J. 415 (1977) (reviewing Dworkin, *Law's Empire* (cited in note 3)); Philip Soper, *Legal Theory and the Obligation of the Judge: The Hart/Dworkin Dispute*, 75 Mich. L. Rev. 473 (1977).

5. On the meaning and importance of undertheorized agreement in constitutional interpretation, see Cass R. Sunstein, *One Case at a Time* 13 (Harvard U. Press, 1999).

6. Dissenting in *Miranda*, Justice White put it this way:

That the court's holding today is neither compelled nor even strongly suggested by the language of the Fifth Amendment, is at odds with American and English legal history, and involves a departure from a long line of precedent does not prove either that the Court has exceeded its powers or that the court is wrong or unwise in its present reinterpretation of the Fifth Amendment. It does, however, underscore the obvious—that the Court has not discovered or found the law in making today's decision, nor has it derived it from irrefutable sources; what it has done is to make new law and new public policy in much the same way that it has in the course of interpreting other great clauses of the Constitution. This is what the Court historically has done. Indeed, it is what it must do and will continue to do until and unless there is some fundamental change in the constitutional distribution of governmental powers.

Miranda v. Arizona, 384 U.S. 436, 531–32 (1966) (White, J., dissenting) (footnote omitted).

7. Herbert L. Packer, *Two Models of the Criminal Process*, 113 U. Pa. L. Rev. 1 (1964).

8. Mirjan Damaska, *Evidentiary Barriers to Conviction and Two Models of Criminal Procedure: A Comparative Study*, 121 U. Pa. L. Rev. 506 (1973).

9. For some examples of this latter tendency, see, e.g., Arnold Loewy, *Criminal Law: Cases and Materials* 1 (Anderson Publishing, 1991) ("In asking whether particular activity ought to be criminal, we are asking whether it ought to be punished."); Peter W. Low, John Calvin Jeffries, Jr., & Richard J. Bonnie, *Criminal Law: Cases and Materials* 1 (Foundation Press, 4th ed. 1986) ("It is essential to the study of substantive criminal law to focus on the purpose of the enterprise—that is, to ask why the criminal process is used to punish people who engage in designated behavior. This inquiry requires consideration of the rationales or purposes of punishment."); Wayne LaFave & Austin Scott, Jr., *Criminal Law* 22 (West, 2d ed. 1986) ("Purposes of the Criminal Law—Theories of Punishment"). All of these astute authors recognize the priority of legality over the purposes of punishment; only on the assumption that the criminal law possesses society's sole means of punishment does the conflation of punishment's purposes and the criminal law's purposes make sense. Only by explicitly recognizing the distinctive purposes of law and punishment, however, can the moral and political foundations of criminal procedure be exposed.

10. I borrow this scheme of classification from H.L.A. Hart, *Punishment and Responsibility* (Oxford U. Press, 1968).

11. See, e.g., John Kaplan & Robert Weisberg, *Criminal Law: Cases and Materials* 954–55 (Little, Brown, 2d ed. 1991) (characterizing legality as one of the "further requisites of just punishment").

12. See, e.g., Glanville Williams, *Criminal Law: The General Part* 575 (Stevens, 2d ed. 1961) ("In its Latin dress of *Nullum crimen sine lege, Nulla poena sine lege*—[the principle] that there must be no crime or punishment except in accordance with fixed, predetermined law . . . has been regarded by most thinkers as a self-evident principle of justice ever since the French Revolution."); *Keeler v. Superior Court of Amador County*, 470 P.2d 617 (Cal. 1970) (intentional killing of fetus in womb of defendant's ex-wife could not be punished as murder absent explicit legislation equating a fetus with "human being" for purpose of murder statute).

13. See H.L.A. Hart, *Punishment and Responsibility* at 11–13, 17–24 (cited in note 10); Joseph Raz, *The Rule of Law and its Virtues*, 93 Law Q. Rev. 195, 202–05 (1977).

14. See Donald Dripps, *The Constitutional Status of the Reasonable Doubt Rule*, 75 Cal. L. Rev. 1665, 1684–85 (1987):

[T]he legality principle ensures a degree of neutrality among persons in the administration of justice. Rules made in advance cannot as easily be directed toward despised individuals. Even absent oppressive motives, the legality principle helps to prevent punishment that is merely gratuitous and arbitrary. The legality principle expresses the judgement that punishment must be justified by some public purpose important enough to be articulated generally and prospectively. Without that declaration, the state may not argue that the general interest requires the suffering of a particular person. The chance that such an argument is meritorious is too remote, the chance that the argument is feigned too immediate, to justify its temptation in every case.

15. See Chapter 1, § 5.

16. 4 William Blackstone, *Commentaries* *358.

17. See Hans Zeisel, *The Limits of Law Enforcement* 57 (U. Chicago Press, 1982) ("The search for the means of identifying the habitual criminal has been going on for some two-hundred years and has been stepped up during recent decades. Yet whenever the efficiency of these identification efforts was examined, it was found wanting.") (footnote omitted); Jacqueline Cohen, *Selective Incapacitation: An Assessment*, 1984 U. Ill. L. Rev. 253, 264–76. The instant offense is not a reliable predictor of future offenses, in part because plea bargaining may result in a conviction for a crime that does not describe the offender's actual conduct, and more fundamentally because criminals do not specialize. Today's auto thief may be tomorrow's burglar or mugger.

18. Horton, it will be recalled, raped a woman while furloughed from a Massachusetts prison, thereby becoming grist for the 1984 presidential election campaign. See *Dukakis Now Supports Ban on Furloughs for Murderers*, N.Y. Times § I, at 30, col. 6. (Mar. 24, 1988).

19. James Q. Wilson summarizes the problem well:

Imagine a young man walking down the street at night with nothing on his mind but a desire for good times and high living. Suddenly he sees a little old lady standing alone on a dark corner stuffing the proceeds of her recently cashed social security check into her purse. There is nobody else in view. If the boy steals the purse, he gets the money immediately. That is a powerful incentive, and it is available immediately and without doubts. The costs of taking it are uncertain; the odds are at least fourteen to one that the police will not catch a given robber, and even if he is caught the odds are very good that he will not go to prison, unless he has a long record. On the average, no more than three felonies out of one hundred result in the imprisonment of the offender. In addition to this uncertainty, whatever penalty may come his way will come only after a long delay; in some jurisdictions, it might take a year of more to complete the court disposition of the offender, assuming he is caught in the first place. Moreover, this young man may, in his ignorance of how the world works, think the odds in his favor are even greater and that the delay will be even longer.

Thinking About Crime 118 (BasicBooks, rev. ed. 1983). I quite agree with Wilson's conclusion that punishment does deter in a general way, in the same way that incentives influence behavior generally. But the precise question is whether a criminal process as concerned with the escape of the guilty as with the punishment of the innocent would reap substantial crime control benefits. Given that the major infirmities of the legal threat concern the likelihood of arrest and the scarcity of prison space, even a major increase in the probability that the arrested will be convicted might add nothing perceptible to the credibility of the legal threat.

20. See, e.g., Brian Forst, *Criminal Justice System: Measurement of Performance*, in 2 Ency. of Crime & Justice 479, 481 (Free Press, Sanford Kadish ed. 1983).

21. U.S. Dept. of Justice, Bureau of Justice Statistics, *Sourcebook of Criminal Justice Statistics* 1993, 252 (table 3.6) (1994). For all offenses, the rate of reporting of crimes mentioned in the national victimization survey was 38.7%. Victims reported only 52.5% of rapes, 51.1% of robberies, and 29.5% of thefts.

22. See id. at 452 (table 4.24) (in 1992, police cleared 21.4% of all offenses, 44.6% of violent crimes, and 17.7% of property crimes).

23. John Rawls, *A Theory of Justice* § 87 (Belknap Press, 1971). Rawls criticizes utilitarianism for failing to "take seriously the distinction between persons." Id., § 5, at 27. The utilitarian is indifferent to the distribution of happiness, caring only about its aggregate amount. Thus a utilitarian is willing to confer great happiness on a few at the expense of a small cost to many, or to confer a small benefit to many by imposing a high cost on a few. One can agree with Rawls's objection to this form of utilitarianism, however, without agreeing with the rigid difference principle Rawls derives from this objection.

24. R.M. Hare, a leading exponent of justifying categorical moral principles on utilitarian grounds, offers the security of the innocent against criminal penalties as an example of the kind of principle generated by his ethical system. See R.M. Hare, *Moral Thinking* 162 (Clarendon Press, 1981):

Prima facie moral principles are needed for the conduct of those who administer the law, and critical thinking has to select these principles. . . . Thus the grounds of selection will be utilitarian; but the principles selected may not themselves look utilitarian at all. They are likely to be, rather, of the sort dear to deontologists and intuitionists; they will insist on things like not punishing the innocent, not condemning people unheard, observing procedures in court which are calculated to elicit the truth from witnesses and cause the jury to attend to it, and so on. These prima facie principles of substantial, including procedural, justice in the administration of the law will be selected by critical thinking because their general acceptance is likely to further the interests of those affected, all in all, considered impartially, i.e. with formal justice. So, though the principles may accord with those defended by intuitionists, their justification is utilitarian.

25. For utilitarian views, compare Hare, *Moral Thinking* (cited in note 24) with H.L.A. Hart, *Punishment and Responsibility* at 22 (cited in note 10). See also John Rawls, *Two Concepts of Rules*, 64 Phil. Rev. 1, 7–8 (1955) (*system* of criminal justice that permitted conviction of the innocent for consequentialist ends would not serve utility). For a deontological view, see Charles Fried, *Expressive Aspects of Criminal Procedure* in *An Anatomy of Values* 125–32 (Harvard U. Press, 1970).

26. See, e.g., Philip Bean, *Punishment* 29 (Martin Robertson, 1981); H.J. McCloskey, *A Nonutilitarian Approach to Punishment* in *Contemporary Utilitarianism* (Michael D. Bayles ed. 1968).

27. See Fried, *An Anatomy of Values* at 126 (cited in note 25).

28. See *Addington v. Texas*, 441 U.S. 418, 423–33 (1979) (government must prove mental illness and danger to self or others by clear and convincing evidence at adversary hearing); *United States v. Salerno*, 481 U.S. 739, 750–57 (1987) (preventive detention constitutional pending trial provided government proves by clear and convincing evidence that only confinement can protect the public, and conditions of detention are minimally punitive).

29. For the suggestion, see, e.g., Fried, *An Anatomy of Values* (cited in note 25).

30. On the role of criminal procedure safeguards in checking potential totalitarianism, see Donald Dripps, *The Exclusivity of the Criminal Law: Toward a "Regulatory Model" of, or "Pathological Perspective" on, the Civil/Criminal Distinction*, 7 J. Contemp. Legal Issues 199 (1996).

31. See Sunstein, *One Case at a Time* (cited in note 5).

32. United States Department of Justice, *Sourcebook of Criminal Justice Statistics* 1998 at 328 table 4.1 (1999).

33. See, e.g., *Benton v. Maryland*, 395 U.S. 784, 808 (1969) (Harlan, J., dissenting) ("the 'selective incorporation' doctrine finds no support either in history or in reason") (quoting *Duncan v. Louisiana*, 391 U.S. 145, 171 (1968)); *Miranda v. Arizona*, 384 U.S. 436, 505 (1966) (Harlan, J., dissenting) (majority's approach "require[d] a strained reading of history and precedent and a disregard of the very pragmatic concerns that alone may on occasion justify such strains"); *Mapp v. Ohio*, 367 U.S. 643, 682 (1961) (Harlan, J., dissenting) ("I do not believe that the Fourteenth Amendment empowers this Court to mould state remedies effectuating the right to freedom from 'arbitrary intrusion by the police' to suit its own notions of how things should be done").

Justice Harlan expounded his view most completely in *Duncan v. Louisiana*, 391 U.S. 145, 174–76 (1968) (Harlan, J., dissenting):

A few members of the Court have taken the position that the intention of those who drafted the first section of the Fourteenth Amendment was simply, and exclusively, to make the provisions of the first eight Amendments applicable to state action. This view has never been accepted by this Court. In my view, often expressed elsewhere, the first section of the Fourteenth Amendment was meant neither to incorporate, not to be limited to the specific guarantees of the first eight Amendments. The overwhelming historical evidence marshaled by Professor Fairman demonstrates, to me conclusively, that the Congressmen and state legislators who wrote, debated, and ratified the Fourteenth Amendment did not think they were "incorporating" the Bill of Rights and the very breadth and generality of the Amendment's provisions suggest that its authors did not suppose that the Nation would always be limited to mid-19th century conceptions of "liberty" and "due process of law" but that the increasing experience and evolving conscience of the American people would add new "intermediate premises." In short, neither history, nor sense, supports using the Fourteenth Amendment to put the States in a constitutional straightjacket with respect to their own development in the administration of criminal or civil law.

(footnotes omitted).

34. See *Duncan*, 391 U.S. at 173–83 (Harlan, J., dissenting).

35. Id. at 174.

36. For example, Robert Bork criticizes substantive due process as illegitimate, but then cites Joseph Grano, the leading academic defender of fundamental fairness analysis, as one of the few real originalists in the academy. See Robert Bork, *The Tempting of America* 31–34 & 223–24 (Free Press, 1990).

37. See *Estelle v. Williams*, 425 U.S. 501, 509–13 (1976) (holding that defendant had waived right in instant case).

38. *Doyle v. Ohio*, 426 U.S. 610, 617–20 (1976).

39. *Chambers v. Mississippi*, 410 U.S. 284, 283–303 (1973).

40. *Interstate Commerce Commission v. Louisville & Nashville Railroad*, 227 U.S. 88, 91–92 (1913); *Londoner v. Denver*, 210 U.S. 373, 380–86 (1908).

41. *Betts v. Brady*, 316 U.S. 455, 462 (1942).

42. See *Duncan*, 391 U.S. at 173 (Harlan, J., dissenting) (prior justices who rejected incorporation "were wont to believe rather that the security of liberty in America rested primarily upon the dispersion of governmental power across a federal system.") (footnote omitted).

43. See Jesse H. Choper, *Judicial Review and the National Political Process* 175–84 (U. Chicago Press, 1980); Herbert Wechsler, *The Political Safeguards of Federalism: The Role of the States in the Composition and Selection of the National Government*, 54 Colum. L. Rev. 543 (1954).

44. See William E. Nelson, *The Fourteenth Amendment* 197 (Harvard U. Press, 1988) ("The two key facts about the framing and ratification of section one were that the victorious Northern public demanded that the postwar South be restrained in the future from discriminating against blacks and Northerners, and that this restraint be imposed without altering radically the structure of the federal system or increasing markedly the powers of the federal government. Perhaps these two Northern wishes were inconsistent, but the political leaders who framed and ratified the Fourteenth Amendment were bound by them and had striven to draft an amendment that accommodated them.").

45. See Chapter 2, § 3.

46. See Brief for Petitioner at 33, *Gideon v. Wainwright*, 372 U.S. 335 (1963) (No. 63–155) ("*Betts v. Brady* has engendered conflict between the federal and state courts because of the case by case review it entails and because it does not prescribe a clear-cut standard which the state courts can follow.").

47. See, e.g., Lawrence M. Friedman, *Crime and Punishment in American History* 360–63 (BasicBooks, 1993).

48. See, e.g., id. at 374–77; *Southern Justice* (Pantheon, Leon Friedman ed. 1965).

49. See note 61 *infra* (appellate courts upheld trial court refusals to appoint counsel under *Betts* rule in 124 out of 139 cases). Presumably, only a fraction of the self-represented indigent were able to perfect an appeal.

50. See, e.g., Frank T. Read & Lucy S. McGough, *Let Them Be Judged: The Judicial Integration of the Deep South* 328–29 (Scarecrow Press, 1978) ("There was every indication that blacks, traditionally excluded, were continuing to be intentionally foreclosed from participation as jurors in the judicial process in the states of the Fifth Circuit. . . . As late as 1954, no black had ever served on a jury in Carroll County, Mississippi. Fifty-seven per cent of the population of that county was black. . . . ").

51. E.g., *Lyons v. Oklahoma*, 322 U.S. 596, 601–05 (1944).

52. This characterization is from *Betts*, 316 U.S. at 463.

53. 316 U.S. at 472.

54. Id.

55. Id. at 474 (Black, J., dissenting).

56. See Yale Kamisar, Gideon v. Wainwright *A Quarter Century Later*, 10 Pace L. Rev. 343, 351–52 (1990); Yale Kamisar, *The Right to Counsel and the Fourteenth Amendment: A Dialogue on "the Most Pervasive Right" of an Accused*, 30 U. Chi. L. Rev. 1, 42–56 (1962).

57. Francis A. Allen, *The Supreme Court, Federalism, and State Systems of Criminal Justice*, 8 DePaul L. Rev. 213, 230 (1959) (emphasis in original).

58. *Betts*, 316 U.S. at 473.

59. See *Betts*, 316 U.S. at 472–73; Allen, 8 DePaul L. Rev. at 228 (cited in note 57) ("The crucial question posed by the Court's counsel rule in the noncapital cases relates to those special circumstances under which want of legal representation may be taken to result in denial of a fair hearing.").

60. 316 U.S. at 472 n. 31 (quoting Judge Bond's opinion for the court below).

61. See Brief for the American Civil Liberties Association and the Florida Civil Liberties Association, *Amici Curiae*, at Appendix II, *Gideon v. Wainwright*, 372 U.S. 335 (1963) (No. 62–155) (out of 139 reported state court decisions applying the special circumstances rule, 124 found no special circumstances and affirmed convictions rendered without counsel for the defense; only fourteen of these cases were reviewed by writ of certiorari in the Supreme Court, and of the fourteen, eleven were reversed).

62. For example, in *Shaffer v. Warden*, 126 A.2d 573, 574 (Md. 1956), the court rejected the defendant's claim that the court and the stenographer had misunderstood his request for counsel because of the defendant's congenital speech impediment. The court felt itself bound by the record, even though the record was made by a nineteen-year-old defendant of limited intelligence suffering from a speech impediment.

To a like effect is Commonwealth ex rel. *Ringer v. Maroney*, 110 A.2d 801, 801–02 (Pa. Super. 1955), rejecting a collateral attack on a guilty plea entered by a defendant with a third grade education, who claimed to have signed written confessions although he was illiterate, and who was classified by the correctional authorities as a "moron." Again the basic idea is that the defendant could not go outside a record made without counsel to impugn his plea.

63. For example, in *Gryger v. Burke*, 334 U.S. 728 (1948), the defendant claimed that the trial judge mistakenly imposed a life sentence on the defendant out of the mistaken belief that state law made that sentence mandatory. In *Townsend v. Burke*, 334 U.S. 736 (1948), the trial judge's remarks at sentencing evinced a mistaken belief that the defendant had been convicted of two charges for which he had, in fact, been acquitted. In both cases the defendants argued that, had counsel been appointed, the judge's errors would have been corrected and a lesser penalty imposed. Despite the similarity of these cases, decided the same day under the same standard, the Court split the difference, and vacated Townsend's sentence but not Gryger's.

64. 343 U.S. 181, 184–91 (1952).

65. 373 U.S. 503, 513–15 (1963).

66. 356 U.S. 560, 567–69 (1958).

67. 356 U.S. 390, 400–03 (1958).

68. See id. at 400.

69. See Yale Kamisar, *A Dissent from the* Miranda *Dissents: Some Comments on the "New" Fifth Amendment and the Old "Voluntariness" Test*, 65 Mich. L. Rev. 59, 94–104 (1966); Anthony Amsterdam, *The Supreme Court and the Rights of Suspects in Criminal Cases*, 45 N.Y.U. L. Rev. 685, 806–08 (1970).

70. See Chapter 3, § 4.

71. *Rochin v. California*, 342 U.S. 165, 172–73 (1952), discussed in Chapter 2, § 2.

72. *Irvine v. California*, 347 U.S. 128, 132–34 (1954), discussed in Chapter 2, § 2.

73. *Breithaupt v. Abram*, 352 U.S. 432, 435–40 (1957).

74. See, e.g., Michael Mushlin, *Foreword*, 10 Pace L. Rev. 327, 327–28 (1990):

In *Gideon v. Wainwright*, the Supreme Court unanimously held that indigent state felony defendants are constitutionally entitled to the appointment of trial counsel. The opinion aroused wide support, and even enthusiasm, almost from the moment it was announced in 1963. Two and a half decades later this support has not diminished. Even former Attorney General Edwin Meese III approves.

(footnotes omitted).

75. The Court has gone no further than to require the appointment of a defense psychiatric expert in a case in which an indigent defendant's insanity plea was rejected in a capital case. *Ake v. Oklahoma*, 470 U.S. 68, 74, 86–87 (1985). The Court adopted a balancing test that entitles the accused to "the basic tools of an adequate defense." Id. at 77 (quoting *Britt v. North Carolina*, 404 U.S. 226, 227 (1971)). Lower courts generally have given this test a restrictive application. See David A. Harris, *The Constitution and Truth Seeking: A New Theory on Expert Services for Indigent Defendants*, 83 J. Crim. L. Criminology 469, 483–91 (1992).

76. See, e.g., Michael McConville & Chester L. Mirsky, *Criminal Defense of the Poor in New York City*, 15 N.Y.U. J. L & Soc. Change 581 (1986–87) (indigent defenders miss 40% of required court appearances, requiring appointment of substitute counsel; few pretrial motions are made, and defense attorneys view pleading cases as goal of system); *Indigent Defense System KO'd*, Nat'l L. J. 3, 10 (Feb. 24, 1992) (Louisiana state court judge found that the "likelihood, under the current system, that an innocent person will choose a plea of guilty at arraignment, because of no meaningful representation, is great"); Stephen Bright, Stephen Kinnard & David Webster, *Keeping Gideon from Being Blown Away*, 4 Crim. Just. 10, 11 (1990) ("The vice-president of the Georgia trial Lawyers Association once described the standard for competence of counsel in many Georgia counties as the 'mirror test.' 'You put a mirror under the court-appointed attorney's nose, and if the mirror clouds up, that's adequate counsel.'"); Andy Court, *Is There a Crisis?*, Am. Lawyer 46 (Jan./Feb. 1993) ("As our reporters fanned out across the country, they did not look exclusively at the worst places, but they did find serious problems that should disturb the conscience of every American concerned about equal justice."); David L. Bazelon, *The Defective Assistance of Counsel*, 42 U. Cin. L. Rev. 1, 2 (1973) ("a great many—if not most—indigent defendants do not receive the effective assistance of counsel guaranteed them by the 6th Amendment"). See also Donald Dripps, *Ineffective Assistance of Counsel: The Case for an Ex Ante Parity Standard*, 88 J. Crim. L. & Crimin. 242, 245–52 (1997) (reviewing studies); Note, *Gideon's Promise Unfulfilled: The Need for Litigated Reform of Indigent Defense*, 113 Harv. L. Rev. 2062, 2063–65 (2000) (noting broad agreement on inadequacy of indigent defense).

The principal defense of indigent defense is a study by Roger A. Hanson, et al., *Indigent Defenders Get the Job Done and Done Well* (1992), performed for the National Center for State Courts. They compared the outcomes of cases in nine different courts according to representation by private counsel or by a public defender or an assigned lawyer. Although they found that defendants represented by private counsel fared better than the rest, the differences were not catastrophic.

Three points need to be borne in mind about the Hanson research. First, there certainly appear to be many jurisdictions not studied by the Hanson group in which the defense function is grossly deficient. Second, the Hanson data indeed suggest that private representation has some benefits. In five large systems with public defender offices, defendants represented by publicly appointed counsel were incarcerated 71.5% of the time; those represented by private counsel were incarcerated only 50.5% of the time, although, in the smaller courts, the difference was negligible. See id. at 59. There may be problems with both the size, and the selection, of the sample, but such inferences as can be drawn from the study cast no great credit on public defenders.

Finally, it needs to be recalled that most criminal defendants are poor, even if they are not indigent. Many of those who can afford counsel can still afford only the services of the bar's bottom-feeders. Thus, a comparison between appointed counsel and retained counsel is not necessarily a comparison between appointed counsel and effective counsel. See Floyd Feeney & Patrick Jackson, *Public Defenders, Assigned Counsel, Retained Counsel: Does the Type of Criminal Defense Counsel Matter?*, 22 Rutgers L.J. 361, 409–10 (1991):

> The studies to date clearly do not establish, nor does this article claim, that all attorneys lack effect. The record compiled by the top criminal defense attorneys clearly indicates to the contrary. The best lawyers do make a difference. Wealthy defendants, or those who have access to these superior forms of counsel, are likely to fare better in the criminal courts than those who lack this advantage. Only a few of the defendants who retain their own criminal defense counsel, however, fall into this group. Most criminal defendants who hire their own counsel or who have private counsel appointed for them are poor, and only marginally different, if at all, from the public defender's clients.

(footnotes omitted).

77. See Chapter 3, § 4.

78. See Chapter 4, § 4.

79. *Massiah v. United States*, 377 U.S. 201, 206 (1964), discussed in Chapter 3, § 3.

80. Professor Grano struggles to distinguish the right to refuse to answer from the right to be free from questions; but at any event he acknowledges the former right. See Joseph D. Grano, *Confessions, Truth and the Law* 44–45 & 141–43 (U. Michigan Press, 1993).

81. 142 U.S. 547 (1892).

82. See Richard A. Leo, *Police Interrogation and Social Control*, 3 Soc. & Legal Stud. 93, 99 (1994) ("Although virtually all suspects waive their *Miranda* rights, police officers are keenly aware that a suspect may terminate questioning at any time during the interrogation.") (citation omitted); Chapter 4, § 2, nn.114–17.

83. 378 U.S. 1, 8 (1964).

84. The two precedents are *Adamson v. California*, 332 U.S. 46 (1947) and *Twining v. New Jersey*, 211 U.S. 78 (1908).

85. For one possible argument along these lines, see George C. Thomas III, *Separated at Birth but Siblings Nonetheless:* Miranda *and the Due Process Notice Cases*, 99 Mich. L. Rev. 1081 (2001).

86. 392 U.S. 1 (1968).

87. See *State v. Terry*, 214 N.E.2d 114, 118–20 (Ohio Ct. App. 1966).

88. Id. at 117–18.

89. Id. at 120 ("Are we to allow him the right of inquiry and then, when this right is exercised, reward him with an assailant's bullet?").

90. 392 U.S. at 10.

91. Id. at 12–14.

92. Id. at 16.

93. Id.

94. Id.

95. Id. at 19.

96. 392 U.S. at 36 (Douglas, J., dissenting).

97. 392 U.S. at 23.

98. Id. In footnote 16, the majority explained that *Terry* did not raise a question about "the constitutional propriety of an investigative 'seizure' upon less than probable cause for purposes of 'detention' and/or 'investigation,'" because the record did not clearly

indicate whether there had been a seizure prior to the frisk, or whether the seizure and the frisk were in reality a single simultaneous transaction. 392 U.S. at 19 n.16.

99. See id. at 26–27.

100. 392 U.S. at 31–34 (Harlan, J., concurring).

101. Id. at 33 (Harlan, J., concurring).

102. 392 U.S. at 62.

103. See id. at 63–65.

104. See id. at 66–68; Yale Kamisar, *The Warren Court (Was it Really so Defense-Minded), the Burger Court (Is it Really so Prosecution Oriented?), and Police Investigatory Practices*, in Vincent Blasi ed., *The Burger Court: The Counter-Revolution that Wasn't* 62, 65 (Yale University Press 1983) (the Court "strained a good deal to avoid explaining how the police, after opening an *opaque* envelope from a 'frisked' suspect's pocket could open the envelope to see what was inside").

105. *Sibron*, 392 U.S. at 63 (citing *Terry*).

106. *Terry*, 392 U.S. at 31 (Harlan, J., concurring) (emphasis added).

107. Due process by itself requires that restrictions on individual liberty be justified by interests proportionate to the intrusion, so that the basic idea of creating categories of intrusions coupled with standards of suspicions comports quite naturally with a due process paradigm. On the role of the proportionality principle in *Terry* see Christopher Slobogin, *Let's Not Bury* Terry: *A Call For Rejuvenation of the Proportionality Principle*, 72 St. John's L. Rev. 1053 (1998).

108. As one of the prosecutors in *Sibron v. New York*, one of the companion cases to *Terry*, put it after the fact: "It was a daunting task to defend the right of the police to stop and frisk persons abroad on the public streets on less than probable cause. . . ." Michael R. Juviler, *A Prosecutor's Perspective*, 72 St. John's L. Rev. 741, 741 (1998). "[I]n the brief six years under the exclusionary rule," Judge Juviler recollects, "we had been trained and developed in a culture of probable cause." Id. at 742. It is illuminating that the justices at the conference were unanimous in voting to affirm Terry's conviction, and that they were equally unanimous in categorizing the stop-and-frisk as a Fourth Amendment search. See John Q. Barrett, *Deciding the Stop and Frisk Cases: A Look Inside the Supreme Court's Conference*, 72 St. John's L. Rev. 749, 791 (1998). Chief Justice Warren's draft opinion attempted to rationalize the stop-and-frisk as supported by probable cause, but in the face of various objections from the other justices he ultimately adopted Justice Brennan's suggestion of relying on the reasonableness clause. See id. at 793–830.

109. *United States v. Calandra*, 414 U.S. 338, 349–55 (1974).

110. *Harris v. New York*, 401 U.S. 222, 224–26 (1971); *United States v. Havens*, 446 U.S. 620, 624–28 (1980).

111. *United States v. Janis*, 428 U.S. 433, 447–58 (1976).

112. *Harris v. New York*, 401 U.S. 222, 225–26 (1971), discussed in Chapter 4, § 3.

113. *New York v. Quarles*, 467 U.S. 649, 655–58 (1984), discussed in Chapter 4, § 5.

114. *Edwards v. Arizona*, 451 U.S. 477, 481–87 (1981), discussed in Chapter 4, § 4.

115. *Minnick v. Mississippi*, 498 U.S. 146, 150–56 (1990).

116. *Michigan v. Mosley*, 423 U.S. 96, 104–07 (1975), discussed in Chapter 4, § 4.

117. *Rhode Island v. Innis*, 446 U.S. 291, 297–304 (1980), discussed in Chapter 4, § 4.

118. *Oregon v. Bradshaw*, 462 U.S. 1039, 1044–47 (1983).

119. Compare *Berger v. New York*, 388 U.S. 41, 54–60 (1967) with *Lopez v. United States*, 373 U.S. 427, 438–40 (1963) and *Rathbun v. United States*, 355 U.S. 107, 109–11 (1957).

120. *Massiah v. United States*, 377 U.S. 201, 204–07 (1964).

121. *California v. Acevedo*, 500 U.S. 565, 569–80 (1982).

122. *Arizona v. Hicks*, 480 U.S. 321, 324–29 (1987).

123. *United States v. Watson*, 423 U.S. 411, 414–24 (1976).

124. *Hoffa v. United States*, 385 U.S. 293, 300–03 (1966).

125. *Smith v. Maryland*, 442 U.S. 735, 739–46 (1979).

126. *United States v. Miller*, 425 U.S. 435, 440–47 (1976).

127. *Strickland v. Washington*, 466 U.S. 668, 684–98 (1984), discussed in Chapter 3, § 4.

128. *In re Winship*, 397 U.S. 358, 361–68 (1970).

129. *Mullaney v. Wilbur*, 421 U.S. 684, 690–704 (1975).

130. *Martin v. Ohio*, 480 U.S. 228, 231–36 (1987).

131. 410 U.S. 284, 294–303 (1973).

132. 488 U.S. 51, 55–59 (1988).

133. Views on the force of precedent in constitutional cases diverge widely. At one extreme, Gary Lawson has argued that the authority of the constitutional text deserves priority over decisional law, so that *any* reliance on precedent is unjustified. See Gary Lawson, *The Constitutional Case Against Precedent*, 17 Harv. J.L. & Pub. Pol. 23 (1994). For similar but less categorical views, see William Douglas, *Stare Decisis*, 49 Colum. L. Rev. 735 (1949); Bork, *The Tempting of America* at 155–59 (cited in note 36). For an account of precedent as relevant but of only modest force, not confined to constitutional cases, see Michael Moore, *Precedent, Induction, and Ethical Generalization*, in *Precedent in Law* 183 (Oxford U. Press, Laurence Goldstein ed. 1987).

For stronger, but still heavily qualified, theories of precedent in constitutional cases, see *Planned Parenthood of Southeastern Pennsylvania v. Casey*, 112 S. Ct. 2791, 2815 (1992) (plurality opinion) ("[t]o overrule under fire in the absence of the most compelling reason to reexamine a watershed decision would subvert the Court's legitimacy beyond any serious question"); Henry Paul Monaghan, *Stare Decisis and Constitutional Adjudication*, 88 Colum. L. Rev. 723 (1988).

134. In *Tucker* Justice Rehnquist wrote that "the police conduct at issue here did not abridge respondent's constitutional privilege against compulsory self-incrimination, but departed only from the prophylactic standards later laid down by this Court in *Miranda* to safeguard that privilege." 417 U.S. at 446. In *Dickerson* he wrote that *Miranda* "being a constitutional decision of this Court, may not be in effect overruled by Congress," 530 U.S. 428, 431, "that *Miranda* is a constitutional decision," id. at 438, that "*Miranda* is of constitutional origin," id. at 439 n.3, that "*Miranda* is constitutionally based," id. at 440, and that "*Miranda* announced a constitutional rule that Congress may not supersede legislatively." Id. at 444.

135. See Chapter 4, § 5.

136. See *Oregon v. Elstad*, 470 U.S. 298, 364 (1980) (Stevens, J., dissenting).

137. See *United States v. Dickerson*, 166 F.3d 667, 676 (4th Cir. 1999), reversed 530 U.S. 428 (2000) ("Although the district court suppressed the statement obtained in violation of *Miranda*, it nevertheless denied Dickerson's motion to suppress the evidence found as a result thereof, *e.g.*, the statement made by Rochester identifying Dickerson as the getaway driver.").

138. *California Attorneys for Criminal Justice v. Butts*, 195 F.3d 1039 (9th Cir. 1999), cert. denied sub nom. *Butts v. McNally*, 530 U.S. 1261 (2000).

139. See Charles D. Weisselberg, *Saving* Miranda, 84 Cornell L. Rev. 109, 132–40 (1998).

140. See Donald Dripps, *Is the* Miranda *Caselaw Really Inconsistent? A Proposed Fifth Amendment Synthesis*, 17 Const. Comment. 19, 27–34 (2000).

141. See id. at 38–40.

142. See 414 U.S. at 347–48 ("[T]he rule is a judicially created remedy designed to safeguard Fourth amendment rights generally through its deterrent effect, rather than a personal constitutional right of the party aggrieved.") (citations omitted).

143. See id. at 351–52.

144. See, e.g., Wayne R. LaFave, 1 *Search & Seizure* § 1.2(a) at 22–24 (West, 1987).

145. See *Malley v. Briggs*, 475 U.S. 335, 344–45 (1986).

146. See *Leon*, 468 U.S. at 977 (Stevens, J., dissenting) ("Today, for the first time, the Court holds that although the Constitution has been violated, no court should do anything about it at any time and in any proceeding.") (footnote omitted).

147. See my paper, *Living with* Leon, Yale L.J. 906 (1986).

148. *People v. DeFore*, 150 N.E. 585, 587 (N.Y. 1926) (Cardozo, J.).

149. See, e.g., *United States v. Janis*, 428 U.S. 433, 449–54 (1976).

150. Bradley C. Canon, *Is the Exclusionary Rule in Failing Health? Some New Data and a Plea Against a Precipitous Conclusion*, 62 Ky. L.J. 681, 708–11 (1974) (warrant use in Cincinnati rose from 3, 0 and 7 per year in 1958, 1959, and 1960 to 100, 113, and 89 in 1963, 1964, and 1965; in Boston, the numbers rose from 176, 186, and 267 in 1958, 1959, and 1960 to 940, 574, and 560 in 1963, 1964, and 1965); Michael Murphy, *Judicial Review of Police Methods in Law Enforcement*, 44 Texas L. Rev. 939, 941–42 (1966) (prior to *Mapp*, search warrants "had been rarely used"; as of December, 1965, 17,889 had been obtained). The magnitude of the increase, and the time and trouble associated with the application process, make it highly unlikely that any other factor accounted for the change.

151. Dallin H. Oaks, *Studying the Exclusionary Rule in Search and Seizure*, 37 U. Chi. L. Rev. 665, 681–89 (1970); James E. Spiotto, *Search and Seizure: An Empirical Study of the Exclusionary Rule and Its Alternatives*, 2 J. Legal Stud. 243, 245–69 (1973).

152. See Peter F. Nardulli, *The Societal Cost of the Exclusionary Rule: An Empirical Assessment*, 1983 A.B.F. Res. J. 585, 598 (successful motions to suppress physical evidence occurred in 0.69% of 7,484 criminal cases sampled); Thomas Y. Davies, *A Hard Look at What We Know (and Still Need to Learn) About the Costs of the Exclusionary Rule: The NIJ Study and Other Studies of "Lost" Arrests*, 1983 A.B.F. Res. J. 611, 617–22 (NIJ study indicates that California prosecutors decline fewer than 1% of felony arrests because of search-and-seizure problems; other studies indicate that exclusionary rule's combined effects at all stages of arrest processing "only results in the nonprosecution and/or nonconviction of in the range of 0.6% to 2.35% of felony arrests in the jurisdictions studied"); Report of the Comptroller General, *Impact of the Exclusionary Rule on Federal Criminal Prosecutions* (Rep. No. CDG-79-45) (1979) (suppression motions based on Fourth Amendment granted in 1.3% of sample of 2,804 federal cases; convictions obtained in half of the cases in which motions granted); Richard Van Duizend, L. Paul Sutton, & Charlotte Carter, *The Search Warrant Process: Preconceptions, Perceptions, and Practices* 43 (table 25) (National Center for State Courts, 1985) (in study of search warrants in seven cities, motions to suppression were granted in 5% of the prosecutions involving warrants).

Perhaps defense attorneys fail to file suppression motions in a great many meritorious cases, so that these data could be squared with the hypothesis that the rule does not deter. The low suppression rate holds in warrant cases, in which suppression motions are relatively common. See id. (suppression motions filed in 39% of warrant cases). Nor does the rate of motions granted vary coherently with the frequency of motions filed. See Nardulli, *The Societal Cost of the Exclusionary Rule* at 596, 598 (table 9).

It might also be the case that judges refuse to grant meritorious motions. This, however, would nonetheless mean that the rule deters police conduct that genuinely offends the judges, whether or not they should be offended by other behavior. In any event, the low suppression rate holds in both state and federal courts, at different times and in different places. Judicial hostility to Fourth Amendment rights therefore seems an unlikely explanation for the data.

153. See William J. Mertens & Silas Wasserstrom, *The Good Faith Exception to the Exclusionary Rule: Deregulating the Police and Derailing the Law*, 70 Geo. L.J. 365, 400–01 & nn.174–75 (1981).

154. See *The Exclusionary Rule Bills: Hearings on S. 101, S. 755, and S. 1995 Before the Subcomm. on Criminal Law of the Senate Comm. on the Judiciary*, 97th Cong., 1st & 2d sess. 335–36 (Statement of G. Robert Blakey) ("To the degree that I have been involved in [criminal justice] for 20 years, I will tell you unequivocally that the suppression rule, in fact, deters. . . . Anyone who suggests to you the contrary, in my judgment, doesn't know what he is talking about."); Stephen H. Sachs, *The Exclusionary Rule: A Prosecutor's Defense*, Crim. Just. Ethics 28, 30 (Summer/Fall 1982); Stern, *Letter from Judge Herbert Stern to Senator Charles McC. Mathias* (May 12, 1982) ("I have spent my entire career working within the criminal justice system. . . . It is, I think, a slander to suggest that our law enforcement authorities are either so stupid or uncaring that they are . . . undeterred by what the courts say they must do. . . . ") (quoted in Yale Kamisar, *Does (Did) (Should) the Exclusionary Rule Rest on a "Principled Basis" Rather than an "Empirical Proposition"?*, 16 Creighton L. Rev. 565, 599 n.211 (1983)).

155. See Fed. R. Evid. 407, Advisory Committee Note ("The rule rests on two grounds. (1) The conduct is not in fact an admission, since the [subsequent remedial measures are] equally consistent with injury by mere accident or through contributory negligence. . . . (2) The other, and more impressive, ground for exclusion rests on a social policy of encouraging people to take, or at least not discouraging them from taking, steps in furtherance of added safety.").

156. 447 U.S. 727, 729–30 (1980).

157. *Michigan v. Tucker*, 417 U.S. 433, 444 (1974).

158. *New York v. Quarles*, 467 U.S. 649, 657 (1984).

159. See Grano, *Confessions, Truth and the Law* at 218 (cited in note 80) ("The current situation is doctrinally unstable, with two lines of irreconcilable cases coexisting to give the Court a choice between allowing or disallowing the police to have the necessary tools for effective interrogation.")

160. See David Simon, *Homicide: A Year on the Killing Streets* 202–03 (1991):

Even if a suspect does indeed ask for a lawyer, he must—at least according to the most aggressive interpretation of *Miranda*—ask definitively: "I want to talk to a lawyer and I don't want to answer questions until I do."

Anything less leaves room for a good detective to maneuver. The distinctions are subtle and semantic:

"Maybe I should get a lawyer."

"Maybe you should. But why would you need a lawyer if you don't have anything to do with this?"

Or: "I think I should talk to a lawyer."

"You better be sure. Because if you want a lawyer then I'm not going to be able to do anything for you."

161. See Martin Yant, *Presumed Guilty* ch. 4 (Prometheus Books, 1991).

162. 391 U.S. 145, 147–48 (1968) (holding that the Fourteenth Amendment gives state defendants the right to a jury trial).

163. *Williams v. Florida*, 399 U.S. 78, 86–103 (1970).

164. *Apodaca v. Oregon*, 406 U.S. 404, 410–14 (1972); *Johnson v. Louisiana*, 406 U.S. 356, 359–63 (1972).

165. 380 U.S. 400, 403–06 (1965) (stating that the Fourteenth Amendment incorporates the Sixth Amendment confrontation clause).

166. See *Bourjaily v. United States*, 483 U.S. 171, 175–84 (1987) (upholding the admissibility of coconspirator statements without either general or particular evidence of trustworthiness).

167. 397 U.S. 358, 361–68 (1970) (due process requires that government prove guilt beyond reasonable doubt).

168. *Patterson v. New York*, 432 U.S. 197, 201–16 (1977).

169. *Strickland*, 466 U.S. at 687.

CHAPTER 6

1. See Chapter 1, § 1.

2. See, e.g., *Cleveland Board of Educ. v. Loudermill*, 470 U.S. 532 (1985); *Perry v. Sinderman*, 408 U.S. 593 (1972); Charles A. Reich, *The New Property*, 73 Yale L.J. 733 (1964).

3. See, e.g., *Loudermill*, 470 U.S. 532; Douglas Laycock, *Due Process and Separation of Powers: The Effort to Make the Due Process Clause Nonjusticiable*, 60 Texas L. Rev. 875 (1982).

4. If one reads "vel" in Chapter 39 as "and," it follows that the "judgment of peers" provides the procedure by which the "law of the land" will be applied. See George Burton Adams, *The Origin of the English Constitution* 266 (Yale U. Press, 1912). If one reads "vel" as "or," however, Chapter 39 should still be read as a royal pledge to comply with preexisting, largely customary, law. Whether the form of trial was a judgment of peers, or by battle, compurgation, or ordeal as provided by the "law of the land," in either case the *substance* of the law to be applied was customary, as opposed to the royal prerogative. See F.M. Powicke, *Per Iudicium Parium vel per Legem Terrae*, in *Magna Carta: Commemorative Essays* 96, 100–103 (Royal Historical Society, Henry Elliot Malden ed. 1917); Paul Vinogradoff, *Magna Carta, C. 39*, in id. 78, 85 ("The struggle was waged to secure trial in properly constituted courts of justice and in accordance with established law. The latter requirement would apply equally to substantive rules as far as they existed, and to procedure; it was in fact a declaration in favour of legality all around.").

5. See *Reno v. Flores*, 507 U.S. 292, 316 (1993) (O'Connor, J., concurring) ("The institutionalization of an adult by the government triggers heightened, substantive due process scrutiny. There must be a 'sufficiently compelling' governmental interest to justify such action, usually a punitive interest in imprisoning the convicted criminal or a regulatory interest in forestalling danger to the community."); *Foucha v. Louisiana*, 504 U.S. 71, 80–81 (1992); *United States v. Salerno*, 481 U.S. 739, 748 (1987) ("[S]ufficiently compelling governmental interests can justify detention of dangerous persons.").

6. See *Jacobson v. Massachusetts*, 197 U.S. 11, 22–39 (1905).

7. *Salerno*, 481 U.S. at 745–55.

8. See *Kansas v. Hendricks*, 521 U.S. 346, 356–60 (1997); *Addington v. Texas*, 441 U.S. 418, 425–33 (1979).

9. E.g., *Lochner v. New York*, 198 U.S. 45 (1905).

10. See, e.g., John Hart Ely, *Democracy and Distrust* 18 (Harvard U. Press, 1980).

11. See, e.g., Raoul Berger, *Liberty and the Constitution* 29 Ga. L. Rev. 585, 586 (1995).

12. See, e.g., *Adamson v. California*, 332 U.S. 46, 89–92 (1947) (Black, J., dissenting).

13. Ely, *Democracy and Distrust* at 18 (cited in note 10).

14. See, e.g., Suzanna Sherry, *Natural Law in the States*, 61 U. Cin. L. Rev. 171 (1992). The role of natural law in legal thought, Sherry notes, diminished during the antebellum years. To the degree that our positive law directs us to understand nineteenth-century legal thought, however, we should recognize that positivism is far more prevalent now than then.

15. See Robert E. Riggs, *Substantive Due Process in 1791*, 1990 Wis. L. Rev. 941, 977–84.

16. See *Murray's Lessee v. Hoboken Land & Improvement Co.*, 59 U.S. (18 How.) 272, 276–80 (1856).

17. Id. at 276.

18. 55 U.S. 539, 547–48 (1853).

19. 55 U.S. at 553.

20. 60 U.S. (19 How.) 393 (1857).

21. See 60 U.S. at 450–53.

22. Edward S. Corwin, *The Doctrine of Due Process of Law Before the Civil War*, 24 Harv. L. Rev. 460, 476–77 (1911).

23. Ely, *Democracy and Distrust* at 16 (cited in note 10).

24. 60 U.S. at 624 (Curtis, J., dissenting).

25. See 60 U.S. at 626 (referring to Fifth Amendment due process clause as "this restriction on the legislative power").

26. See, e.g., Michael Kent Curtis, *No State Shall Abridge: The Fourteenth Amendment and the Bill of Rights* 46–47 (Duke U. Press, 1986) (Republican platforms in 1856 and 1860 declared that the due process clause of Fifth Amendment barred congressional support of slavery in the territories.).

27. See, e.g., Cong. Globe, 38th Cong., 1st Sess. 1479–83 (1864) (statement of Sen. Sumner) (describing pending Thirteenth Amendment as redundant but desirable, and explaining theory that Fifth Amendment due process clause always had prohibited slavery).

28. See Laurence H. Tribe, *Taking Text and Structure Seriously: Reflections on Free-Form Method in Constitutional Interpretation*, 108 Harv. L. Rev. 1221, 1297 n.247 ("Although the Fourteenth Amendment of course overruled certain key aspects of *Dred Scott*—principally its holding that slaves, former slaves, and their descendants could not be citizens for federal purposes—there is no evidence that the Fourteenth Amendment was understood by anyone to be overruling *Dred Scott*'s structural premise that not every formally proper legislative enactments meets the constitutional definition of 'law.' ")

29. Cong. Globe, 39th Cong., 1st Sess. 1090 (Feb. 28, 1866) (statement of Rep. Bingham). Bingham argued that the antebellum Constitution did not confer power on Congress to legislate for the protection of individual rights against state government. He then said:

And I am perfectly confident that that grant of power would have been there [i.e., in the antebellum constitution] but for the fact that its insertion in the Constitution would have been utterly incompatible with the existence of slavery in any State; for although slaves might not have been admitted to be citizens they must have been admitted to be persons. That is the only reason why it was not there. . . .

As slaves were not protected by the Constitution, there might be some color of excuse for the slave States in their disregard for the requirement of the bill of rights as to slaves and refusing them protection in life or property. . . . Gentlemen who oppose this amendment oppose the grant of power to enforce the bill of rights.

The apparent upshot is that where the due process clause applies, it forbids slavery.

30. John Norton Pomeroy, *An Introduction to the Constitutional Law of the United States* § 250 at 160 (Hurd and Houghton, 1868).

31. Thomas M. Cooley, *A Treatise on the Constitutional Limitations Which Rest Upon the Legislative Power of the States of the American Union* 351–58 (Little, Brown, and Co., 1st ed. 1868).

32. Id. at 386.

33. Id. at 390–91.

34. See id. at 582–84; id. at 596.

35. 80 U.S. 654, 655–56 (1872).

36. 80 U.S. at 662.

37. See John V. Orth, *Taking from A and Giving to B: Substantive Due Process and the Case of the Shifting Paradigm*, 14 Const. Comment. 337 (1997).

38. I would not go so far as to say that only specific practices thought to violate due process in 1868 should be held to violate due process today. Professor Tribe makes an important point when he says that "reading part of the Fourteenth Amendment's first section through an 1868 lens and part of the same section through an evolving lens—seems more than a bit schizophrenic." Tribe, 108 Harv. L. Rev. at 1298 n.247 (cited in note 28). It is, however, entirely possible for positive law to incorporate morality by reference. A positive law forbidding "unreasonable searches" or "negligence" does not necessarily freeze the content of reasonableness or negligence. A positive law forbidding "gross injustice" likewise need not freeze the content of "gross injustice." But a positive law forbidding *gross* injustice does suppose a distinction between gross and considerable injustice; simple injustice according to contemporary lights would never be enough.

In any event, the framers who argued that Fifth Amendment due process forbade slavery *in the states* surely realized they were making an argument that would not have prevailed in 1791. So it seems fair to say that at least with respect to the Fourteenth Amendment due process clause, there was some realization that the content of natural law was not fixed by the ideas of the founding generation.

39. See Chapter 2, § 1.

40. See, e.g., Ely, *Democracy and Distrust* at 25–30 (cited in note 10).

41. For a striking illustration, *Gitlow v. New York* relies on *Coppage v. Kansas*. See *Gitlow v. New York*, 268 U.S. 652, 666 n.9 (1925).

42. Different theories have been offered to support the sexual privacy cases, but their strongest defense probably lies with substantive due process as articulated by Justice Harlan in *Poe v. Ullman*, 367 U.S. 497, 539–45 (1961) (Harlan, J., dissenting). In any event this seems to be the theory on which *Roe* and *Griswold* now depend. See *Planned Parenthood of Southeastern Pa. v. Casey*, 505 U.S. 833, 846–49 (1992).

43. *Meyer v. Nebraska*, 262 U.S. 390 (1923); *Pierce v. Society of Sisters*, 268 U.S. 510 (1925); *Skinner v. Oklahoma*, 316 U.S. 535 (1942).

44. See Ely, *Democracy and Distrust* at 43–54 (cited in note 10).

45. For an excellent analysis and critique of this feature of our constitutional law, see Sherry F. Colb, *Freedom from Incarceration: Why is this Right Different from All other Rights?*, 69 N.Y.U. L. Rev. 781 (1994). Whatever the merits of her suggested strict scrutiny of laws authorizing imprisonment, more rigorous judicial scrutiny of the substantive criminal law would not alter my arguments about constitutional criminal procedure. Surely the state has a compelling interest in punishing murder, but that does not justify punishing people during murder investigations or convicting innocent people on murder charges.

46. *Robinson v. California*, 370 U.S. 660 (1962).

47. Compare *Solem v. Helm*, 463 U.S. 277 (1983) with *Harmelin v. Michigan*, 501 U.S. 957 (1991).

48. Consider, for example, *Foucha v. Louisiana*, 504 U.S. 71 (1992). Foucha was acquitted on grounds of insanity, committed, and then pronounced sane. His continued detention was subject to strict scrutiny, even though only rational basis scrutiny would have applied to a state statute abolishing the insanity defense.

49. *Schall v. Martin*, 467 U.S. 253, 263–68 (1984).

50. *United States v. Salerno*, 481 U.S. 739, 746–50 (1987).

51. See Wayne R. LaFave, *Arrest: The Decision to Take a Suspect into Custody* 437–38 (Little, Brown, and Co., 1965).

52. See Adams, *English Constitution* at 266 (cited in note 4).

53. See Powicke, *Magna Carta* at 100–03 (cited in note 4); Riggs, 1990 Wis. L. Rev. at 949–52 (cited in note 15).

54. See sources cited in note 4, *supra*.

55. See Chapter 1, § 1.

56. See *Johnson v. Glick*, 481 F.2d 1028, 1030–34 (2d Cir. 1973); Bradley M. Campbell, Comment, *Excessive Force Claims: Removing the Double Standard*, 53 U. Chi. L. Rev. 1369, 1390–91 (1986) ("The underlying concern when police use excessive force is precisely that the police have been able to 'skip the trial' and proceed directly to punishing the detainee.").

57. See *Graham v. Connor*, 490 U.S. 386, 392–99 (1989).

58. See *Tennessee v. Garner*, 471 U.S. 1, 7 (1985).

59. See *United States v. Russell*, 411 U.S. 423, 432 (1973); *Hampton v. United States*, 425 U.S. 484, 495 n.7 (1976) (Powell, J., concurring).

60. 424 U.S. 319, 334–35 (1976).

61. See *United States v. Raddatz*, 447 U.S. 667, 677–79 (1980); *Ake v. Oklahoma*, 470 U.S. 68, 77–83 (1985).

62. *Medina v. California*, 505 U.S. 437, 442–53 (1992).

63. See 2 John Henry Wigmore, *Evidence in Trials at Common Law* § 508 (Little, Brown, and Co., James H. Chadbourn ed. 1979) (citing Hale and describing common-law rebuttable presumption of incompetence below ages fourteen and seven).

64. See id. at § 575.

65. At common-law joint defendants were barred from testifying as parties, although they could give evidence if charged separately. See id. at § 580.

66. For the common-law pedigree of the so-called voucher rule, see 3A John Henry Wigmore, *Evidence in Trials at Common Law* § 896 (Little, Brown, and Co., James H. Chadbourn ed. 1970).

67. See *Washington v. Texas*, 388 U.S. 14 (1967) (striking down bar on coconspirator testimony under Sixth Amendment compulsory process clause); *Chambers v. Mississippi*,

410 U.S. 284 (1973) (striking down voucher rule on due process grounds); *Rock v. Arkansas*, 483 U.S. 44 (1987) (striking down on compulsory process grounds ban on testimony by accused who had been subjected to hypnosis prior to trial).

68. See Jerold H. Israel, *Free Standing Due Process and Criminal Procedure: The Supreme Court's Search for Interpretive Guidelines*, 45 St. L. U. L.J. 303, 417–18 (2001).

69. *Rideau v. Louisiana*, 373 U.S. 723, 726–27 (1963).

70. *United States v. Bagley*, 473 U.S. 667, 674–78 (1985); *Brady v. Maryland*, 373 U.S. 83, 86–88 (1963).

71. *Foster v. California*, 394 U.S. 440, 442–43 (1969) (excluding suggestive lineup on due process grounds).

72. *Crane v. Kentucky*, 476 U.S. 683, 687–91 (1986) (conducting a due process and compulsory process analysis); *Chambers v. Mississippi*, 410 U.S. 284, 294–302 (1973).

73. *Napue v. Illinois*, 360 U.S. 264, 269–71 (1959); *Mooney v. Holohan*, 294 U.S. 103, 112 (1935).

74. See *Estelle v. Williams*, 425 U.S. 501, 503–12 (1976) (holding that defendant had waived right to appear in street clothes).

75. *Miller v. Pate*, 386 U.S. 1, 6 (1967).

76. *In re Winship*, 397 U.S. 358, 361–68 (1970).

77. 316 U.S. 455, 461–62 (1942).

78. As Judge Friendly put it, in the article that mapped out *Mathews* before that decision came down:

The required degree of procedural safeguards varies directly with the importance of the private interest affected and the need for and usefulness of the particular safeguard in the given circumstances and inversely with the burden and any other adverse consequences of affording it. Even amplified in this way, such a balancing test is uncertain and subjective, but the more elaborate specification of the relevant factors may help to produce more principled and predictable decisions.

"Some Kind of Hearing," 123 U. Pa. L. Rev. 1267, 1278 (1975) (footnotes omitted).

79. See, e.g., Alfred C. Aman & William T. Mayton, *Administrative Law* § 7.65 at 184 (West, 1993) ("[T]he Court emphasized that in applying this three-part test the courts should not address the circumstances of the individual claiming due process, but the courts should instead consider the 'generality' of cases. The balancing process prescribed by the Court is, therefore, overtly utilitarian and legislative-like.") (footnote omitted).

80. See Jerry L. Mashaw, *The Supreme Court's Due Process Calculus for Administrative Adjudication in* Mathews v. Eldridge: *Three Factors in Search of a Theory of Value*, 44 U. Chi. L. Rev. 28 (1976).

81. See Israel, 45 St. L. U. L.J. at 423–24 (cited in note 68):

In the course of applying the traditional fundamental fairness standard as prescribed by *Medina*, a court, in its analysis of the impact of the challenged state procedure upon the structural prerequisites of fairness, is likely to consider many of the same factors as it would in applying *Mathews*. However, it will do so from a perspective that prohibits only a serious undermining of the structural prerequisite rather than one that considers whether the state has struck a reasonable balance in failing to produce a procedure that would better implement that structural prerequisite. . . . In this sense, the *Medina* Court does appear to eschew balancing and to utilize an inquiry that is "narrower."

(footnotes omitted).

82. 470 U.S. 68 (1985).

83. See Chapter 1, § 1.

84. See *supra* notes 69–76 and accompanying text.

85. *Atwater v. City of Lago Vista*, 531 U.S. 990 (2001) (holding that the Fourth Amendment does not prohibit custodial arrest, booking, and jailing of motorist for offenses of driving without seatbelt and driving children without seatbelts).

86. 392 U.S. 1 (1968).

87. 453 U.S. 454 (1981).

88. On the inevitability of this project, see Richard H. Fallon, Jr., *Foreword: Implementing the Constitution*, 111 Harv. L. Rev. 54 (1997).

89. Compare *Maryland v. Craig*, 497 U.S. 836 (1990) (upholding testimony of a child witness by closed-circuit television only when trial court makes fact-specific finding of likely trauma from live testimony) with *White v. Illinois*, 502 U.S. 346 (1992) (admitting a child declarant's unrecorded, uncross-examined statements under the statements for purposes of medical diagnosis exception to the hearsay rule).

90. 378 U.S. 1 (1964). For the argument that *Malloy* should be overruled, see my paper, *Foreword: Against Police Interrogation—and the Privilege Against Self-Incrimination*, 78 J. Crim. L. & Criminology 699 (1988).

91. 395 U.S. 784 (1969).

92. See my paper, *At the Borders of the Fourth Amendment: Why a Real Due Process Test Should Replace the Outrageous Government Conduct Defense*, 1993 U. Ill. L. Rev. 261.

93. See *United States v. Dixon*, 509 U.S. 688 (1993). *Dixon* overruled *Grady v. Corbin*, 495 U.S. 508 (1990), which had held that the double-jeopardy clause bars prosecution for an offense if the government's proof must include proof of conduct that constitutes an offense for which the defendant had previously been prosecuted. *Grady* was too rigid by far, for in many instances the government has a good excuse for not joining more serious charges to lesser ones arising from the same transaction. *Dixon*'s return to a same-evidence, as distinct from a same-conduct test, however, is as undemanding as *Grady* was rigid. Once again, preoccupation with the specific text of the Bill of Rights deflected the Court from asking sensible questions about whether a challenged procedure risks erroneous convictions or amounts to punishment in its own right.

94. 397 U.S. 436, 437–44 (1970).

95. See *Ashe*, 397 U.S. at 443–44. Even a Bill of Rights maven like Akhil Amar admits that collateral estoppel "cannot easily be crammed into the Double Jeopardy Clause in light of the syntax, grammar, purpose and history of the Clause." Akhil Reed Amar, *Double Jeopardy Law Made Simple*, 106 Yale L.J. 1807, 1816 (1997) (footnote omitted).

96. See, e.g., Wayne R. LaFave & Jerold H. Israel, 2 *Criminal Procedure* § 17.4(a) (West, 1984).

97. See id.; *Ashe*, 397 U.S. at 448, 459 (Brennan, J., concurring).

98. For illustrative approaches, see LaFave & Israel, 2 *Criminal Procedure* at § 17.4 (cited in note 96).

99. For an excellent discussion of rules that could reduce the risk of misidentification, see Gary L. Wells & Eric P. Seelau, *Eyewitness Identification: Psychological Research and Legal Policy on Lineups*, 1 Psychol. Pub. Policy & L. 765 (1995).

100. 391 U.S. 145 (1968).

101. *Apodaca v. Oregon*, 406 U.S. 404, 407–14 (1972); *Johnson v. Louisiana*, 406 U.S. 356, 359–63 (1972). When, however, the jury is composed of six, rather than twelve, unanimity is required. *Burch v. Louisiana*, 441 U.S. 130, 134–39 (1979).

102. *Singer v. United States*, 380 U.S. 24, 27–34 (1965).

103. William Blackstone, 1 *Commentaries* *134.

104. See my paper, *Criminal Procedure, Footnote Four, and the Theory of Public Choice: OR, Why Don't Legislatures Give a Damn About the Rights of the Accused?*, 44 Syr. L. Rev. 1079 (1993).

105. This is not to deny that ordinary citizens may overrate the risk of victimization. See Sarah Sun Beal, *What's Law Got to Do with It? The Political, Social, Psychological and other Non-Legal Factors Influencing the Development of (Federal) Criminal Law*, 1 Buffalo Crim. L. Rev. 23 (1997).

106. See, e.g., Sarah Sun Beal, *Reporters Draft for the Working Group on Principles to Use When Considering the Federalization of Criminal Law*, 46 Hastings L.J. 1277 (1995).

107. See Chapter 1, § 1.

108. Thomas M. Cooley, *Preface to Blackstone's Commentaries* xxv (Callaghan & Cockroft, 2d ed. 1871).

109. Pomeroy, *Introduction to the Constitutional Law of the United States* §§ 235–38 at 149–52 (cited in note 30).

110. Id. § 231 at 145–46.

111. Id. § 242 at 154–55.

112. Id.

113. *Prudential Insurance Co. of Am. v. Cheek*, 259 U.S. 530, 543 (1922).

114. *Gitlow v. New York*, 268 U.S. 652, 666 (1925).

115. *O'Neil v. Vermont*, 144 U.S. 323, 332 (1892).

116. See Chapter 1, § 3; Chapter 2, § 2.

117. See Chapter 1, § 3; Chapter 2, § 1.

118. 316 U.S. 455 (1942).

119. 287 U.S. 45, 59–66 (1932).

120. 297 U.S. 278, 285–87 (1936).

121. *Weeks v. United States*, 232 U.S. 383, 389–95 (1914).

122. *Agnello v. United States*, 269 U.S. 20, 35 (1925).

123. *Carroll v. United States*, 267 U.S. 132, 147–53 (1925).

124. *Olmstead v. United States*, 277 U.S. 438, 462–64 (1928).

125. In *Chimel v. California*, 395 U.S. 752, 755 (1969), Justice Stewart noted for the Court that prior decisions on the scope of search incident to arrest "have been far from consistent, as even the most cursory review makes evident." Justice Harlan, concurring, characterized the body of precedent as "bad Fourth Amendment law." 395 U.S. at 769 (Harlan, J., concurring).

126. *New York v. Belton*, 453 U.S. 454, 460–61 (1981).

127. *United States v. Ross*, 456 U.S. 798 (1982).

128. 451 U.S. 477, 481–87 (1981).

129. For the argument that Article III prohibits the Court from formulating doctrine in rule-like terms, see Joseph D. Grano, *Prophylactic Rules in Criminal Procedure: A Question of Article III Legitimacy*, 80 Nw. U.L. Rev. 100 (1985).

130. See, e.g., *Craig v. Boren*, 429 U.S. 190, 195–97 (1976); *Eisenstadt v. Baird*, 405 U.S. 438, 443–46 (1972); *Barrows v. Jackson*, 346 U.S. 249, 257 (1953).

131. There is a large literature comparing and contrasting rules and standards. See, e.g., Frederick Schauer, *Playing by the Rules: A Philosophical Examination of Rule-Based Decisionmaking in Law and in Life* (Oxford U. Press, 1991); Duncan Kennedy, *Form and Substance in Private Law Adjudication*, 89 Harv. L. Rev. 1685 (1976); Colin S. Diver, *The Optimal Precision of Administrative Rules*, 93 Yale L.J. 65 (1983). An early contribution

focusing on rule-making by the police is Kenneth Culp Davis, *Discretionary Justice: A Preliminary Inquiry* (Louisiana State U. Press, 1969).

132. See Louis Kaplow, *Rules Versus Standards: An Economic Analysis*, 42 Duke L.J. 557 (1992).

133. See, e.g., Anthony G. Amsterdam, *Perspectives on the Fourth Amendment*, 58 Minn. L. Rev. 349, 378–91 (1974); Wayne R. LaFave, *"Case by Case Adjudication" Versus "Standardized Procedures": The* Robinson *Dilemma*, 1974 S. Ct. Rev. 127, 141.

134. Wayne R. LaFave, 3 *Search and Seizure: A Treatise on the Fourth Amendment* § 7.1(c) at 446 (West, 3d ed. 1996).

135. See Albert W. Alschuler, *Bright Line Fever and the Fourth Amendment*, 45 U. Pitt. L. Rev. 227 (1984); Craig M. Bradley, *The Failure of the Criminal Procedure Revolution* (U. Pennsylvania Press, 1993); Christopher Slobogin, *The World Without a Fourth Amendment*, 39 U.C.L.A. L. Rev. 1 (1991).

136. Alschuler, 45 U. Pitt. L. Rev. at 287 (cited in note 135).

137. Slobogin, 39 U.C.L.A. L. Rev. at 72 (cited in note 135).

138. Id. at 74 n.237.

139. Craig M. Bradley & Joseph L. Hoffmann, *Public Perception, Justice, and the "Search for Truth" in Criminal Cases*, 69 S. Cal. L. Rev. 1267, 1278 n.32 (1996).

140. Professor Alschuler, for example, finds *Miranda* clear enough to deliver a biting disparagement of the Burger Court's infidelities to that decision. See Albert W. Alschuler, *Failed Pragmatism: Reflections on the Burger Court*, 100 Harv. L. Rev. 1436, 1442 (1987).

141. See *Belton*, 453 U.S. at 470 (Brennan, J., dissenting); Alschuler, 45 U. Pitt. L. Rev. at 281–82 (cited in note 135); Wayne R. LaFave, *The Fourth Amendment in an Imperfect World: On Drawing "Bright Lines" and "Good Faith*," 43 U. Pitt. L. Rev. 307, 326 (1982).

142. See H.L.A. Hart, *The Concept of Law*, ch. 7 (Clarendon Press, 1961).

143. See Alschuler, 45 U. Pitt. L. Rev. at 286 (cited in note 135).

144. See LaFave, 3 *Search and Seizure* § 7.1(c) at 451 n.86 & 452 n.88 (cited in note 134).

145. See id. at 451 n.86.

146. Id. at 448 (footnote omitted).

147. This is the conclusion of a survey of the cases conducted six years after the decision. See David M. Silk, Comment, *When Bright Lines Break Down: Limiting* New York v. Belton, 136 U. Pa. L. Rev. 281 (1987).

148. See William J. Stuntz, *Warrants and Fourth Amendment Remedies*, 77 Va. L. Rev. 881, 897 (1991) ("[I]n the ordinary case the probable cause standard is likely to be fairly predictable to those who apply it.").

149. The discussion of constitutional *stare decisis* repeats the claims I made in *Constitutional Theory for Criminal Procedure*: Miranda, Dickerson, *and the Continuing Quest for Broad-but-Shallow*, 43 Wm. & Mary L. Rev. 1 (2001).

150. For accessible discussions of Arrow's Theorem, see Daniel A. Farber & Philip P. Frickey, *Law and Public Choice* 38–42 (U. Chicago Press, 1991); Herbert Hovenkamp, *Arrow's Theorem: Ordinalism and Republican Government*, 75 Iowa L. Rev. 949 (1990). Both discussions focus on the application of the theorem to legislatures. The seminal contribution on the application of Arrow's theorem to the Supreme Court is Frank H. Easterbrook, *Ways of Criticizing the Court*, 95 Harv. L. Rev. 802 (1982).

151. See Maxwell L. Stearns, *Standing Back from the Forest: Justiciability and Social Choice*, 83 Cal. L. Rev. 1309 (1995); Maxwell L. Stearns, *Standing and Social Choice: Historical Evidence*, 144 U. Pa. L. Rev. 309 (1995).

152. There is an interesting debate in the social choice literature about the relative merits of issue voting and outcome voting. Appellate courts in the United States rely on outcome voting; that is to say, rather than take separate votes on each issue necessary for decision, the judges take a single vote on whether to affirm or reverse. The downside to outcome voting is that decisions need not resolve the issues clearly or consistently; the downside to issue voting is that defining the issues and selecting the order in which they are considered could have dramatic and arbitrary influences on the development of the law. Scrupulous *stare decisis* takes a middle course between issue and outcome voting. Outcome voting is retained, but resolutions of particular issues in prior cases would be deemed controlling. This would minimize the incoherence risked by outcome voting, without risking the manipulation of the agenda that issue voting might invite. On issue voting and outcome voting, see Lewis A. Kornhauser & Lawrence G. Sager, *Unpacking the Court*, 96 Yale L.J. 82 (1986); David Post & Steven C. Salop, *Rowing Against the Tidewater: A Theory of Voting by Multijudge Panels*, 80 Geo. L.J. 743 (1992); John M. Rogers, *"I Vote This Way Because I'm Wrong": The Supreme Court Justice as Epimenides*, 79 Ky. L.J. 439 (1991); Colloquy, *Appellate Court Voting Rules*, 49 Vand. L.J. 993 (1996).

153. See *Dickerson*, 530 U.S. at 465 ("I dissent from today's decision, and until § 3501 is repealed, will continue to apply it in all cases where there has been a sustainable finding that the defendant's confession was voluntary.") (Scalia, J., dissenting).

154. Justice Brennan, who dissented from the prophylactic-rules cases (*Tucker* excepted, where he concurred in the result on a retroactivity theory), suspected as much. See *Mosley*, 423 U.S. at 112 (Brennan, J., dissenting) ("Today's distortion of *Miranda*'s constitutional principals can be viewed only as yet another stop in the erosion and, I suppose, ultimate overruling of *Miranda*'s enforcement of the privilege against self-incrimination.").

155. 358 U.S. 1 (1958).

156. See *United States v. Nixon*, 418 U.S. 683, 704 (1974) ("responsibility of this Court as ultimate interpreter of the Constitution"); *Powell v. McCormack*, 395 U.S. 486, 549 (1974) ("the responsibility of this Court to act as the ultimate interpreter of the Constitution.").

157. See 530 U.S. at 437 ("But Congress may not legislatively supersede our decisions interpreting and applying the Constitution.").

158. See *City of Boerne v. Flores*, 521 U.S. 507, 516–20 (1997).

159. See, e.g., Daniel A. Farber, *The Supreme Court and the Rule of Law*: Cooper v. Aaron *Revisited*, 1982 U. Ill. L. Rev. 387, 388–89 (reviewing criticism of *Cooper*).

160. For an exhaustive defense of coordinate review, see Michael Stokes Paulsen, *The Most Dangerous Branch: Executive Power to Say What the Law Is*, 83 Geo. L.J. 217 (1994).

161. See Larry Alexander & Frederick Schauer, *On Extrajudicial Constitutional Interpretation*, 110 Harv. L. Rev. 1359 (1997).

162. Id. at 1377 ("When the Constitution is subject to multiple interpretations, a preconstitutional norm must referee among interpretations to decide what is to be done.").

163. See Suzanna Sherry, *Justice O'Connor's Dilemma: The Baseline Question*, 39 Wm. & Mary L. Rev. 865, 892 (1998):

Although the Court has never squarely faced the question of whether its own decisions should be taken as a baseline by dissenting members, it has frequently reiterated the broader view that its decisions are the binding law of the land. Usually it does so in the course of chastising some rebellious state or federal official—or some recalcitrant lower federal court—for ignoring the Court's pronouncements. The language that the Court has used in this context tends to confirm the unitary nature of the Supreme Court, brushing off the views of individual Justices as largely irrelevant.

164. See William J. Brennan, Jr., *In Defense of Dissents*, 37 Hastings L.J. 427, 437 (1986):

This kind of dissent, in which a judge persists in articulating a minority view of the law in case after case presenting the same issue, seeks to do more than simply offer an alternative analysis—that could be done in a single dissent and does not require repetition. Rather, this type of dissent constitutes a statement by the judge as an individual: "Here I draw the line." Of course, as a member of a court, one's general duty is to acquiesce in the rulings of that court and to take up the battle behind the court's new barricades. But it would be a great mistake to confuse this unquestioned duty to obey and respect the law with an imagined obligation to subsume entirely one's own views of constitutional imperatives to the views of the majority.

Justice Brennan certainly did not claim any moral advantage over lower court judges; he began his lecture *In Defense of Dissents* with fulsome praise of Mathew Tobriner. Nor do I readily imagine that great egalitarian claiming a moral advantage over a humble citizen called for jury duty in a capital case. What seems unjustified in Justice Brennan's explanation is the equation of a right to express a different view and a right to have that view alter the legal rights and liabilities of parties in litigation. A judge is of course free to follow precedent but file a concurring opinion criticizing that precedent. Justice Harlan did just that with respect to *Miranda* in *Orozco v. Texas*. In a nutshell, Justice Brennan seems to be equating the unquestioned right of every person to express political dissent with the dubious right of an outvoted judge to influence the outcome of a lawsuit contrary to the governing law. Interestingly, the most plausible defense of the Brennan and Marshall death penalty dissents takes the view that these dissenting votes actually followed the logic of *Gregg*, their expressed abolitionist justifications notwithstanding. See Jordan M. Steiker, *The Long Road Up From Barbarism: Thurgood Marshall and the Death Penalty*, 71 Tex. L. Rev. 1131 (1993).

165. Cf. *Webster v. Doe*, 486 U.S. 592, 608 (1988) (Scalia, J., concurring and dissenting) ("there are many governmental decisions that are not at all subject to judicial review.").

166. As a representative in Congress, James Madison argued that Congress had no constitutional power to charter a national bank. His view was later rejected by the Supreme Court, and when, as president, he had to decide whether to veto a bill reauthorizing the bank—an experience in his view had proved the bank to be in the public interest—he deferred to prevailing constitutional opinion and signed the bill. See Drew R. McCoy, *The Last of the Fathers: James Madison and the Republican Legacy* 81 (Cambridge U. Press, 1989).

167. 428 U.S. 153 (1976).

168. The proposition that precedents count as law is of course a conclusion, not a justification. A necessary, if not sufficient, condition of that status is that they must, like statutes and the Constitution itself, be accepted widely as authoritative. See Kent Greenawalt, *The Rule of Recognition and the Constitution*, 85 Mich. L. Rev. 621, 630 (1987) ("In sum, one cannot imagine any normative theory of law [normative in the sense that the theory opposes conventionalist theories of law] in which the law of a particular society could be identified wholly independently of socially accepted practices."). The observation that constitutional law consists mostly of Supreme Court cases, however, has become commonplace. See, e.g., David A. Strauss, *Common Law Constitutional Interpretation*, 63 U. Chi. L. Rev. 877, 877 (1996) ("when people interpret the Constitution, they

rely not just on the text but also on the elaborate body of law that has developed, mostly through judicial decisions, over the years."); Edward Rubin, *Politics, Doctrinal Coherence, and the Art of Treatise Writing* (review of Chemerinksy, *Constitutional Law: Principles and Policies* (Aspen Law & Business, 1997)), 21 Seattle U.L. Rev. 837, 837 (1998) ("The common law character of constitutional law makes a treatise on the subject a necessity."); Henry Paul Monaghan, *Stare Decisis and Constitutional Adjudication*, 88 Colum. L. Rev. 723 (1988) (fact that much constitutional doctrine is at odds with original understanding proves the precedent is source of constitutional law that may trump original understanding); Farber, 1982 U. Ill. L. Rev. 387 (cited in note 159) (acceptance of *Brown* and *Cooper* by many who disagreed with those decisions indicates that constitutional precedents are law, although where precedent fits in hierarchy of constitutional law is debatable).

169. See Charles Fried, *Impudence*, 1992 S. Ct. Rev. 155 (1992) (elegant argument too nuanced to be captured accurately by parenthetical).

170. See, e.g., *Buchanan v. Kentucky*, 483 U.S. 402, 407–08 n.6 (1987) ("A death-qualified jury is one from which prospective jurors have been excluded for cause in light of their inability to set aside their views about the death penalty that would prevent or substantially impair the performance of [their] duties as [jurors] in accordance with [their] instructions and [their] oath. The prosecutor may remove such potential jurors. . . . ") (citations and internal quotations marks omitted; brackets original in *Buchanan*).

171. Compare *Woodson v. North Carolina*, 428 U.S. 280 (1976) (five-justice majority, including Brennan and Marshall, holds mandatory death penalty statute unconstitutional) and *Sumner v. Shuman*, 483 U.S. 66 (1987) (six-justice majority, including Brennan and Marshall, holds that statute mandating death penalty for murder committed by prisoner serving life-without-parole is unconstitutional) with *Lockett v. Ohio*, 438 U.S. 586 (1978) (four justices conclude that state statute gives insufficient scope to consideration of mitigating circumstances; Justice Marshall concurs on ground that death penalty is *per se* unconstitutional; two other justices concur on yet other, but respective, grounds) and *Eddings v. Oklahoma*, 455 U.S. 104 (1982) (five-justice majority, including Brennan and Marshall, holds that death penalty jury must be allowed to consider any mitigating factor proffered by the defense). The tension in the Eighth Amendment cases is generally agreed on, regardless of ideological attitudes toward the death penalty. See *Callins v. Collins*, 510 U.S. 1141, 1141–42 (1994) (Scalia, J., concurring in denial of certiorari) ("this Court has attached to the imposition of the death penalty two quite incompatible sets of commands: The sentencer's discretion to impose death must be closely confined, but the sentencer's discretion *not* to impose death (to extend mercy) must be unlimited.") (citations omitted); id. at 1149 (Blackmun, J., dissenting from the denial of certiorari) ("Experience has shown that the consistency and rationality promised in *Furman* are inversely related to the fairness owed the individual when considering a sentence of death. A step toward consistency is a step away from fairness."); Carol S. Steiker & Jordan M. Steiker, *Sober Second Thoughts: Reflections on Two Decades of Constitutional Regulation of Capital Punishment*, 109 Harv. L. Rev. 355, 382 (1995) ("This tension between *Gregg*'s seeming insistence on channeling and *Woodson*'s seeming insistence on uncircumscribed consideration of mitigating evidence constitutes the central dilemma in post-*Furman* capital punishment law.").

172. Justice Brennan himself recognized a judge's "general duty . . . to acquiesce in the rulings of that court" and equated this with an "unquestioned duty to obey and respect the law." See Brennan, 37 Hastings L.J. at 437 (cited in note 164).

173. *Burnet v. Coronado Oil & Gas Co.*, 285 U.S. 393, 405–10 (1932) (Brandeis, J., dissenting).

174. 505 U.S. 833, 867 (1992) (plurality opinion).

175. See, e.g., Wayne R. LaFave, Jerold H. Israel, & Nancy J. King, 1 *Criminal Procedure* § 2.6(c) (West, 3d ed. 2000) ("Acceptance of Selective Incorporation in the Post-1960s").

176. See U.S. News & World Rep. 27 (June 3, 1996).

177. See Chapter 3, § 2.

178. See, e.g., Morgan Cloud, *The Dirty Little Secret*, 43 Emory L.J. 1311 (1994).

179. See, e.g., *United States v. Bayless*, 921 F. Supp. 211 (S.D.N.Y. 1996) (district judge reversed prior suppression order regarding large quantities of drugs after popular outcry against decision).

180. In 1992 I served as a reporter for a series of seminars for Illinois judges. It was there that I learned of two unwritten exceptions to the exclusionary rule: the kilogram exception (exclusionary rule does not apply to narcotics seizures in excess of one kilogram) and the retention exception (exclusionary rule does not apply in the six months prior to a judge's retention election).

181. A phrase made famous by John Kaplan, *The Limits of the Exclusionary Rules*, 26 Stan. L. Rev. 1027, 1037 (1974).

182. For a fuller account, see Donald Dripps, *Akhil Amar on Criminal Procedure and Constitutional Law: "Here I Go Down that Wrong Road Again,"* 74 N.C.L. Rev. 1559, 1616–21 (1996).

183. See *Manson v. Brathwaite*, 432 U.S. 98 (1977); *Neil v. Biggers*, 409 U.S. 188 (1972).

184. See, e.g., Wayne R. LaFave & Jerold H. Israel, 1 *Criminal Procedure* § 7.4 at 585–86 (West, 1984).

185. *Arizona v. Youngblood*, 488 U.S. 51 (1988).

186. Those who would abolish the exclusionary rule in favor of tort suits typically insist on these or similar modifications. See, e.g., Richard Posner, *Rethinking the Fourth Amendment*, 1981 S. Ct. Rev. 49, 62–68.

187. A point emphasized in William J. Stuntz, *The Virtues and Vices of the Exclusionary Rule*, 20 Harv. J.L. & Pub. Pol'y 443 (1997).

188. See id. at 446; Dripps, 74 N.C.L. Rev. at 1618 n.268 (cited in note 182).

189. For a fuller defense of the contingent exclusionary rule, see Donald A. Dripps, *The Case for the Contingent Exclusionary Rule*, 38 Am. Crim. L. Rev. 1 (2001). For a thoughtful but skeptical comment, see George C. Thomas III, *Judges are not Economists and Other Reasons to be Skeptical of Contingent Suppression Orders: A Response to Professor Dripps*, 38 Am. Crim. L. Rev. 47 (2001).

190. See Dripps, 74 N.C.L. Rev. at 1618–19 (cited in note 182).

191. See National Criminal Justice Commission, *The Real War on Crime* 115 (Steven Donziger ed. 1996); Michael Tonry, *Malign Neglect—Race, Crime, and Punishment in America* 109–11 (Oxford U. Press, 1995).

192. See, e.g., David Cole, *The Paradox of Race and Crime: A Comment on Randall Kennedy's "Politics of Distinction,"* 83 Geo. L.J. 2547, 2557 (1995).

193. David Cole, *No Equal Justice: Race and Class in the American Criminal Justice System* 190 (New Press, 1999).

194. See Tracey Maclin, *Race and the Fourth Amendment*, 51 Vand. L. Rev. 333, 344–54 (1998); David A. Harris, *Factors for Reasonable Suspicion: When Black and*

Poor Means Stopped and Frisked, 69 Ind. L.J. 659 (1994); Cole, *No Equal Justice* at 34–41 (cited in note 193).

195. See *Washington v. Davis*, 426 U.S. 229 (1976).

196. See *Personnel Administrator v. Feeney*, 442 U.S. 256, 276–80 (1979).

197. See *Village of Arlington Heights v. Metropolitan Housing Dev. Corp.*, 429 U.S. 252, 266–68 (1977).

198. Id. at 265–66.

199. 517 U.S. 806 (1996).

200. For the most part the courts have rejected equal protection challenges to police practices. The Supreme Court's treatment of *prosecutorial* discretion is usually carried over to analysis of *police* discretion, hardly an inevitable move. Compare *United States v. Armstrong*, 517 U.S. 456 (1996) with *United States v. Avery*, 128 F.3d 974 (6th Cir. 1997); *United States v. Bullock*, 94 F.3d 896 (4th Cir. 1996); *United States v. Bell*, 86 F.3d 820 (8th Cir. 1996). But cf. *United States v. Jennings*, 985 F.2d 562, 1993 WL 5927 (6th Cir. Jan. 13, 1993) (unpublished decision) (adopting burden-shifting approach but rejecting claim on the facts).

201. See, e.g., Randall Kennedy, *Race, Crime, and the Law* 19–20 (Pantheon, 1997).

202. On the disproportionate frequency of black offending and victimization, see, e.g., id. at 145; James Q. Wilson & Richard Herrnstein, *Crime and Human Nature* 461–66 (Simon and Schuster, 1985); Tonry, *Malign Neglect* ch. 2 (cited in note 191).

203. 517 U.S. 456 (1996).

204. For cogent criticism of *Armstrong*, see Cole, *No Equal Justice* at 158–61 (cited in note 193); Richard McAdams, *Race and Selective Prosecution: Discovering the Pitfalls of* Armstrong, 73 Chi.-Kent L. Rev. 605 (1998).

205. See *supra* notes 191–94.

206. See, e.g., Cole, *No Equal Justice* at 23–25 (cited in note 193); Kennedy, *Race, Crime, and the Law* at 151–53 (cited in note 201).

207. *United States v. Martinez-Fuerte*, 428 U.S. 543, 563 (1976).

208. See, e.g., John E. Nowak & Ronald D. Rotunda, *Constitutional Law* § 14.4 at 633–34 n.63 (West, 5th ed. 1995).

209. See *United States v. Prandy-Binett*, 995 F.2d 1069, 1075 (D.C. Cir. 1993) (Edwards, J., dissenting) ("The real harm done is not fully apparent, because we usually do not hear of the cases of the innocent people who are stopped by the police.") (footnote omitted).

210. See Kennedy, *Race, Crime, and the Law* at 159–61 (cited in note 201).

211. See, e.g., *United States v. Avery*, 128 F.3d at 984 n.5.

212. On the basic incompatibility of objective Fourth Amendment standards and the motivational inquiry in equal protection jurisprudence, see Andrew D. Leipold, *Objective Tests and Subjective Bias: Some Problems of Discriminatory Intent in the Criminal Law*, 73 Chi.-Kent L. Rev. 559 (1998).

213. Many commentators have advocated such a development. See, e.g., Leipold, 73 Chi.-Kent L. Rev. at 594–95 (cited in note 212); Carl J. Schifferle, *After* Whren v. United States: *Applying the Equal Protection Clause to Racially Discriminatory Enforcement of the Law*, 2 Mich. L. & Pol'y Rev. 159 (1997).

214. As Michael Tonry writes in the book from which I borrow the "malign neglect" phrase:

The criminal law's mens rea analyses, for example, offer the law's most highly developed schema for analyzing culpability and moral responsibility. In the criminal law, purpose and knowledge are equally culpable states of mind. An action taken with a purpose to kill is no more culpable than an action taken with some other purpose in mind but with knowledge that a death will probably result. . . . By analogy with the criminal law, the responsibility of the architects of contemporary crime control policies is the same as if their primary goal had been to lock up disproportionate numbers of young blacks.

Tonry, *Malign Neglect* at 32 (cited in note 191).

CHAPTER 7

1. See, e.g., *United States v. Garsson*, 291 F. 646, 649 (S.D.N.Y. 1923) (L. Hand, J.) (specter of innocent man being convicted is "unreal dream"); Alan M. Dershowitz, *The Best Defense* xxi (Random House, 1982) ("Almost all criminal defendants are, in fact, guilty.").

2. See, e.g., *More Money for the Defense*, Chi. Trib. § 1, at 22 (May13, 1999) (since capital punishment was reinstated in 1977, "Illinois has condemned to death 11 men who later were determined to be innocent—the worst wrongful conviction record of any state besides Florida.").

3. See Edward Connors et al., *Convicted by Juries, Exonerated by Science: Case Studies in the Use of DNA Evidence to Establish Innocence After Trial* 20 (U.S. Dept. Of Justice, 1996) (Justice Department survey of more than 21,000 cases found that 16% of tests were inconclusive, 23% exonerating, and the remainder inculpatory). The exculpatory tests account for about 27% of the conclusive results.

4. See, e.g., C. Ronald Huff et al., *Convicted But Innocent: Wrongful Conviction and Public Policy* 66 (Sage Publications, 1996).

5. See *United States v. Wade*, 388 U.S. 218, 223–39 (1967).

6. See *Kirby v. Illinois*, 406 U.S. 682, 687–91 (1972).

7. See *United States v. Ash*, 413 U.S. 300 (1973).

8. See *Manson v. Braithwaite*, 432 U.S. 98, 109–17 (1977); *Neil v. Biggers*, 409 U.S. 188, 196–201 (1972).

9. See Wayne R. LaFave & Jerold H. Israel, 1 *Criminal Procedure* § 7.4(d) (West, 2d ed. 1992).

10. See, e.g., Elizabeth F. Loftus, *Eyewitness Testimony* 33 (Harvard U. Press, 1979).

11. The discussion that follows is based on Gary L. Wells & Eric P. Seelau, *Eyewitness Identification: Psychological Research and Legal Policy on Lineups*, 1 Psychol. Pub. Pol'y & L. 765 (1995), which summarizes the psychological research and recommends both the reasonable-resemblance rule and the veil-of-ignorance requirement.

12. It would be possible to go further by involving defense counsel in choosing the foils in a process similar to jury selection. See my paper *Miscarriages of Justice and the Constitution*, 2 Buffalo Crim. L. Rev. 635, 656–64 (1999). A reasonableness standard enforced by the exclusionary rule, or by a contingent exclusionary rule, would be less complicated and might achieve nearly as much.

13. See Brian L. Cutler et al., *Conceptual, Practical, and Empirical Issues Associated with Eyewitness Identification Test Media*, in *Adult Eyewitness Testimony: Current Trends and Developments* 163, 175 (Press Syndicate of the University of Cambridge, David Frank Ross et al. eds., 1994).

14. See *United States v. White*, 401 U.S. 745, 749 (1971) (plurality opinion).

15. See *United States v. Simpson*, 813 F.2d 1462, 1465–71 (9th Cir. 1987).

16. See *United States v. Penn*, 647 F.2d 876, 889–82 (9th Cir. 1980); *United States v. Levasseur*, 699 F. Supp. 995, 1002–08 (D. Mass. 1988), aff'd sub nom., *United States v. Curzi*, 867 F.2d 36 (1st Cir. 1989).

17. See Mark Curriden, *The Informant Trap: Secret Threat to Justice*, Nat. L.J. at A1, A30 (Feb. 20, 1995):

Practically all warrants now rely on information from CIs [confidential informants] in some manner. In 1980, 46% of the warrants cited an informant's word; in 1993, 92% of them did.

More disturbing is a trend toward the use of only one confidential source by agents applying for warrants. Reliance on a single CI has jumped from 24% of the warrants in 1980 to 71% in 1993.

18. Cf. *Hoffa. v. United States*, 385 U.S. 293, 319 (1966) (Warren, C.J., dissenting) (the informant "became the equivalent of a bugging device which moved with Hoffa wherever he went.").

19. See, e.g., Lawrence Marshall, *What Do We Owe People Who Have Been Wrongly Convicted?*, Chi. Trib. C17 (July 7, 1996) (role of informants in false convictions of the Ford Heights Four); Mark Curriden, *Making Crime Pay*, A.B.A. J. at 42, 43 (June 1991) ("Informants have lied under oath, sending innocent people to jail, just to make deals with authorities.").

20. *United States v. Caceres*, 440 U.S. 741, 744 (1979); *United States v. White*, 401 U.S. 745, 748–49 (1971) (plurality opinion); *Hoffa*, 385 U.S. at 300–02; *Lewis v. United States*, 385 U.S. 206, 209–11 (1966); *Osborn v. United States*, 385 U.S. 323, 326–29 (1966); *Lopez v. United States*, 373 U.S. 427, 437–40 (1963); *On Lee v. United States*, 343 U.S. 747, 751–58 (1952).

21. For the argument that the Fourth Amendment could be applied to informants, see Tracey Maclin, *Informants and the Fourth Amendment: A Reconsideration*, 74 Wash. U. L.Q. 573 (1996).

22. See *Hoffa*, 385 U.S. at 317 (Warren, C.J., dissenting) ("I see nothing wrong with the Government's thus verifying the truthfulness of the informer and protecting his credibility in this fashion.") (footnote omitted). In *On Lee*, however, Warren took the view that the informant must testify for a recording to be admissible, a position that seems at war with itself. If a recording is better evidence than an informant's word, why not just admit the tape and leave it to the defense to call the informant if the tape is claimed to be inaccurate?

23. See, e.g., Andrew Jay McClurg, *Bringing Privacy Law Out of the Closet: A Tort Theory of Liability for Intrusions in Public Places*, 73 N.C. L. Rev. 989, 1018 (1995) ("Whatever snooping devices concerned Warren and Brandeis, it is safe to say they are to modern surveillance technology what the slide rule is to the personal computer.") A typical law enforcement body recorder is the size of a paperback novel and costs about $6,000. See Joseph Sjostrom, *Du Page Has a Beef About Bugs*, Chi. Trib. 1 (Feb. 1, 1991). Transmitters that might be hidden in a prison cell might be much smaller. The cost, compared to what is now paid to informants, is paltry.

The equipment sometimes malfunctions and background noises can make conversations difficult to hear. Where the government did everything possible to obtain an accurate record of conversations between suspect and informant but for technical reasons the recording failed, I would not penalize the government by excluding the informant's testimony.

24. *Kuhlmann v. Wilson*, 477 U.S. 436, 459 (1986) approves admitting the defendant's post-indictment admissions to an informant so long as the informant took no action "beyond merely listening, that was designed deliberately to elicit incriminating remarks."

25. See, e.g., Huff et al., *Convicted But Innocent* at 77 (cited in note 4); *More Money for the Defense* (cited in note 2) ("Although each of the 11 bungled death penalty cases is unique, a recurring factor has been inept, bargain-basement legal counsel during the initial, and crucial, phases of the adjudicatory process.").

26. See my paper, *Ineffective Assistance of Counsel: The Case for an* ex Ante *Parity Standard*, 88 J. Crim. L. & Criminology 242, 245–51 (1997) (reviewing research).

27. See, e.g., Richard Klein & Robert Spangenberg, *The Indigent Defense Crisis* 6 (The Association, 1993) (noting that in Knox County, Kentucky, hourly rates were *cut* from $20 per hour for out-of-court and $30 per-hour for in-court time; Virginia caps compensation at $350 for most felonies).

28. See, e.g., Charles J. Ogletree, Jr., *An Essay on the New Public Defender for the 21st Century*, Law & Contemp. Probs. 81, 85 (Winter 1995) ("the typical public defender is burdened by a dramatic lack of resources, limited training and supervision, an unconscionable caseload, unhealthy working conditions, and unsympathetic police, prosecutors, judges, witnesses, and jurors with whom she must work.") (footnotes omitted).

29. See Tony Kennedy, *Public Defenders Outside Hennepin, Ramsey Counties Vote to Join Union*, Minn. Star-Trib. D3 (May 14, 1999). The Hennepin and Ramsey County public defenders had previously joined AFSCME.

30. See Dripps, 88 J. Crim. L. & Criminology at 286–91 (cited in note 26).

31. As that notorious sentimentalist, Judge Easterbrook, puts it:

Compulsion to represent criminal defendants is scandalous, as are the payment scales offered to these involuntary agents. You get what you pay for. Unwilling workers do not provide the level of care that not only defendants but also society are entitled to expect. At average expenses *per case* as low as $63, states are providing so little legal time to defendants that much exculpatory evidence and many valid defenses go begging. A shortfall is less pressing at the bargaining stage than at trial . . . but is unjustifiable in either setting. A society professing the inestimable value of liberty, yet prepared to pay more than $20,000 per year to incarcerate a person, should be willing to pay the market cost of supplying defense services. . . . The medicare system pays the market price for medical services; the military system pays the market price for soldiers and aircraft carriers; the criminal justice system should pay the market price for legal services.

Frank H. Easterbrook, *Plea Bargaining as Compromise*, 101 Yale L.J. 1969, 1973–74 (1992) (footnotes omitted).

32. See *Strickland*, 466 U.S. 668, 687 (1984) (establishing deficient performance under the first prong of the test "requires showing that counsel made errors so serious that counsel was not functioning as the 'counsel' guaranteed the defendant by the Sixth Amendment.").

33. See, e.g., Yale Kamisar et al., *Modern Criminal Procedure* 25 (West, 8th ed. 1994); Brian Forst, *Criminal Justice System: Measurement of Performance*, in 2 *Encyclopedia of Crime and Justice* 479 (Free Press, Stanford Kadish ed. 1983).

34. See Floyd Feeney et al., *Arrests Without Conviction: How Often They Occur and Why* 243 (U.S. Dept. of Justice, 1983) ("Most suspects who are arrested but not convicted are thought by police and prosecutors to be guilty. Many cases of this kind are dropped for evidentiary reasons but could and probably ought to be salvaged.").

35. See *The Jury and the Search for Truth: The Case Against Excluding Relevant Evidence at Trial*, Hearings before the Senate Judiciary Committee, 104th Cong., 143 (1995) (statement of Thomas Y. Davies).

36. See Feeney et al., *Arrests Without Conviction* at 196–99 (cited in note 34) (summarizing studies); Brian Forst et al., *Arrest Convictability as a Measure of Police Performance* 9–10 (U.S. Dept. of Justice, 1982) (in every jurisdiction studied, evidence and witness problems were cited as reasons for rejecting at least 50% of the arrests declined for prosecution; in three jurisdictions the figure was 70% or higher); Michael Graham, *Witness Intimidation: The Law's Response* 1–8 (Quorum Books, 1985) (reviewing studies).

37. See *Pointer v. Texas*, 380 U.S. 400, 408–09 (1965) (Harlan, J., concurring).

38. See Jeremy A. Blumenthal, *A Wipe of the Hands, A Lick of the Lips: The Validity of Demeanor Evidence in Assessing Witness Credibility*, 72 Neb. L. Rev. 1157 (1993); Olin Guy Wellborn III, *Demeanor*, 76 Cornell L. Rev. 1075 (1991).

39. John Henry Wigmore, V *Evidence* § 1367 at 32 (Little, Brown, and Co., James H. Chadbourn rev. 1974).

40. Graham, *Witness Intimidation* at 252–80 (cited in note 36).

41. See *Country of Riverside v. McLaughlin*, 500 U.S. 44, 52–59 (1991).

42. See Walter V. Schaefer, *The Suspect and Society: Criminal Procedure and Converging Constitutional Doctrines* (Northwestern U. Press, 1967); Marvin E. Frankel, *From Private Rights Toward Public Justice*, 51 N.Y.U. L. Rev. 516 (1976); Paul G. Kauper, *Judicial Examination of the Accused: A Remedy for the Third Degree*, 30 Mich. L. Rev. 1224 (1932); Roscoe Pound, *Legal Interrogation of Persons Accused or Suspected of Crime*, 24 J. Crim. L. & Crimin. 1014 (1934).

43. 380 U.S. 609 (1965).

44. 378 U.S. 1 (1964).

45. Jeremy Bentham, 5 *Rationale of Judicial Evidence* 229–47 (Hunt and Clarke, 1827).

46. The most thorough modern reexamination of the privilege concludes that the privilege has no accessible justification. See David Dolinko, *Is There a Rationale for the Privilege Against Self-Incrimination?*, 33 U.C.L.A. L. Rev. 1063 (1986).

47. See *Adamson v. California*, 332 U.S. 46, 50–53 (1947); *Twining v. New Jersey*, 211 U.S. 78, 91–99 (1908). Dicta in *Palko v. Connecticut*, 302 U.S. 319 (1937) also declared that the privilege was not "fundamental" for purposes of the Fourteenth Amendment due process.

48. Donald A. Dripps, Foreword: *Against Police Interrogation—and the Privilege Against Self-Incrimination*, 78 J. Crim. L. & Criminology 699 (1988).

49. See *Crist v. Bretz*, 437 U.S. 28, 52–53 (1978) (Powell, J., dissenting); *Apodaca v. Oregon*, 406 U.S. 404, 373 (1972) (Powell, J., concurring); *Duncan v. Louisiana*, 391 U.S. 145, 181 (1968) (Harlan, J., dissenting).

50. See 380 U.S. at 615.

51. See id. at 613 (quoting *Wilson v. United States*, 149 U.S. 60, 66 (1893)).

52. See Fed. R. Evid. 801(D)(1); Fed. R. Evid. 804(B)(1).

53. See *California v. Green*, 399 U.S. 149, 153–64 (1970) (defense cross-examination of witness at preliminary hearing satisfies confrontation clause); *Ohio v. Roberts*, 448 U.S. 56, 67–73 (1980) (defense cross-examination at preliminary hearing of witness unavailable for trial satisfies confrontation clause).

54. See Graham, *Witness Intimidation* at 280 n.1 (cited in note 36).

55. See id. at 270–71.

56. See *White v. Illinois*, 502 U.S. 346, 358 (1992) (Thomas, J., concurring).

57. See *Coy v. Iowa*, 487 U.S. 1012, 1015–20 (1988). The majority in *Maryland v. Craig*, 497 U.S. 836, 844–50 (1990), over Justice Scalia's dissent, upheld very limited use of trial testimony by means of closed-circuit television in cases in which in-court testimony might traumatize a child witness so as to impair the truth-finding mission.

58. *White v. Illinois*, 502 U.S. 346 (1992).

59. See Albert W. Alschuler, *Implementing the Criminal Defendant's Right to Trial: Alternatives to the Plea Bargaining System*, 50 U. Chi. L. Rev. 931, 1023–24 (1983); Gerald Miller et al., *The Effects of Videotape Testimony in Jury Trials: Studies on Juror*

Decision Making, Information Retention, and Emotional Arousal, 1975 B.Y.U. L. Rev. 331; Diane M. Hartmus, *Videotrials*, 23 Ohio N.U. L. Rev. 1, 6–11 (1996).

60. See *supra* note 38.

61. See *Morse v. Hanks*, 172 F.3d 983, 985 (7th Cir. 1999); *United States v. Horsley*, 864 F.2d 1543, 1545 (11th Cir. 1989).

62. See, e.g., David Cole, *No Equal Justice: Race and Class in the American Criminal Justice System* 120–23 (New Press, 1999).

63. See Michael A. Fletcher, *Driven to Extremes: Black Men Take Steps to Avoid Police Stops*, Wash. Post A1 (Mar. 29, 1996).

64. As Randall Kennedy puts it, "[e]ven when rightful rules are underenforced, they are still worth fighting for because they set the standard for legitimacy, standards which, like magnets, exert a pull that affects the order of things." *Race, Crime, and the Law* 163 (Pantheon, 1997) (footnote omitted).

65. See Cole, *No Equal Justice* at 53 (cited in note 62) (advocating warning of right to refuse consent to search, and noting that the FBI routinely provides just such a warning).

66. See Adrian J. Barrio, *Rethinking* Schneckloth v. Bustamonte: *Incorporating Obedience Theory into the Supreme Court's Conception of Voluntary Consent*, 1997 U. Ill. L. Rev. 215.

67. See William J. Stuntz, *Race, Class, and Drugs*, 98 Colum. L. Rev. 1795, 1799 (1998) ("It is easier, often a great deal easier, to catch and punish sellers and buyers in lower-class markets than it is to catch and punish their higher-end counterparts.").

EPILOGUE

1. H.L.A. Hart, *Essays on Bentham: Jurisprudence and Political Theory* 39 (1982).

Bibliography

BOOKS

Adams, George Burton. *The Origin of the English Constitution*. Yale U. Press, 1912.

Aman, Alfred C., & William T. Mayton. *Administrative Law*. West, 1993.

Baker, Liva. Miranda: *Crime, Law, and Politics*. Atheneum, 1983.

Bean, Philip. *Punishment*. Martin Robertson, 1981.

Beaney, William M. *Right to Counsel*. U. Michigan Press, 1955.

Bentham, Jeremy. 5 *Rationale of Judicial Evidence*. Hunt and Clarke, 1827.

Berger, Raoul. *The Fourteenth Amendment and the Bill of Rights*. U. Oklahoma Press, 1989.

Bishop, Joel Prentiss. 1 *Commentaries on the Law of Criminal Procedure*. Little, Brown, and Co., 2d ed. 1872.

Bishop, Joel Prentiss. 1 *New Criminal Procedure*. T.H. Flood, 4th ed. 1895.

Bishop, Joel Prentiss. 1 *Commentaries on the Law of Criminal Procedure*. Little, Brown, and Co., 1866.

Bishop, Joel Prentiss. 1 *Commentaries on the Law of Criminal Procedure*. Little, Brown, and Co., 3d ed. 1880.

Blackstone, William. 1 *Commentaries*. 1765.

Blackstone, William. 4 *Commentaries*.

Bond, James E. *No Easy Walk to Freedom: Reconstruction and the Ratification of the Fourteenth Amendment*. Praeger, 1997.

Bork, Robert. *The Tempting of America*. Free Press, 1990.

Bradley, Craig M. *The Failure of the Criminal Procedure Revolution*. U. Pennsylvania Press, 1993.

Breckenridge, Adam Carlyle. *Congress Against the Court.* U. Nebraska Press, 1970.

The Burger Court: The Counter-Revolution that Wasn't. Vincent Blasi ed. Yale University Press, 1983.

Busch, Francis. *Guilty or Not Guilty?* Bobbs-Merrill, 1952.

Choper, Jesse H. *Judicial Review and the National Political Process.* U. Chicago Press, 1980.

Church, William. *A Treatise on the Writ of Habeas Corpus.* Bancroft-Whitney, 1893.

Clark, W.L. *Handbook on Criminal Procedure.* West Publishing, 1895.

Cole, David. *No Equal Justice: Race and Class in the American Criminal Justice System.* New Press, 1999.

Connors, Edward et al. *Convicted by Juries, Exonerated by Science: Case Studies in the Use of DNA Evidence to Establish Innocence After Trial.* U.S. Dept. of Justice, 1996.

Cooley, Thomas M. *Preface to Blackstone's Commentaries.* Callaghan & Cockroft, 2d ed. 1871.

Cooley, Thomas M. *A Treatise on the Constitutional Limitations Which Rest Upon the Legislative Power of the States of the American Union.* Little, Brown, and Co., 1st ed. 1868.

Cooley, Thomas. *Treatise on the Constitutional Limitations.* Little, Brown, and Co., 2d ed. 1871.

Cortner, Richard. *The Supreme Court and the Second Bill of Rights.* U. Wisconsin Press, 1981.

Currie, David P. *The Constitution in the Supreme Court.* U. Chicago Press, 1985.

Curtis, Michael Kent. *No State Shall Abridge: The Fourteenth Amendment and the Bill of Rights.* Duke U. Press, 1986.

Cutler, Brian L. et al. *Conceptual, Practical, and Empirical Issues Associated with Eyewitness Identification Test Media,* in *Adult Eyewitness Testimony: Current Trends and Developments.* Press Syndicate of the University of Cambridge, David Frank Ross et al. eds., 1994.

Davis, Kenneth Culp. *Discretionary Justice: A Preliminary Inquiry.* Louisiana State U. Press, 1969.

Dershowitz, Alan M. *The Best Defense.* Random House, 1982.

Duker, William. *A Constitutional History of Habeas Corpus.* Greenwood Press, 1980.

Dworkin, Ronald. *Law's Empire.* Belknap Press, 1986.

Ely, John Hart. *Democracy and Distrust.* Harvard U. Press, 1980.

Encyclopedia of Crime & Justice. Free Press, Sanford Kadish ed. 1983.

Fairman, Charles. *History of the Supreme Court of the United States—Reconstruction and Reunion, Part One.* Macmillan, 1974.

Farber, Daniel A., & Philip P. Frickey. *Law and Public Choice.* U. Chicago Press, 1991.

Feeney, Floyd et al. *Arrests Without Conviction: How Often They Occur and Why.* U.S. Dept. of Justice, 1983.

Flack, Horace Edgar. *The Adoption of the Fourteenth Amendment*. The Johns Hopkins Press, 1908.

Forst, Brian et al. *Arrest Convictability as a Measure of Police Performance*. U.S. Dept. of Justice, 1982.

Frankfurter, Felix. *Mr. Justice Holmes and the Supreme Court*. Harvard U. Press, 1938.

Fried, Charles. *Expressive Aspects of Criminal Procedure* in *An Anatomy of Values*. Harvard U. Press, 1970.

Friedman, Lawrence M. *Crime and Punishment in American History*. Basic Books, 1993.

Friedman, Lawrence, & Robert Percival. *The Roots of Justice*. U. North Carolina Press, 1981.

Goodman, James. *Stories of Scottsboro*. Pantheon, 1994.

Graham, Fred P. *The Self-Inflicted Wound*. Macmillan, 1970.

Graham, Michael. *Witness Intimidation: The Law's Response*. Quorum Books, 1985.

Grano, Joseph D. *Confessions, Truth and the Law*. U. Michigan Press, 1993.

Griswold, Erwin. *The Fifth Amendment Today*. Harvard U. Press, 1955.

Hare, R.M. *Moral Thinking*. Clarendon Press, 1981.

Hart, H.L.A. *The Concept of Law*. Clarendon Press, 1961.

Hart, H.L.A. *Essays on Bentham*. Clarendon Press, 1982.

Hart, H.L.A. *Punishment and Responsibility*. Oxford U. Press, 1968.

Huff, C. Ronald et al. *Convicted But Innocent: Wrongful Conviction and Public Policy*. Sage Publications, 1996.

Kaczorowski, Robert. *The Politics of Judicial Interpretation: The Federal Courts, Department of Justice and Civil Rights, 1866–1876*. Oceana Publications, 1985.

Kalven Jr., Harry, & Hans Zeisel. *The American Jury*. U. Chicago Press, Phoenix ed. 1971.

Kamisar, Yale et al. *Modern Criminal Procedure*. West, 8th ed. 1994.

Kamisar, Yale et al. *Modern Criminal Procedure*. West, 9th ed. 1999.

Kamisar, Yale. *What is an "Involuntary" Confession?*, in *Police Interrogations and Confessions: Essays in Law and Policy* 1980.

Kaplan, John, & Robert Weisberg. *Criminal Law: Cases and Materials*. Little, Brown, 2d ed. 1991.

Kennedy, Randall. *Race, Crime, and the Law*. Pantheon, 1997.

Kent, James. 1 *Commentaries on American Law*. Little, Brown, and Co., Oliver Wendell Holmes, Jr. ed. 1873.

Klein, Richard, & Robert Spangenberg. *The Indigent Defense Crisis*. The Association, 1993.

LaFave, Wayne R. *Arrest: The Decision to Take a Suspect into Custody*. Little, Brown, and Co., 1965.

LaFave, Wayne R. 1 *Search & Seizure*. West, 1987.

LaFave, Wayne R. 3 *Search and Seizure: A Treatise on the Fourth Amendment*. West, 3d ed. 1996.

LaFave, Wayne, & Austin Scott, Jr. *Criminal Law*. West, 2d ed. 1986.

LaFave, Wayne R., & Jerold H. Israel. 1 *Criminal Procedure*. West, 1984.

LaFave, Wayne R., & Jerold H. Israel. 1 *Criminal Procedure*. West, 2d ed. 1992.

LaFave, Wayne R., & Jerold H. Israel. *Criminal Procedure*. West, 2d ed. 1992 & 1997 pocket part.

LaFave, Wayne R., & Jerold H. Israel. 2 *Criminal Procedure*. West, 1984.

LaFave, Wayne R., & Jerold H. Israel. 3 *Criminal Procedure*. West, 1984.

LaFave, Wayne R., Jerold H. Israel, & Nancy J. King. 1 *Criminal Procedure*. West, 3d ed. 2000.

Loewy, Arnold. *Criminal Law: Cases and Materials*. Anderson Publishing, 1991.

Loftus, Elizabeth F. *Eyewitness Testimony*. Harvard U. Press, 1979.

Low, Peter W., John Calvin Jeffries, Jr., & Richard J. Bonnie. *Criminal Law: Cases and Materials*. Foundation Press, 4th ed. 1986.

Maltz, Earl. *Civil Rights, the Constitution, and Congress, 1863–1869*. U. Press of Kansas, 1990.

McCloskey, H.J. *A Nonutilitarian Approach to Punishment* in *Contemporary Utilitarianism*. Michael D. Bayles ed. Anchor Books, 1968.

McCoy, Drew R. *The Last of the Fathers: James Madison and the Republican Legacy*. Cambridge U. Press, 1989.

Mueller, Gerhard O.W. *Crime, Law and the Scholars*. Heinemann Educational, 1969.

National Criminal Justice Commission. *The Real War on Crime*. Steven Donziger ed. 1996.

Nelson, William E. *The Fourteenth Amendment*. Harvard U. Press, 1988.

Newman, Roger K. *Hugo Black*. Pantheon Books, 1994.

Nowak, John E., & Ronald D. Rotunda. *Constitutional Law*. West, 5th ed. 1995.

Nowak, John E., Ronald Rotunda, & J. Nelson Young. 3 *Treatise on Constitutional Law*. West, 1986.

Pomeroy, John Norton. *An Introduction to the Constitutional Law of the United States*. Hurd and Houghton, 1868.

Pound, Roscoe. *The Development of Constitutional Guarantees of Liberty*. Yale U. Press, 1957.

Powicke, F.M. *Per Iudicium Parium vel per Legem Terrae* in *Magna Carta: Commemorative Essays*. Royal Historical Society, Henry Elliot Malden ed. 1917.

Precedent in Law. Laurence Goldstein ed. Oxford U. Press, 1987.

Rawls, John. *A Theory of Justice*. Belknap Press, 1971.

Read, Frank T., & Lucy S. McGough. *Let Them Be Judged: The Judicial Integration of the Deep South*. Scarecrow Press, 1978.

Rotunda, Ronald D., John E. Nowak, & J. Nelson Young. 2 *Treatise on Constitutional Law*. West, 1986.

Scalia, Antonin. *A Matter of Interpretation*. Princeton U. Press, 1997.

Schaefer, Walter V. *The Suspect and Society: Criminal Procedure and Converging Constitutional Doctrines*. Northwestern U. Press, 1967.

Schauer, Frederick. *Playing by the Rules: A Philosophical Examination of Rule-Based Decisionmaking in Law and in Life*. Oxford U. Press, 1991.

Simon, David. *Homicide: A Year on the Killing Streets*. 1991.

Southern Justice. Pantheon, Leon Friedman ed. 1965.

Stephenson, Gilbert. *Race Distinctions in American Law*. D. Appleton, 1910.

Story, Joseph. 2 *Commentaries on the Constitution of the United States*. Little, Brown, and Co., Thomas Cooley ed. 1873.

Story, Joseph. 3 *Commentaries on the Constitution of the United States*. Hilliard, Gray, 1833.

Sunstein, Cass R. *One Case at a Time*. Harvard U. Press, 1999.

Tonry, Michael. *Malign Neglect—Race, Crime, and Punishment in America*. Oxford U. Press, 1995.

Tucker, John Randolph. 2 *The Constitution of the United States*. Henry St. George Tucker ed. Chicago, Callaghan & Co. 1899.

Uviller, H. Richard. *Tempered Zeal*. Contemporary Books, 1980.

Van Duizend, Richard, L. Paul Sutton, & Charlotte Carter. *The Search Warrant Process: Preconceptions, Perceptions, and Practices*. National Center for State Courts, 1985.

Viesselman, P.W. *Abbott's Criminal Trial Practice*. Rochester, N.Y.: Lawyer's Co-Operative Publishing Co., 4th ed. 1939.

Wharton, Francis. 1 *A Treatise on the Criminal Law of the United States, Pleading and Evidence*. Kay and Bro., 6th ed. 1868.

Wharton, Francis. 1 *A Treatise on the Criminal Law of the United States, Principles, Pleading, and Evidence*. Kay and Bro., 7th ed. 1874.

Wharton, Francis. *A Treatise on Criminal Pleading and Practice*. Kay and Bro., 8th ed. 1880.

Wharton, Francis. *A Treatise on Criminal Pleading and Practice*. Kay and Bro., 9th ed. 1889.

Wigmore, John Henry. V *Evidence*. Little, Brown, and Co., James H. Chadbourn rev. 1974.

Wigmore, John. 3 *Evidence*. 3d ed. 1940.

Wigmore, John Henry. 2 *Evidence in Trials at Common Law*. Little, Brown, and Co., James H. Chadbourn ed. 1979.

Wigmore, John Henry. 3A *Evidence in Trials at Common Law*. Little, Brown, and Co., James H. Chadbourn ed. 1970.

Williams, Glanville. *Criminal Law: The General Part*. Stevens, 2d ed. 1961.

Wilson, James Q. *Thinking About Crime*. Basic Books, rev. ed. 1983.

Wilson, James Q., & Richard Herrnstein. *Crime and Human Nature*. Simon and Schuster, 1985.

Yant, Martin. *Presumed Guilty*. Prometheus Books, 1991.

Yarborough, Tinsley E. *Judicial Enigma*. Oxford U. Press, 1995.

Zeisel, Hans. *The Limits of Law Enforcement*. U. Chicago Press, 1982.

PERIODICALS

Alexander, Larry, & Frederick Schauer. *On Extrajudicial Constitutional Interpretation*, 110 Harv. L. Rev. 1359 (1997).

Allen, Francis. *Federalism and the Fourth Amendment: A Requiem for* Wolf, 1961 Sup. Ct. Rev. 1.

Allen, Francis A. *The Supreme Court, Federalism, and State Systems of Criminal Justice*, 8 DePaul L. Rev. 213 (1959).

Allen, Francis. *The Supreme Court and State Criminal Justice*, 4 Wayne L. Rev. 191 (1958).

Alschuler, Albert W. *Bright Line Fever and the Fourth Amendment*, 45 U. Pitt. L. Rev. 227 (1984).

Alschuler, Albert W. *Failed Pragmatism: Reflections on the Burger Court*, 100 Harv. L. Rev. 1436 (1987).

Alschuler, Albert W. *Implementing the Criminal Defendant's Right to Trial: Alternatives to the Plea Bargaining System*, 50 U. Chi. L. Rev. 931 (1983).

Amar, Akhil Reed. *The Bill of Rights and the Fourteenth Amendment*, 101 Yale L.J. 1193 (1992).

Amar, Akhil Reed. *Double Jeopardy Law Made Simple*, 106 Yale L.J. 1807 (1997).

Amar, Akhil Reed. *Fourth Amendment First Principles*, 107 Harv. L. Rev. 757 (1994).

Amsterdam, Anthony G. *Perspectives on the Fourth Amendment*, 58 Minn. L. Rev. 349 (1974).

Amsterdam, Anthony. *The Supreme Court and the Rights of Suspects in Criminal Cases*, 45 N.Y.U. L. Rev. 685 (1970).

Arkin, Marc M. *Rethinking the Criminal Defendant's Right to a Criminal Appeal*, 39 U.C.L.A. L. Rev. 503 (1992).

Aynes, Richard. *On Misreading John Bingham and the Fourteenth Amendment*, 103 Yale L.J. 57 (1993).

Aynes, Richard L. *Charles Fairman, Felix Frankfurter, and the Fourteenth Amendment*, 70 Chi.-Kent L. Rev. 1197 (1995).

Barrett, John Q. *Deciding the Stop and Frisk Cases: A Look Inside the Supreme Court's Conference*, 72 St. John's L. Rev. 749 (1998).

Barrio, Adrian J. *Rethinking* Schneckloth v. Bustamonte: *Incorporating Obedience Theory into the Supreme Court's Conception of Voluntary Consent*, 1997 U. Ill. L. Rev. 215.

Bator, Paul. *Finality in Criminal Law and Federal Habeas Corpus for State Prisoners*, 76 Harv. L. Rev. 441 (1963).

Bazelon, David L. *The Defective Assistance of Counsel*, 42 U. Cin. L. Rev. 1 (1973).

Beal, Sarah Sun. *Reporters Draft for the Working Group on Principles to Use When Considering the Federalization of Criminal Law*, 46 Hastings L.J. 1277 (1995).

Beal, Sarah Sun. *What Law Got to Do with It? The Political, Social, Psychological and other Non-Legal Factors Influencing the Development of (Federal) Criminal Law*, 1 Buffalo Crim. L. Rev. 23 (1997).

Benner, Lawrence A., & Charles T. Samarkos. *Searching for Narcotics in San Diego: Preliminary Findings From the San Diego Search Warrant Project*, 36 Cal. West. L. Rev. 221, (2000).

Berger, Raoul. *Liberty and the Constitution*, 29 Ga. L. Rev. 585 (1995).

Blumenthal, Jeremy A. *A Wipe of the Hands, A Lick of the Lips: The Validity of Demeanor Evidence in Assessing Witness Credibility*, 72 Neb. L. Rev. 1157 (1993).

Bradley, Craig M., & Joseph L. Hoffmann. *Public Perception, Justice, and the "Search for Truth" in Criminal Cases*, 69 S. Cal. L. Rev. 1267 (1996).

Brand, Jeffrey S. *The Supreme Court, Equal Protection, and Jury Selection: Denying That Race Still Matters*, 1994 Wis. L. Rev. 511.

Brennan Jr., William J. *In Defense of Dissents*, 37 Hastings L.J. 427 (1986).

Bright, Stephen, Stephen Kinnard, & David Webster. *Keeping* Gideon *from Being Blown Away*, 4 Crim. Just. 10 (1990).

Campbell, Bradley M. Comment, *Excessive Force Claims: Removing the Double Standard*, 53 U. Chi. L. Rev. 1369 (1986).

Canon, Bradley C. *Is the Exclusionary Rule in Failing Health? Some New Data and a Plea Against a Precipitous Conclusion*, 62 Ky. L.J. 681 (1974).

Carrington, Paul D. *The Twenty-First Wisdom*, 52 Wash. & Lee L. Rev. 333 (1995).

Cassell, Paul G. *The Paths Not Taken: The Supreme Court's Failures in* Dickerson, 99 Mich. L. Rev. 898 (2001).

Cassell, Paul G., & Bret S. Hayman. *Police Interrogation in the 1990s: An Empirical Study of the Effects of* Miranda, 43 U.C.L.A. L. Rev. 839 (1996).

Cassell, Paul G., & Richard Fowles. *Handcuffing the Cops? A Thirty-Year Perspective on* Miranda's *Harmful Effects on Law Enforcement*, 50 Stan. L. Rev. 1055 (1998).

Cloud, Morgan. *The Dirty Little Secret*, 43 Emory L.J. 1311 (1994).

Cloud, Morgan. *The Fourth Amendment During the* Lochner *Era: Privacy, Property, and Liberty in Constitutional Theory*, 48 Stan. L. Rev. 555 (1996).

Cohen, Jacqueline. *Selective Incapacitation: An Assessment*, 1984 U. Ill. L. Rev. 253.

Colb, Sherry F. *Freedom from Incarceration: Why is this Right Different from All other Rights?*, 69 N.Y.U. L. Rev. 781 (1994).

Cole, David. *The Paradox of Race and Crime: A Comment on Randall Kennedy's "Politics of Distinction,"* 83 Geo. L.J. 2547 (1995).

Colloquy. *Appellate Court Voting Rules*, 49 Vand. L.J. 993 (1996).

Comment. *The Coerced Confession Cases in Search of a Rationale*, 31 U. Chi. L. Rev. 313 (1964).

Corwin, Edward S. *The Doctrine of Due Process of Law Before the Civil War*, 24 Harv. L. Rev. 460 (1911).

Court, Andy. *Is There a Crisis?*, Am. Lawyer 46 (Jan./Feb. 1993).

Crosskey, William Winslow. *Charles Fairman, "Legislative History," and the Constitutional Limits on State Authority*, 22 U. Chi. L. Rev. 1 (1954).

Curriden, Mark. *The Informant Trap: Secret Threat to Justice*, Nat. L. J. at A1 (Feb. 20, 1995).

Curriden, Mark. *Making Crime Pay*, A.B.A. J. at 42 (June 1991).

Currie, David. *The Constitution in the Supreme Court: Limitations on State Power, 1865–1873*, 51 U. Chi. L. Rev. 329 (1984).

Damaska, Mirjan. *Evidentiary Barriers to Conviction and Two Models of Criminal Procedure: A Comparative Study*, 121 U. Pa. L. Rev. 506 (1973).

Davies, Thomas Y. *A Hard Look at What We Know (and Still Need to Learn) About the "Costs of the Exclusionary Rule: The NIJ Study and Other Studies of "Lost" Arrests*, 1983 A.B.F. Res. J. 611.

Dershowitz, Alan M., & John Hart Ely. Harris v. New York: *Some Anxious Observations on the Candor and Logic of the Emerging Nixon Majority*, 80 Yale L.J. 1198 (1971).

Developments in the Law—Race and the Criminal Process, 101 Harv. L. Rev. 1472 (1988).

Diamond, Shari Seidman et al. *Realistic Responses to the Limitations of* Batson v. Kentucky, 7 Cornell J. L. & Pub. Pol'y 77 (1997).

Diver, Colin S. *The Optimal Precision of Administrative Rules*, 93 Yale L.J. 65 (1983).

Dolinko, David. *Is There a Rationale for the Privilege Against Self-Incrimination?*, 33 U.C.L.A. L. Rev. 1063 (1986).

Douglas, William. *Stare Decisis*, 49 Colum. L. Rev. 735 (1949).

Dripps, Donald. *Akhil Amar on Criminal Procedure and Constitutional Law: "Here I Go Down that Wrong Road Again,"* 74 N. C. L. Rev. 1559 (1996).

Dripps, Donald. *At the Borders of the Fourth Amendment: Why a Real Due Process Test Should Replace the Outrageous Government Conduct Defense*, 1993 U. Ill. L. Rev. 261.

Dripps, Donald. *Constitutional Theory for Criminal Procedure*: Miranda, Dickerson, *and the Continuing Quest for Broad-but-Shallow*, 43 Wm. & Mary L. Rev. 1 (2001).

Dripps, Donald. *Criminal Procedure, Footnote Four, and the Theory of Public Choice: OR, Why Don't Legislatures Give a Damn About the Rights of the Accused?*, 44 Syr. L. Rev. 1079 (1993).

Dripps, Donald. *Ineffective Assistance of Counsel: The Case for an Ex Ante Parity Standard*, 88 J. Crim. L. & Crimin. 242 (1997).

Dripps, Donald. *Is the* Miranda *Caselaw Really Inconsistent? A Proposed Fifth Amendment Synthesis*, 17 Const. Comment. 19 (2000).

Dripps, Donald. *Living with* Leon, 95 Yale L.J. 906 (1986).

Dripps, Donald. *Miscarriages of Justice and the Constitution*, 2 Buffalo Crim. L. Rev. 635 (1999).

Dripps, Donald. *The Constitutional Status of the Reasonable Doubt Rule*, 75 Cal. L. Rev. 1665 (1987).

Dripps, Donald. *The Exclusivity of the Criminal Law: Toward a "Regulatory Model" of, or "Pathological Perspective" on, the Civil/Criminal Distinction*, 7 J. Contemp. Legal Issues 199 (1996).

Dripps, Donald A. *The Case for the Contingent Exclusionary Rule*, 38 Am. Crim. L. Rev. 1 (2001).

Dripps, Donald A. Foreword: *Against Police Interrogation—and the Privilege Against Self-Incrimination*, 78 J. Crim. L. & Criminology 699 (1988).

Dukakis Now Supports Ban on Furloughs for Murderers, N.Y. Times § I, at 30, col. 6. (Mar. 24, 1988).

Duker, William. *The Fuller Court and State Criminal Process: Threshold of Modern Limitations on Government*, 1980 B.Y.U. L. Rev. 275.

Easterbrook, Frank. *Substance and Due Process*, 1982 Sup. Ct. Rev. 85.

Easterbrook, Frank H. *Plea Bargaining as Compromise*, 101 Yale L.J. 1969 (1992).

Easterbrook, Frank H. *Ways of Criticizing the Court*, 95 Harv. L. Rev. 802 (1982).

Enker, Arnold N., & Sheldon H. Elsen. *Counsel for the Suspect*: Massiah v. United States *and* Escobedo v. Illinois, 49 Minn. L. Rev. 47 (1964).

Fairman, Charles. *Does the Fourteenth Amendment Incorporate the Bill of Rights? The Original Understanding*, 2 Stan. L. Rev. 5 (1949).

Fallon Jr., Richard H. *A Constructivist Coherence Theory of Constitutional Interpretation*, 100 Harv. L. Rev. 1189 (1987).

Fallon Jr., Richard H. Foreword: *Implementing the Constitution*, 111 Harv. L. Rev. 54 (1997).

Fallon Jr., Richard H. *Stare Decisis and the Constitution: An Essay on Constitutional Methodology*, 76 N.Y.U. L. Rev. 570 (2001).

Farber, Daniel A. *The Supreme Court and the Rule of Law*: Cooper v. Aaron *Revisited*, 1982 U. Ill. L. Rev. 387.

Feeney, Floyd, & Patrick Jackson. *Public Defenders, Assigned Counsel, Retained Counsel: Does the Type of Criminal Defense Counsel Matter?*, 22 Rutgers L.J. 361 (1991).

Fletcher, Michael A. *Driven to Extremes: Black Men Take Steps to Avoid Police Stops*, Wash. Post A1 (Mar. 29, 1996).

Foote, Caleb. *Vagrancy-Type Law and its Administration*, 104 U. Pa. L. Rev. 603 (1956).

Frankel, Marvin E. *From Private Rights Toward Public Justice*, 51 N.Y.U. L. Rev. 516 (1976).

Fried, Charles. *Impudence*, 1992 S. Ct. Rev. 155 (1992).

Friendly, Henry J. *Is Innocence Irrelevant? Collateral Attack on Criminal Judgments*, 38 U. Chi. L. Rev. 142 (1970).

Friendly, Henry J. *"Some Kind of Hearing,"* 123 U. Pa. L. Rev. 1267 (1975).

Georgia Pardons Victim 70 Years After Lynching, N.Y. Times A16 (March 12, 1986).

Grano, Joseph D. Rhode Island v. Innis: *A Need to Reconsider the Constitutional Premises Underlying the Law of Confessions*, 17 Am. Crim. L. Rev. 1 (1979).

Grano, Joseph D. *Prophylactic Rules in Criminal Procedure: A Question of Article III Legitimacy*, 80 Nw. U. L. Rev. 100 (1985).

Grano, Joseph D. *Voluntariness, Free Will and the Law of Confessions*, 65 Va. L. Rev. 859 (1979).

Green, Bruce Andrew. *A Functional Analysis of the Effective Assistance of Counsel*, 80 Colum. L. Rev. 1053 (1980).

Greenwalt, Kent. *The Rule of Recognition and the Constitution*, 85 Mich. L. Rev. 621 (1987).

Harris, David A. *The Constitution and Truth Seeking: A New Theory on Expert Services for Indigent Defendants*, 83 J. Crim. L. Criminology 469 (1992).

Harris, David A. *Factors for Reasonable Suspicion: When Black and Poor Means Stopped and Frisked*, 69 Ind. L.J. 659 (1994).

Harrison, John. *Reconstructing the Privileges or Immunities Clause*, 101 Yale L.J. 1385 (1992).

Hart Henry. Foreword: *The Time Chart of the Justices*, 73 Harv. L. Rev. 84 (1959).

Hartmus, Diane M. *Videotrials*, 23 Ohio N.U. L. Rev. 1 (1996).

Hoffman, Joseph L., & William J. Stuntz. *Habeas After the Revolution*, 1993 Sup. Ct. Rev. 65.

Holtzoff, Alexander. *The Right of Counsel Under the Sixth Amendment*, 20 N.Y.U. L. Rev. 1 (1944).

Hovenkamp, Herbert. *Arrow's Theorem: Ordinalism and Republican Government*, 75 Iowa L. Rev. 949 (1990).

Indigent Defense System KO'd, Nat'l L. J. 3 (Feb. 24, 1992).

Israel, Jerold H. *Free Standing Due Process and Criminal Procedure: The Supreme Court's Search for Interpretive Guidelines*, 45 St. L. U. L.J. 303 (2001).

Johnson, Sheri Lynn. *Black Innocence and the White Jury*, 83 Mich. L. Rev. 1611 (1985).

Juviler, Michael R. *A Prosecutor's Perspective*, 72 St. John's L. Rev. 741 (1998).

Kamisar, Yale. Brewer v. Williams, Massiah, *and* Miranda: *What is "Interrogation"? When Does it Matter?*, 67 Geo. L. J. 1 (1978).

Kamisar, Yale. *Can (Did) Congress "Overrule"* Miranda, 85 Cornell L. Rev. 883 (2000).

Kamisar, Yale. *A Dissent from the* Miranda *Dissents: Some Comments on the "New" Fifth Amendment and the Old "Voluntariness" Test*, 65 Mich. L. Rev. 59 (1966).

Kamisar, Yale. *Does (Did) (Should) the Exclusionary Rule Rest on a "Principled Basis" Rather than an "Empirical Proposition"?*, 16 Creighton L. Rev. 565 (1983).

Kamisar, Yale. Foreword: Brewer v. Williams—*A Hard Look at a Discomfiting Record*, 66 Geo. L. J. 209 (1977).

Kamisar, Yale. Gideon v. Wainwright *A Quarter Century Later*, 10 Pace L. Rev. 343, 351–52 (1990).

Kamisar, Yale. *Police Investigatory Practices*, in Vincent Blasi ed., *The Burger Court: The Counter-Revolution that Wasn't* (Yale University Press, 1983).

Kamisar, Yale. *The Right to Counsel and the Fourteenth Amendment: A Dialogue on "the Most Pervasive Right" of an Accused*, 30 U. Chi. L. Rev. 1 (1962).

Kamisar, Yale. *The Warren Court (Was It Really So Defense-Minded), the Burger Court (Is It Really So Prosecution Oriented)?*, in Vincent Blasi ed., *The Burger Court: The Counter-Revolution that Wasn't* (Yale University Press, 1983).

Kamisar, Yale. Wolf *and* Lustig *Ten Years Later: Illegal State Evidence in State and Federal Courts*, 43 Minn. L. Rev. 1083 (1959).

Kaplan, John. *The Limits of the Exclusionary Rules*, 26 Stan. L. Rev. 1027 (1974).

Kaplow, Louis. *Rules Versus Standards: An Economic Analysis*, 42 Duke L.J. 557 (1992).

Kauper, Paul G. *Judicial Examination of the Accused: A Remedy for the Third Degree*, 30 Mich. L. Rev. 1224 (1932).

Kennedy, Duncan. *Form and Substance in Private Law Adjudication*, 89 Harv. L. Rev. 1685 (1976).

Kennedy, Tony. *Public Defenders Outside Hennepin, Ramsey Counties Vote to Join Union*, Minn. Star-Trib. D3 (May 14, 1999).

Klarman, Michael. *The Racial Origins of Modern Criminal Procedure*, 99 Mich. L. Rev. 48 (2000).

Klein, Susan R. *Identifying and (Re)Formulating Prophylactic Rules, Safe Harbors, and Incidental Rights in Constitutional Criminal Procedure*, 99 Mich. L. Rev. 1030 (2001).

Kornhauser, Lewis A., & Lawrence G. Sager. *Unpacking the Court*, 96 Yale L.J. 82 (1986).

LaFave, Wayne R. *"Case by Case Adjudication" Versus "Standardized Procedures": The* Robinson *Dilemma*, 1974 S. Ct. Rev. 127.

LaFave, Wayne R. *The Fourth Amendment in an Imperfect World: On Drawing "Bright Lines" and "Good Faith,"* 43 U. Pitt. L. Rev. 307 (1982).

Lawson, Gary. *The Constitutional Case Against Precedent*, 17 Harv. J. L. & Pub. Pol. 23 (1994).

Lawson, John D. *The Trial of George S. Twitchell for the Murder of Mary E. Hill*, 6 Am. St. Tr. 1 (1916).

Laycock, Douglas. *Due Process and Separation of Powers: The Effort to Make the Due Process Clause Nonjusticiable*, 60 Texas L. Rev. 875 (1982).

Lee, Evan Tsen. *Section 2254(d) of the New Habeas Statute: An (Opinionated) User's Manual*, 51 Vand. L. Rev. 103 (1998).

Leipold, Andrew D. *Objective Tests and Subjective Bias: Some Problems of Discriminatory Intent in the Criminal Law*, 73 Chi.-Kent L. Rev. 559 (1998).

Leo, Richard A. *Inside the Interrogation Room*, 86 J. Crim. L. & Criminology 266 (1996).

Leo, Richard A. *Police Interrogation and Social Control*, 3 Soc. & Legal Stud. 93 (1994).

Liebman, James S. *More than "Slightly Retro:" The Rehnquist Court's Rout of Habeas Corpus Jurisdiction in* Teague v. Lane, 18 N.Y.U. Rev. L. & Soc. Change 537 (1990–91).

Lyons, David. *Principles, Positivism, and Legal Theory*, 87 Yale L.J. 415 (1977).

Maclin, Tracey. *Informants and the Fourth Amendment: A Reconsideration*, 74 Wash. U. L.Q. 573 (1996).

Maclin, Tracey. *Race and the Fourth Amendment*, 51 Vand. L. Rev. 333 (1998).

Marshall, Lawrence. *What Do We Owe People Who Have Been Wrongly Convicted?*, Chi. Trib. C17 (July 7, 1996).

Mashaw, Jerry L. *The Supreme Court's Due Process Calculus for Administrative Adjudication in* Mathews v. Eldridge: *Three Factors in Search of a Theory of Value*, 44 U. Chi. L. Rev. 28 (1976).

McAdams, Richard. *Race and Selective Prosecution: Discovering the Pitfalls of* Armstrong, 73 Chi.-Kent L. Rev. 605 (1998).

McClurg, Andrew Jay. *Bringing Privacy Law Out of the Closet: A Tort Theory of Liability for Intrusions in Public Places*, 73 N.C. L. Rev. 989 (1995).

McConville, Michael, & Chester L. Mirsky. *Criminal Defense of the Poor in New York City*, 15 N.Y.U. J. L & Soc. Change 581 (1986–87).

Medalie, Richard J. et al. *Custodial Police Interrogation in Our Nation's Capital: The Attempt to Implement* Miranda, 66 Mich. L. Rev. 1347 (1968).

Melilli, Kenneth J. Batson *in Practice: What We Have Learned About* Batson *and Peremptory Challenges*, 71 Notre Dame L. Rev. 447 (1996).

Mertens, William J., & Silas Wasserstrom. *The Good Faith Exception to the Exclusionary Rule: Deregulating the Police and Derailing the Law*, 70 Geo. L.J. 365 (1981).

Meyer, Linda. *"Nothing We Say Matters"*: Teague *and New Rules*, 61 U. Chi. L. Rev. 423 (1994).

Milledge, Stanley. Escobedo—*Toward Eliminating Coerced Confessions*, 19 U. Miami L. Rev. 415 (1965).

Miller, Gerald et al. *The Effects of Videotape Testimony in Jury Trials: Studies on Juror Decision Making, Information Retention, and Emotional Arousal*, 1975 B.Y.U. L. Rev. 331.

Mishkin, Paul J. Foreword: *The High Court, the Great Writ, and the Due Process of Time and Law*, 79 Harv. L. Rev. 56 (1965).

Monaghan, Henry Paul. *Stare Decisis and Constitutional Adjudication*, 88 Colum. L. Rev. 723 (1988).

Montoya, Jean. *The Future of the Post-* Batson *Peremptory Challenge: Voir Dire by Questionnaire and the "Blind" Peremptory*, 29 U. Mich. J. L. Ref. 981 (1996).

More Money for the Defense, Chi. Trib. § 1, at 22 (May13, 1999).

Morrison, Stanley. *Does the Fourteenth Amendment Incorporate the Bill of Rights? The Judicial Interpretation*, 2 Stan. L. Rev. 140, 147–48 (1949).

Mosteller, Robert. *Taking the Fifth Amendment Seriously*, 73 Va. L. Rev. 1 (1987).

Murphy, Michael. *Judicial Review of Police Methods in Law Enforcement*, 44 Texas L. Rev. 939 (1966).

Mushlin, Michael. *Foreword*, 10 Pace L. Rev. 327 (1990).

Nardulli, Peter F. *The Societal Cost of the Exclusionary Rule: An Empirical Assessment*, 1983 A.B.F. Res. J. 585.

Newman, Philip H. *Ineffective Assistance of Counsel: The Lingering Debate*, 65 Cornell L. Rev. 659 (1980).

Note. *Gideon's Promise Unfulfilled: The Need for Litigated Reform of Indigent Defense*, 113 Harv. L. Rev. 2062 (2000).

Note. *State Police, Unconstitutionally Obtained Evidence and Section 242 of the Civil Rights Statute*, 7 Stanford L. Rev. 76 (1955).

Oaks, Dallin H. *Studying the Exclusionary Rule in Search and Seizure*, 37 U. Chi. L. Rev. 665 (1970).

Ogletree, Charles J. *Are Confessions Really Good for the Soul? A Proposal to Mirandize Miranda*, 100 Harv. L. Rev. 1826 (1987).

Ogletree Jr., Charles J. *An Essay on the New Public Defender for the 21st Century*, Law & Contemp. Probs. 81 (Winter 1995).

Orth, John V. *Taking from A and Giving to B: Substantive Due Process and the Case of the Shifting Paradigm*, 14 Const. Comment. 337 (1997).

Packer, Herbert L. *Two Models of the Criminal Process*, 113 U. Pa. L. Rev. 1 (1964).

Paulsen, Michael Stokes. *The Most Dangerous Branch: Executive Power to Say What the Law Is*, 83 Geo. L.J. 217 (1994).

Pearson Jr., James O. Annotation, *Use of Peremptory Challenge to Exclude from Jury Persons Belonging to a Class or Race*, 79 A.L.R.3d 14 (1977).

Posner, Richard. *Rethinking the Fourth Amendment*, 1981 S. Ct. Rev. 49.

Post, David, & Steven C. Salop. *Rowing Against the Tidewater: A Theory of Voting by Multijudge Panels*, 80 Geo. L.J. 743 (1992).

Pound, Roscoe. *Legal Interrogation of Persons Accused or Suspected of Crime*, 24 J. Crim. L. & Crimin. 1014 (1934).

Rawls, John. *Two Concepts of Rules*, 64 Phil. Rev. 1 (1955).

Raz, Joseph. *The Rule of Law and its Virtues*, 93 Law Q. Rev. 195 (1977).

Reich, Charles A. *The New Property*, 73 Yale L.J. 733 (1964).

Report on Habeas Corpus in Capital Cases, 45 Crim. L. Rep. 3239 (Sept. 27, 1989).

Riggs, Robert E. *Substantive Due Process in 1791*, 1990 Wis. L. Rev. 941.

Ritz, Wilfred J. *Twenty-Five Years of State Criminal Confession Cases in the U.S. Supreme Court*, 19 Wash. & Lee L. Rev. 35 (1962).

Rogers, John M. *"I Vote This Way Because I'm Wrong": The Supreme Court Justice as Epimenides*, 79 Ky. L.J. 439 (1991).

Royall, William. *The Fourteenth Amendment: The Slaughter-House Cases*, 4 Southern L. Rev. (New Series) 558 (1879).

Rubin, Edward. *Politics, Doctrinal Coherence, and the Art of Treatise Writing*, 21 Seattle U. L. Rev. 837 (1998).

Sachs, Stephen H. *The Exclusionary Rule: A Prosecutor's Defense*, Crim. Just. Ethics 28 (Summer/Fall 1982).

Schifferle, Carl J. *After* Whren v. *United States: Applying the Equal Protection Clause to Racially Discriminatory Enforcement of the Law*, 2 Mich. L. & Pol'y Rev. 159 (1997).

Schmidt, Benno C. *Juries, Jurisdiction, and Race Discrimination: The Lost Promise of* Strauder v. West Virginia, 61 Tex. L. Rev. 1401 (1983).

Schullhofer, Stephen J. *Confessions and the Court*, 79 Mich. L. Rev. 865 (1981).

Schullhofer, Stephen J. Miranda *and Clearance Rates*, 91 Nw. L. Rev. 278 (1996).

Seeburger, Richard H., & R. Stanton Wettick, Jr. Miranda *in Pittsburgh: A Statistical Study*, 29 U. Pitt. L. Rev. 1 (1967).

Seidman, Louis Michael. Brown *and* Miranda, 80 Cal. L. Rev. 673 (1992).

Sherry, Suzanna. *Justice O'Connor's Dilemma: The Baseline Question*, 39 Wm. & Mary L. Rev. 865 (1998).

Sherry, Suzanna. *Natural Law in the States*, 61 U. Cin. L. Rev. 171 (1992).

Silk, David M., Comment. *When Bright Lines Break Down: Limiting* New York v. Belton, 136 U. Pa. L. Rev. 281 (1987).

Sjostrom, Joseph. *Du Page Has a Beef About Bugs*, Chi. Trib. 1 (Feb. 1, 1991).

Slobogin, Christopher. *Let's Not Bury* Terry: *A Call For Rejuvenation of the Proportionality Principle*, 72 St. John's L. Rev. 1053 (1998).

Slobogin, Christopher. *The World Without a Fourth Amendment*, 39 U.C.L.A. L. Rev. 1 (1991).

Soper, Philip. *Legal Theory and the Obligation of the Judge: The Hart/Dworkin Dispute*, 75 Mich. L. Rev. 473 (1977).

Special Project. *Interrogations in New Haven: The Impact of* Miranda, 76 Yale L.J. 1519 (1967).

Spiotto, James E. *Search and Seizure: An Empirical Study of the Exclusionary Rule and Its Alternatives*, 2 J. Legal Stud. 243 (1973).

Stearns, Maxwell L. *Standing Back from the Forest: Justiciability and Social Choice*, 83 Cal. L. Rev. 1309 (1995).

Stearns, Maxwell L. *Standing and Social Choice: Historical Evidence*, 144 U. Pa. L. Rev. 309 (1995).

Steiker, Carol S., & Jordan M. Steiker. *Sober Second Thoughts: Reflections on Two Decades of Constitutional Regulation of Capital Punishment*, 109 Harv. L. Rev. 355 (1995).

Steiker, Jordan M. *The Long Road Up From Barbarism: Thurgood Marshall and the Death Penalty*, 71 Tex. L. Rev. 1131 (1993).

Stone, Geoffrey R. *The Miranda Doctrine in the Burger Court*, 1977 Sup. Ct. Rev. 99.

Strauss, David A. *Common Law Constitutional Interpretation*, 63 U. Chi. L. Rev. 877 (1996).

Strauss, David A. Miranda, *The Constitution, and Congress*, 99 Mich. L. Rev. 958 (2001).

Stuntz, William J. *Race, Class, and Drugs*, 98 Colum. L. Rev. 1795 (1998).

Stuntz, William. *The Substantive Origins of Criminal Procedure*, 105 Yale L.J. 393 (1995).

Stuntz, William J. *The Virtues and Vices of the Exclusionary Rule*, 20 Harv. J. L. & Pub. Pol'y 443 (1997).

Stuntz, William J. *Warrants and Fourth Amendment Remedies*, 77 Va. L. Rev. 881 (1991).

Sutherland Jr., Arthur E. *Crime and Confession*, 79 Harv. L. Rev. 21 (1965).

Symposium, Miranda *after* Dickerson: *The Future of Confession Law*, 99 Mich. L. Rev. (2001).

Thomas III, George C. *Judges are not Economists and Other Reasons to be Skeptical of Contingent Suppression Orders: A Response to Professor Dripps*, 38 Am. Crim. L. Rev. 47 (2001).

Thomas III, George C. *Plain Talk About the* Miranda *Empirical Debate: A "Steady-State" Theory of Confessions*, 43 U.C.L.A. L. Rev. 933 (1996).

Thomas III, George C. *When Constitutional Worlds Collide: Resurrecting the Framers' Bill of Rights and Criminal Procedure*, 100 Mich. L. Rev. 145 (2001).

Tomkovicz, James J. *Standards for Invocation and Waiver of Counsel in Confession Contexts*, 71 Iowa L. Rev. 975 (1986).

Traynor, Roger. Mapp v. Ohio *at Large in the Fifty States*, 1962 Duke L.J. 319.

Tribe, Laurence H. *Contrasting Constitutional Visions: Of Real and Unreal Differences*, 22 Harv. C.R.-C.L. L. Rev. 95 (1987).

Tribe, Laurence H. *Taking Text and Structure Seriously: Reflections on Free-Form Method in Constitutional Interpretation*, 108 Harv. L. Rev. 1221 (1995).

Tushnet, Mark V. *Dia-Tribe*, 78 Mich. L. Rev. 694 (1980).

Urofsky, Melvin. *Myth and Reality: The Supreme Court and Protective Legislation in the Progressive Era*, 1983 Y.B. of the Supreme Court Historical Society.

Wechsler, Herbert. *The Political Safeguards of Federalism: The Role of the States in the Composition and Selection of the National Government*, 54 Colum. L. Rev. 543 (1954).

Weisberg, Robert. *A Great Writ While it Lasted*, 81 J. Crim. L. & Criminology 9 (1990).

Weisselberg, Charles D. *Saving* Miranda, 84 Cornell L. Rev. 109 (1998).

Wellborn III, Olin Guy. *Demeanor*, 76 Cornell L. Rev. 1075 (1991).

Wells, Gary L., & Eric P. Seelau. *Eyewitness Identification: Psychological Research and Legal Policy on Lineups*, 1 Psychol. Pub. Pol'y & L. 765 (1995).

White, Welsh S. *Defending* Miranda: *A Reply to Professor Caplan*, 39 V. and L. Rev. 1 (1986).

CASES

Adams v. New York, 192 U.S. 585 (1904)

Adamson v. California, 332 U.S. 46 (1947)

Addington v. Texas, 441 U.S. 418 (1979)
Agnello v. United States, 269 U.S. 20 (1925)
Ake v. Oklahoma, 470 U.S. 68 (1985)
Alderman v. United States, 394 U.S. 165 (1969)
Anderson v. State, 205 A.2d 281 (Md. 1964)
Andrews v. Swartz, 156 U.S. 272 (1895)
Apodaca v. Oregon, 406 U.S. 404 (1972)
Arizona v. Hicks, 480 U.S. 321 (1987)
Arizona v. Roberson, 486 U.S. 675 (1988)
Arizona v. Youngblood, 488 U.S. 51 (1988)
Arnett v. Kennedy, 416 U.S. 134 (1974)
Ashe v. Swenson, 397 U.S. 436 (1970)
Atwater v. City of Lago Vista, 531 U.S. 990 (2001)
Bailey v. Richardson, 182 F.2d 46 (D.C. Cir. 1950)
Barrows v. Jackson, 346 U.S. 249 (1953)
Batson v. Kentucky, 476 U.S. 79 (1986)
Benton v. Maryland, 395 U.S. 784 (1969)
Berger v. New York, 388 U.S. 41 (1967)
Betts v. Brady, 316 U.S. 455 (1942)
Bishop v. Wood, 426 U.S. 341 (1976)
Bivens v. Six Unknown Named Agents of the Federal Bureau of Narcotics, 403
      U.S. 388 (1971)
Bloomer v. McQuewan, 55 U.S. 539 (1853)
Bolling v. Sharpe, 347 U.S. 497 (1954)
Bostick v. State, 554 So.2d 1153 (Fla. 1989)
Bourjaily v. United States, 483 U.S. 171 (1987)
Bowen v. Johnston, 306 U.S. 19 (1939)
Boyd v. United States, 116 U.S. 616 (1886)
Bozel v. Hudspeth, 126 F.2d 585 (10th Cir. 1942)
Brady v. Maryland, 373 U.S. 83 (1963)
Bram v. United States, 168 U.S. 532 (1897)
Breithaupt v. Abram, 352 U.S. 432 (1957)
Brewer v. Williams, 430 U.S. 387 (1977)
Brooks v. Tennessee, 406 U.S. 605 (1972)
Brown v. Allen, 344 U.S. 443 (1953)
Brown v. Mississippi, 297 U.S. 278 (1936)
Brown v. New Jersey, 175 U.S. 172 (1899)
Brown v. State, 158 So. 339 (Miss. 1935)
Buchanan v. Kentucky, 483 U.S. 402 (1987)
Burch v. Louisiana, 441 U.S. 130 (1979)
Burnet v. Coronado Oil & Gas Co., 285 U.S. 393 (1932)
Butts v. McNally, 530 U.S. 1261 (2000)
Caldwell v. Texas, 137 U.S. 692 (1891)
California Attorneys for Criminal Justice v. Butts, 195 F.3d 1039 (9th Cir. 1999)

California v. Acevedo, 500 U.S. 565 (1982)
California v. Green, 399 U.S. 149 (1970)
California v. Greenwood, 486 U.S. 35 (1988)
Callins v. Collins, 510 U.S. 1141 (1994)
Camara v. Municipal Court, 387 S. 523 (1967)
Cantwell v. Connecticut, 310 U.S. 296 (1940)
Carnley v. Cochran, 369 U.S. 506 (1962)
Carroll v. United States, 267 U.S. 132 (1925)
Chambers v. Florida, 309 U.S. 227 (1940)
Chambers v. Maroney, 399 U.S. 42 (1970)
Chambers v. Mississippi, 410 U.S. 284 (1973)
Chicago, Burlington & Quincy R.R. Co. v. Chicago, 166 U.S. 226 (1897)
Chimel v. California, 395 U.S. 752 (1969)
Cicenia v. LaGay, 357 U.S. 504 (1958)
City of Boerne v. Flores, 521 U.S. 507 (1997)
Cleveland Board of Education v. Loudermill, 470 U.S. 532 (1985)
Cochran v. Kansas, 316 U.S. 255 (1942)
Commonwealth v. Coyle, 203 A.2d 782 (Pa. 1964)
Commonwealth ex rel. Ringer v. Maroney, 110 A.2d 801 (Pa. Super. 1955)
Commonwealth v. Soares, 387 N.E.2d 499 (1979)
Cooper v. Aaron, 358 U.S. 1 (1958)
Cooper v. Commonwealth, 140 S.E.2d 688 (Va. 1965)
Coppage v. Kansas, 236 U.S. 1 (1915)
Corfield v. Coryell, 6 F. Cas. 546, 551–52 (C.C.E.D. Pa. 1823) (No. 3230)
Couch v. United States, 409 U.S. 322 (1973)
Counselman v. Hitchcock, 142 U.S. 547 (1892)
Country of Riverside v. McLaughlin, 500 U.S. 44 (1991)
Coy v. Iowa, 487 U.S. 1012 (1988)
Craig v. Boren, 429 U.S. 190 (1976)
Crane v. Kentucky, 476 U.S. 683 (1986)
Crist v. Bretz, 437 U.S. 28 (1978)
Crooker v. California, 357 U.S. 433 (1958)
Culombe v. Connecticut, 367 U.S. 568 (1961)
Dartmouth College v. Woodward, 17 U.S. (4 Wheat.) 518 (1819)
Davis v. United States, 160 U.S. 469 (1895)
Dickerson v. United States, 530 U.S. 428 (2000)
Diggs v. Welch, 148 F.2d 667 (D.C. Cir. 1945)
Douglas v. California, 372 U.S. 353 (1963)
Dowd v. Cook, 340 U.S. 206 (1951)
Doyle v. Ohio, 426 U.S. 610 (1976)
Dred Scott v. Sandford, 60 U.S. (19 How.) 393 (1857)
Duncan v. Louisiana, 391 U.S. 145 (1968)
Duncan v. Missouri, 152 U.S. 377 (1894)
Duren v. Missouri, 439 U.S. 357 (1979)

Eddings v. Oklahoma, 455 U.S. 104 (1982)

Edwards v. Arizona, 451 U.S. 477 (1981)

Eisenstadt v. Baird, 405 U.S. 438 (1972)

Entick v. Carrington, 19 Howell's St. Tr. 1029 (1765)

Escobedo v. Illinois, 378 U.S. 478 (1964)

Estelle v. Williams, 425 U.S. 501 (1976)

Eury v. Huff, 146 F.2d 17 (D.C. Cir. 1944)

Ex Parte Bigelow, 113 U.S. 328 (1885)

Ex Parte Harding, 120 U.S. 782 (1887)

Ex Parte Lange, 85 U.S. 163 (1877)

Ex Parte Siebold, 100 U.S. 371 (1879)

Ex Parte Watkins, 28 U.S. (3 Pet.) 193 (1830)

Ex Parte Wilson, 114 U.S. 417 (1885)

Fare v. Michael C., 442 U.S. 707 (1979)

Fay v. Noia, 372 U.S. 391 (1963)

Feldman v. United States, 322 U.S. 487 (1944)

Felker v. Turpin, 518 U.S. 651 (1996)

Felts v. Murphy, 201 U.S. 123 (1906)

Fikes v. Alabama, 352 U.S. 191 (1957)

Fisher v. United States, 425 U.S. 391 (1976)

Flagg v. United States, 233 F. 481 (2d Cir. 1916)

Fleming v. Collins, 954 F.2d 1109 (5th Cir. 1992)

Florida v. Bostick, 501 U.S. 429 (1991)

Foster v. California, 394 U.S. 440 (1969)

Foucha v. Louisiana, 504 U.S. 71 (1992)

Fowler v. Hunter, 164 F.2d 668 (10th Cir. 1947)

Fox v. Washington, 236 U.S. 273 (1915)

Frank v. Mangum, 237 U.S. 309 (1915)

Gallegos v. Nebraska, 342 U.S. 55 (1951)

Geders v. United States, 425 U.S. 80 (1976)

Gideon v. Wainwright, 372 U.S. 335 (1963)

Gilbert v. Minnesota, 254 U.S. 325 (1920)

Gitlow v. New York, 268 U.S. 652 (1925)

Goss v. Lopez, 419 U.S. 565 (1975)

Gouled v. United States, 255 U.S. 298 (1921)

Grady v. Corbin, 495 U.S. 508 (1990)

Graham v. Connor, 490 U.S. 386 (1989)

Gregg v. Georgia, 428 U.S. 153 (1976)

Griffin v. California, 380 U.S. 609 (1965)

Griffin v. Illinois, 351 U.S. 12 (1956)

Griffin v. Wisconsin, 483 U.S. 868 (1987)

Gryger v. Burke, 334 U.S. 728 (1948)

Hale v. Henkel, 201 U.S. 43 (1906)

Hallinger v. Davis, 146 U.S. 314 (1892)

Hampton v. United States, 425 U.S. 484 (1976)
Harmelin v. Michigan, 501 U.S. 957 (1991)
Harris v. New York, 401 U.S. 222 (1971)
Haynes v. Washington, 373 U.S. 503 (1963)
Herring v. New York, 422 U.S. 853 (1975)
Hicks v. United States, 150 U.S. 442 (1893)
Hodgson v. Vermont, 168 U.S. 262 (1897)
Hoffa v. United States, 385 U.S. 293 (1966)
Holland v. Illinois, 493 U.S. 474 (1990)
Hopt v. Utah, 110 U.S. 574 (1884)
Hurtado v. California, 110 U.S. 516 (1884)
Illinois v. Gates, 462 U.S. 213 (1983)
Illinois v. Krull, 480 U.S. 340 (1987)
In re Converse, 137 U.S. 624 (1891)
In re Kemmler, 136 U.S. 436 (1890)
In re Medley, 134 U.S. 160 (1890)
In re Nielsen, 131 U.S. 176 (1889)
In re Winship, 397 U.S. 358 (1970)
Interstate Commerce Commission v. Louisville & Nashville Railroad, 227 U.S.
    88 (1913)
Irvine v. California, 347 U.S. 128 (1954)
Jack v. Kansas, 199 U.S. 372 (1905)
Jackson v. Denno, 378 U.S. 368 (1964)
Jacobson v. Massachusetts, 197 U.S. 11 (1905)
James v. Illinois, 493 U.S. 307 (1990)
Johnson v. Glick, 481 F.2d 1028 (2d Cir. 1973)
Johnson v. Louisiana, 406 U.S. 356 (1972)
Johnson v. Zerbst, 304 U.S. 458 (1938)
Kalloch v. Superior Court, 56 Cal. 229 (1880)
Kansas v. Hendricks, 521 U.S. 346 (1997)
Kastigar v. United States, 406 U.S. 441 (1972)
Katz v. United States, 389 U.S. 347 (1967)
Kaufman v. United States, 394 U.S. 217 (1969)
Keeler v. Superior Court of Amador County, 470 P.2d 617 (Cal. 1970)
Kirby v. Illinois, 406 U.S. 682 (1972)
Kirby v. United States, 174 U.S. 47 (1899)
Kuhlmann v. Wilson, 477 U.S. 436 (1986)
Leeper v. Texas, 139 U.S. 462 (1891)
Lewis v. United States, 385 U.S. 206 (1966)
Linkletter v. Walker, 381 U.S. 618 (1965)
Lisenba v. California, 314 U.S. 219 (1941)
Lochner v. New York, 198 U.S. 45 (1905)
Lockett v. Ohio, 438 U.S. 586 (1978)
Londoner v. Denver, 210 U.S. 373 (1908)

Lopez v. United States, 373 U.S. 427 (1963)

Lyons v. Oklahoma, 322 U.S. 596 (1944)

Malley v. Briggs, 475 U.S. 335 (1986)

Mallory v. United States, 354 U.S. 449 (1957)

Malloy v. Hogan, 378 U.S. 1 (1964)

Manson v. Brathwaite, 432 U.S. 98 (1977)

Mapp v. Ohio, 367 U.S. 643 (1961)

Martin v. Ohio, 480 U.S. 228 (1987)

Maryland v. Craig, 497 U.S. 836 (1990)

Massiah v. United States, 377 U.S. 201 (1964)

Mathews v. Eldridge, 424 U.S. 319 (1976)

Mattox v. United States, 156 U.S. 237 (1895) & 146 U.S. 140 (1892)

Maxwell v. Dow, 176 U.S. 581 (1900)

Mayer v. Chicago, 404 U.S. 189 (1971)

McCray v. Abrams, 750 F.2d 1113 (2d Cir. 1984)

McKane v. Durston, 153 U.S. 684 (1894)

McLaughlin v. Florida, 379 U.S. 184 (1964)

McMann v. Richardson, 397 U.S. 759 (1970)

McNabb v. United States, 318 U.S. 332 (1943)

Meyer v. Nebraska, 262 U.S. 390 (1923)

Michigan v. Mosley, 423 U.S. 96 (1975)

Michigan v. Tucker, 417 U.S. 433 (1974)

Miller v. Pate, 386 U.S. 1 (1967)

Mincey v. Arizona, 437 U.S. 385 (1978)

Minnick v. Mississippi, 498 U.S. 1465 (1990)

Miranda v. Arizona, 384 U.S. 436 (1966)

Mooney v. Holohan, 294 U.S. 103 (1935)

Moore v. Dempsey, 261 U.S. 86 (1923)

Morse v. Hanks, 172 F.3d 983 (7th Cir. 1999)

Mullaney v. Wilbur, 421 U.S. 684 (1975)

Murphy v. Waterfront Commission, 378 U.S. 52 (1964)

Murray v. Carrier, 477 U.S. 478 (1986)

Murray's Lessee v. Hoboken Land and Improvement Co., 59 U.S. (18 How.) 272
    (1855)

Napue v. Illinois, 360 U.S. 264 (1959)

Neal v. Delaware, 103 U.S. 370 (1880)

Near v. Minnesota, 283 U.S. 697 (1931)

Neil v. Biggers, 409 U.S. 188 (1972)

New Jersey v. Portash, 440 U.S. 450 (1979)

New York v. Belton, 453 U.S. 454 (1981)

New York v. Quarles, 467 U.S. 649 (1984)

Nix v. Williams, 467 U.S. 431 (1984)

Norris v. Alabama, 294 U.S. 587 (1935)

North Carolina v. Butler, 441 U.S. 369 (1979)

Ohio v. Roberts, 448 U.S. 56 (1980)
Olmstead v. United States, 277 U.S. 438 (1928)
O'Neil v. Vermont, 144 U.S. 323 (1892)
On Lee v. United States, 343 U.S. 747 (1952)
Oregon v. Bradshaw, 462 U.S. 1039 (1983)
Oregon v. Elstad, 470 U.S. 298 (1980)
Oregon v. Hass, 420 U.S. 714 (1975)
Oregon v. Mathiason, 429 U.S. 492 (1977)
Orozco v. Texas, 394 U.S. 324 (1969)
Osborn v. Nicholson, 80 U.S. 654 (1872)
Osborn v. United States, 385 U.S. 323 (1966)
Palko v. Connecticut, 302 U.S. 319 (1937)
Patterson v. Colorado, 205 U.S. 454 (1907)
Patterson v. New York, 432 U.S. 197 (1977)
Patton v. Yount, 467 U.S. 1025 (1984)
Payne v. Arkansas, 356 U.S. 560 (1958)
Pennsylvania v. Finely, 481 U.S. 551 (1987)
People v. Cahan, 282 P.2d 905 (1955)
People v. DeFore, 150 N.E. 585 (N.Y. 1926)
People v. Dorado, 398 P.2d 361 (Cal. 1965)
People v. Escobedo, 190 N.E.2d 825 (1963)
People v. Gonzales, 124 P.2d 44 (1942)
People v. Hartgraves, 202 N.E.2d 33 (Ill. 1964)
People v. Kulis, 221 N.E.2d 541 (1966)
People v. Wheeler, 583 P.2d 748 (1978)
Perry v. Sinderman, 408 U.S. 593 (1972)
Personnel Administrator v. Feeney, 442 U.S. 256 (1979)
Pierce v. Society of Sisters, 268 U.S. 510 (1925)
Pierce v. United States, 160 U.S. 355 (1896)
Planned Parenthood of Southeastern Pa. v. Casey, 505 U.S. 833 (1992)
Poe v. Ullman, 367 U.S. 497 (1961)
Pointer v. Texas, 380 U.S. 400 (1965)
Powell v. Alabama, 287 U.S. 45 (1932)
Powell v. McCormack, 395 U.S. 486 (1974)
Prescott v. Ohio, 19 Ohio St. 184 (1870)
Price v. Johnston, 125 F.2d 806 (9th Cir. 1942)
Prudential Insurance Co. of Am. v. Cheek, 259 U.S. 530 (1922)
Purkett v. Elem, 514 U.S. 765 (1995)
Rakas v. Illinois, 439 U.S. 128 (1978)
Rathbun v. United States, 355 U.S. 107 (1957)
Rawlings v. Kentucky, 448 U.S. 98 (1980)
Reed v. Reed, 404 U.S. 71 (1971)
Reno v. Flores, 507 U.S. 292 (1993)
Rhode Island v. Innis, 446 U.S. 291 (1980)

Riddle v. Dyche, 262 U.S. 333 (1923)
Rideau v. Louisiana, 373 U.S. 723 (1963)
Roberts v. LaVallee, 389 U.S. 40 (1967)
Robinson v. California, 370 U.S. 660 (1962)
Rochin v. California, 342 U.S. 165 (1952)
Rock v. Arkansas, 483 U.S. 44 (1987)
Rogers v. Richmond, 365 U.S. 534 (1961)
Ross v. Moffitt, 417 U.S. 600 (1974)
Rowan v. State, 30 Wis. 129 (1872)
Schaefer v. United States, 251 U.S. 466 (1920)
Schall v. Martin, 467 U.S. 253 (1984)
Schmerber v. California, 384 U.S. 757 (1966)
Scott v. Sandford, 60 U.S. (19 How.) 393 (1857)
Shaffer v. Warden, 126 A.2d 573 (Md. 1956)
Shelley v. Kraemer, 334 U.S. 1 (1948)
Silverthorne Lumber Co. v. United States, 251 U.S. 385 (1920)
Singer v. United States, 380 U.S. 24 (1965)
Skinner v. Oklahoma, 316 U.S. 535 (1942)
Slaughterhouse Cases, 83 U.S. (16 Wall.) 36 (1873)
Smith v. Maryland, 442 U.S. 735 (1979)
Smith v. Murray, 477 U.S. 527 (1986)
Solem v. Helm, 463 U.S. 277 (1983)
Spano v. New York, 360 U.S. 315 (1959)
Sparf & Hansen v. United States, 156 U.S. 51 (1895)
State v. Dufour, 206 A.2d 82 (R.I. 1965)
State v. Jackson, 21 La. Ann. 574 (August 1869)
State v. Schumpert, 1 S.C. 85 (1869) (30 West's S.C. Reports 40
        (Nov./Dec. 1868))
State v. Smith, 202 A.2d 669 (N.J. 1964)
State v. Terry, 214 N.E.2d 114 (Ohio Ct. App. 1966)
State v. Wells, 46 Iowa 662 (1877)
State v. Williams, 182 N.W.2d 396 (Iowa 1970)
Stein v. New York, 346 U.S. 156 (1953)
Strauder v. West Virginia, 100 U.S. 303 (1879)
Strickland v. Washington, 466 U.S. 668 (1984)
Stroble v. California, 343 U.S. 181 (1952)
Stromberg v. California, 283 U.S. 359 (1931)
Sumner v. Shuman, 483 U.S. 66 (1987)
Swain v. Alabama, 380 U.S. 202 (1965)
Tague v. Louisiana, 444 U.S. 469 (1980)
Taylor v. Louisiana, 419 U.S. 522 (1975)
Teague v. Lane, 489 U.S. 288 (1989)
Tennessee v. Garner, 471 U.S. 1 (1985)
Terry v. Ohio, 392 U.S. 1 (1968)

Thomas v. Arizona, 356 U.S. 390 (1958)

Townsend v. Burke, 334 U.S. 736 (1948)

Townsend v. Sain, 372 U.S. 293 (1963)

Trapnell v. United States, 725 F.2d 149 (2d Cir. 1983)

Twining v. New Jersey, 211 U.S. 78 (1908)

Twitchell v. Commonwealth, 74 U.S. 321 (1869)

Twitchell v. Pennsylvania, 74 U.S. 321 (1869)

United States v. Armstrong, 517 U.S. 456 (1996)

United States v. Ash, 413 U.S. 300 (1973)

United States v. Avery, 128 F.3d 974 (6th Cir. 1997)

United States v. Bagley, 473 U.S. 667 (1985)

United States v. Bayless, 921 F. Supp. 211 (S.D.N.Y. 1996)

United States v. Bell, 86 F.3d 820 (8th Cir. 1996)

United States v. Brady, 819 F.2d 884 (9th Cir. 1987)

United States v. Bullock, 94 F.3d 896 (4th Cir. 1996)

United States v. Caceres, 440 U.S. 741 (1979)

United States v. Calandra, 414 U.S. 338 (1974)

United States v. Chadwick, 423 U.S. 411 (1976)

United States v. Cone, 354 F.2d 119 (2d Cir. 1965)

United States v. Crosby, 25 F. Cas. 701 (C.C.D.S.C. 1871)

United States v. Cruikshank, 92 U.S. 542 (1876)

United States v. Curzi, 867 F.2d 36 (1st Cir. 1989)

United States v. Dickerson, 166 F.3d 667 (4th Cir. 1999)

United States v. Dickerson, 530 U.S. 428 (2000)

United States v. Dixon, 509 U.S. 688 (1993)

United States v. Doe, 465 U.S. 605 (1984)

United States v. Hall, 26 F. Cas. 701 (C.C.S.D.Al. 1871) (no. 15,282)

United States v. Havens, 446 U.S. 620 (1980)

United States v. Horsley, 864 F.2d 1543 (11th Cir. 1989)

United States v. Hubbell, 530 U.S. 27 (2000)

United States v. Garsson, 291 F. 646 (S.D.N.Y. 1923)

United States v. Inadi, 475 U.S. 387 (1986)

United States v. Janis, 428 U.S. 433 (1976)

United States v. Jennings, 985 F.2d 562, 1993 WL 5927 (6th Cir. Jan. 13, 1993) (unpublished decision)

United States v. Lawrence, 952 F.2d 1034 (8th Cir. 1992)

United States v. Leon, 468 U.S. 897 (1984)

United States v. Levasseur, 699 F. Supp. 995 (D. Mass. 1988)

United States v. Martinez-Fuerte, 428 U.S. 543 (1976)

United States v. Miller, 425 U.S. 435 (1976)

United States v. Nixon, 418 U.S. 683 (1974)

United States v. Payner, 447 U.S. 727 (1980)

United States v. Penn, 647 F.2d 876 (9th Cir. 1980)

United States v. Prandy-Binett, 995 F.2d 1069 (D.C. Cir. 1993)

United States v. Raddatz, 447 U.S. 667 (1980)

United States v. Robinson, 414 U.S. 218 (1973)

United States v. Ross, 456 U.S. 798 (1982)

United States v. Russell, 411 U.S. 423 (1973)

United States ex rel Russo v. New Jersey, 351 F.2d 429 (3d Cir. 1965)

United States v. Salerno, 481 U.S. 739 (1987)

United States v. Simpson, 813 F.2d 1462 (9th Cir. 1987)

United States v. Wade, 388 U.S. 218 (1967)

United States v. Watson, 423 U.S. 411 (1976)

United States v. White, 401 U.S. 745 (1971)

Veronia School Dist. 47J v. Acton, 515 U.S. 646 (1995)

Village of Arlington Heights v. Metropolitan Housing Dev. Corp., 429 U.S. 252
    (1977)

Virginia v. Rives, 100 U.S. 313 (1879)

Wainwright v. Sykes, 433 U.S. 72 (1977)

Walder v. United States, 347 U.S. 62 (1954)

Waley v. Johnston, 316 U.S. 98 (1942)

Walker v. Sauvinet, 92 U.S. 90 (1875)

Warden v. Hayden, 387 U.S. 294 (1967)

Washington v. Davis, 426 U.S. 229 (1976)

Washington v. Texas, 388 U.S. 14 (1967)

Watts v. Indiana, 338 U.S. 49 (1949)

Webster v. Doe, 486 U.S. 592 (1988)

Weeks v. United States, 232 U.S. 383 (1914)

Weimer v. Bunbury, 30 Mich. *201 (1874)

Wesberry v. Sanders, 376 U.S. 1 (1964)

West v. Louisiana, 194 U.S. 258 (1904)

White v. Illinois, 502 U.S. 346 (1992)

Whren v. United States, 517 U.S. 806 (1996)

Williams v. Brewer, 509 F.2d 227 (8th Cir. 1974)

Williams v. Florida, 399 U.S. 78 (1970)

Williamson v. Lee Optical of Oklahoma, Inc., 348 U.S. 483 (1955)

Wilson v. United States, 149 U.S. 60 (1893)

Wilson v. United States, 162 U.S. 613 (1896)

Withrow v. Williams, 507 U.S. 680 (1993)

Wolf v. People, 187 P.2d 926 (Colo. 1947)

Wolf v. Colorado, 338 U.S. 25 (1949)

Woodson v. North Carolina, 428 U.S. 280 (1976)

Wright v. Dickson, 336 F.2d 878 (9th Cir. 1964)

Yick Wo v. Hopkins, 118 U.S. 356 (1886)

MISCELLANEOUS

28 U.S.C. § 2254(e)

28 U.S.C. § 2254

28 U.S.C. § 2261–2264 & 2244(b)

28 U.S.C. §§ 2254(d)(1) & (2)

90 Cong. Rec. 14,177 (1968)

90 Cong. Rec. 12,937 (1968)

90 Cong. Rec. 14,183 (1968)

90 Cong. Rec. 14,184–86 (1968)

90 Cong. Rec.16,299–300 (1968)

American Law Institute, Model Code of Pre-Arraignment Procedure, Tentative Draft No. 1 (March 1, 1966)

Anti-Terrorism and Effective Death Penalty Act of 1996, Pub. L. No. 104–132, 110 Stat. 1214 (1996)

Brief of the National District Attorneys Association, as Amicus Curiae, *Miranda v. Arizona* (Nos. 584, 759, 760, & 762)

Brief for Petitioner, *Malloy v. Hogan* (No. 110)

Brief for Respondent, *Malloy v. Hogan* (No. 110)

Brief for Defendant in Error, *Hurtado v. California*, 110 U.S. 516 (1884)

Brief for Respondent, *Miranda v. Arizona* (No. 759)

Brief for Petitioner, *Miranda v. Arizona* (No. 759)

Brief of the State of New York, et al., as Amici Curiae, *Miranda v. Arizona* (Nos. 584, 759, 760, & 762)

Brief for the Petitioner, *New York v. Quarles* (No. 82–1213)

Brief for the Respondent, *Escobedo v. Illinois* (No. 615)

Brief for the United States as Amicus Curiae, *New York v. Quarles* (No. 82–1213)

Brief for Petitioner, *Brewer v. Williams* (No. 74–1263)

Brief for Petitioner, *Vignera v. New York* (No. 760)

Brief of the American Civil Liberties Union as Amicus Curiae, *Miranda v. Arizona* (Nos. 584, 759, 760, 761, & 762)

Brief for Petitioner, *Westover v. United States* (No. 761)

Brief for Respondent, *Westover v. United States* (No. 761)

Brief for Respondent, *Brewer v. Williams* (No. 74–1263)

Brief for Petitioner (No. 75–1721), *United States v. Chadwick*, 423 U.S. 411 (1976)

Brief for Petitioner (No. 658), *Schmerber v. California*, 384 U.S. 757 (1966)

Brief for Petitioner (No. 155), *Gideon v. Wainwright*, 372 U.S. 335 (1963)

Brief Amicus Curiae of Americans for Effective Law Enforcement et al., *Brewer v. Williams* (No. 74–1263)

Brief for Petitioner, *Wolf v. People*, 187 P.2d 926 (Colo. 1947)

Brief for Defendant in Error, *Walker v. Sauvinet*, 92 U.S. 90 (1875)

Brief for Plaintiff in Error, *Maxwell v. Dow*, 176 U.S. 581 (1900)

Brief for Petitioner, *Johnson v. Zerbst*, 304 U.S. 458 (1938)

Brief for the American Civil Liberties Association and the Florida Civil Liberties Association, Amici Curiae, *Gideon v. Wainwright*, 372 U.S. 335 (1963) (No. 62–155)

Brief for Plaintiff in Error, *Hurtado v. California*, 110 U.S. 516 (1884)

Brief for Petitioner, *Gideon v. Wainwright*, 372 U.S. 335 (1963) (No. 63–155)

Brief of National District Attorneys' Association, Amicus Curiae, *Malloy v. Hogan* (No. 110)

Cong. Globe, 39th Cong., 1st Sess. 2765–66 (1866) (statement of Sen. Howard)

Cong. Globe, 39th Cong., 1st Sess. 1090 (Feb. 28, 1866) (statement of Rep. Bingham)

Cong. Globe, 39th Cong., 1st Sess. (1866) (Statement of Rep. Bingham)

Cong. Globe, 39th Cong., 1st Sess. 1089–90 (1866) (Statement of Rep. Bingham)

Cong. Globe, 39th Cong., 1st Sess. at 2462–63 (Statement of Rep. Garfield)

Cong. Globe, 38th Cong., 1st Sess. 1479–83 (1864) (Statement of Sen. Sumner)

Cong. Globe, 39th Cong., 1st Sess. at 2498 (Statement of Rep. Eliot)

Cong. Globe, 39th Cong., 1st Sess. (1866) (Statement of Sen. Howard)

Cong. Globe, 42d Cong., 1st Sess. app. 84 (1871) (Statement of Rep. Bingham)

Fed. R. Evid. 407, Advisory Committee Note

Fed. R. Evid. 804(B)(1)

Fed. R. Evid. 801(D)(1)

Hanson, Roger A. et al., *Indigent Defenders Get the Job Done and Done Well* (1992) (study performed for the National Center for State Courts)

Harris v. New York (No. 206), Appendix

Harris v. New York (No. 206), Petition for Certiorari

Report of the Comptroller General, *Impact of the Exclusionary Rule on Federal Criminal Prosecutions* (Rep. No. CDG-79-45) (1979)

The Jury and the Search for Truth: The Case Against Excluding Relevant Evidence at Trial, Hearings before the Senate Judiciary Committee, 104th Cong., 143 (1995) (Statement of Thomas Y. Davies)

The President's Commission on Law Enforcement and Administration of Justice, *The Challenge of Crime in a Free Society* (U.S. Government Printing Office, 1967)

The Exclusionary Rule Bills: Hearings on S. 101, S. 755, and S. 1995 Before the Subcomm. on Criminal Law of the Senate Comm. on the Judiciary, 97th Cong., 1st & 2d sess. (Statement of G. Robert Blakey)

Transcript of Oral Argument in *Miranda v. Arizona*, in 63 Landmark Briefs and Arguments of the Supreme Court (U. Publications of America, Phillip B. Kurland & Gerhard Casper eds., 1975)

U.S. Department of Justice, Bureau of Justice Statistics, *Sourcebook of Criminal Justice Statistics* 1993 (1994)

U.S. News & World Rep. 27 (June 3, 1996)

United States Department of Justice, *Sourcebook of Criminal Justice Statistics* 1998 (1999)

Subject Index

Name Index

Case Index

About the Author

DONALD A. DRIPPS is the James Levee Professor of Law and Criminal Procedure at the University of Minnesota Law School.